ESSAY'D 2

ESSAY'D 2 // 30 DETROIT ARTISTS

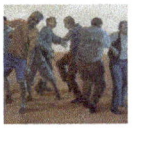 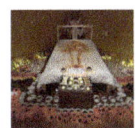 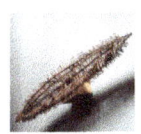 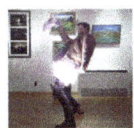 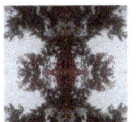 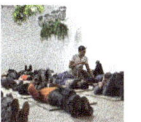

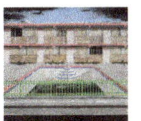 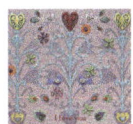 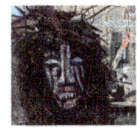 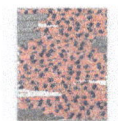 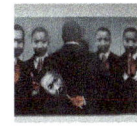 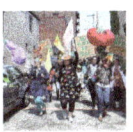

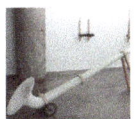 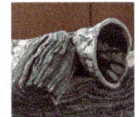 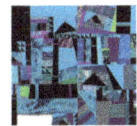 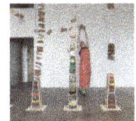 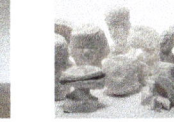 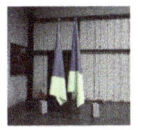

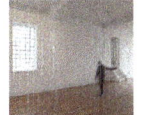 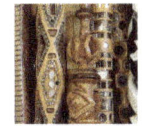 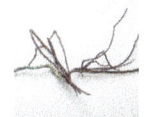 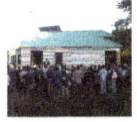 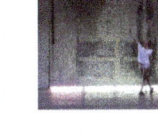 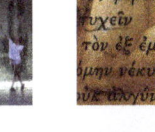

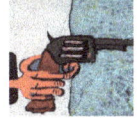 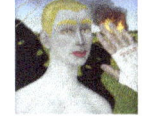 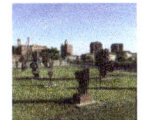 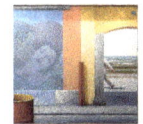 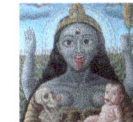 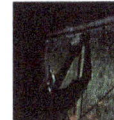

Written, Edited, and Compiled by
Dennis Alan Nawrocki,
Steve Panton, Matthew Piper,
and Sarah Rose Sharp

A Painted Turtle book
DETROIT, MICHIGAN

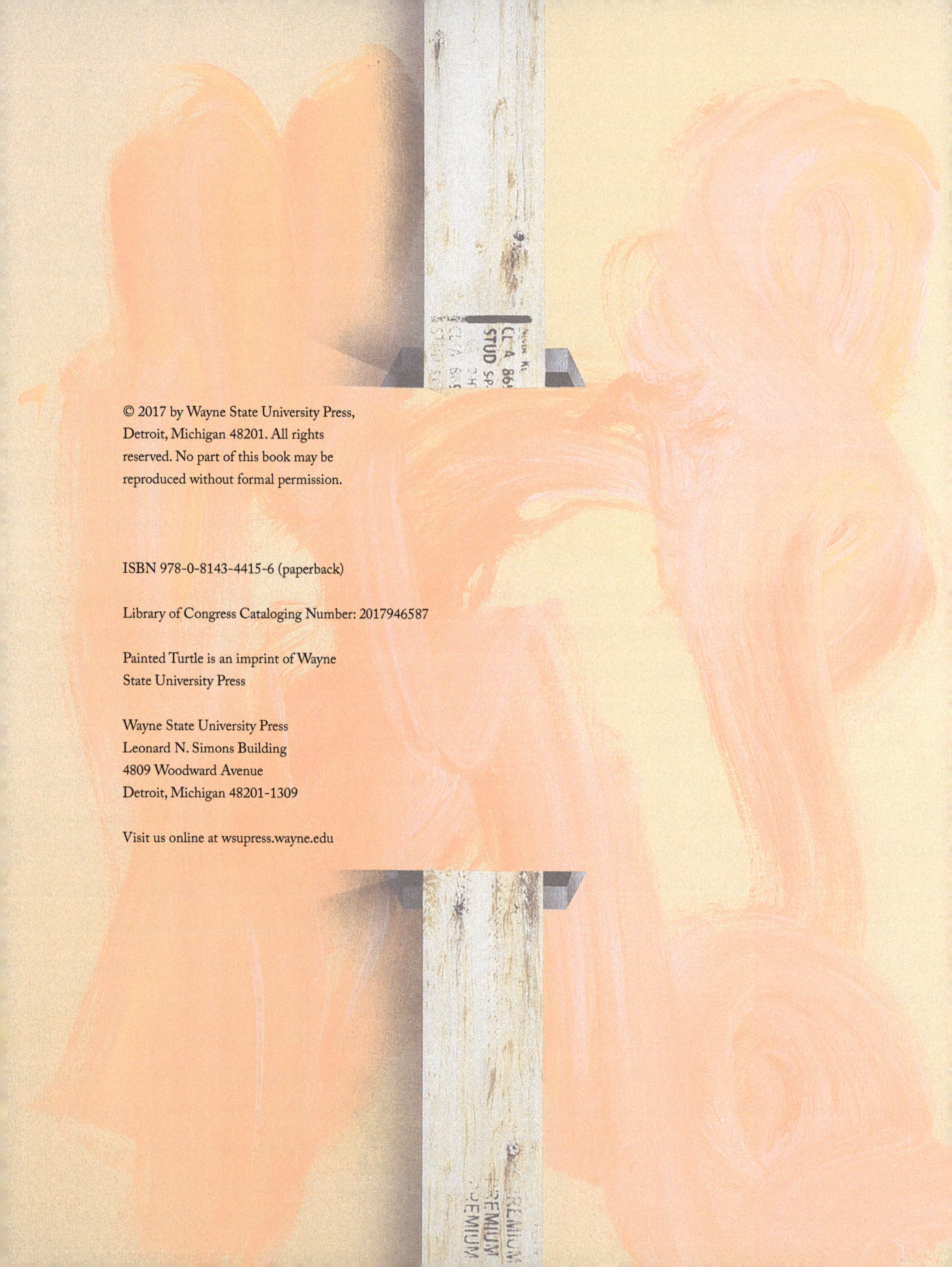

ISBN 978-0-8143-4415-6 (paperback)

Library of Congress Cataloging Number: 2017946587

Painted Turtle is an imprint of Wayne
State University Press

Wayne State University Press
Leonard N. Simons Building
4809 Woodward Avenue
Detroit, Michigan 48201-1309

Visit us online at wsupress.wayne.edu

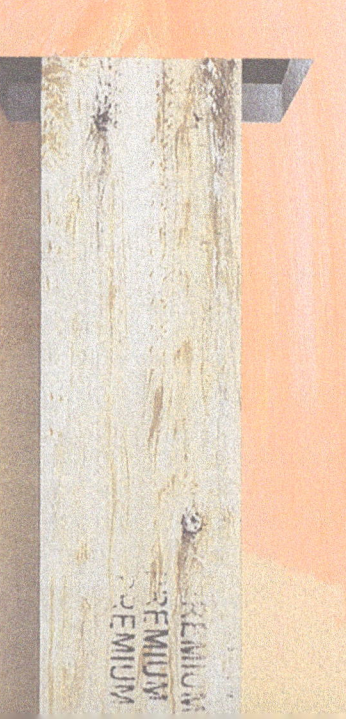

CONTENTS

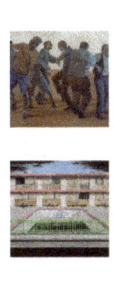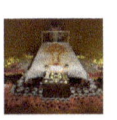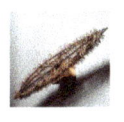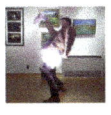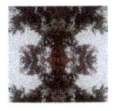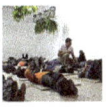
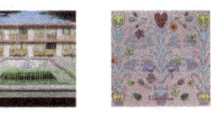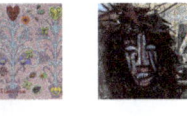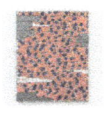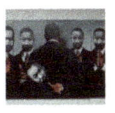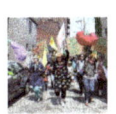
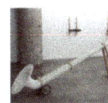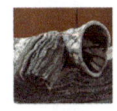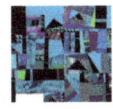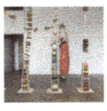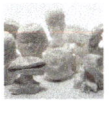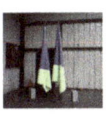
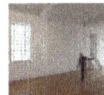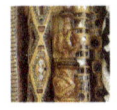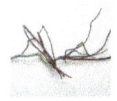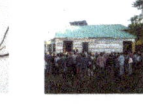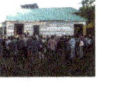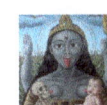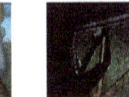

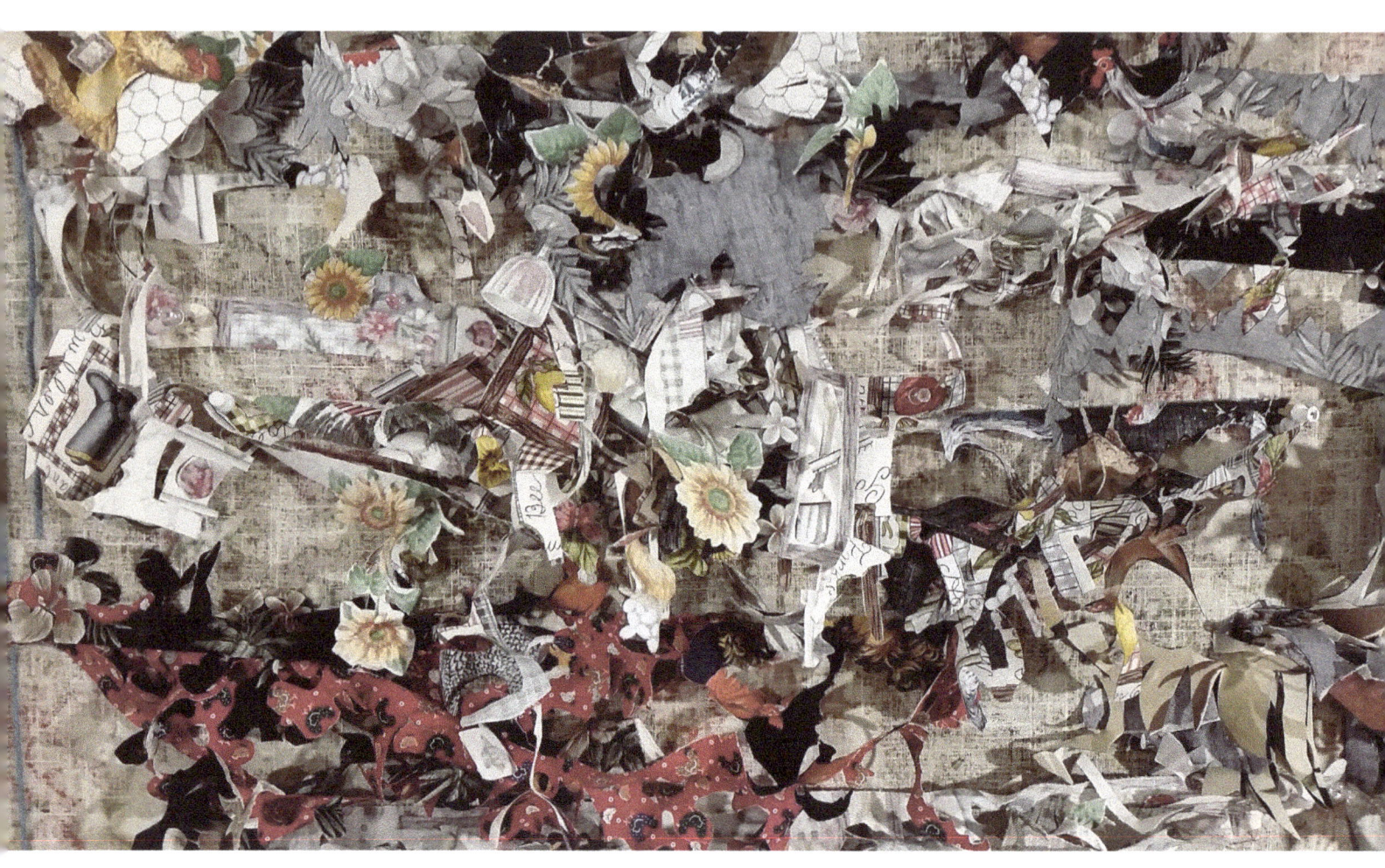

ACKNOWLEDGMENTS

We wish to first thank the readers and supporters, buyers and sellers, enthusiasts and critics of our first collection of essays. You have each contributed to the vitality of our project, and we are deeply grateful for your interest, your thoughtful reactions, and your support of Detroit artists and writers.

Next—and again—we offer profound thanks to our attorney, Noel French, who single-handedly invalidates all the lawyer jokes, and whose fine-grained mind and seemingly tireless dedication has kept the Essay'd train running on the right track and on time, with minimal bumps along the way.

We remain grateful to our partners at Wayne State University Press, namely Jane Ferreyra, Kathryn Wildfong, Kristin Harpster, Emily Nowak, Kristina Stonehill, and Jamie Lee Jones, for their continued belief in and support of this project; to Rebecca Emanuelsen, copyeditor extraordinaire; and to designer Rachel Ross, whose deft repurposing of Bryce Schimanski's original design has yielded an elegant follow-up volume that is at once complementary and distinctive.

For his timely and knowledgeable technical assistance, we are indebted to Ian Chapp of the James Pearson Duffy Department of Art and Art History at Wayne State.

Sincere thanks as well to guest writers Steve Hughes, Rebecca Mazzei, Anthony Marcellini, and Kathy Rashid, whose singular voices diversify the scope of our effort and enliven the pages that follow.

We are grateful to our friends at area art institutions for their help growing the reach and impact of our project, including Amy Corle at the Museum of Contemporary Art Detroit, Phil Gilchrist of the Anton Art Center, and Annie Van-Gelderen of the Birmingham Bloomfield Art Center.

For their generous material support, we thank the following individual and institutional friends of Essay'd: Lynne Avadenka, Kim Fischer, Dan Graschuk, Addie Langford and Michael Stone-Richards, Sharon Zimmerman, and the Birmingham Bloomfield Art Center.

Finally—for their participation and help in completing this book, but more importantly, for the inspiration to undertake it at all—we thank the thirty profiled artists.

DAN, SP, MP

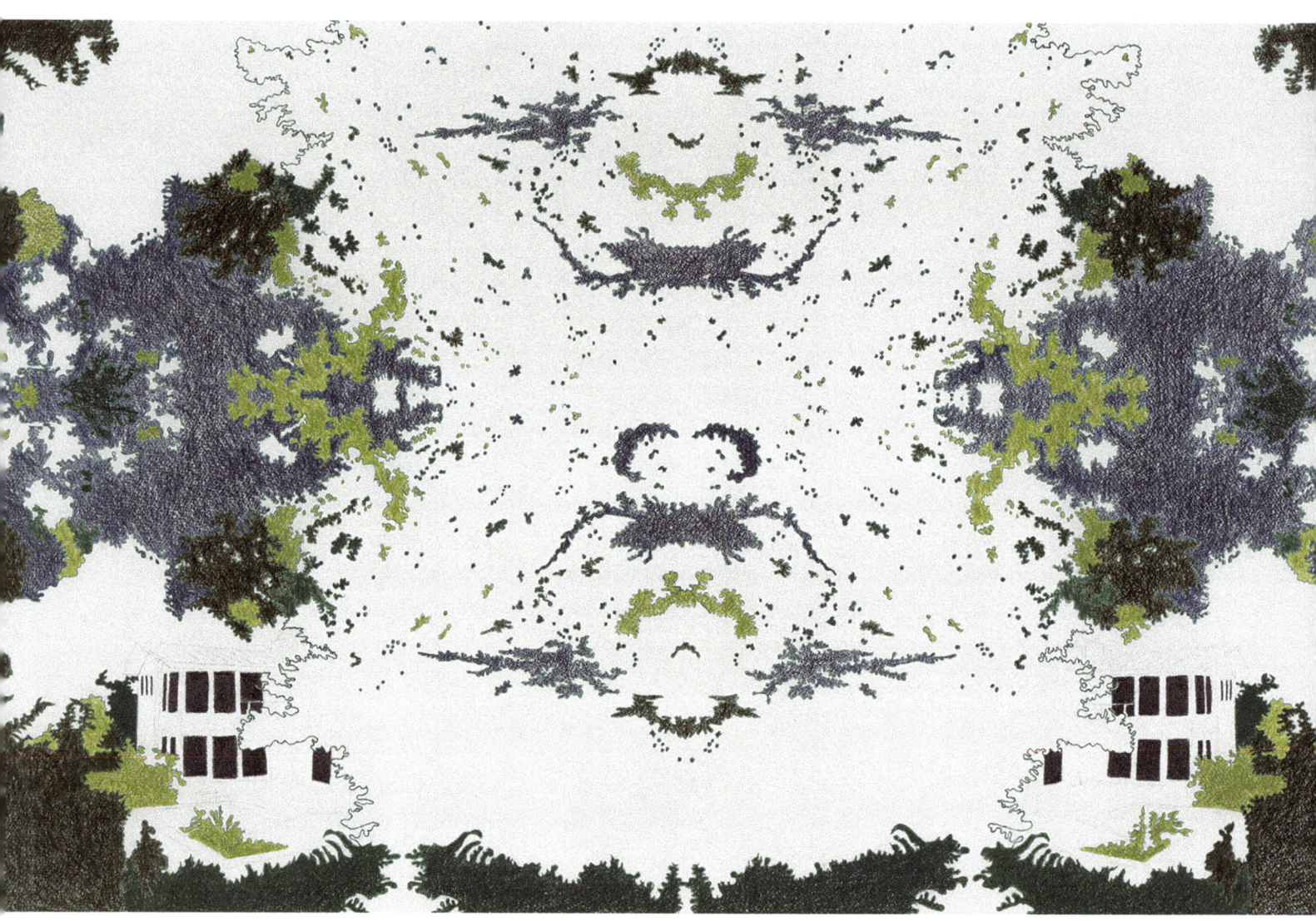

INTRODUCTION

Essay'd is an ongoing effort to document and uplift Detroit's thriving contemporary art community, one artist at a time. Following on the heels of our first printed collection, published in August 2016, Essay'd 2 presents a fresh selection of thirty career-survey profiles of Detroit-area artists. Their subjects, themes, and modes of practice have been singled out from the populous mix of the local scene, in which no single style dominates, but where art production tends to be marked, instead, by a shared spirit of resourcefulness, cooperation, and creative freedom.

Among the kaleidoscopic variety of work to be encountered on the pages that follow lie, for example, both the intimate, fraught vignettes of Jo Powers and the masked denizens of Tylonn Sawyer's claustrophobic interiors; the rambling outdoor installations of Olayami Dabls and Robert Sestok; the evocative fiber art of Carole Harris and Levon Kafafian; Scott Northrup's revelatory video sculptures and Mel Rosas's mysterious streetscapes; David Philpot's richly carved, bejeweled staffs alongside Megan Heeres's eco- and community-conscious paper-making workshops.

The principal authors/editors of Essay'd, who write from our own distinctive perspectives about artists we're personally interested in, are joined, in vol. 2, by four guest writers, whose presence has fostered an even broader array of artists under consideration. This increase (we published just one guest essay in vol. 1) attests to the Essay'd

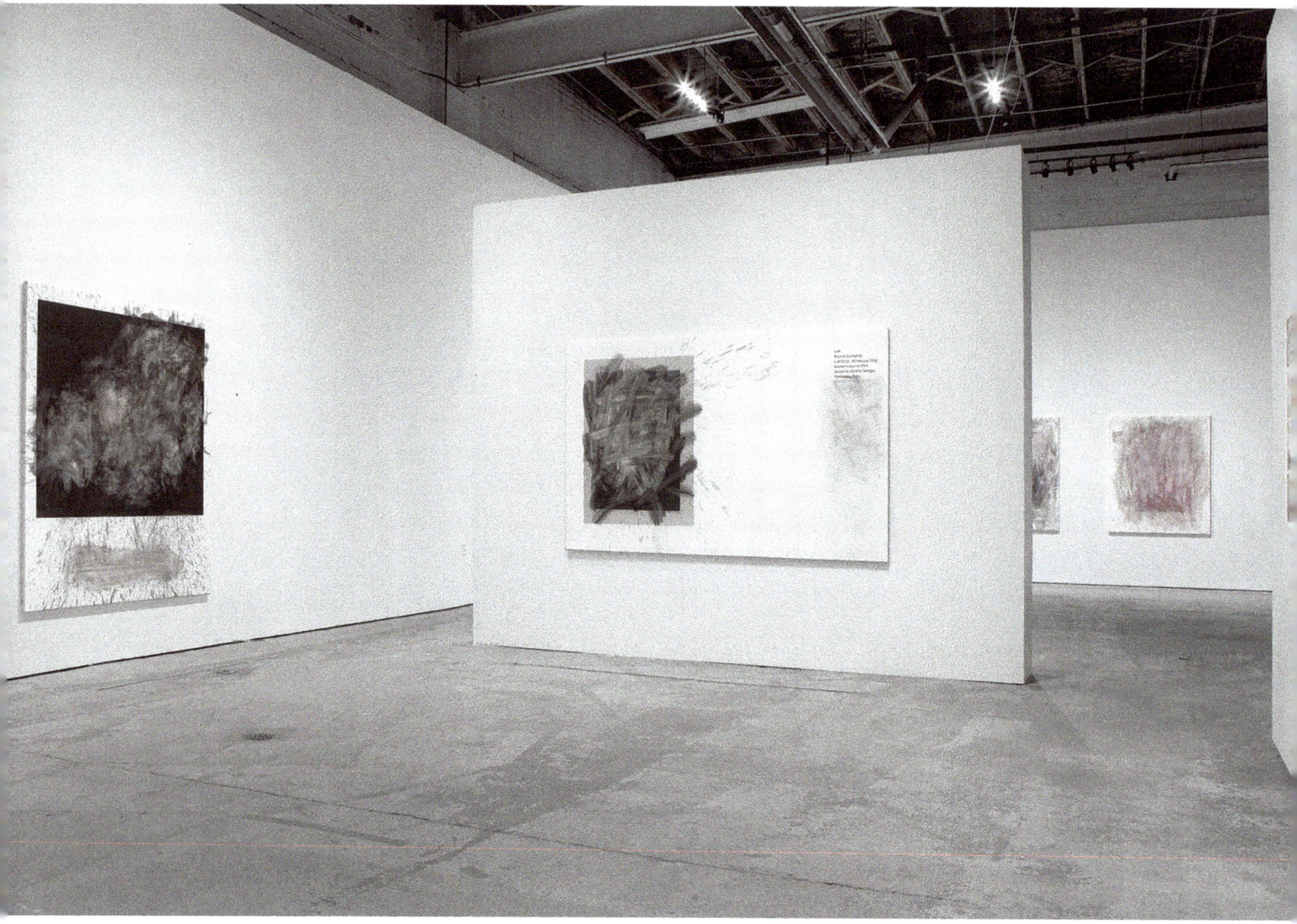

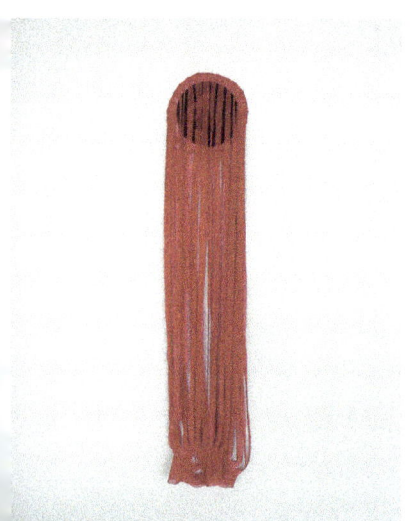

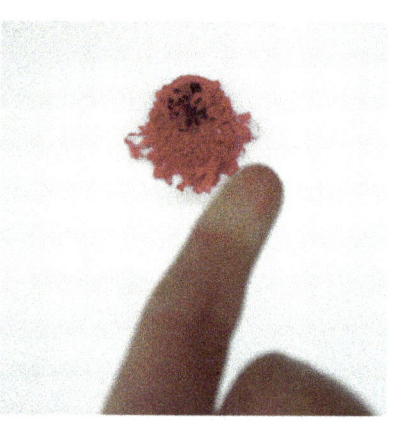

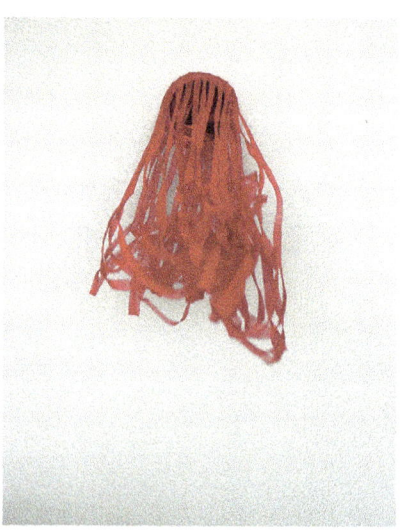

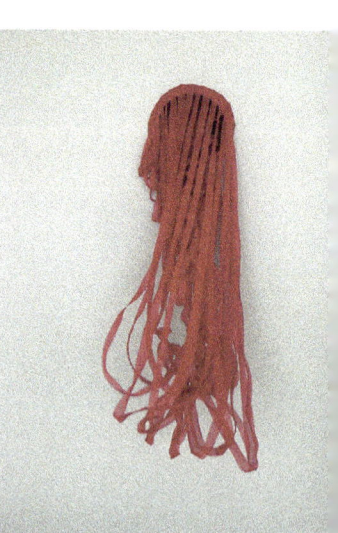

project's expansion in spirit and reach in the last year. Additional developments include our first-ever art-writing workshop, coordinated in partnership with the Museum of Contemporary Art Detroit (MOCAD), and our ongoing series of Essay'd artist talks, held at both the Anton Art Center in Mount Clemens and the Birmingham Bloomfield Art Center. Through these efforts, we have advanced our respective goals of fostering and supporting a local art-writing ecosystem, and promoting regional awareness and understanding of the art made in and of Detroit.

Our buoyant launch of vol. 1 at MOCAD in 2016 was decidedly affirmative and encouraging, as have been the regular installations of our subjects' artwork, presented first at the 9338 Campau gallery and subsequently at other venues, including the N'Namdi Center for Contemporary Art, the Art Department Gallery at Wayne State University, and the Atrium Gallery at the Detroit Symphony Orchestra's Max M. and Marjorie S. Fisher Music Center. Our grateful receipt in late 2016 of a matching grant from the Knight Foundation, meanwhile, has enabled us to not only put our ambitious endeavor on sound financial footing but to begin to grow it—no small feat for a small, grassroots art-writing project.

Now, as volume 2 of our collective undertaking becomes a reality and rolls off the presses, we ask ourselves, can volume 3 be far behind? Will *Essay'd* morph from individual volumes to a trilogy, and thence to a multivolume compendium, as envisioned in our cautiously worded but surely immodest foundational claim that: "With time, we expect a fairly comprehensive survey to emerge"? We suspect, in fact, that we are well on our way.

DAN, SP, MP

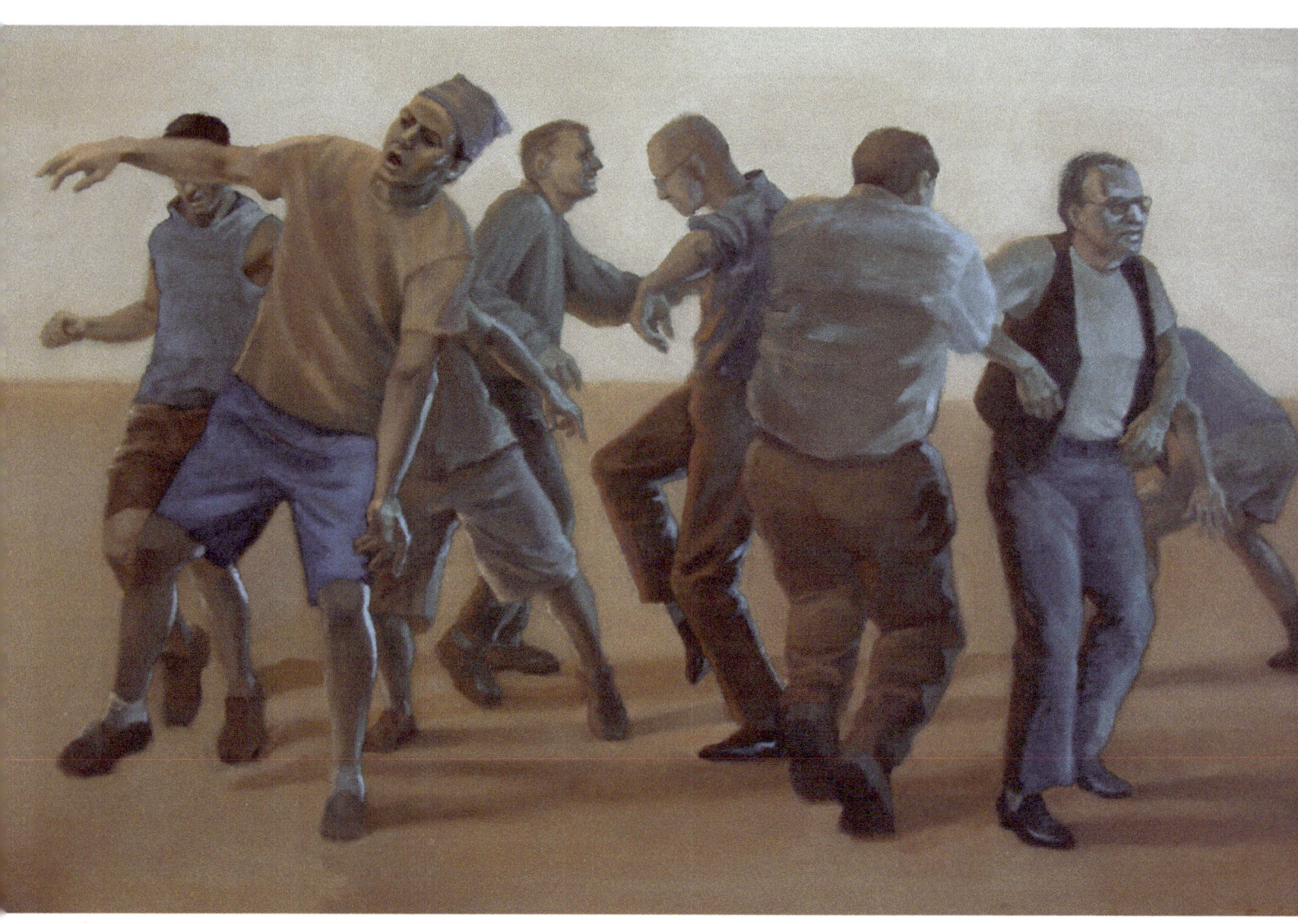

Man Dance. 2007. Oil on wood, 13 x 21 in.

Born Detroit, 1951
BFA, Wayne State University; MFA,
Syracuse University, New York
Lives in Royal Oak, Michigan

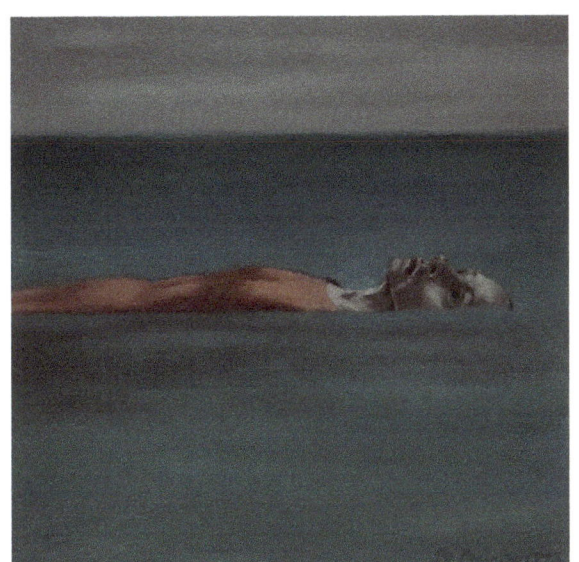

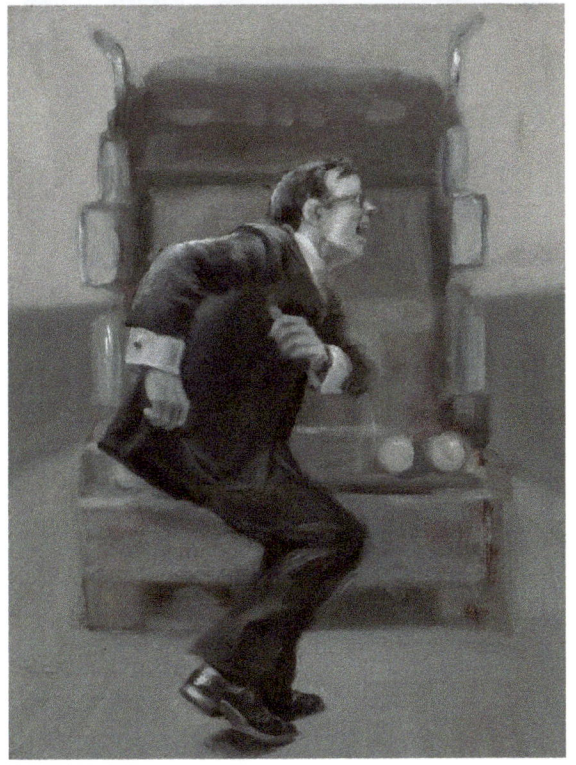

Soundlessly, without stirring a ripple, a woman glides into view in Jo Powers's **Lake**, the painter's haunting self-portrait of 1993. Garbed in pink and borne on a watery expanse of azure, she drifts, Ophelia-like, calm, composed, and with eyes wide open, all-seeing. Albeit "at sea" in life's journey, this "swimmer" ruminates on her present, pressured state of mind, rebooting as she floats along. Several arresting self-portraits, in similarly tiny oil-on-wood format—**Lake** is a mere six by six inches—punctuate Powers's three-decades-long career. Her spare, sometimes austere compositions, petite scale, low-key color, suppressed emotion, and painterly facture, offset by startling scenarios, is the raw material of a consummate pictorialist. Painter,

(Top) Lake. 1993. Oil on wood, 6 x 6 in.
(Bottom) Highway Dance. 2011. Oil on wood, 11 x 8 in.

1

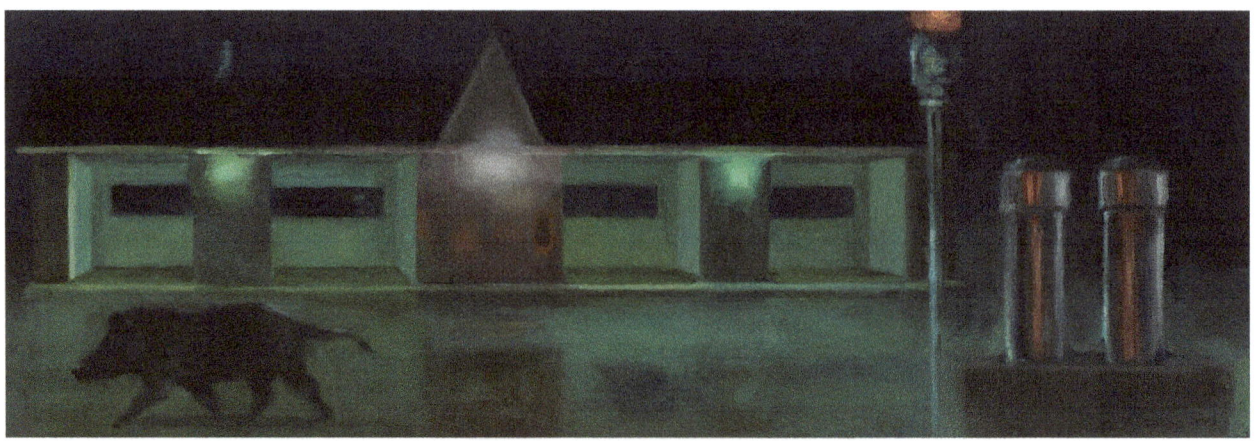

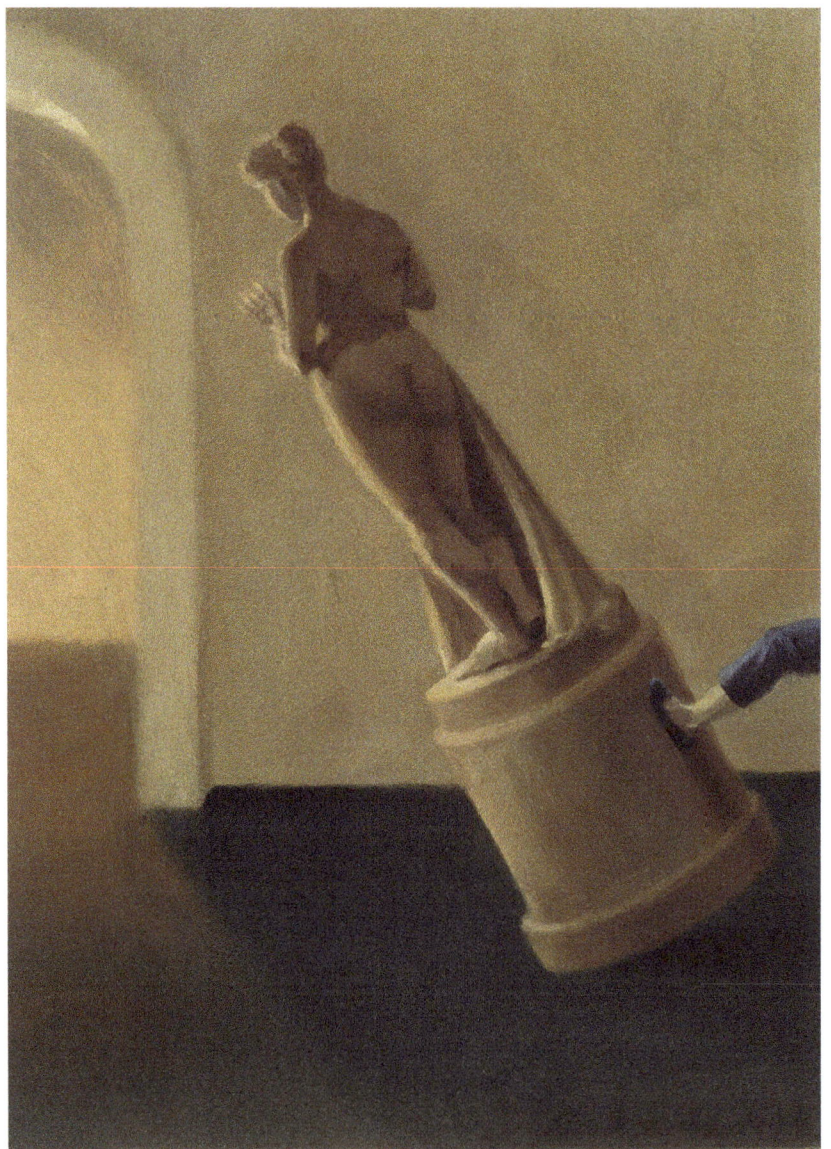

(Top) Car Wash. 2013. Oil on wood, 4 1/2 x 13 1/2 in.
(Bottom) Pandora. 1994. Oil on wood, 9 x 6 in.

illustrator, and art faculty at Macomb and Oakland Community Colleges, Powers has participated in numerous group and solo shows, her images uniformly described as "mysterious" and "powerful."

Indeed, Powers's themes and scenes of resilience, agitation, turmoil, soul searching, and stoicism (and sporadic celebration) reverberate with universal ramifications. In a series of "museum pictures," including **Pandora** (1994) and **Museum Dance** (1996), for instance, the stultifying presence of old art, embodied by nineteenth-century white marble sculptures, provoked several encounters of human and marmoreal figures set amidst the galleries of the Detroit Institute of Arts. In the former, a slim female leg, shod in a ballet flat, thrusts in from the right to topple a chiton-clad statue depicting "Pandora's

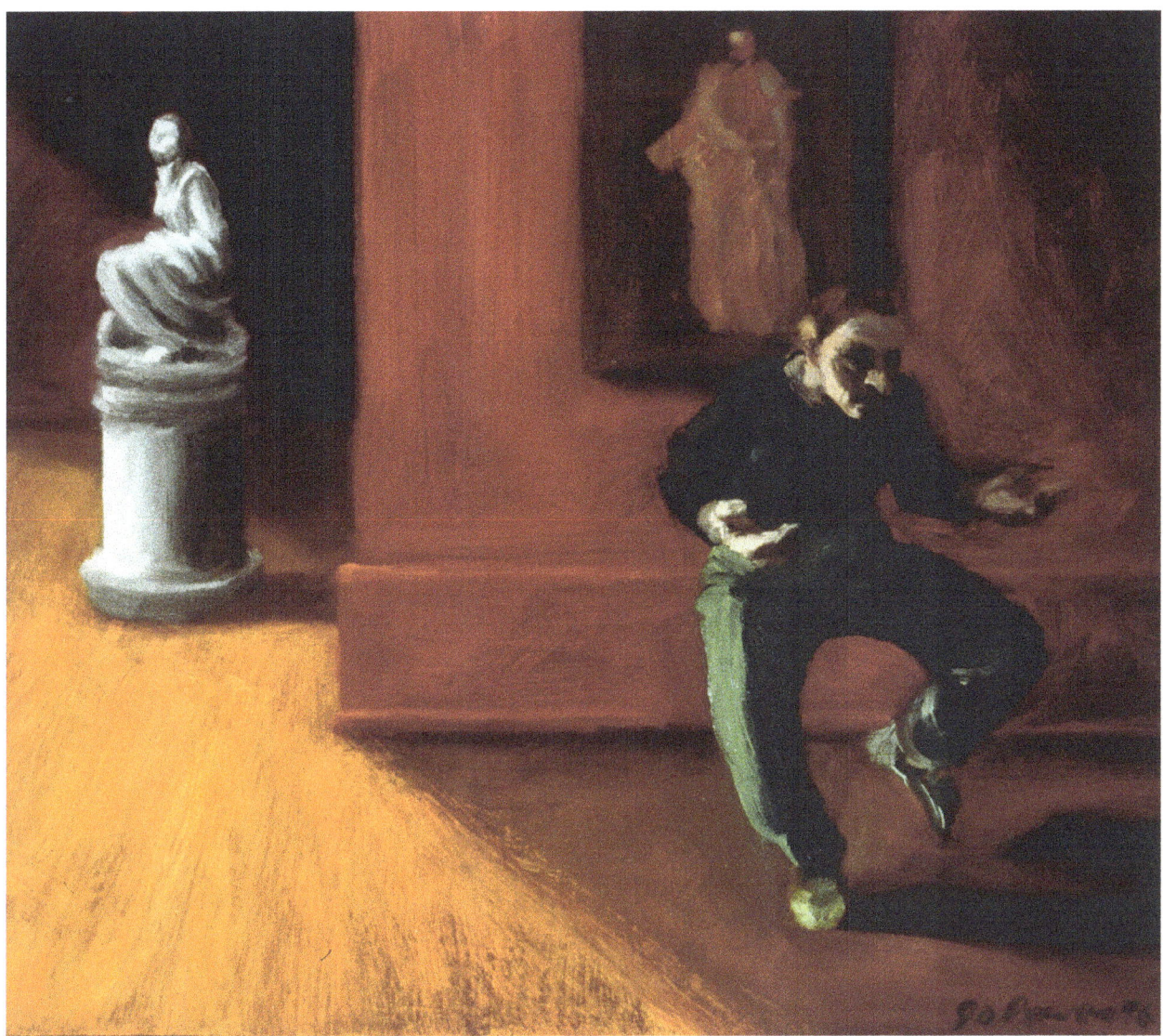

Museum Dance. 1996. Oil on wood, 11 x 12 in.

box," while in the latter, a male visitor/artist is caught in a spirited dance, the gyrations of which the crouching marble figure is completely oblivious to. In this episode, the inflamed red of the wall is strikingly complemented by the green-attired dancer unleashing his id just around the corner and out of sight of the ivory-hued effigy in the background.

Dance, frenzied or decorous, is a recurring motif in Powers's images, either of solitary hoofers or, more rarely, of a group, a subject prompted in part by collaborative ventures she undertook with the Detroit Dance Collective in the nineties. ***Man Dance*** (2007) highlights a fully realized example of such scenes, rendered in comparatively large scale at

thirteen by twenty-one inches. In a warm, harmonious palette and indeterminate space, eight men of divers ages and modes of dress—apparently unaware of us observing their gambol—are caught up in singularly individual dance steps. The middle-aged couple at the right, familiar with one another's body language, dance sedately, while the younger pair at

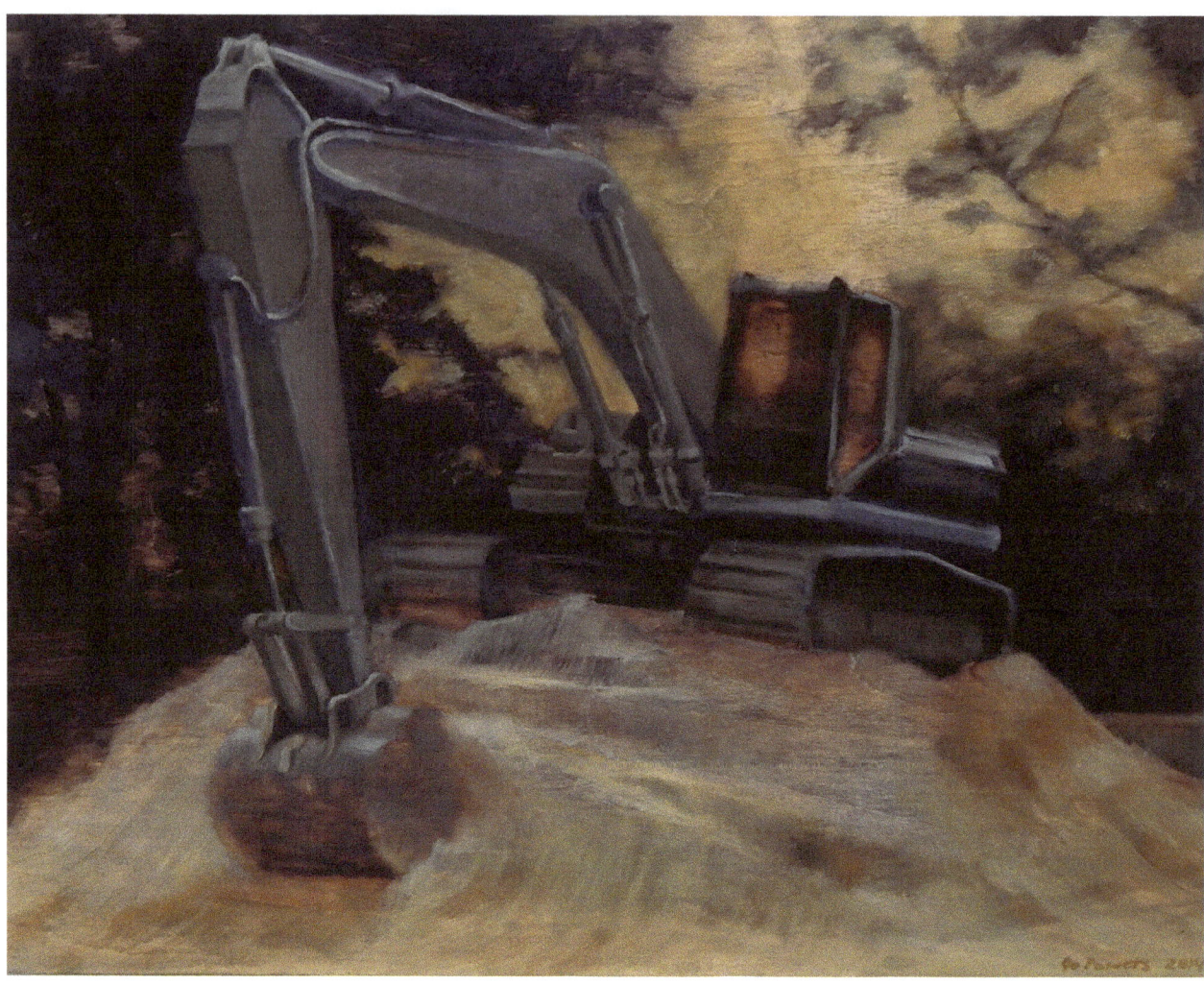

Neighborhood. 2014. Oil on wood, 9 x 12 in.

the left, albeit partners, turn and twist to their individual drummers. The man in front, his back turned to his companion, seems about to execute an improvised move that will shatter the shapely oval formed by the group. Indeed, the lusty camaraderie of this rhythmic ensemble, even absent a soundtrack, is positively palpable.

In Powers's universe, threats to one's equilibrium, however, are never far from home, originating as they do from the streets or precincts of one's neighborhood. In **Street Scene** (1998), a sidewalk skirmish has erupted in front of a bridal salon as two men grapple with one another. And then there are the boars (!) that incongruously roam through Powers's scenes, whether in solitude, as in **Car Wash** (2013), or in clusters, from as early as

1996. Fascinated by their sleek, bullet-like bodies rather than their reputed aggressiveness, she renders her boars as unsettling, blurred presences lurking about, or here as a loner trotting past an empty, acidic green car wash in the middle of the night. More recently, as construction sites have metastasized across the city, hulking, heavy-duty vehicles have begun to populate Powers's image

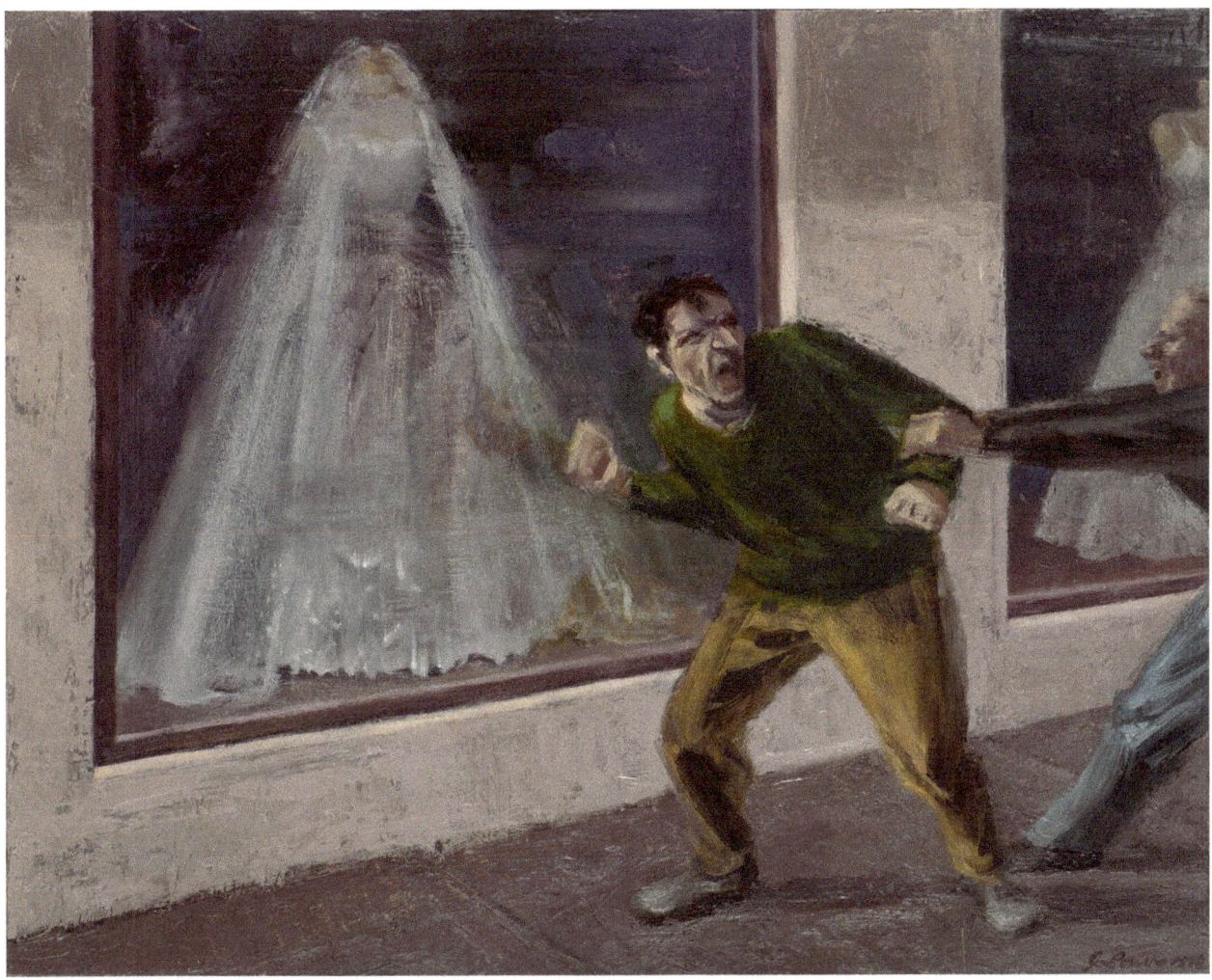

Street Scene. 1998. Oil on wood, 16 x 20 in.

bank. The steam shovel in 2014's ***Neighborhood***, with its pulsing, rosy-hued cab and dinosaurian armature, attests to the invasive nature of these mechanized beasts.

Yet the dance of life insistently bursts forth, as in 2011's ***Highway Dance***, where, in a muted grisaille palette, a suit—cuff links conspicuously visible—shouts, swings, and sways as fast as he can in front of the looming cab of a

massive eighteen-wheeler. Is the truck parked or bearing down; is the "Watusi" dancer venting frustration, recklessly oblivious, savoring a victory, or defying an incarnation of brute force, in an echo of David vs. Goliath? Thus is the scope of Powers's self-defined "narrative realism," a rather terse phrase for an oeuvre of charged, intimate panel paintings—small but roomy—imbued

with the scale, scope, and, yes, mystery of actual life.

DENNIS ALAN NAWROCKI, SEPTEMBER 2015

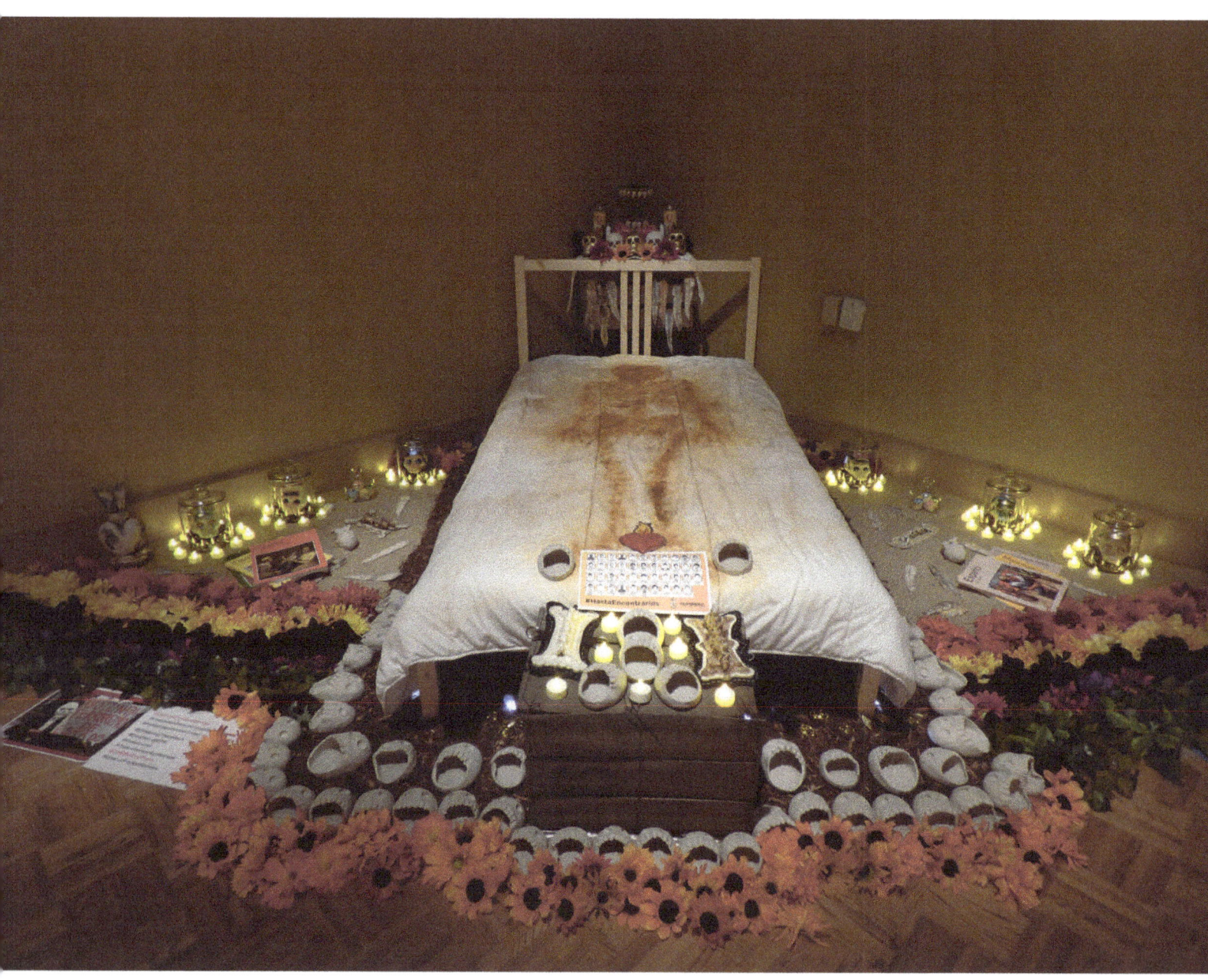

Ayotzinapa. 2014. Bed, sand, salt, unfired clay, silk flowers, elementary school books from Mexico, sugar skulls, and bullet shells. Photography by Larry McMann.

Born Cuernavaca Morelos, Mexico, 1976
BFA, Universidad del Sol,
Cuernavaca, Mexico
Lives in Ferndale, Michigan

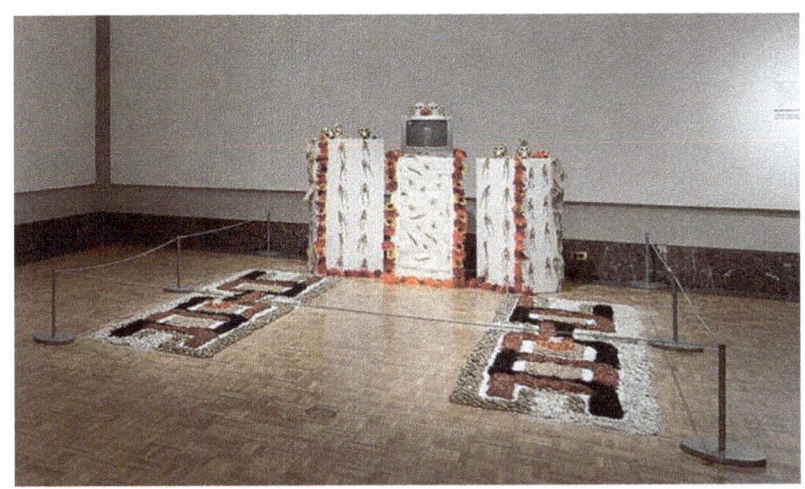

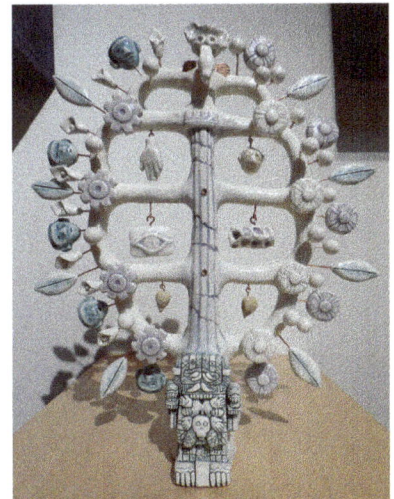

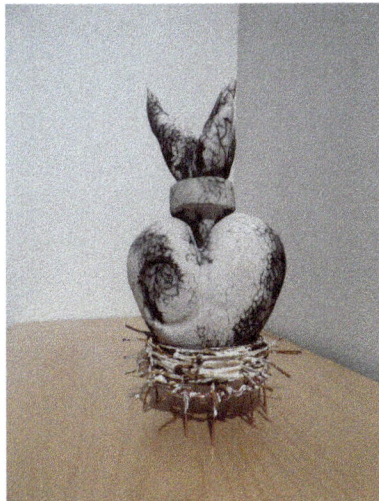

For artist Kia Arriaga, there are ways in which existing is an act of resistance; Arriaga deeply identifies with her Aztek roots and works in multiple media to "rescue the traditional ways of the original people of Mexico." Powerful and oppositional, Arriaga's art has the rare capacity to offer resistance in a form so beautiful, so alluring, that it may be courted by the very institutions it seeks to disrupt.

These media include her primary work as a blacksmith, ceramics (her "new lover"), stained glass, and mural painting (her degree is in graphic design/illustration)—but also extends

(*Top*) *Ephemeral.* 2013. Mulch, gravel, sand, salt, silk flowers, papier-mâché skulls, paint. Photography by Larry McMann.
(*Bottom, left*) *Frida and Diego, Arbol de la vida.* 2015. Porcelain, copper, 15 x 13 x 3 in. Photography by Larry McMann.
(*Bottom, right*) *Milagro.* 2011. Naked raku, found object, 14 x 6 x 5 in. Photography by Larry McMann.

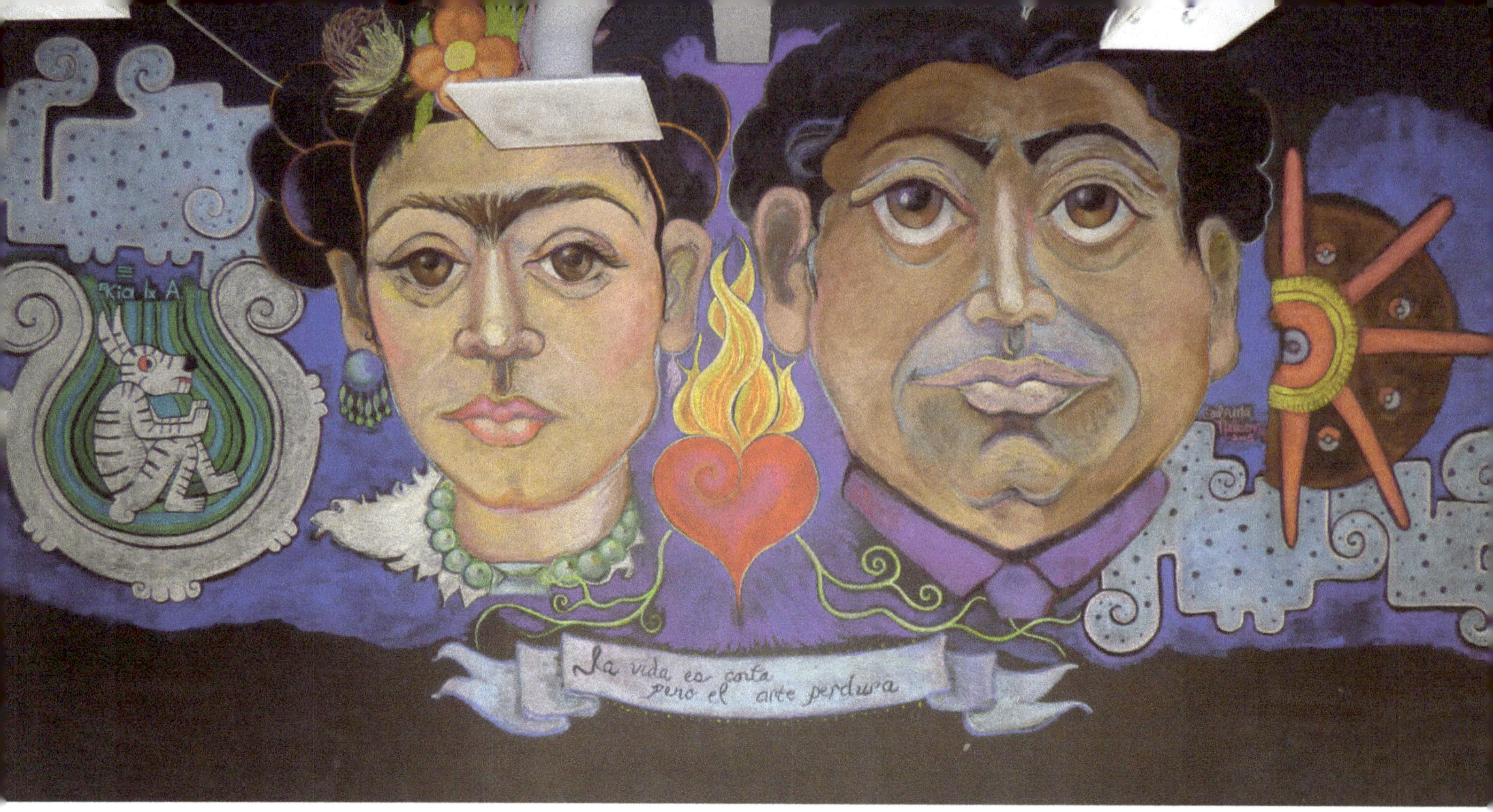

Frida y Diego; La vida es corta, pero el arte perdura (collaboration with painter Sabrina Nelson). 2015. Chalk mural, 10 x 22 ft.

through her **practice as an Aztek Dancer** and member of the Aztek group Kalpulli Tlahuikayotl. This practice, which Arriaga has pursued since the age of thirteen, involves not only dancing but the transfer of knowledge about many aspects of Aztek culture, including the Aztek calendar and the count of time, traditional food preparation, traditional healing, regalia-making, codex painting and interpretation, philosophy, and agriculture. "You learn to love learning, in general," Arriaga says, and it seems to be a lesson she has learned well. Though she lacks a formal degree from either institution, she has pursued her fine art studies at both Wayne

State University and the College for Creative Studies since moving to the Detroit metro area in 1998. "I am probably going to be the oldest student ever," she enthuses.

In fact, Arriaga's bubbly manner is striking when contrasted with the seriousness of her themes. Across all her various expressive media, Arriaga's work is deeply personal and draws from a treasure trove of heritage that includes both Aztek and Latin American roots, Mexican culture—including Lucha Libre (Mexican professional wrestling), as with **Santo, el Enmascarado de Plata** (2014), and Día de Muertos (Day of the Dead)—and a familial affinity for multimedia

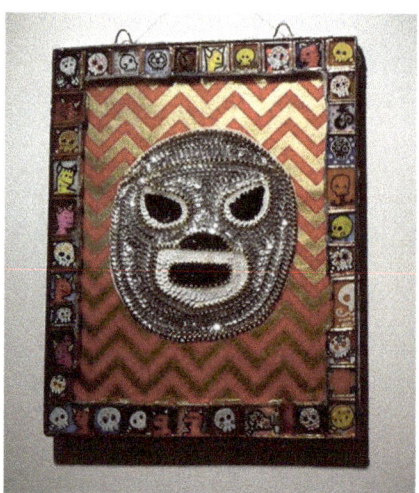

Santo, el Enmascarado de Plata. 2014. Stained glass, sequins, mixed media, 11 x 10 x 1 1/2 in. Photography by Larry McMann.

arts, learning, and teaching, as well as her grandfather's specialized trade as a blacksmith. All of these have synthesized within Arriaga's work and manifest in the form of ceramic and metal works that range from whimsical to gothic, and highly political installations, including elaborate *ofrendas* (traditional altars that are temporarily constructed to celebrate Mexican Día de Muertos and Aztek rites of summer). Arriaga has been a fixture of local Día de Muertos celebrations, as well as a two-time contributor to the Detroit Institute of Arts' annual *ofrenda* exhibit. In 2013, Arriaga created **Ephemeral**, a seed mandala—"Tlalmanalli" in the Aztek language (Nahuatl), meaning "offering to earth"—combined with a video feed of static. In 2014, still reeling from the horrific news of the kidnapping and murder of a bus full of teachers in training near her hometown, Arriaga scrapped her original *ofrenda* plans, replacing them with **Ayotzinapa**, an arresting installation around a bed, the white sheets of which were marred with the rusty imprint of a skeleton. Clustered around the foot of the bed, open-mouthed ceramic skulls stand like empty sets of slippers, with the faces of hungry spirits.

Arriaga's installation work typically contains specific, personally crafted components of this nature, many of which are art objects in their own right—for example,

the **Milagro** (2011) that formed a detail of *Ayotzinapa*. Her more recent focus on ceramics has seen the development of stand-alone ceramic and wire pieces, such as the **Frida and Diego, Arbol de la vida** (2015), which incorporates ceramic and metal working, the traditional tree of life motif, and Arriaga's interest in Mexican cultural icons Frida Kahlo and Diego Rivera, who she recently also commemorated in a wall-sized chalk mural, a collaboration with painter Sabrina Nelson in the DIA's Learning Annex—**Frida y Diego; La vida es corta, pero el arte perdura** (2015). "*La vida es corta, pero el arte perdura,*" the mural's inscription reads—"Life is short, but art endures." With each craft learned, each tradition remembered and passed on, and each work of art—be it temporary or fired in clay or iron—Arriaga is forming an enduring cultural legacy, one which begins from the deeply personal and moves out through her community to touch and offer teaching to all who encounter her work. Like the Azteks, who buried key monuments and artifacts in an effort to preserve their culture in the face of Spanish colonialism, Arriaga's life and work stands as an act of

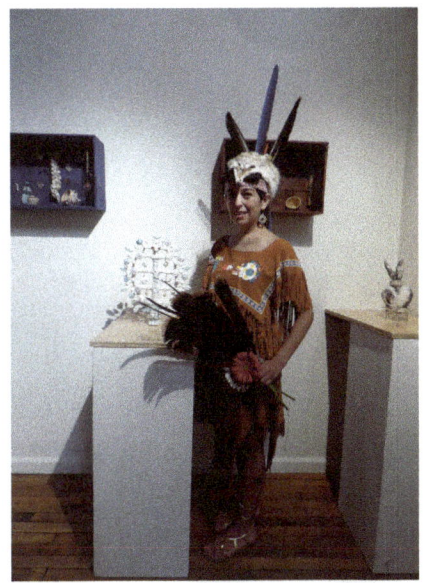

Kiauitzin in Aztek Regalia (performance at the N'Namdi Center for Contemporary Art). 2015. Leather, feathers, beads, acrylic, and sacred objects. Photography by Larry McMann.

resistance against any forces that would seek to wipe the slate of history, politics, or tradition clean.

SARAH ROSE SHARP,
SEPTEMBER 2015

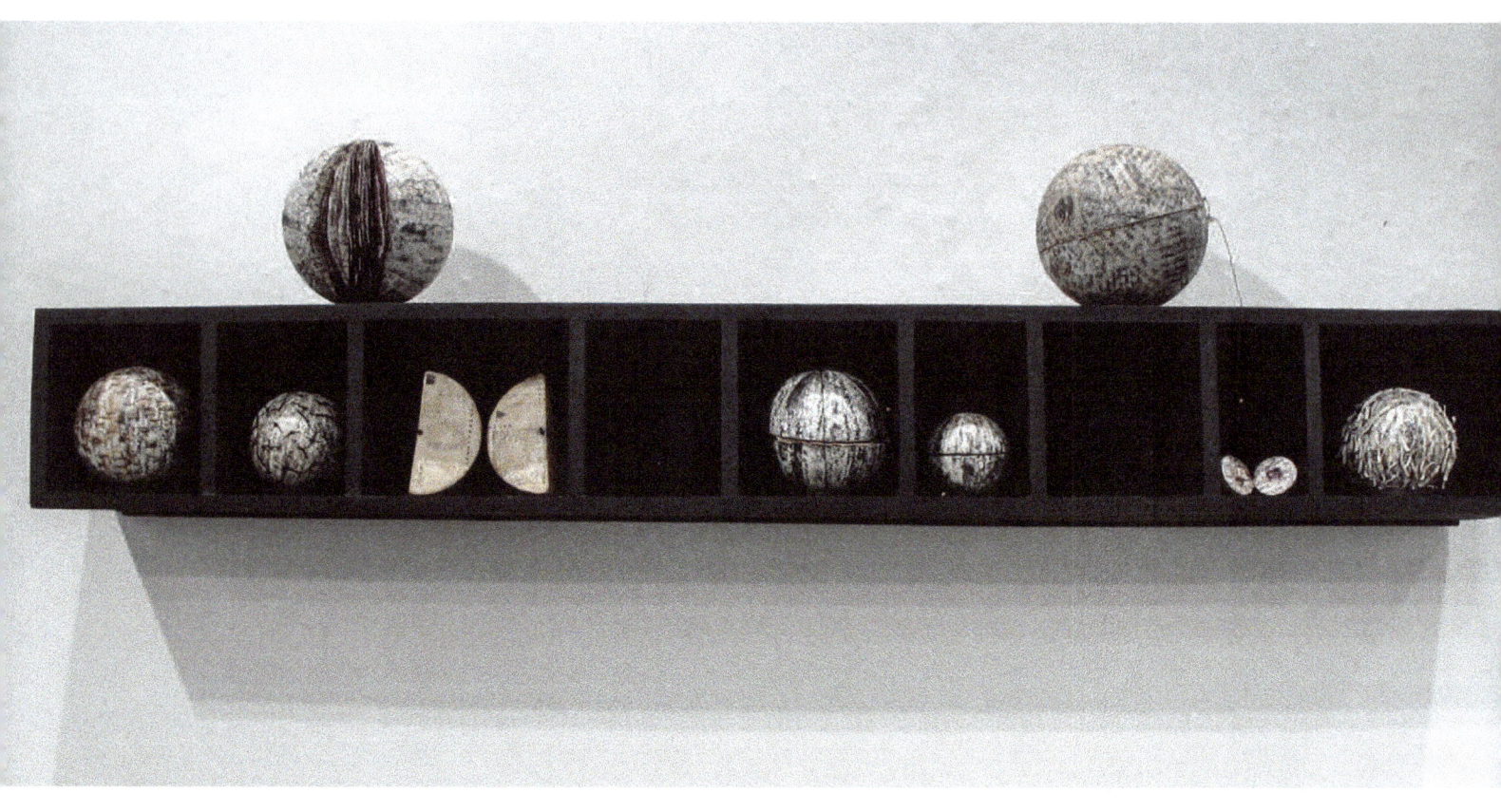

Impossible Books. 2003. Paper, ink, assorted objects, 60 x 10 x 10 in.

Born Detroit, 1949
BFA, Wayne State University; MFA,
Eastern Michigan University
Lives in Troy, Michigan

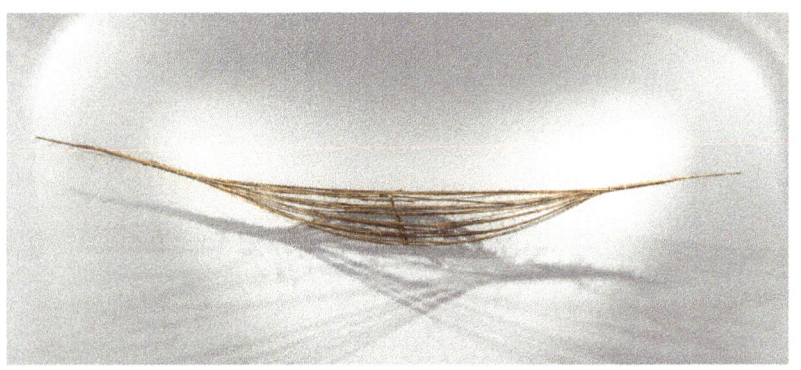

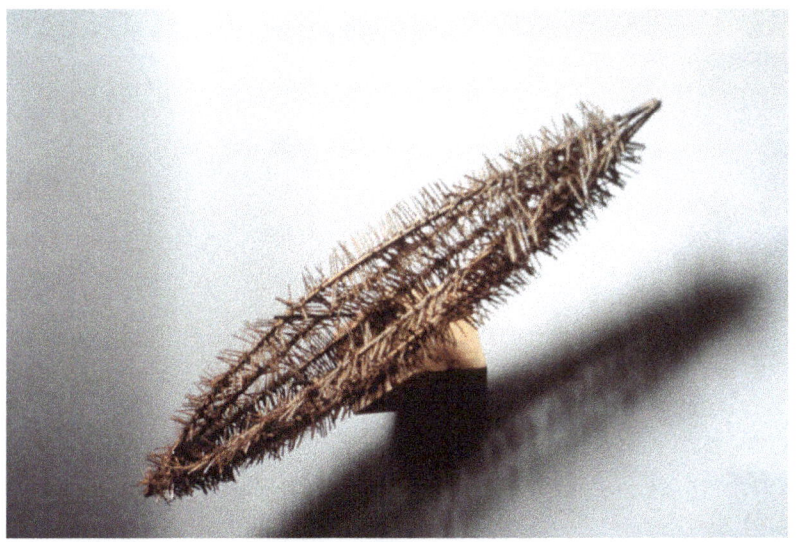

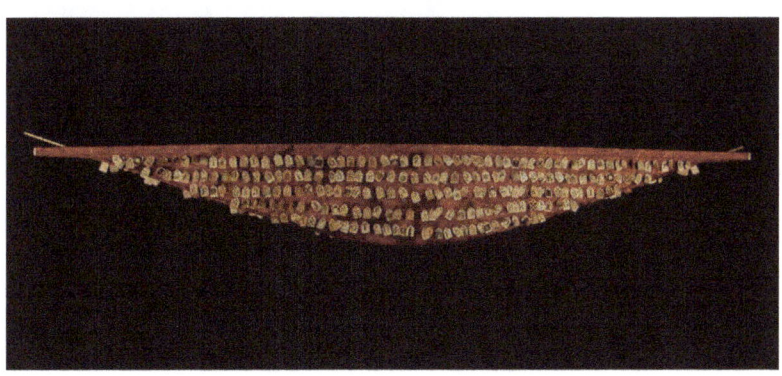

Christine Hagedorn's hands are impressively large, the skin cracked and calloused in places: a worker's hands, which belie the slender, elegant lines of her overall stature. A similar duality runs through her practice as an artist. Her fine sense of order and aesthetics temper her essential impulse to let materials speak for her, by means of letting them speak for themselves, through her immersion in rigorous, sometimes obsessive handwork. But a third motive breaks between these channels in her art-making. Hagedorn recalls her childhood habit of finding something—a necklace, a shell, a stone—unearthing it from the ground, and wrapping it with string or

(*Top*) *Spirit Boat.* 1996. Reeds, waxed sinew, 168 x 12 x 10 in.
(*Middle*) *Psychology of Desire.* 1996. Steel, nails, wire, 72 x 12 x 10 in.
(*Bottom*) *Alternative Communication.* 2007. Hand-dyed paper, tags, ink, 72 x 11 x 8 in.

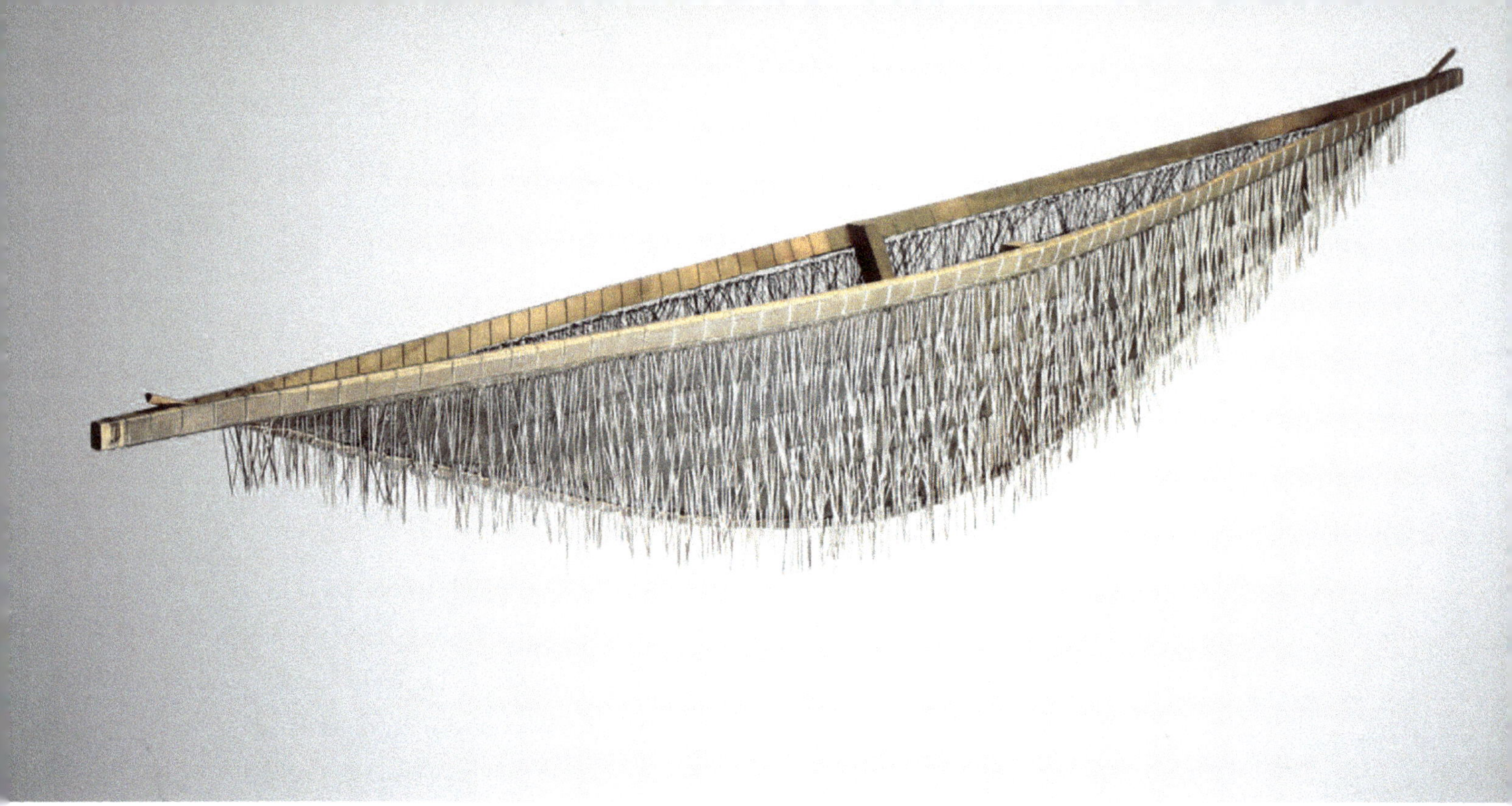

Implication. 2000. Wood, screen, needles, thread, 72 x 10 x 8 in.

yarn, then hiding it again, in order to recover it later and deem it "powerful" or "magic." This engagement with otherworldliness through self-made ritual circulates through all her creative work.

Her early work reflects the influence of a transformative exposure to African art and ritual, particularly the practice of pounding nails into ancestral images to represent prayers and promises of sacrifice as a means of personal and communal healing. The starkly expressive **Prayers for the City** (1994) is an old, burned, weather-beaten board she scavenged off the street and hammered with a fringe of rusted nails along its singed edge. Similar

works, using a wooden pole or fence post, begin to allude more literally to the human figure and, by implication, the self. One of these, **Coming through the Fire** (1995), she wrapped with wire to a bier of wire mesh and set on fire behind the old Michigan Gallery in a cleansing ritual that invited viewers to throw their own tokens into the flames.

This performance also marked a transition in her work away from the flat, vertical wall pieces that retained the 2-D influence of her background in printmaking. Packing her figure pieces horizontally for transport one day, she suddenly saw them take on the form of a boat in motion and realized that this form was

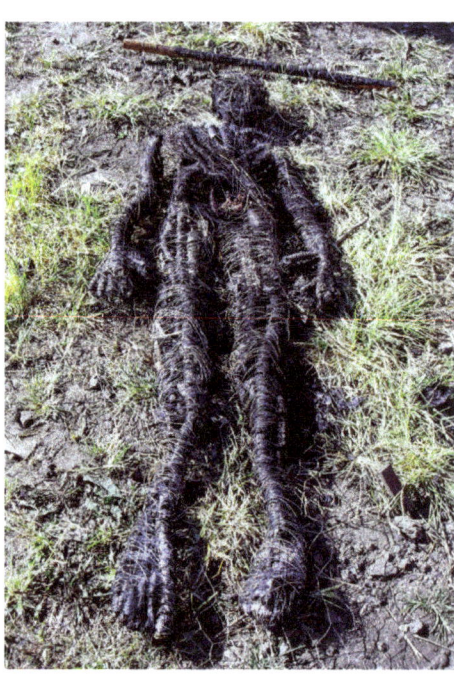

Coming through the Fire. 1995. Wood, wire, ashes, 67 x 18 x 5 in.

an even more apt vessel to express the ambiguous interior/exterior nature of the self. Many of the boats in her subsequent work allude to paradoxical aspects of identity—fear and desire—conveying a sense of protection and survival as well as vulnerability and self-destruction. The first in the series, *Spirit Boat* (1996), is simply a bundle of reed-like grasses, held in its center by a single rib and bound on either end into a long bowing arc, appearing light enough to float, but completely open and penetrable by air and water. Another seminal work in the series is *Psychology of Desire* (1996), a vessel wrought of scavenged, heavy-gauge, twisted wire, studded with rusted nails, in a posture of menace bound with a sense of tragic destiny. A stunning example of her obsessive handwork is *Implication* (2000), its outer surface threaded entirely with sewing needles, hanging like rain through the screen of its armature, the thread ends left to carpet the inside like the soft fur of an animal.

Eventually, script and text begin to mark the surface of Hagedorn's work, propelling it into another dimension of reference. She intentionally obscures interpretation by cutting up and jumbling alphabets, numbers, signs, and narrative, using this practice as a way to represent a sense of exile and alienation from lost systems of language and meaning. In *Alternative Communication* (2007), old sales tags she stamped with signs and symbols hang along a boat's contours in dense and illegible sequences.

This reference to irretrievable human knowledge finds its fuller expression when Hagedorn shifts from the boat form to the sphere or globe, as representations of the self move from the individual to her context in human history and culture. *Impossible Books* (2003) condenses three years of her journals, handwritten on sumi paper, which she copied, inverted, and sliced into strips, then built up in layers to cover the surfaces of a series of spheres and hemispheres, some severed and opening into actual pages, with an inscrutable geology. Through the ritual practice of her art, in these "spheres of hidden knowledge," Hagedorn manages to universalize her lifelong desire to touch and hold the numinous power which is lost, forgotten, and collectively yearned for by our unmoored culture, yet still hidden inside the world.

KATHLEEN RASHID,
SEPTEMBER 2015

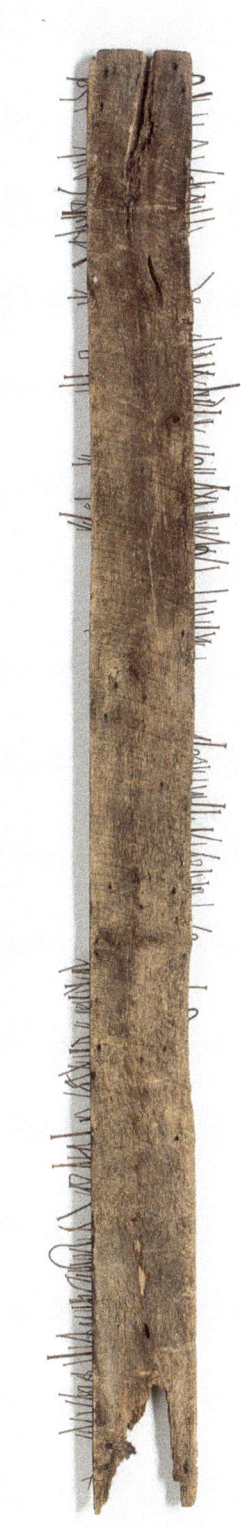

Prayers for the City. 1994.
Found wood, nails,
94 x 12 x 2 in.

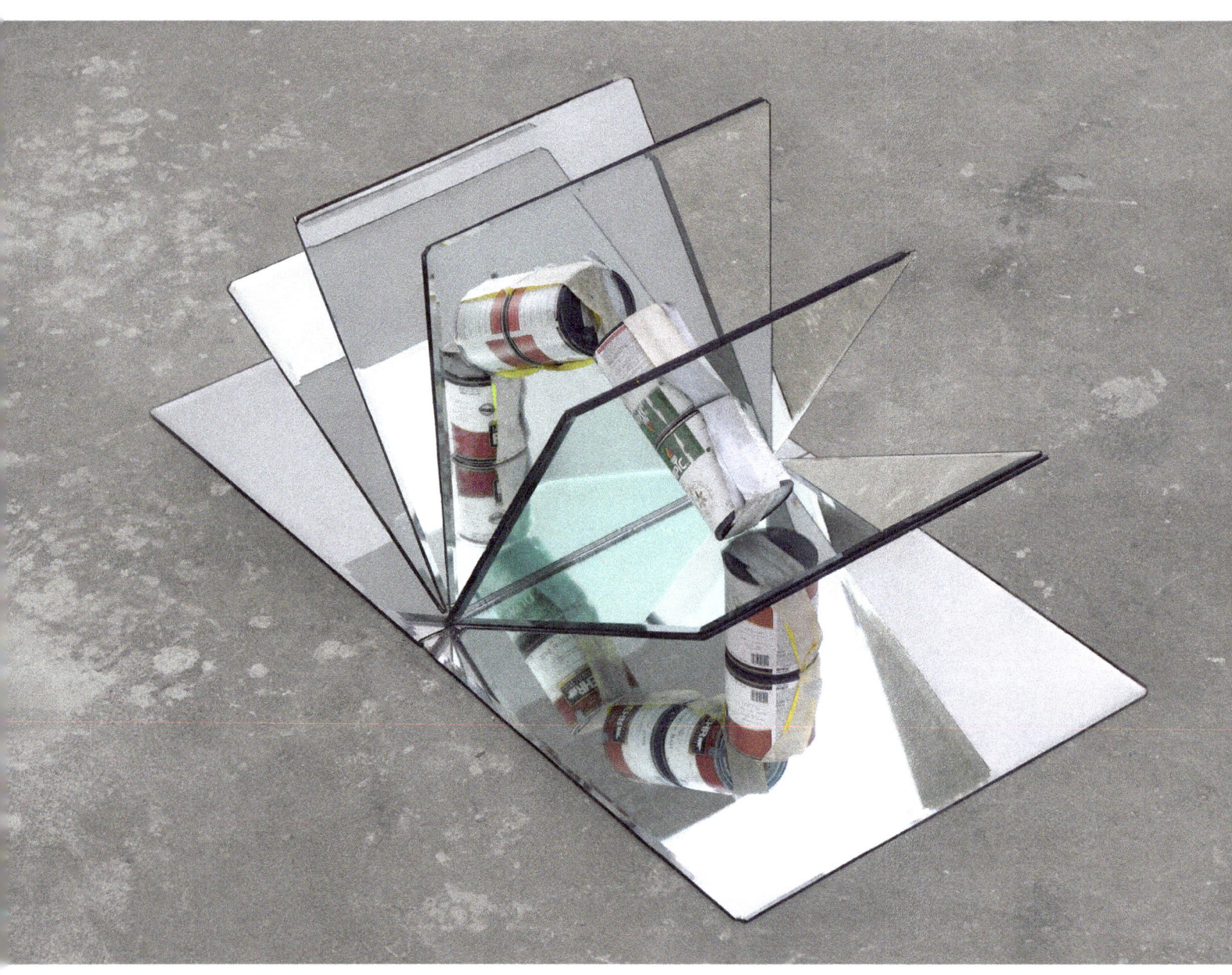

Untitled. 2013. Mirrors, paint cans, duct tape, 20 x 20 x 20 in.

Born Raleigh, North Carolina, 1986
BA, Bennington College, Vermont
Lives in Detroit

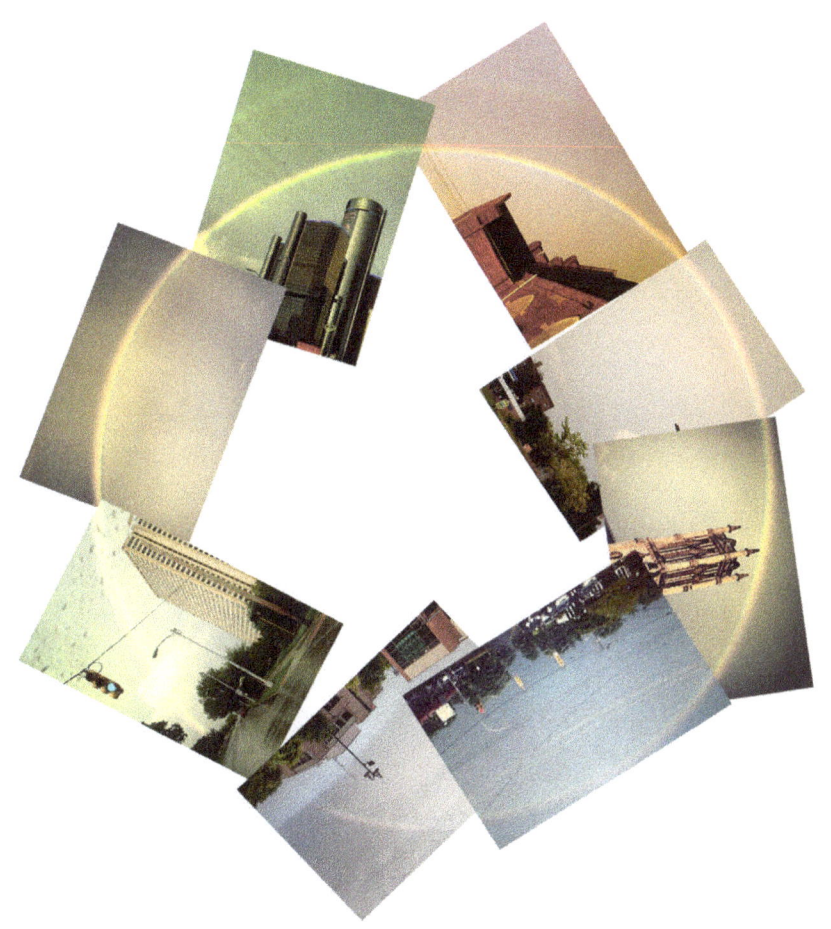

Hamilton Poe's artist statement is a comprehensive neuropsychological evaluation in which he, the patient, a "27-year-old right handed male," is characterized in modern scientific terms. It details everything from his previous diagnoses of attention deficit/hyperactivity disorder and dyslexia to his superior "non-verbal concept formation and reasoning skills." The statement could be read in many ways: as an observation of one individual's state of mind; as a comment on the way America addresses mental health; as a critique of an art world that revels in myth-making; or as a subversion of a system he claims "requires written justifications for the inexplicable."

It can be difficult to touch upon all of the subjects within

9/4/2014 Detroit, MI @urbano-madic @b17carla @hamtownhxc @cuteculturechick @curzlyn @carladianeb @slamari @winterton. 2015. CVS kiosk prints, 22 x 22 in.

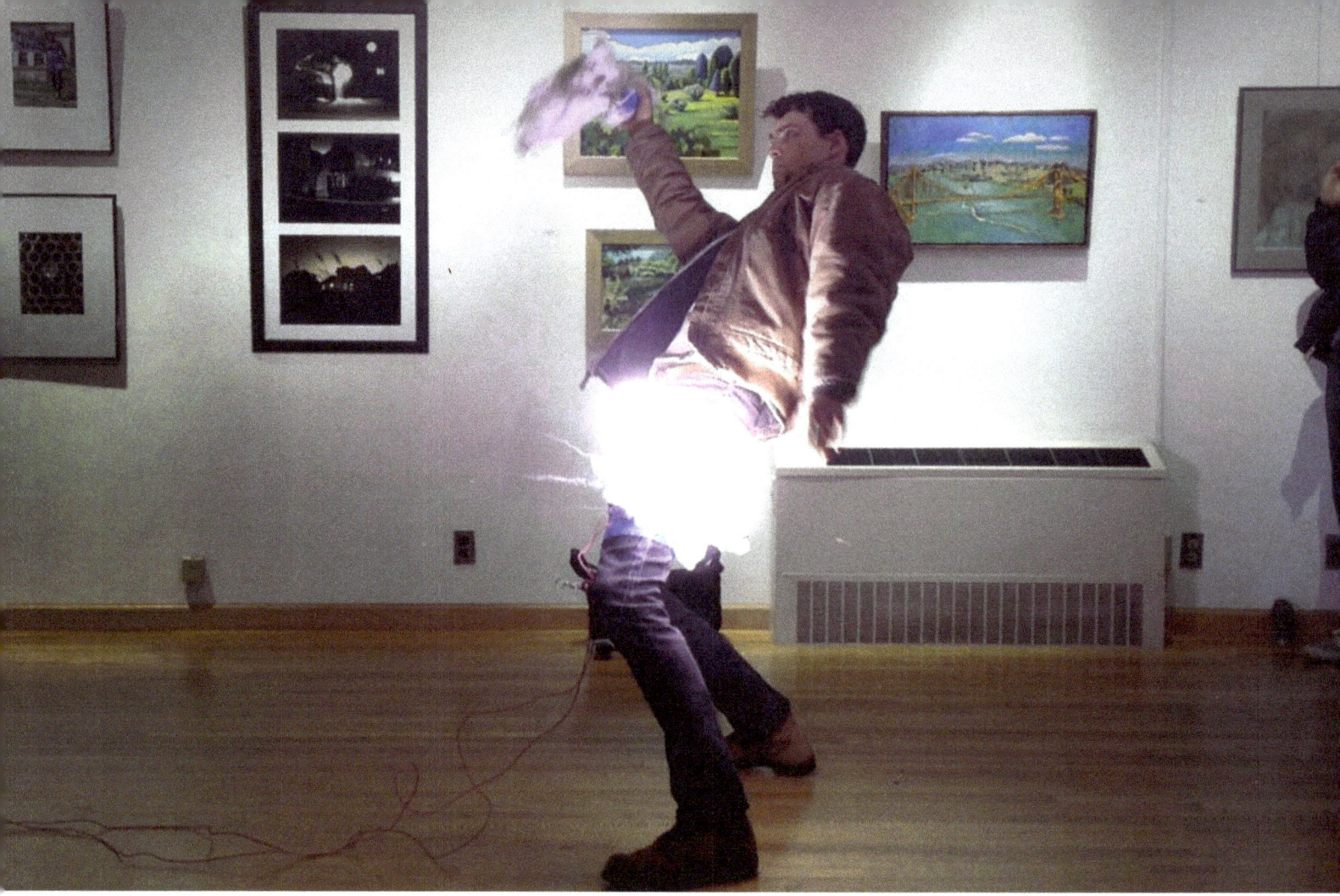

Bullet. 2014. Performance/documentation still.

Poe's artwork because he reflects on topics from many angles, but acknowledgment of that fact clears the path toward an over-arching explanation. The human instinct to filter life through one perspective preoccupies Poe, who seeks to dislodge himself and others from a fixed understanding of reality. The way to get to know his art is to hear him talk about living life, because his approach leads to the ideas and the mak-ing. Running, swimming, and biking long distance propel Poe into a suspended state of being,

in which he meditates on the transitory nature of art and life.

"I've become obsessed with trust, value, and transmutation," he says. A couple of years ago, on one of his long runs around Detroit, he came across dog skeletons by train tracks near Magnolia Street and Vinewood on the near west side. It led him to conceive of a project that foregrounds the moral conflict of right vs. wrong. He rode his bike to the Humane Society with a dog in a trash bag and inquired about cremation, planning to send

the dog's ashes to an online com-pany that purports to transform remains into diamonds. Because the dog didn't belong to him, the agency could not give him the ashes, and ***Doggie Bag*** (2015) resolved itself as an artwork then and there, a conception of an idea that might be considered mor-ally responsible or reprehensible.

The parameters that define contemporary art are much wider through Poe's lens. He references two men in admiration of their intentionality and authenticity: Terry, a stranger who dances in

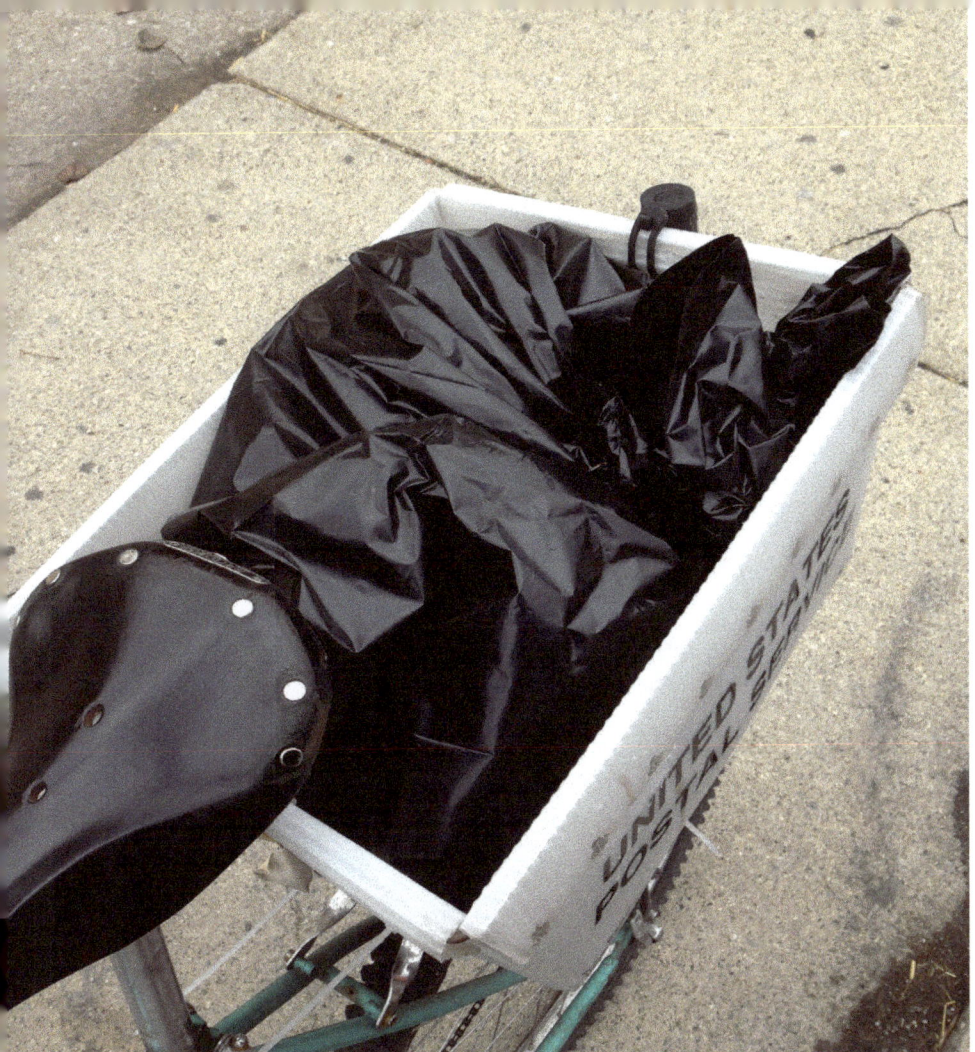

Doggie Bag. 2015. Dog remains, plastic bag, mail crate, 20 in x 15 in x 15 in.

common household materials: paint cans, duct tape, and mirrors. Arranged within a matrix, the paint cans and their reflected images appear as a single continuous circuit that connects distinct yet interrelated perspectives.

His video ***Bullet*** (2014) experiments with the concept of dislocated reality. In front of a live audience at Cranbrook Art Museum, Poe reenacted the famous slow-moving bullet-dodging scene in the 1999 feature film *The Matrix*—a scene that became so pervasive in action flicks that Warner Bros. trademarked the term "bullet time" in 2005 to describe the special effect. Poe's two-minute video was a compilation of stills by audience members, who were sharing in the production of a confounding paradigm: a knockoff of an alternate reality that had become the new norm.

REBECCA MAZZEI, OCTOBER 2015

public space with headphones on, and a man named Tom Bell, who built for himself and occupies a hut made out of recycled materials near the riverfront. Poe is one of several artists who have documented Terry's performances in the Cass Corridor. While many would be dissuaded by the notion of sharing a subject with other artists, Poe has instead gathered images by other observers to produce his own work—proof that he does not equate intellectual proprietorship with originality. This project also exemplifies his interest in "the trinity of arts

creation," in which artist is viewer, viewer is subject, and subject is artist. Similarly, ***9/4/2014 Detroit, MI @urbanomadic @b17carla @ hamtownhxc @cuteculturechick @ curzlyn @carladianeb @slamari @ winterton*** (2015) is a photographic composite including pictures of the same rainbow taken by many people. He contacted strangers who had posted photos on social media, arranged for a group meeting, and followed up with a book documenting the project.

Untitled (2013) unifies disparate realities in sculptural form. The floor piece is made of three

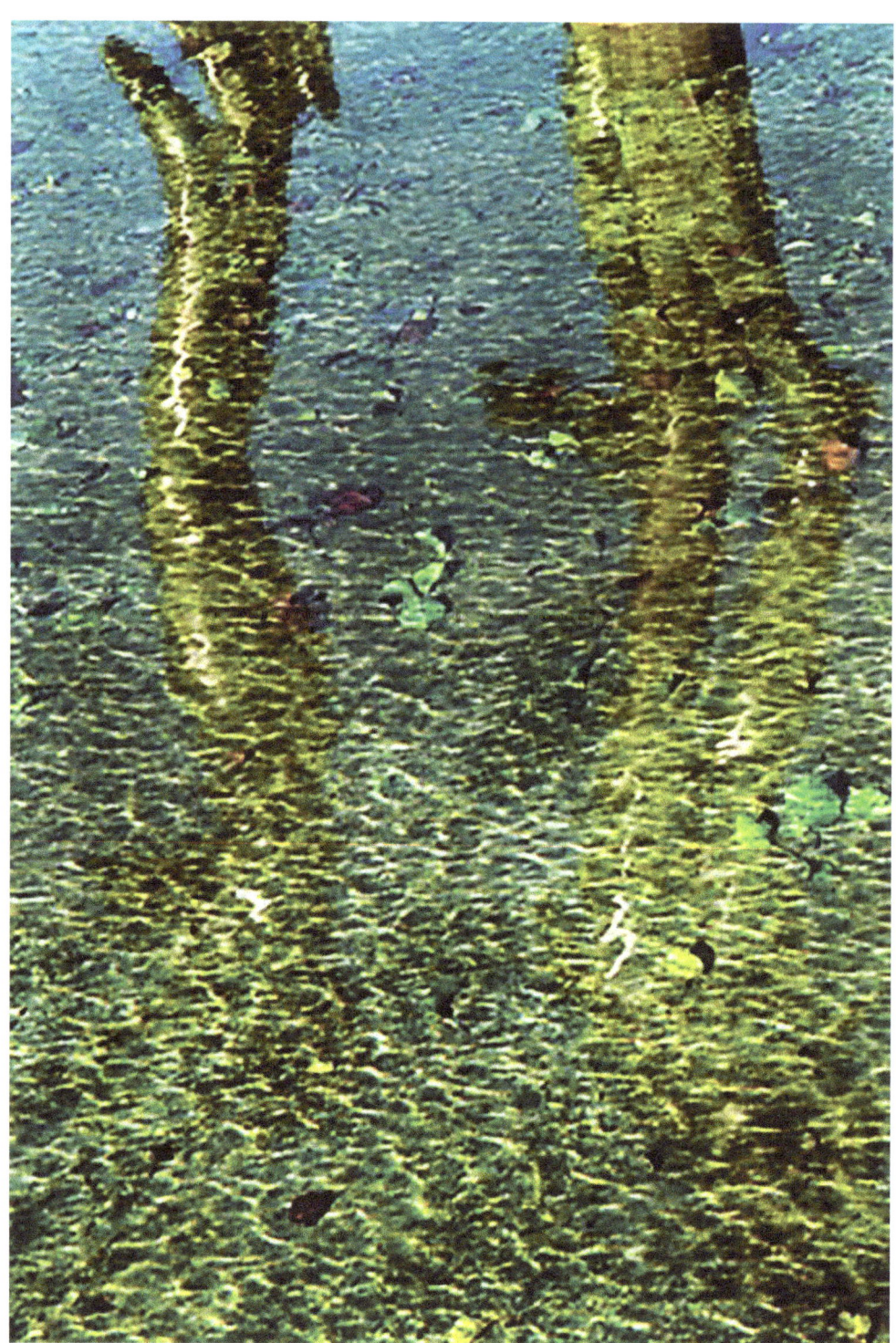

CB Sculpture. 1998. Pigment print, 24 x 20 in.

Born Manchester, Tennessee, 1952
Studied College for Creative Studies
Lives in Detroit

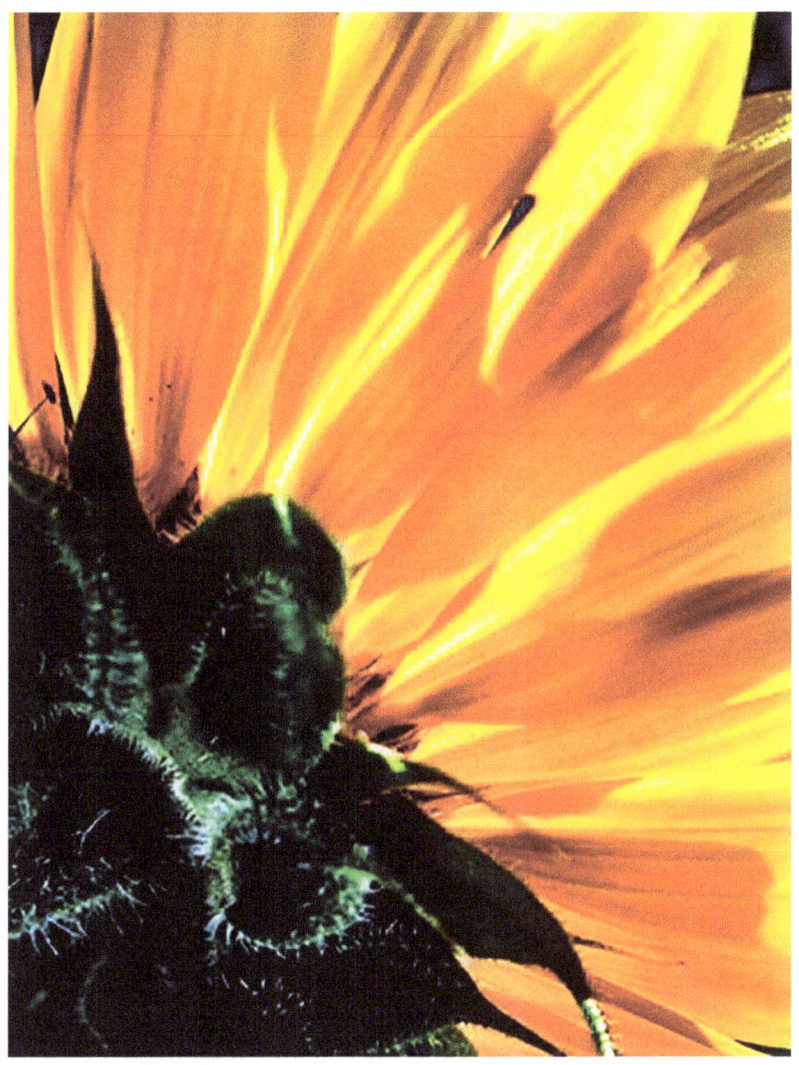

"I've been a tree hugger all my life," recalls S. Kay Young, a long-time venerator of the natural world (and primarily of her Michigan environs). Of Cherokee descent, she describes herself as an "urban Indian" who became enamored of photography from an early age, acknowledging that, "Photography began as inspiration from paintings and a lust for immediate, finished art." *Sunflower*, with its flaming palette of red and yellow, and *CB Sculpture* (both 1998), with its upside-down reflections of a duo of trees bathed in blue-green hues, are choice examples of such serendipitous, quickly captured images. Circa 2011, after a decades-long accumulation of a trove of silver prints, cibachromes, and film stills numbering in the thousands—and counting—Young shifted her

Sunflower. 1998. Cibachrome, 14 x 11 in.

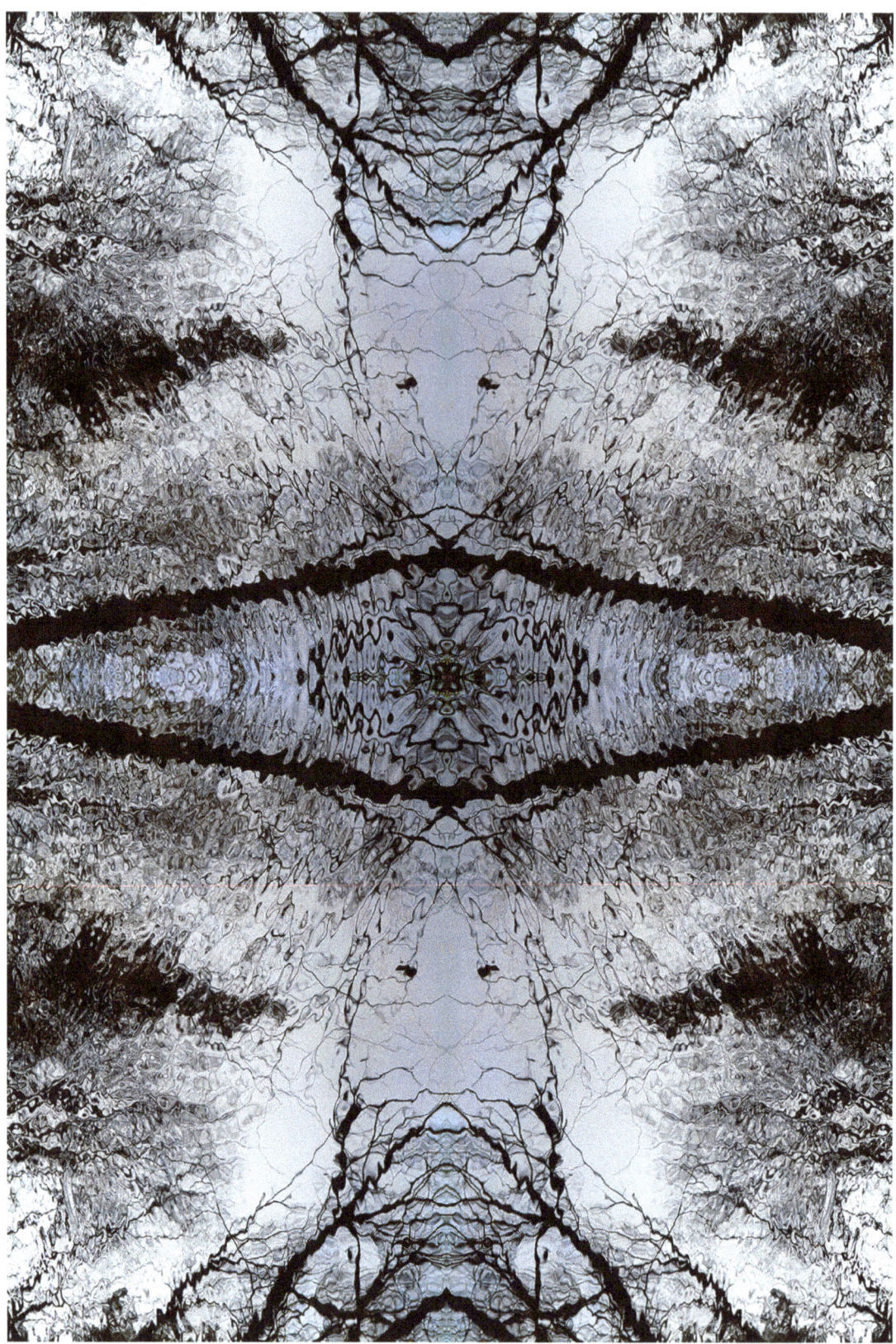

Heartbeat. 2013. Pigment print on archival paper, 68 x 44 in. Courtesy of the University of Michigan.

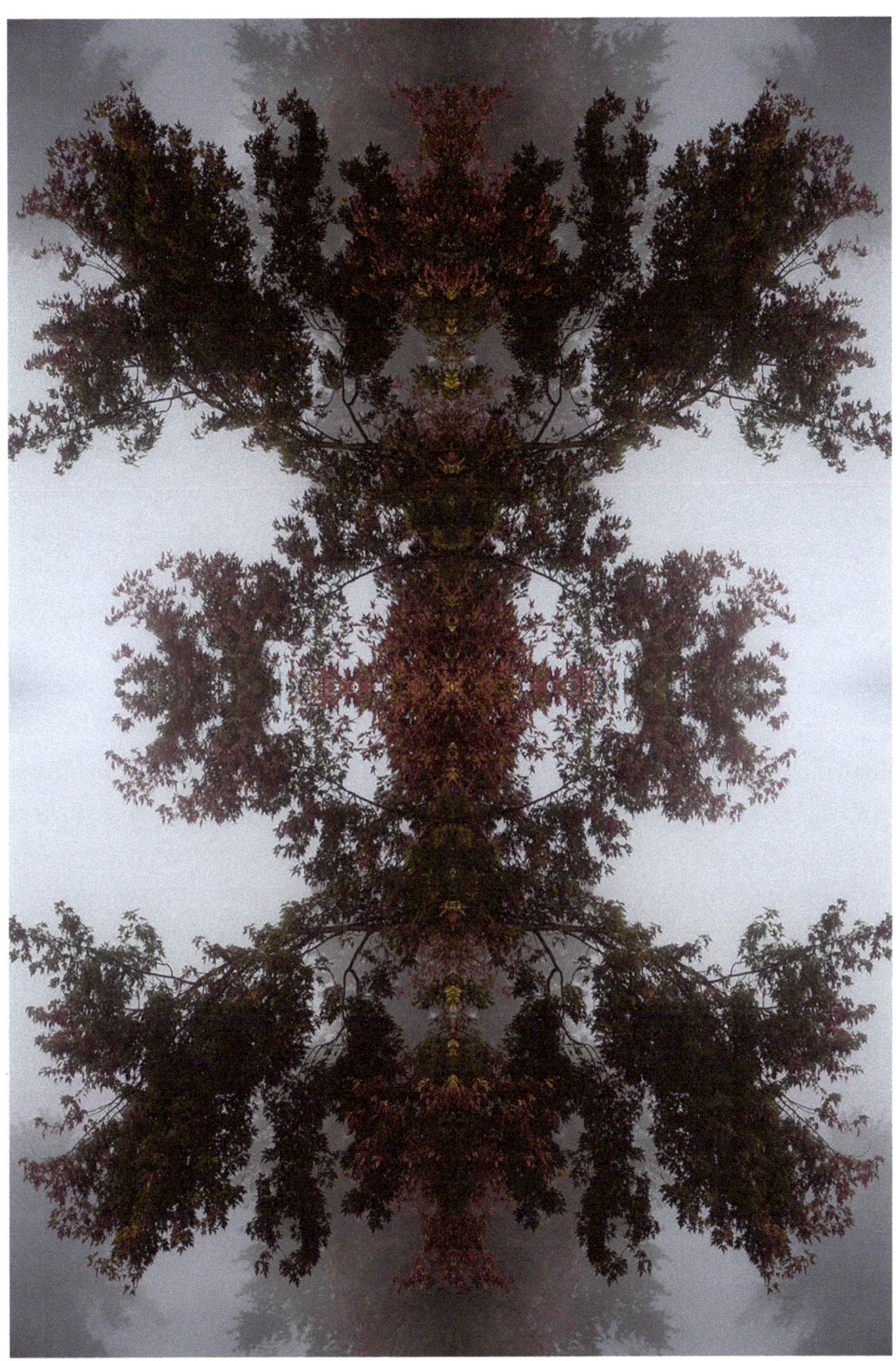

Fog. 2013. Pigment print on archival paper, 68 x 44 in.

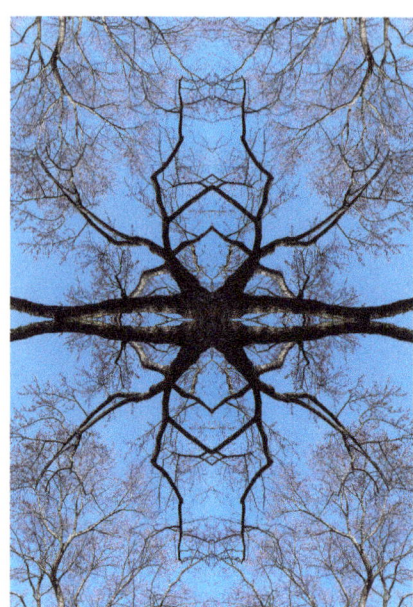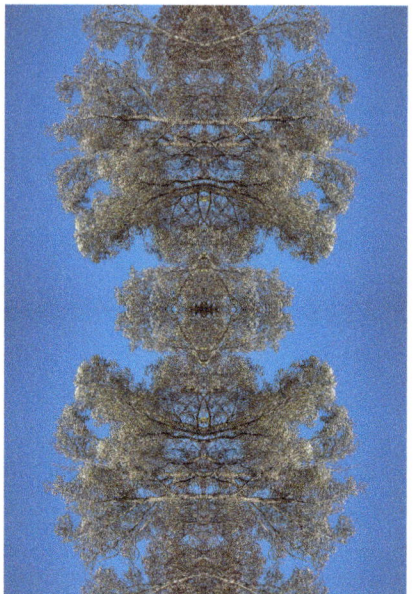

(Left) Dancing Alappin. 2013. Pigment print on archival paper, 44 x 68 in.
(Right) My Big White Alien Boy Friend. 2013. Pigment print on archival paper, 68 x 44 in.

emphasis to the sizable, labor-intensive, digitally manipulated images that have consumed her art-making to the present.

Having studied photography at the College for Creative Studies, followed by a ten-year position at the Detroit Institute of Arts, Young has served over the last decade as adjunct instructor of photography at Oakland Community College. Also a photography instructor of special needs adults at Macomb Oakland Regional Center, Inc., in Clinton Township for a number of years, she is currently working with the Suzanne Haskew Arts Center in Milford in a similar capacity. The synchronicity between Young's

art and teaching practice enables both student-surveyors and tutor-guide to light upon surprising images and points of view. Frequently escorting her students into the surrounding woods on photographic expeditions, she notes that they "shoot from angles I don't see" as they discover their individual voices. Their exploratory efforts were on view at the Scarab Club in the 2015 exhibition *True Nature*, organized by Young. A film of a journey into the forest with another band of nascent photographers, shown on PBS's "Detroit Performs," was awarded an Emmy for documentary shorts.

Young's own solo treks into the woods in weather foul and

fair are often prompted by dreams in which a Native Elder serves as guide. A few years ago, after he told her where to enter the forest, look up, and capture the faces in the Spirit Trees anew, she launched a commanding, ongoing series of large-scale photographs. The results of these woodland excursions offer such contrasting moods and images as ***Fog*** (2013) and ***Dancing Alappin*** (2013), one set against a wan gray miasma, and the other, in a rare horizontal layout, silhouetted against a cloud-free, cerulean sky. The time of year differs as well as the formats, one vertical, one lateral. Both, however, are strictly symmetrical, a consequence of the mirroring of the original shot, which is repeated and rotated three times. Each composition, measuring an outsize sixty-eight by forty-four inches, is actually comprised of four quadrants that the artist refers to as "four-ups"; she also produces "two-folds," generally more modestly sized designs. In either format, however, "when they meet in the middle, human faces, eyes, vaginas, penises, bodies, animals, insects, and spirits" may be espied (per the artist), visions intensified through Photoshop "painting," especially of hues at the center or along the vertical axis.

Sheer radiance of color—and heightened emotion—is readily apparent in **My Big White Alien Boy Friend** (2013) and **Lady Cranbrook** (2013) in particular. The crimson oval of the latter floats like a halo or apparition in the firmament, while the blond, delicately detailed contour of the former hovers like a mythical shower of gold. Perhaps an explanation for the imposing scale and vertical orientation of many of the fourfolds is to evoke the literal dimensions of the trees and their stilled, capacious canopies, as well as to raise eyes and uplift the spirit.

Nor has Young abandoned the aquatic realms and reflections so prevalent in her early work, as witnessed in **Heartbeat** (2013), a frame-filling, icy blue, rippling surface whose quartet of quadrants yield a cross, a pair of faces (with eyes, mouth), and a stained-glass, cruciform jewel within an oval surround at center. Young's paean to water—"The ability to see energy as it blows across a body of water, reflecting reality upside-down and skewed"—attests to the centrality of this essential, life-giving element. Yet, from her formative

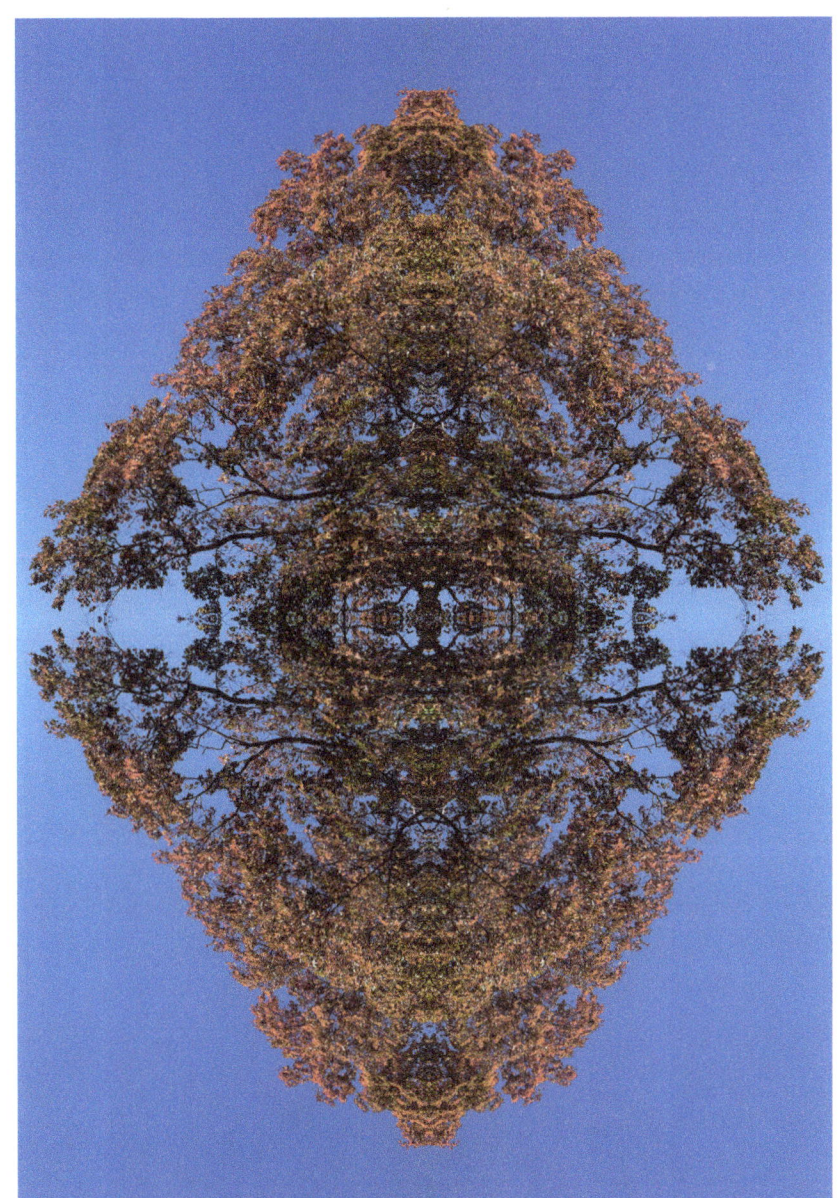

Lady Cranbrook. 2013. Pigment print on archival paper, 68 x 44 in.

tree-hugging passion to her aesthetic practice today, towering trees reign ascendant over Young's oeuvre: "I have found my ultimate muse—the breath-giving trees."

DENNIS ALAN NAWROCKI,
OCTOBER 2015

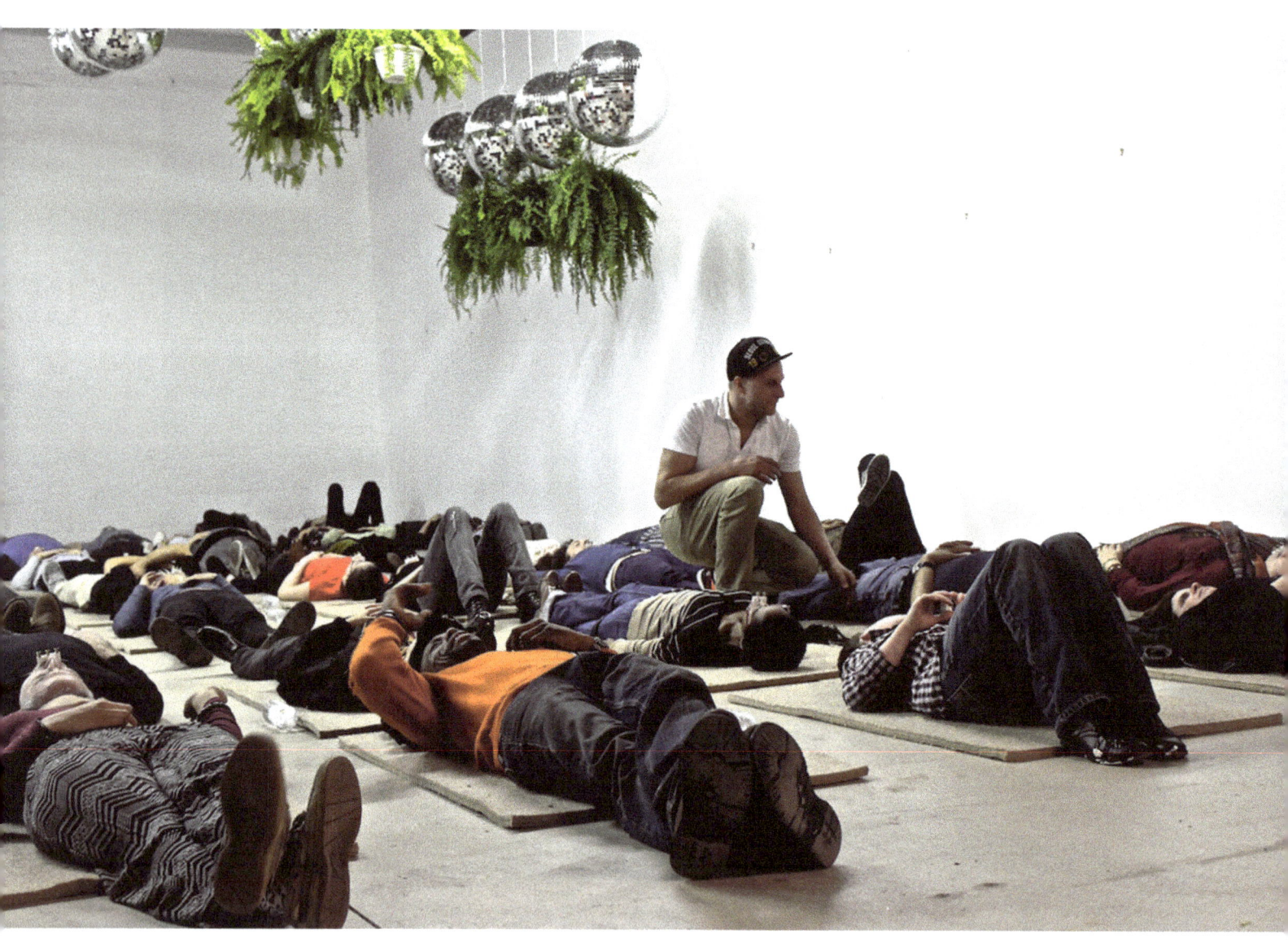

Midperformance of *Windbag for Thirty-Six Sets of Lungs*. 2015. Photography by Sarah Rose Sharp.

Born Detroit, 1977
BFA, Bennington College, Vermont;
MFA, Columbia University, New York
Lives in Hamtramck, Michigan

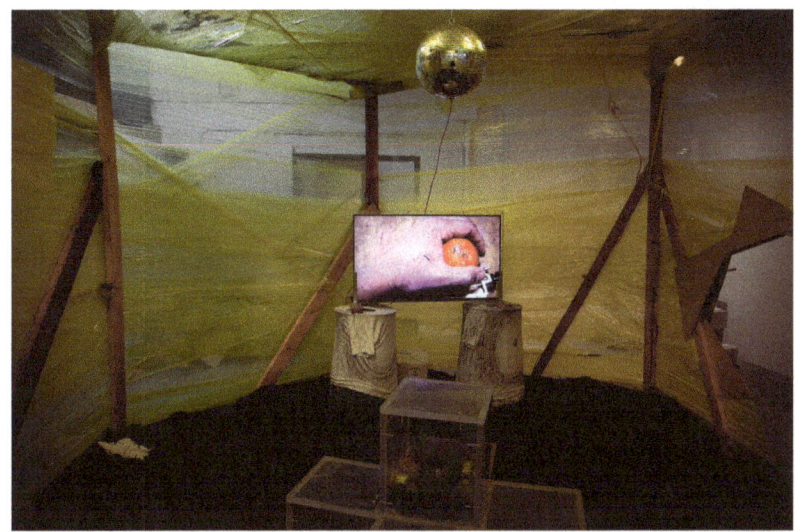

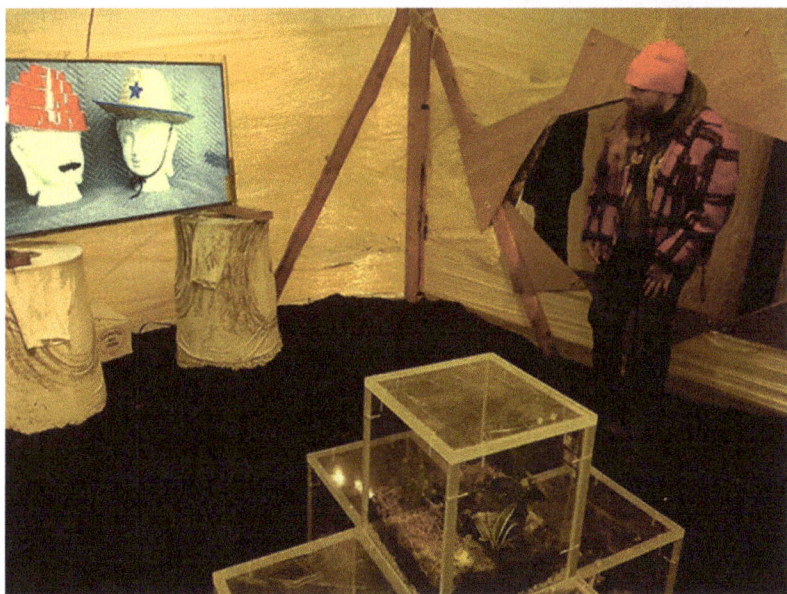

"I am trying the least hard to be an artist of anyone you've met," says Ben Hall, by way of contextualizing art in the diverse constellation of his interests and responsibilities. Like most things Hall says, there are varying degrees of truth to this complicated matter. Fanatical about language, obsessive about details, and meticulous in his planning, Hall is clearly moving toward something with great determination—and that something includes receiving an MFA from

(Top) Dollar Show (collaborative work with Andrew Mehall). 2014. Disco ball, stretch wrap, lumber, wire trash cans, mulch, Vimeo TV, bulletproof screen, print, graphite, T-shirts, banquette terrarium with bulletproof glass, Duck Quack Echo, shovel, atomizer, Winston menthol, 18 x 18 x 14 ft.
(Bottom) Detail from *Dollar Show*, featuring single-channel video: *Screen Tests for the Life of the Buddha & His Cousin Ananda, Mi Primo.* 2014. Photography by Sarah Rose Sharp.

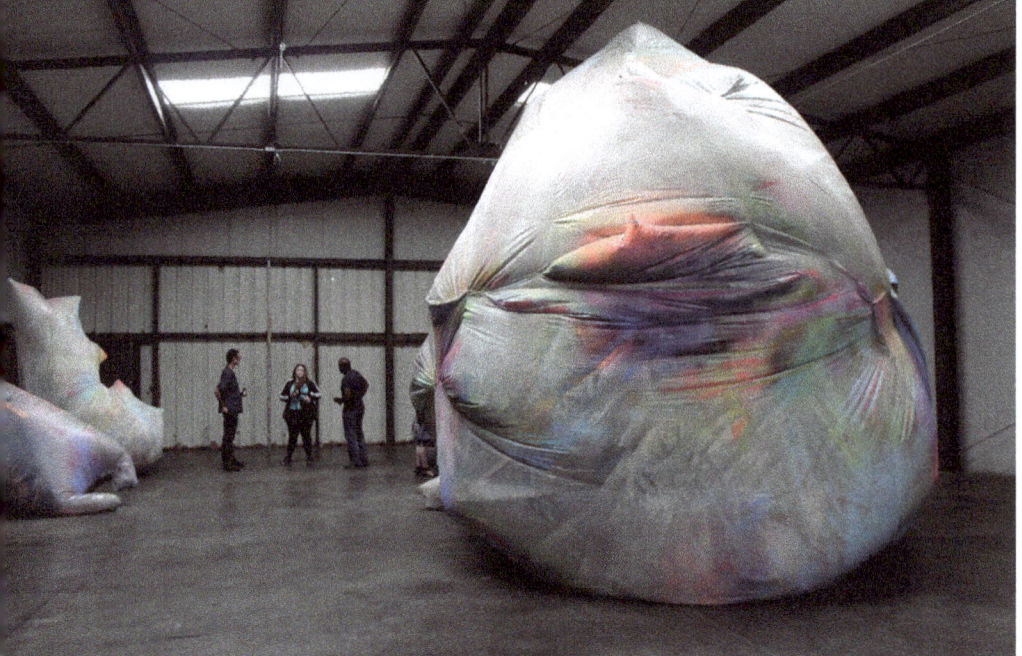

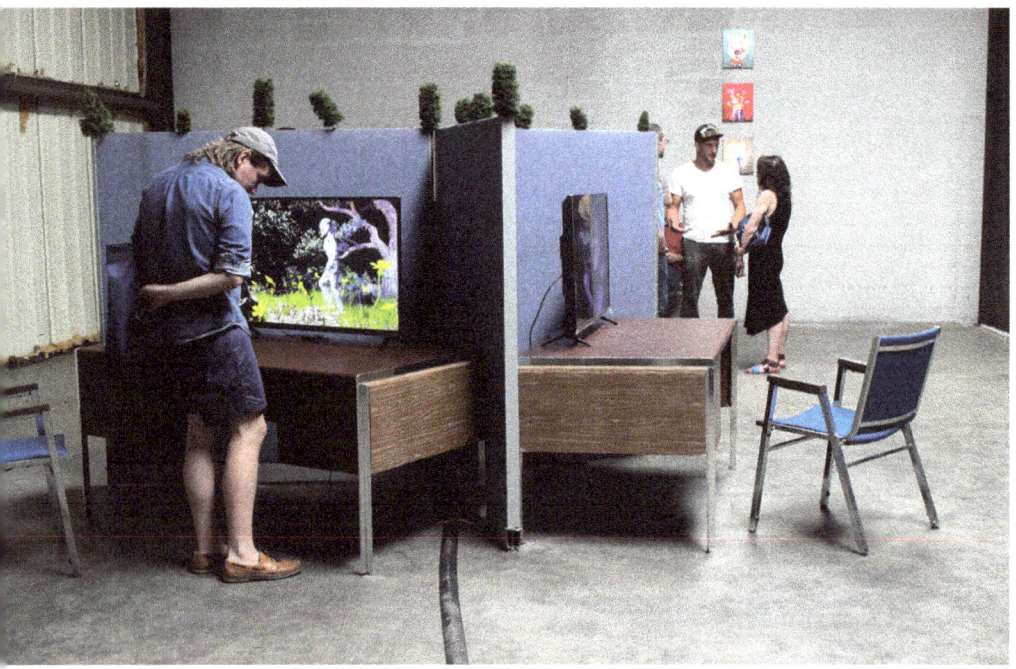

(Top) LANK LIMP LEMONS SUCK by Claire Ashley at Young World (installation view). 2015. Photography by Sarah Rose Sharp. *(Bottom) BELIEVES IN REINCARNATION, HATES HUGS* by Jeremy Couillard at Young World (installation view). 2015. Photography by Sarah Rose Sharp.

placemaking, efficiency, generative curatorial models, and especially social mobility. "My people are neither learned nor educated," Hall is quick to offer. "They are Wal-Marters, through and through." ("Wal-martyrs?" he ponders, finding a new linguistic layer in his own rhetoric, mid-conversation.) While Hall places no apparent judgment on various levels of social strata, he is keenly aware of them and cites their signifiers as a kind of shorthand—both conversationally but also in the deployment of materials in various iterations of his art practice.

This practice, which is developed and executed in close conjunction with his "primary interlocutors" Andrew Mehall (with whom he administrates the Detroit gallery space Young World) and Jason Murphy (who is his partner in the popular Eastern Market eatery, Russell St. Deli), involves a kind of creative generalism that allows all materials and mechanisms to be in play for any given piece, performance, or installation. These materials might include shopping carts, soda cans, and a puffy jacket, as they did in *She Shells*, part of a 2013 showing of largely sculptural

one of the country's most prestigious universities. But a deeper look at the projects and lifestyle infrastructure that Hall has constructed indicate that he is not, as he says, trying to "be an artist," and especially not trying to make things that "look like art." Rather,

art is just one of a number of mechanisms—one which, it must be noted, he manipulates with dexterity—that he's using to drive toward bigger priorities.

What, then, are these aims? Hall is concerned with ideas, first and foremost, but also works at 2739 Edwin; or ceramic Buddha heads, live plants, and bulletproof glass, as with *Dollar Show*, the giant terrarium-like installation he and Mehall created for *Zookeepers*, their 2014 collaborative show at Popps Packing. This last, which also features a fourteen-minute looping video, *Screen Tests for the Life of the Buddha & His Cousin Ananda, Mi Primo.*, is an excellent example of Hall's driving obsession with the relationship between material details and viewer experience. "We talked a lot about how deep the mulch in this piece needed to be to create a degree of verisimilitude in making the viewer feel like they'd entered a completely new space," Hall says. "We discovered that's about eighteen inches."

Verisimilitude—that is, the appearance or semblance of truth—is a useful concept when it comes to reckoning with Hall. He is concerned, always, with the mindset of the consumer as a reflection of his ability to curate an experience. This might be a "die-in," like his 2015 Art X performance piece, *Windbag for Thirty-Six Sets of Lungs*, which laid out rows of volunteers beneath disco balls and hanging ferns on felted mats, in- and

exhaling through pitch pipes to generate an approximately half-hour passive breathing symphony that leaves viewers acutely aware of their own, limited breath. It might involve his role as curator for Young World, an unfinished exindustrial space lacking running water or an electric hookup, which favors **immersive exhibits** that fill the space with oversize and dislocating displays. In terms of his curatorial vision, Hall describes an awareness developed over time spent in a touring band, emphasizing the importance of working with people he enjoys. Spending time hanging out with the people he likes the most is as ardent a goal for Hall as "being an artist."

On the short list of these, of course, are Mehall and Murphy, with whom Hall has generated a kind of symbiotic system that manifests in creative exchange, but also in literal terms as a kind of time banking that allows them to martial their collective resources in support of each other's projects. One suspects that access to the deepest layers of truth in Hall's verisimilitudinous existence is likewise reserved for those within his closest circle, but whether or not he is, in the end, trying to be an artist, Hall

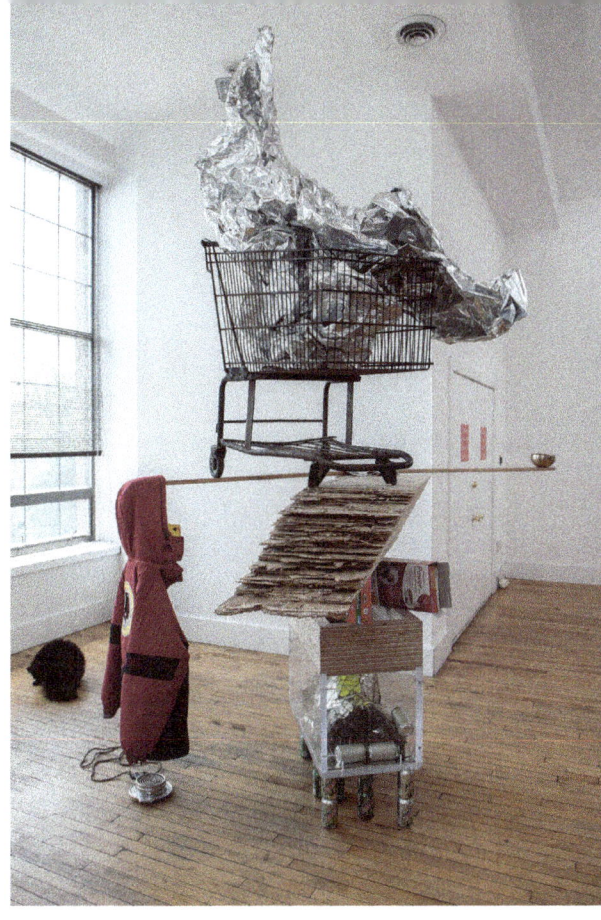

She Shells. 2013. CDX, 3X Fat Goose resewn with albatross feathers, Mountain Dew, scrapped bulletproof glass, mirror, cart, aluminum sheeting, prayer bowl, Master Lock, and Froot Loops, 60 x 60 x 144 in.

has at least achieved the requisite layer of depth to create a pretty good impression of one.

SARAH ROSE SHARP,
OCTOBER 2015

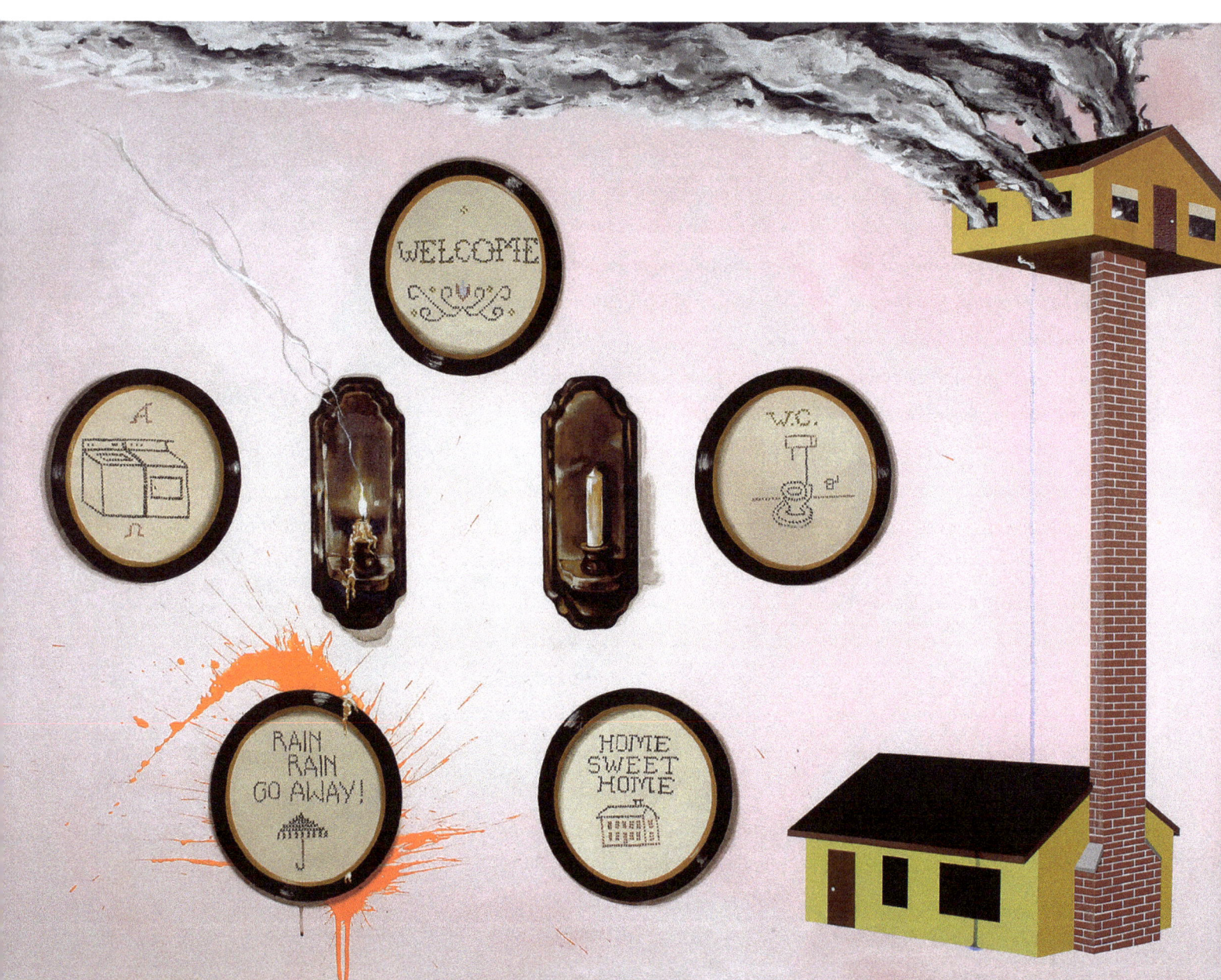

Home Sweet Home. 2009. Acrylic on canvas over panel, 48 x 64 in. Photography by Nicola Kuperus.

Born Indianapolis, Indiana, 1970
BFA, College for Creative Studies
Lives in Detroit

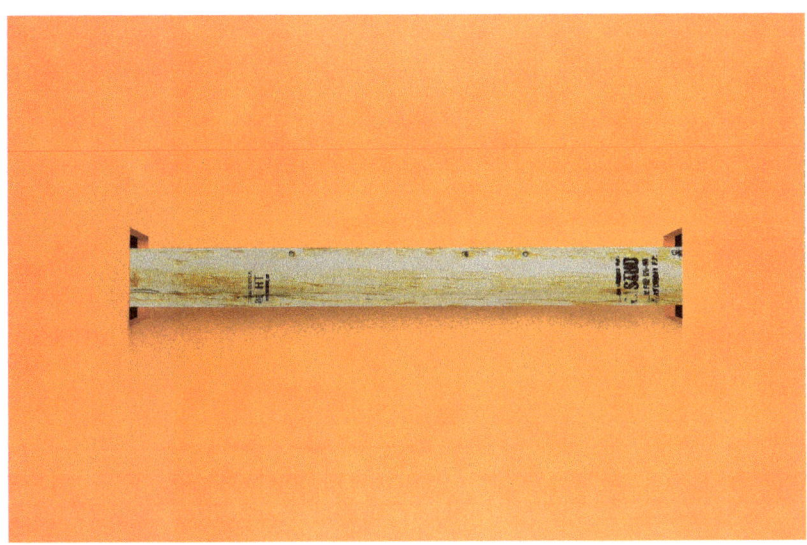

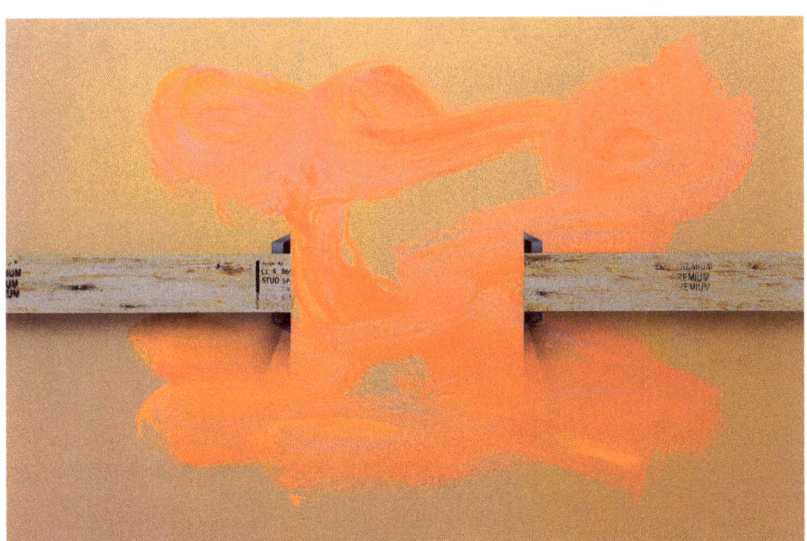

The Oasis Motel, a meticulous 2008 depiction of a shuttered motor lodge arrayed beneath a sky bruised by an inky, foreboding blackness, marks Adam Lee Miller's return to painting after a nearly decade-long hiatus. The intervening years were all but consumed by ADULT., the electro band that he and his wife Nicola Kuperus formed in the late nineties that catapulted them to the forefront of a thriving, transatlantic underground music scene. But before he ever picked up a synth or programmed a drum machine, Miller was a painter, and *The Oasis Motel* marks a return to purely visual expression that he describes as a necessary corrective to the monomania of the music business:

(Top) Stud. 2015. Acrylic on canvas over panel, 32 x 48 in. Photography by Nicola Kuperus. *(Bottom) Messy Stud.* 2015. Acrylic on canvas over panel, 32 x 48 in. Photography by Nicola Kuperus.

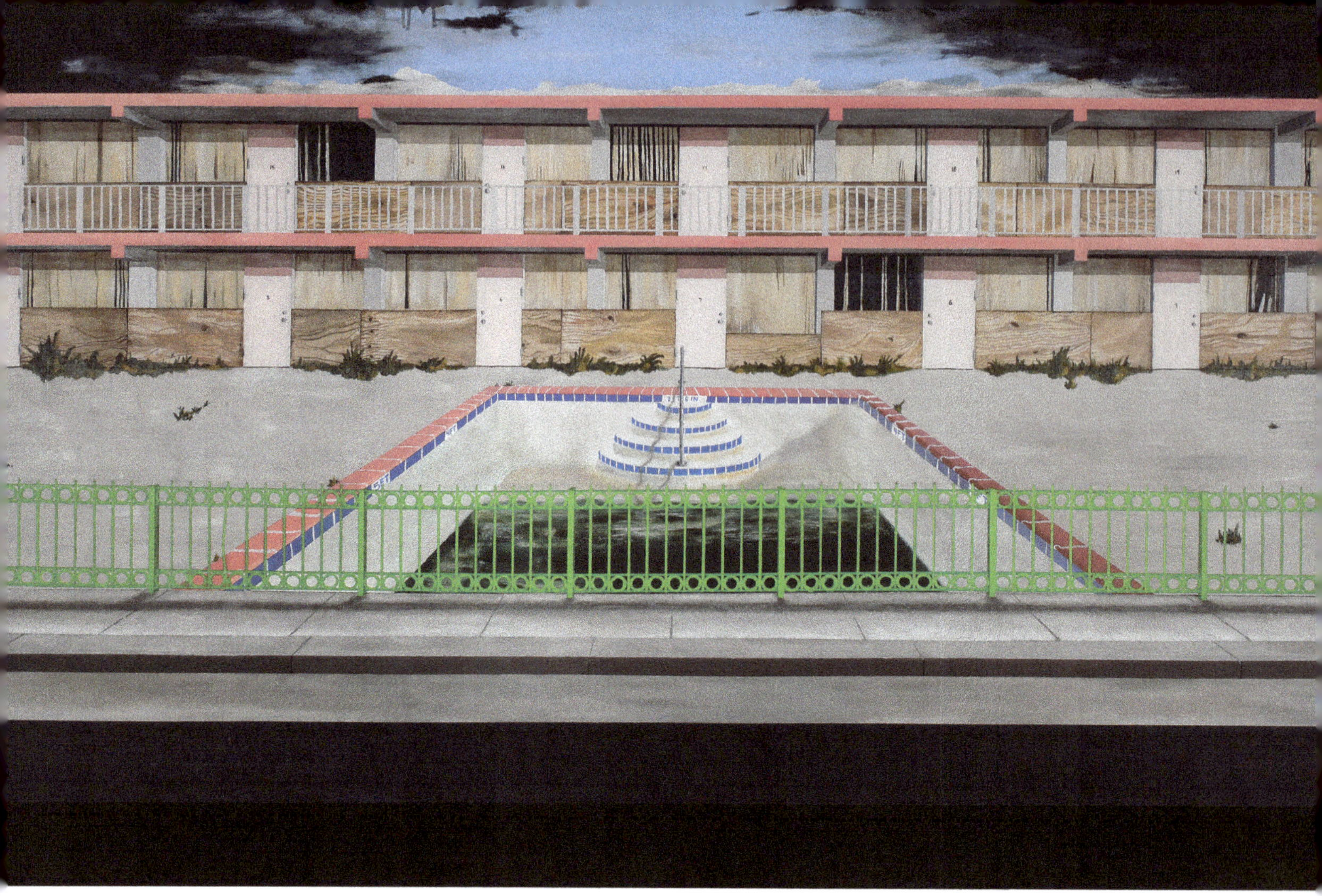

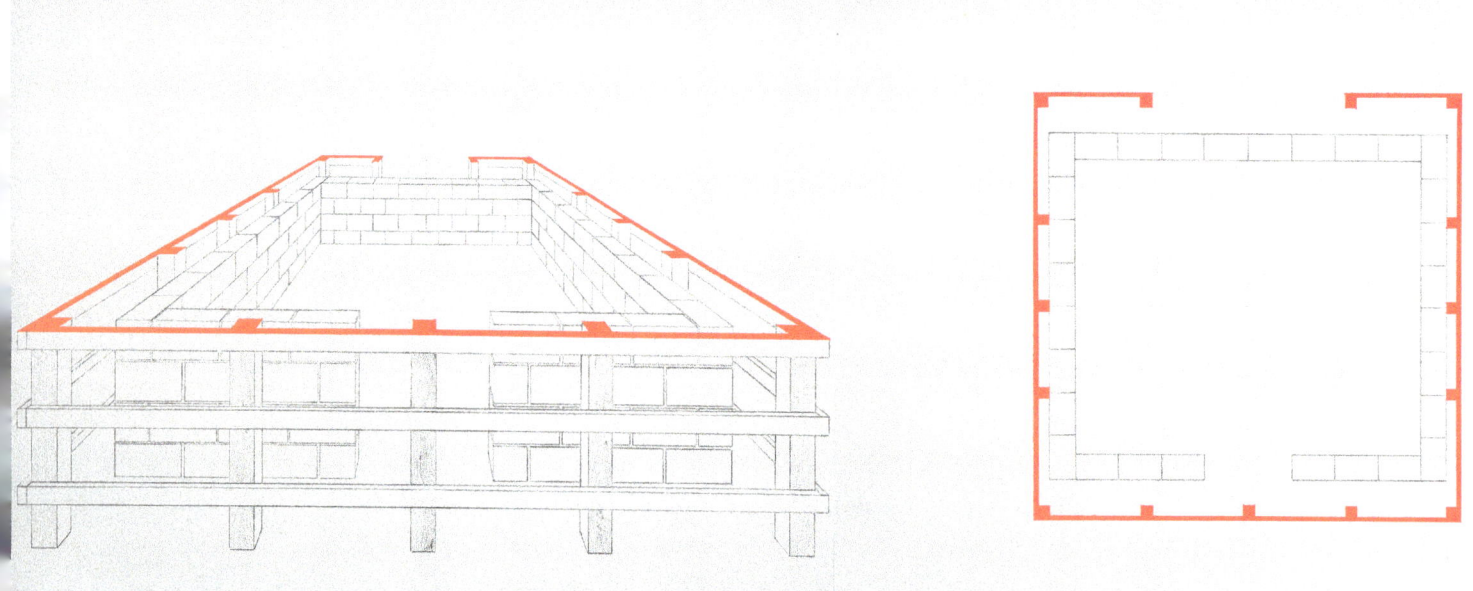

(Top) The Oasis Motel. 2008. Acrylic on canvas, 42 x 72 in. Photography by Nicola Kuperus.
(Bottom) Openings (diptych). 2014. Acrylic, gouache, and pencil on watercolor paper, 36 x 24 in.
Photography by Nicola Kuperus.

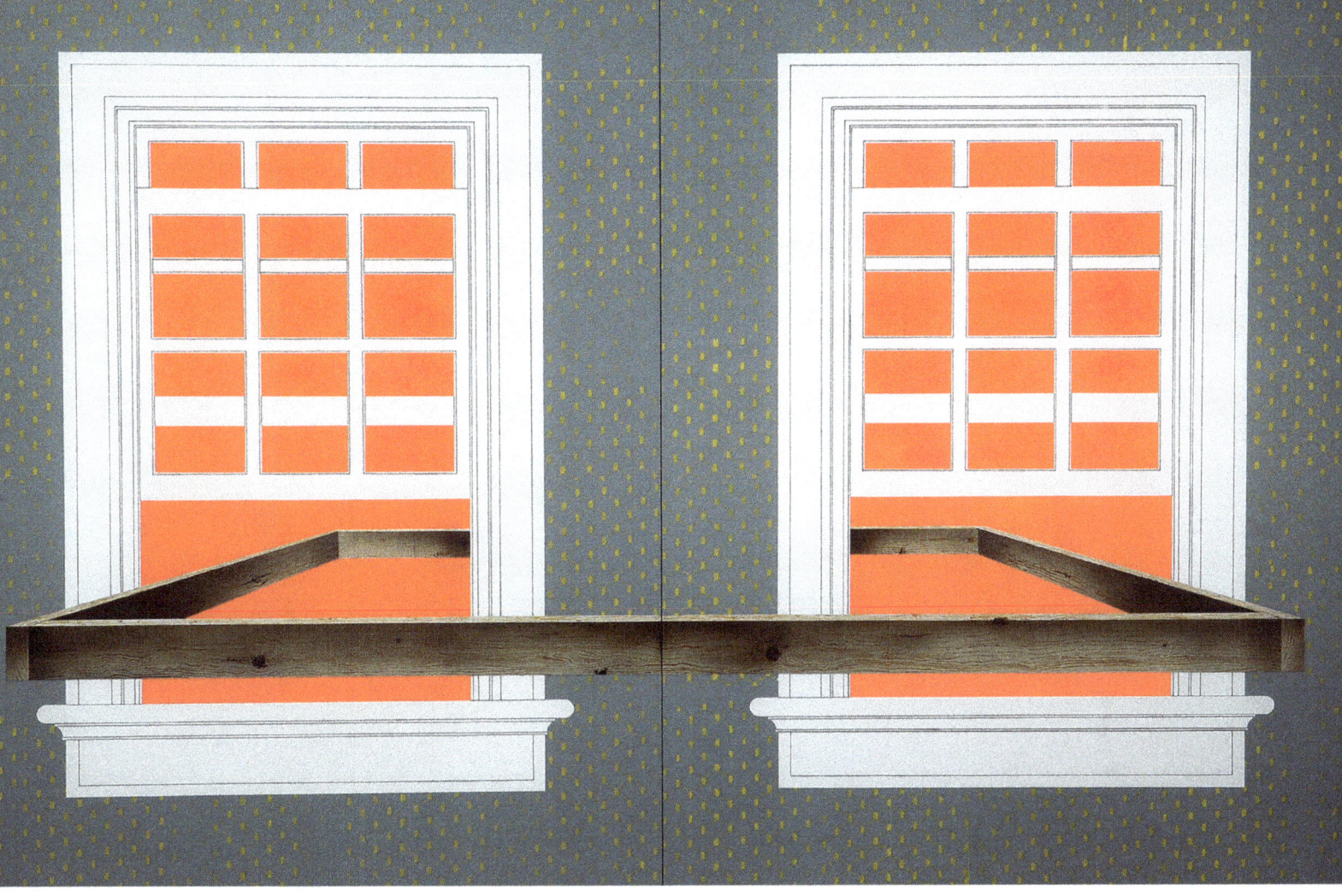

Obstruction (Window No. 1) (diptych). 2014. Acrylic on canvas over panel, 64 x 48 in. (each panel). Photography by Nicola Kuperus.

"We're multidisciplinary artists," he says, "and ADULT. was getting to be too much of one discipline." As the inaugural entry in a growing body of new work, *The Oasis Motel* typifies some of Miller's key thematic and formal concerns, while also functioning as a point of departure for the continued refinement of his evolving visual universe: an elegant, everyday place that's at once familiar and strange, inviting and unsettling, and that is indelibly inscribed by the artist's droll gallows humor and refined, mannerist style.

In terms of subject, Miller returns repeatedly to architecture and its basic constituent parts. But whereas the Oasis Motel is a recognizable building, Miller is increasingly moved to draw and paint what he calls "pointless architecture," curious, invented structures that evoke perturbed psychological states or the futility and folly of human endeavor. Consider, for instance, his hilarious and straightforwardly titled 2011 *Vapor Corrals* (a triptych divided into "basic," "incorrectly installed," and "deluxe") or *Openings* (2014), one of a series of deadpan, two-perspective elevation drawings that expertly depict irrational structures no architect would ever build. *Openings* is comprised of a cinder-block wall nested within a wood fence,

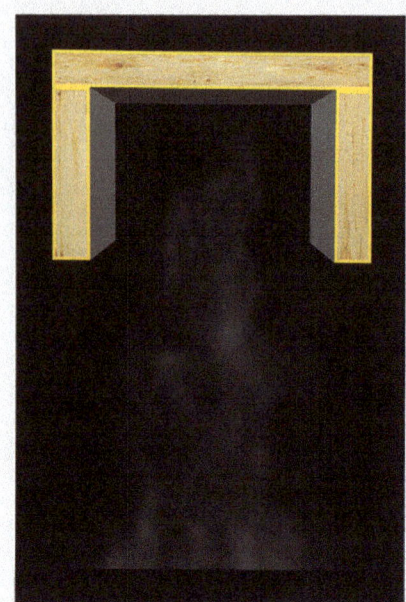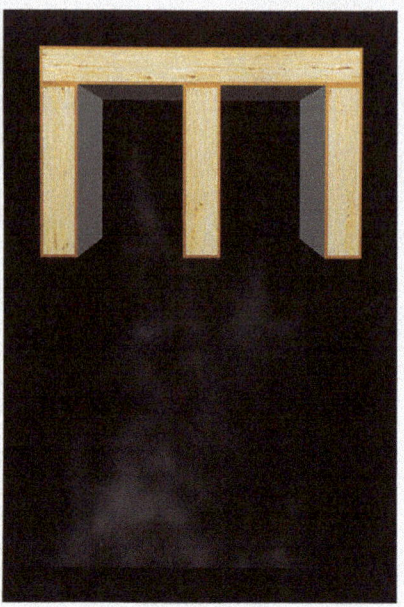

Basic Vapor Corral, Incorrectly Installed Vapor Corral, Deluxe Vapor Corral (triptych). 2011. Acrylic on canvas over panel, 48 x 32 in. (each panel). Photography by Nicola Kuperus.

each containing a single point of entry made inaccessible by the other: a closed-circuit frustration machine, in duplicate. ("I like how systems of order are undermined," Miller says.)

Openings was one of several pieces displayed at the Cranbrook Art Museum during its recent *Theater of the Mind* exhibition, a curatorial choice that underscores the work's psychological quality. *Obstruction (Window No. 1)* (2014) was another. In this diptych, a photorealistic wood frame hovers, impossibly but persistently, half inside a room and half outside of it: a glaring *idée fixe*, a paralyzing memory, a mental block that prevents an implied subject

from achieving literal closure. If, thematically, the piece evokes a surrealist concern with the irrational fathoms of the mind, its characteristically painstaking formal precision owes more to the rational techniques of hard-edge painting (employed as part of a catholic, thoroughly postmodern pastiche). The lurid but finely applied orange of the windows is one of a handful of "safety colors" that appear frequently in Miller's recent drawings and paintings; their judicious distribution contributes to the abundant intrigue and visual appeal of his work, but also to the sense that underneath these carefully controlled surfaces lurks something alarming, perhaps

even dangerous. The silkscreen "wallpaper," meanwhile, evokes his longstanding engagement with Midwestern vernacular forms. His penchant for incorporating Americana into his paintings, from the needlepoint in **Home Sweet Home** (2009) to the folksy light fixture and sign that adorn **Entrance** (2011), makes clear that Miller's idiosyncratic, minor-key vision is, at heart, rooted in the American Midwest.

That vision can also be a hyperlocal one. After all, the kid from Indianapolis who used to draw elaborate scenes of alien invasion on graph paper came of age as an artist here, in Detroit, the national capital of

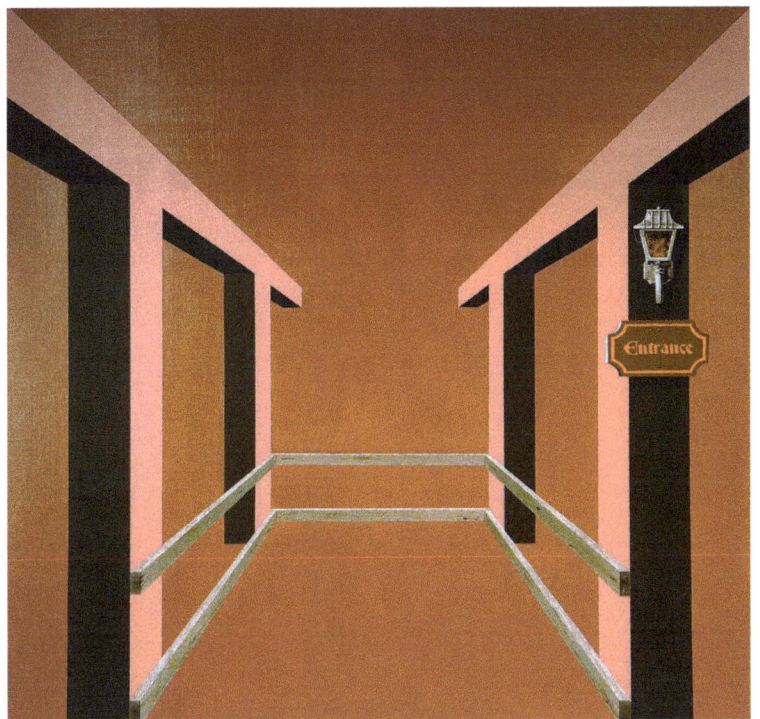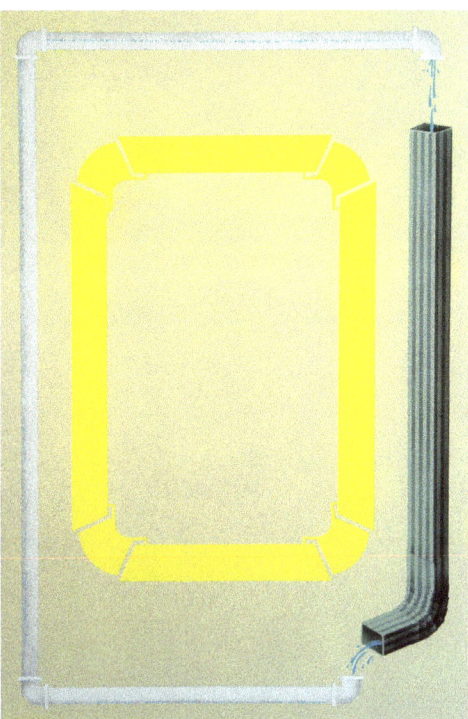

(Left) Entrance. 2011. Acrylic on canvas over panel, 48 x 48 in. Photography by Nicola Kuperus.
(Right) Swappin' Spit. 2015. Acrylic on canvas, 48 x 32 in. Photography by Nicola Kuperus.

undermined systems of order. (His first gallery show out of school was in 1994 at the now-defunct Willis Gallery, where artists staffed their own exhibitions and were given a metal bar to protect themselves in case of trouble.) But the Detroit-ist quality of his work can be apprehended in more than his representations of decaying buildings and broken systems. It is more subtly evident in his probing depictions of the commonplace materials that undergird the built environment, an environment that Miller, well versed in building renovation, knows a thing or two about. There is an echo, even, of the Cass Corridor in his matter-of-fact elevation of plumbing fixtures and two-by-fours to fine art subjects, to active players in his lively, figureless formulations (see ***Swappin' Spit***, ***Stud***, and ***Messy Stud***, all 2015). But an echo is just an echo, and as Miller's compelling body of new work continues to unfold, his peculiar, plainspoken sensibility becomes ever more his own.

MATTHEW PIPER, NOVEMBER 2015

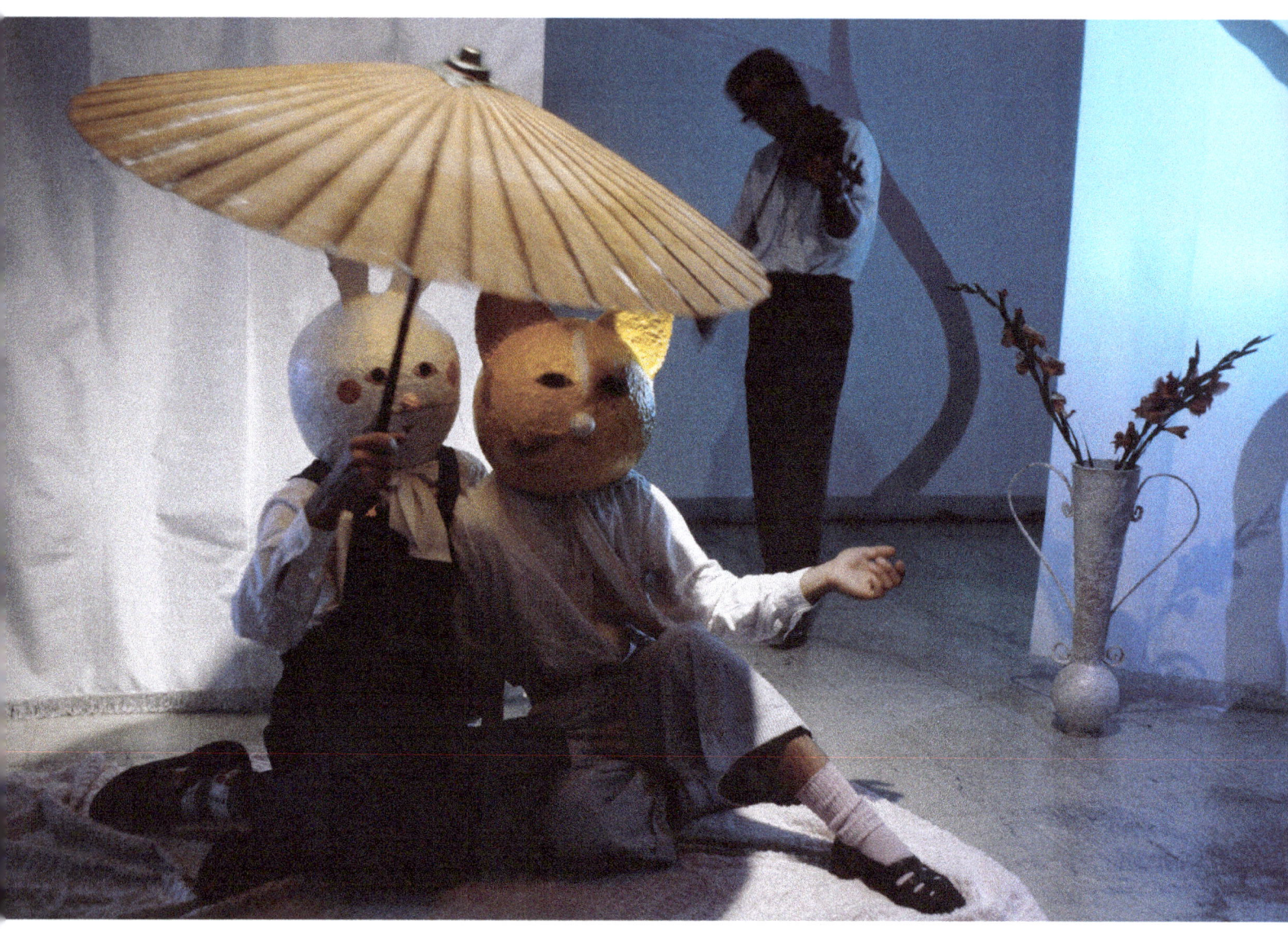

Love Tales and Broken Hearts (Randolph Street Gallery, Chicago). 1983. Photographic still. Photography by S. Kay Young.

Born Detroit
BFA, School of the Art Institute of
Chicago; MLS, University of Detroit
Lives in Detroit

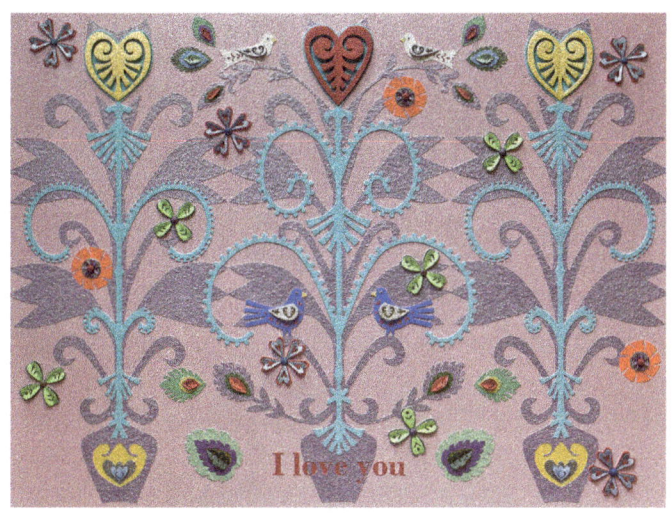

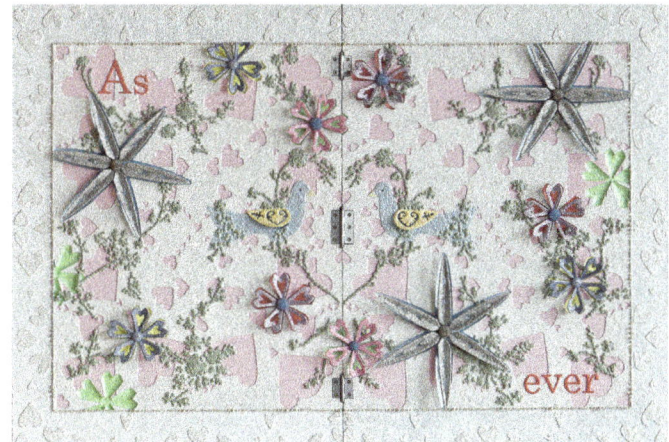

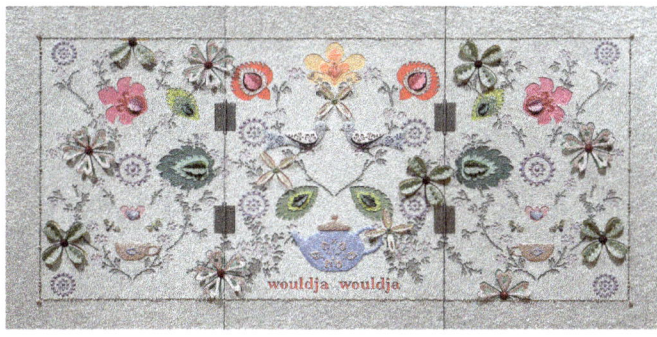

"Perchance," "we two," "yesterdays," and "wouldja wouldja" are a few of the words that embellish and echo across Patrick Burton's richly ornate paintings. Their plaintive and conditional overtones urge a viewer—albeit in low-key, lowercase font—to wonder: "Perchance" what? "We two" who? "Wouldja wouldja" do what? Nestled here and there (center top or bottom, lower or upper right) and incised or raised slightly above the surface, these messages are of a piece with the soft, silvery pastels and three-dimensional blossoms, hearts,

(Top) My Life Lies Elsewhere. 2013. Acrylic, papier-mâché, Swarovski crystals, wood panel, 68 x 90 in.
(Middle) As Ever, I Give You Me. 2003. Acrylic, papier-mâché, Swarovski crystals, sterling silver beads, wood panel, 41 x 57 in.
(Bottom) The Real Patrick Burton Story as Told by Zora Neale Hurston and Carl Van Vechten. 2005. Acrylic, papier-mâché, Swarovski crystals, sterling silver beads, wood panel, 37 x 63 1/2 in.

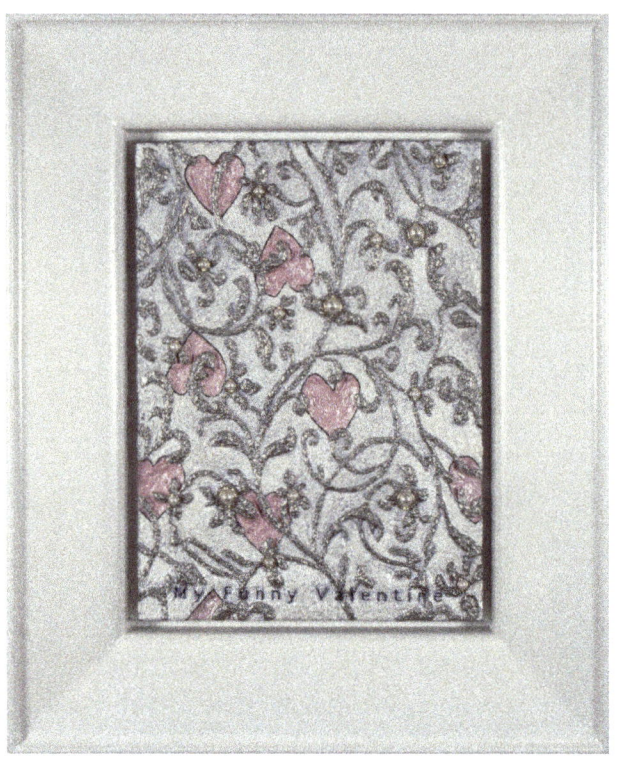 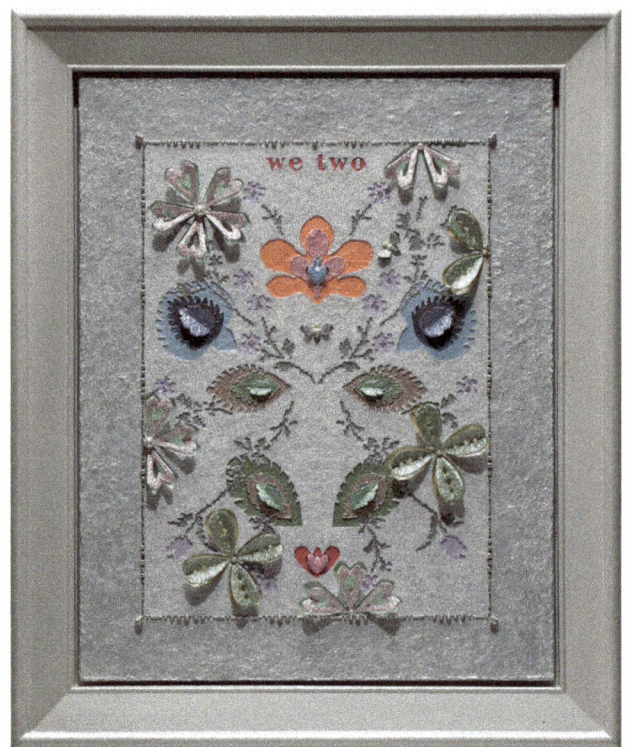

(Left) Thrice Told Tales (central panel). 1999. Acrylic, papier-mâché, pearls, wood panel, 11 x 8 in.
(Right) He Loves You, So. 2003. Acrylic, papier-mâché, pearls, sterling silver beads, wood panel, 28 x 22 in.

leaves, fronds, and vines that proliferate across Burton's low-relief compositions.

In fact, the inscriptions—or poesies, as Burton refers to them, after the fifteenth-century practice of gifting a lover with a "posy ring" etched with a word or two suggestive of love—are the enigmatic starting points for his images, to which the artist also appends longish literary titles: "Perchance," for example, is formally titled ***For a Time the Story Must Go Back Somewhat and Tell All That Had Chanced the First Night We Met*** (2007); and "As ever," writ on another composition, becomes ***As Ever, I Give***

You Me (2003). This literary flair is attributable in large measure to Burton's omnivorous reading regimen from an early age (Gertrude Stein, Langston Hughes, Jean Genet, Carl Van Vechten); his studies at UD toward the master of liberal studies degree and subsequent years of teaching both English and fine arts in Detroit Public Schools until recently; and his fifteen-year foray into scripting and producing performances—among them ***Love Tales and Broken Hearts*** (1983) and *Beauty*, *Until*, and *Punk* (throughout the 1990s). By the end of the decade, as he yearned for a format with longevity and

permanence, painting beckoned as an alternative to theater.

When Burton returned to painting in 1999 with ***Thrice Told Tales***, a triptych, he developed his fastidious, detail-oriented technique of measuring and laying out the composition to the millimeter; cutting, painting, and beading wood or papier-mâché forms; and finally, layering and gluing down the numerous, delicate elements that furnish a completed work. The free-form patterning in this original effort gives way to tightly patterned, symmetrically organized arrangements, as in ***I'll Keep Your Kiss with Mine*** (2014).

Yet, at the same time as structural elements—stems, trunks, branches—anchor compositions, the balanced but irregular placement of birds, blossoms, hearts, or four-leaf clovers relieves the rigid precision of the underlying grid. Valentine hearts also proliferate in numerous works, as many positioned upside down as right side up, to imply, as Burton notes, the perils that accompany a lived life.

A perhaps surprisingly prosaic element in Burton's rarefied world are the generic, silver-toned hinges that link together the panels of dip- and triptychs to highlight pairing and partnering of individuals. (Many bear dedications to Burton's "chosen family" members.) The hinges are emphatically nonfunctional, however, and the abutting panels are locked within their artist-designed frames. Yet these multipanel formats allude as well to portable, domestically scaled, memory-laden objects (screens, altarpieces, picture frames) that, when moved from place to place, live on again in their new setting. Indeed, one might belatedly realize that beyond the dazzling, decorative elements that seize the eye and lure one in, the titles address the often intimate

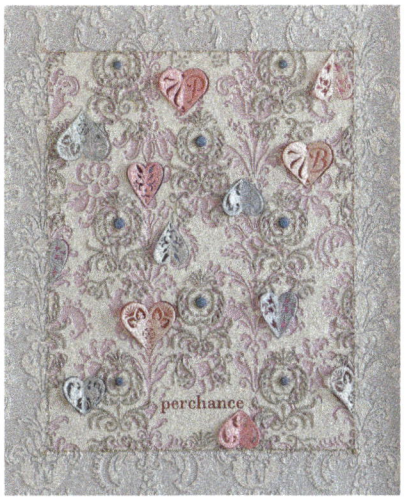

For a Time the Story Must Go Back Somewhat and Tell All That Had Chanced the First Night We Met. 2007. Acrylic, papier-mâché, Swarovksi crystals, sterling silver beads, wood panel, 42 x 34 in.

relationship between artist and observer: *As Ever, I Give You Me*; **The Real Patrick Burton Story as Told by Zora Neale Hurston and Carl Van Vechten** (2005); *He Loves You, So* (2003).

Other stately, large-scale, recent works, such as **My Life Lies Elsewhere** (2013), with "I love you" adorning its surface, posit a firm, declarative assertion, heralded by both image and inscription. The sturdy, anthropomorphic trio of vases, with tall, rising stems and "heart-heads," visited by doves of peace and bluebirds of happiness, all aglitter with Swarovski crystal beads, mark a singular moment in Burton's oeuvre. The romantic

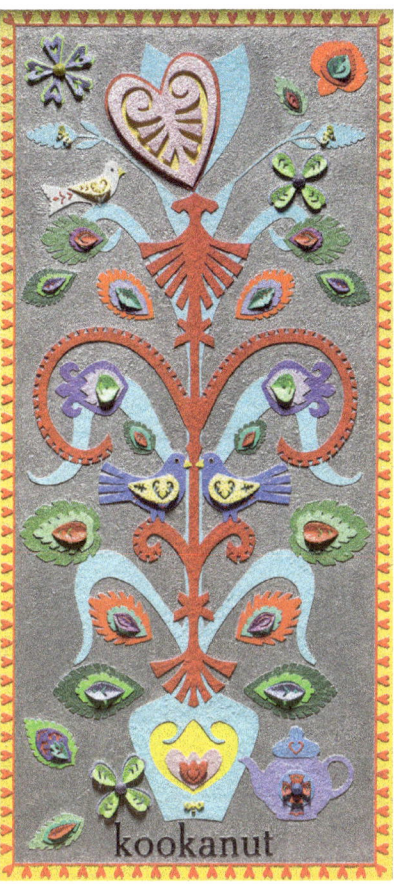

I'll Keep Your Kiss with Mine. 2014. Acrylic, papier-mâché, Swarovski crystals, wood panel, 70 x 32 in.

declaration is counterpointed, however, by its pragmatically nuanced title, frankly intimating that really and truly—but out of sight and handwritten on the back of the support—life lies elsewhere. For, much as he might love his progeny (and this one entailed a year from gestation to completion), an artist invariably harbors a longing to move on.

DENNIS ALAN NAWROCKI, NOVEMBER 2015

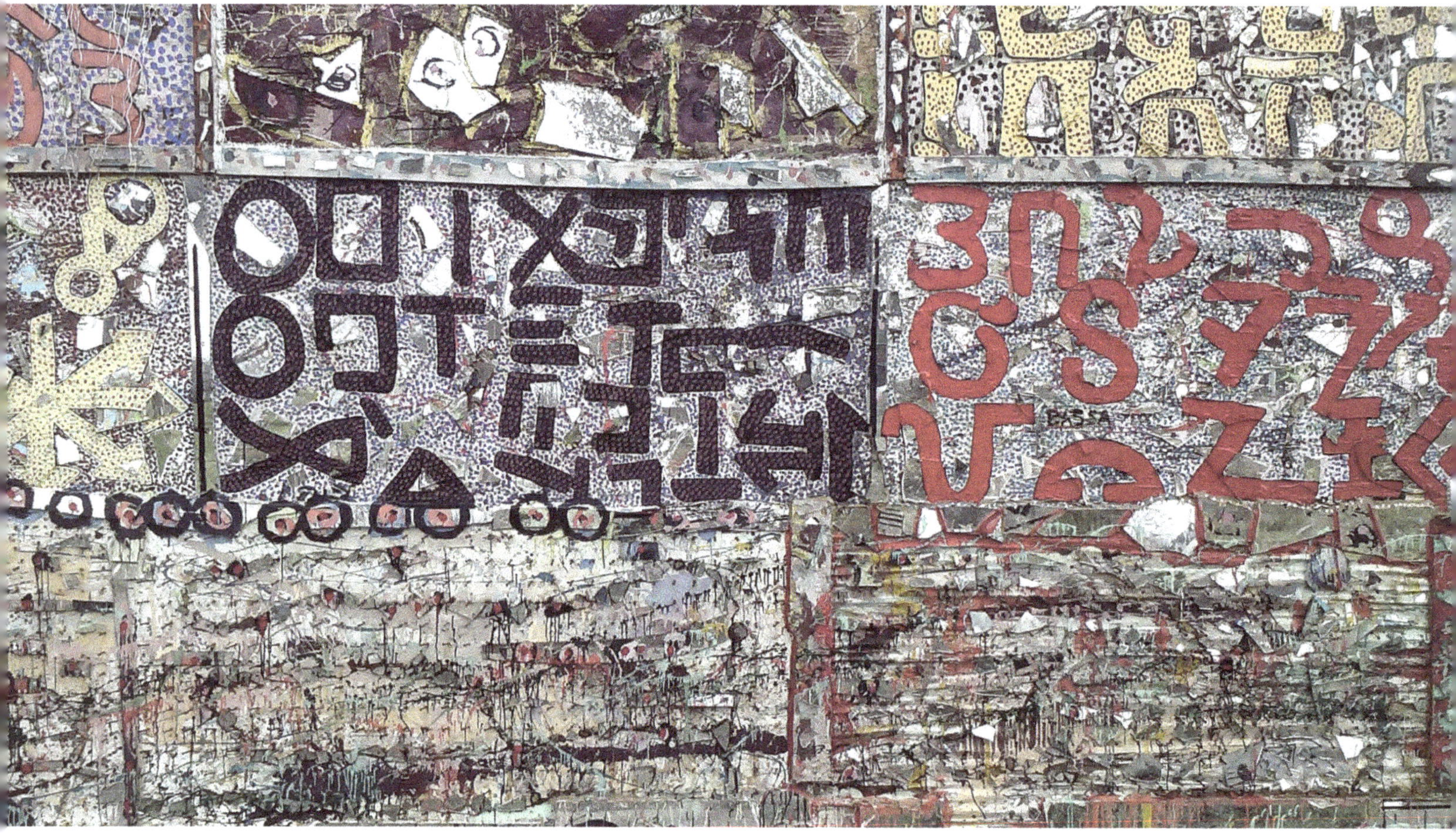

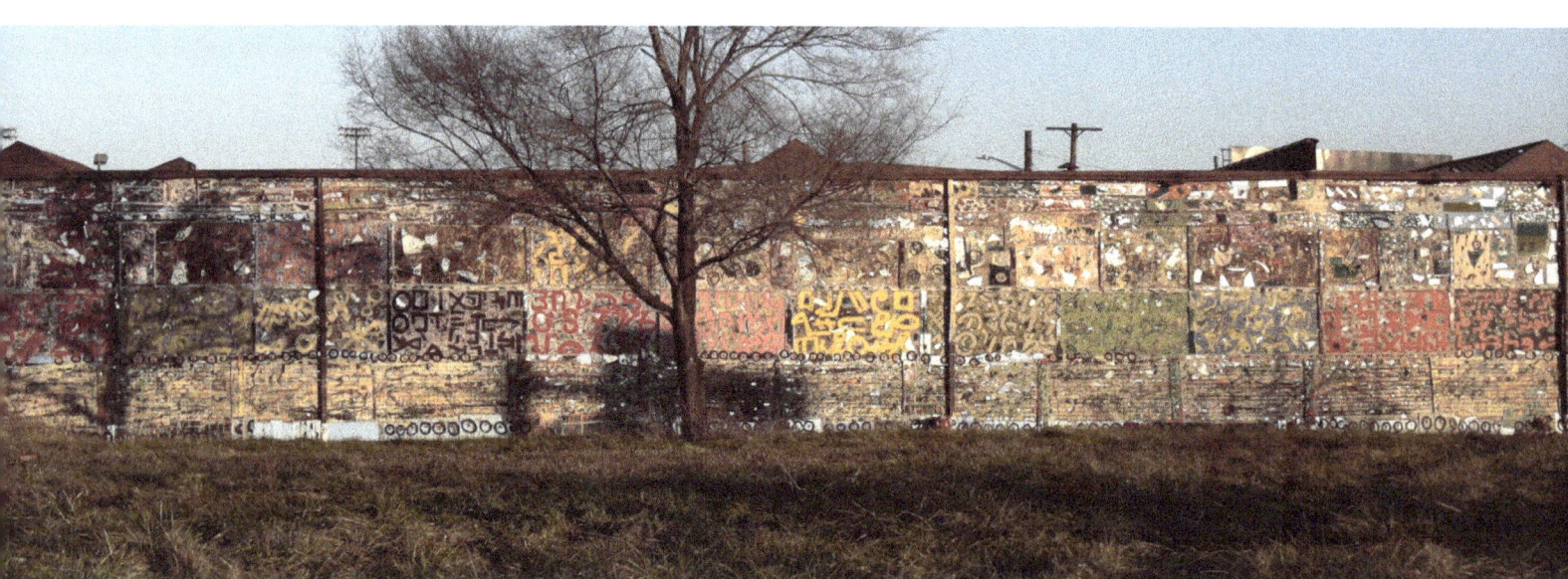

(Top) Rock's Language Wall (detail). 1998–present.
(Bottom) Rock's Language Wall. 1998–present. Photography by Rebecca Cook.

39 // OLAYAMI DABLS

Born Canton, Mississippi, 1948
Studies in Mechanical Engineering and
Art, Wayne State University
Lives in Detroit

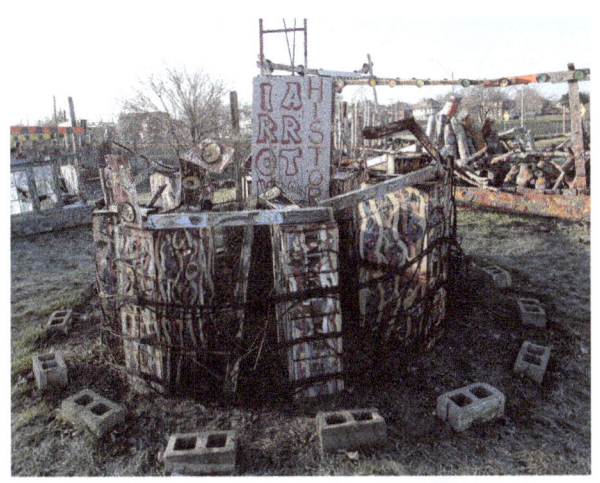

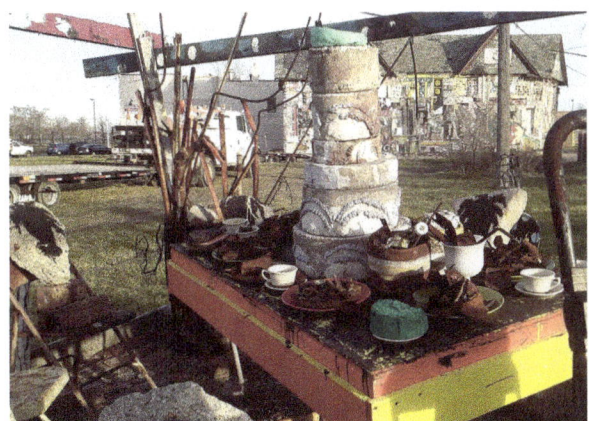

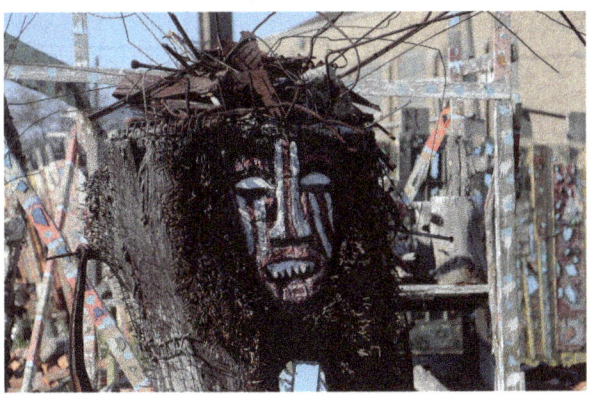

Olayami Dabls's sprawling outdoor installation at Grand River and West Grand Boulevard verges on a world where America rushes by, cocooned in tons of rusting metal—in other words, it overlooks Interstate 96. Dabls knows that world. He trained as a mechanical engineer and worked as a draftsman for Chevrolet Motors. Then in 1975 he had a serious car accident that hospitalized him for three years. During that time he turned to painting (his minor in college) as an escape from the constant physical and psychic pain. He left the hospital

(Top) History Cabinets (from the installation Iron Teaching Rocks How to Rust). 1998–present. Photography by Rebecca Cook. (Middle) Iron Teaching Rocks Table Manners (from the installation Iron Teaching Rocks How to Rust). 1998–present. (Bottom) Nkisi (from the installation Iron Teaching Rocks How to Rust). 1998–present. Photography by Rebecca Cook.

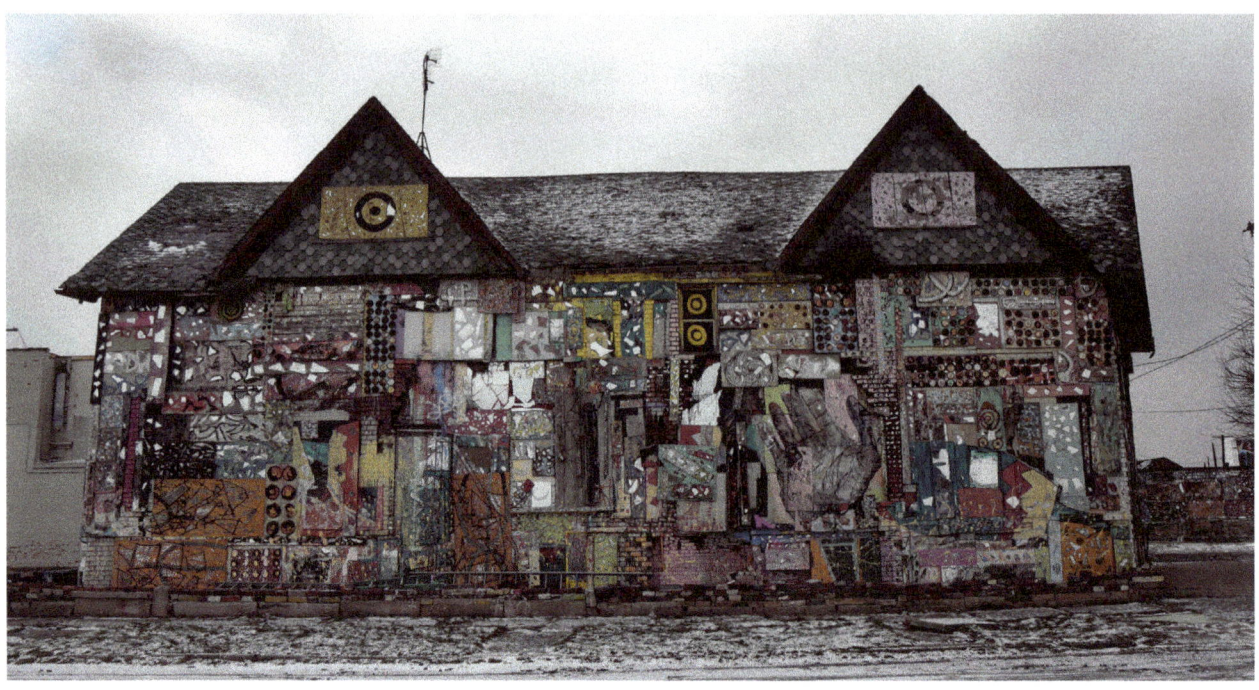

Nkisi House. 1998–present. Photography by Rebecca Cook.

and never looked back, taking stints with the original African American museum, and various theater companies, before eventually founding a gallery with his wife. Around 1998 he moved to the present location, starting the African Bead Museum that carries his name, and transitioning from an artist/gallerist to an educator/storyteller.

To understand the installation *Iron Teaching Rocks How to Rust* (1998–present), it helps to know that it tells a story of the interaction between African culture (symbolized by rock) and European culture (symbolized by iron). Hence, the apparently oxymoronic title can be read as a commentary on how the (European) education system coerces "rocks" (i.e., Africans) to "rust" (i.e., aspire to a veneer of European-ness), despite the obvious implications that such attempts are at best futile, and at worst set people of African descent on the road to personal decay. Clearly education is both the subject and the objective of Dabls's art.

Other than rocks and rusting iron, the most obvious materials used throughout the installation are wood (often symbolizing Native American culture) and thousands of mirror fragments, which represent communication with the ancestors and provide an integrated feeling over the extensive site. Everything other than nails and paint has been sourced for free—Dabls is very proud of that. Looking over the project is an ***Nkisi*** tasked with protecting the work from vandalism and the land from the eyes of the city. By all accounts it's been very successful. Looking south, a massive glass-encrusted ***Nkisi House*** provides a formidable backdrop. Behind that, every scrap of ***Rock's Language Wall*** is covered in a tribute to the twenty-six pre-European written African languages Dabls has researched. The wall's ever-changing surface texture ranges from grids of nails and dowels to Jackson Pollock–like drips and splashes. The

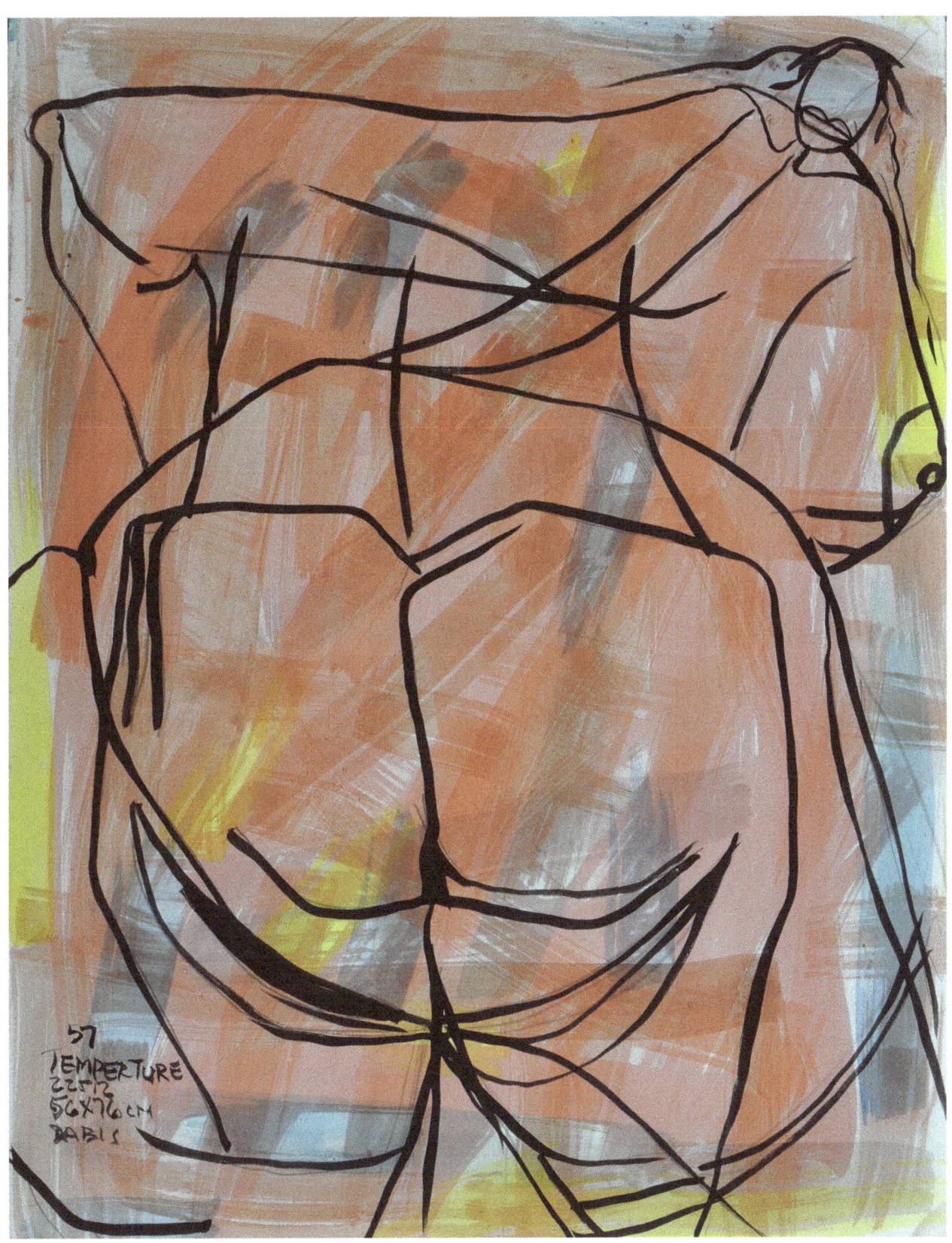

Temperature. 2011. Mixed media on plyboard, 46 x 48 in. Photography by Steve Hughes.

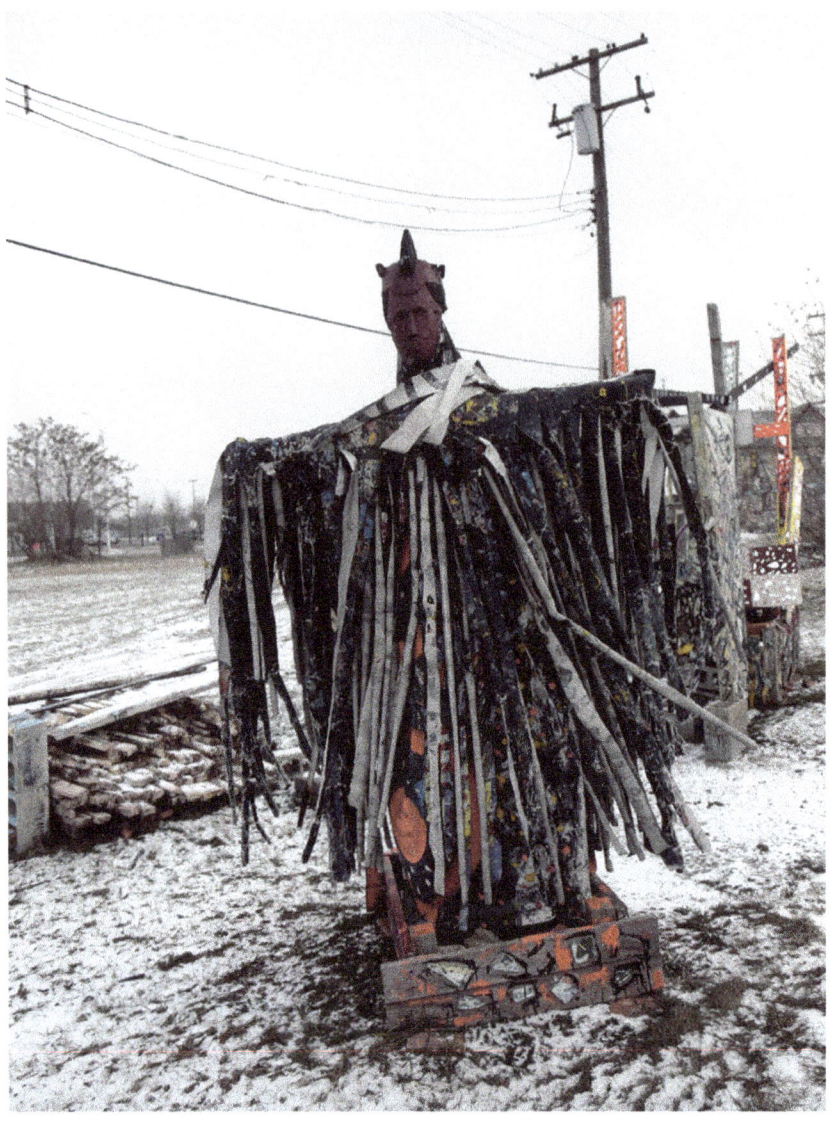

Figure with Ibo Mask (from the installation *Iron Teaching Rocks How to Rust)*. 1998–present.

institutional control. Further examples are provided by ***Iron Teaching Rocks Table Manners*** and ***History Cabinets***. The former has parallels to Dabls's series of paintings ***Normal Nudity*** (2011), which similarly question Western cultural norms, in this case relating to nudity and sexuality. In *History Cabinets*, rock's cultural heritage is shown incarcerated in filing cabinets, symbolizing the Western art museum's need to categorize and isolate objects which in rock's world are simply part of society; as Dabls points out, there was no word for art in traditional African languages. The antithesis of the previous three scenes is provided by ***Figure with Ibo Mask***, which symbolizes the freedom that we all—even iron— really strive for. By consciously starting from an African-centered view of history, Dabls's work may be particularly relevant for African Americans, but fundamentally his message is the universal one that "we are all 99% the same."

Ultimately Dabls is asking us to investigate how historical processes such as colonization and slavery have led us to what we consider normal. Academics might see parallels to postmodern historiography, and even to Paolo

plethora of mirrors, and intricacy of details, means, as with everything else in the project, that the visitor's experience is constantly changing; evening twilight is an especially magical time to see it.

Another way to visualize the project, and the way Dabls himself describes it, is as a series of scenes from a broader story—one which we all enter through a world preconfigured by European modes of thought. In one critical scene, rocks sit attentively in rows of metal frame chairs, invoking the feeling of a ***Classroom*** (or equally a church). It illustrates a recurring theme throughout the project— that of European culture's mission to reproduce itself through

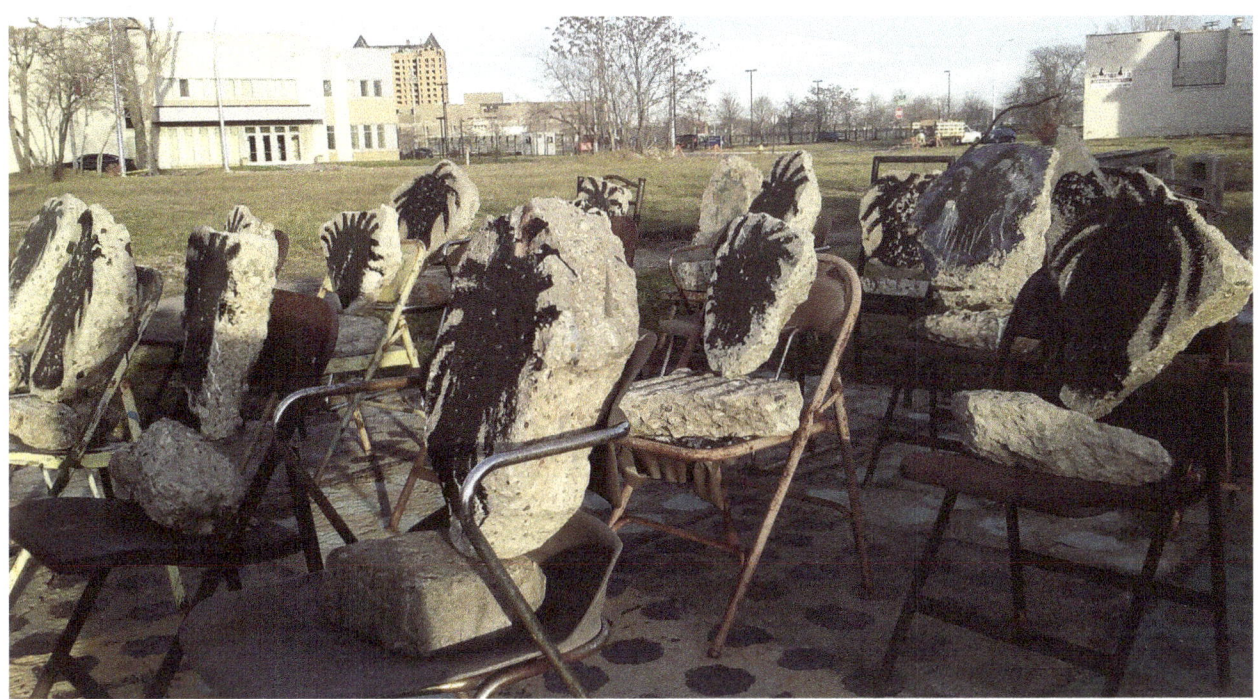

Classroom (from the installation *Iron Teaching Rocks How to Rust*). 1998–present.

Freire's radical pedagogy, but by constructing such a creatively overwhelming installation *and* using it for the educational purpose of unmasking the totalitarian impulses of Western culture, he manages to both question how we've arrived at this point and imagine a world free of that death drive. That it sits by a freeway in the center of the Motor City makes it even more poignant.

STEVE PANTON, DECEMBER 2015

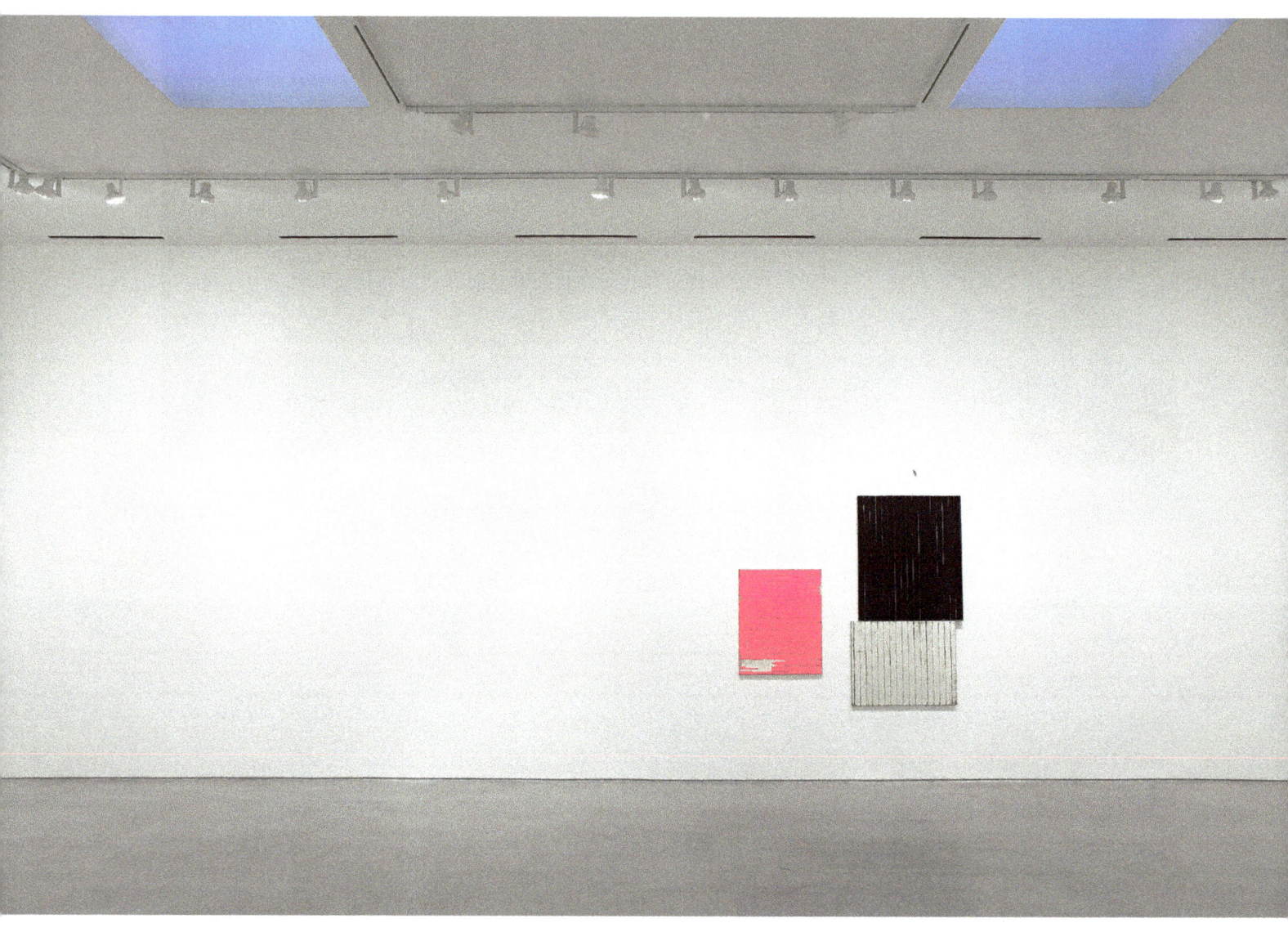

Agalma (installation view). 2015.

40 // GREG FADELL

Born Detroit, 1970
BA, University of Michigan
Lives in Clarkston, Michigan

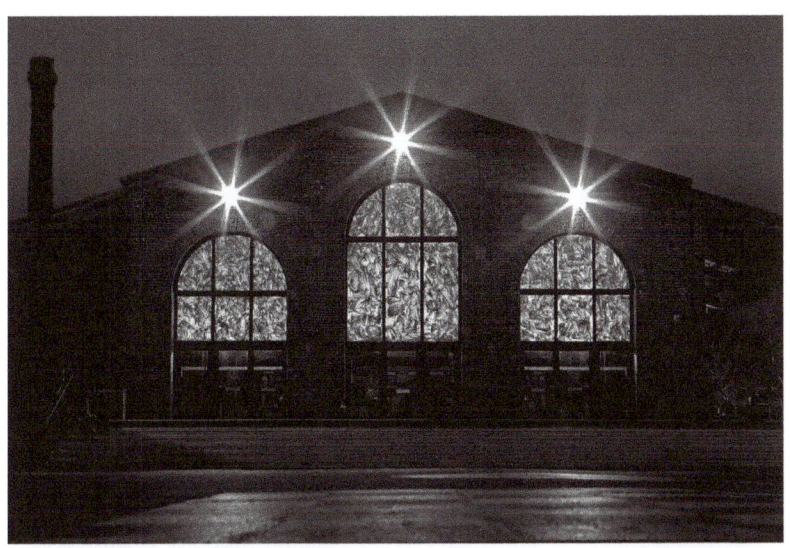

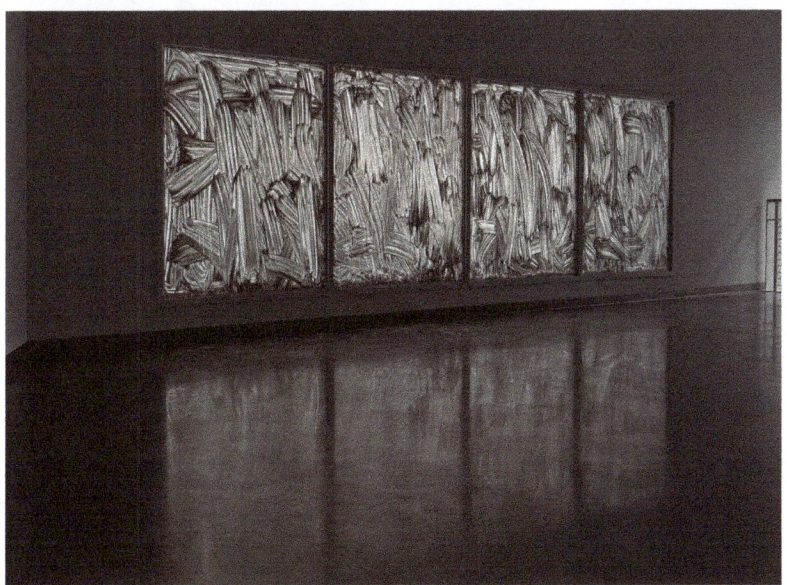

Greg Fadell's work and his persona can be seen as a series of deliberate choices. The work of some artists begins and ends within the frame, but for Fadell, wall, lighting, surfaces, and gallery are just as important as the pieces he brings to hang . . . and all that before his attention to the forces that shape the art world itself. Every aspect of Fadell's practice is deeply considered, even those that might read as casual or irreverent vestiges of his early pro-skater career and personal aesthetic. His body of work draws in the viewer with its ostensible simplicity, but ask an informed question and be astonished by the volubility and the substance of his answer.

For example, his 2012 show ***Nothingness*** at Simone DeSousa

(Top) Lille 3000. 2015. Installation/paint on window glass. (Bottom) UICA. 2013. Installation/paint on window glass.

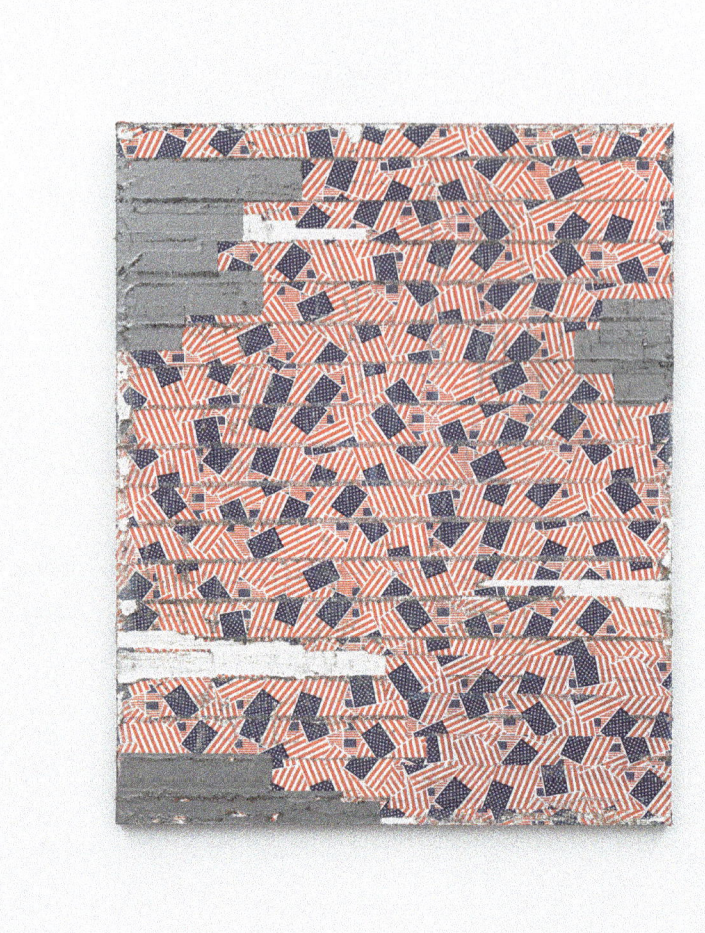
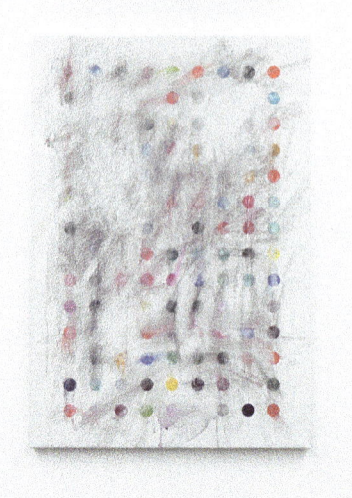
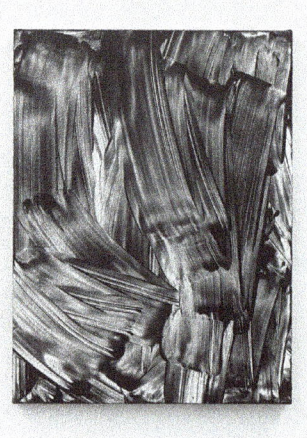

(Top, Left) Untitled. 2015. Duct tape on Baltic birch, 36 x 30 in.
(Top, right) Untitled (Dots). 2014. Chemically altered digital print, 40 1/2 x 27 1/2 in.
(Bottom, right) Nothing (1). 2012. Custom-formulated graphite, 24 x 18 in.

Gallery (then Re:View) presented large-scale paintings in stark black and white that resemble an attempt to vigorously scrub washes of paint in random, vaguely geometric directions. While the content of each canvas would seem to suggest its eponymous "nothing"—see, for example, *Nothing (1)*—Fadell is drawing upon the philosophy laid out by Jean-Paul Sartre's 1943 book-length essay on ontology, *Being and Nothingness.* Fadell rightly identifies the art world as the perfect system within which to exploit ideas of expectation and negation, and effectively does so with these simple forms that he presents repeatedly, having revisited the aesthetics of this body for a *2013 installation* on windows at UICA in Grand Rapids, as well as his *2015 contribution* to the Lille 3000 cultural expo in France.

With his 2015 *solo show* at the Museum of Contemporary Art Detroit, Fadell takes on the art canon *en masse,* displaying museum-issued posters of iconic works of art, altered by application of chemicals to become compromised versions of the image. Fadell shies away from the term "erasure" here, pointing out that none of the pigment is removed, just relocated around the canvas.

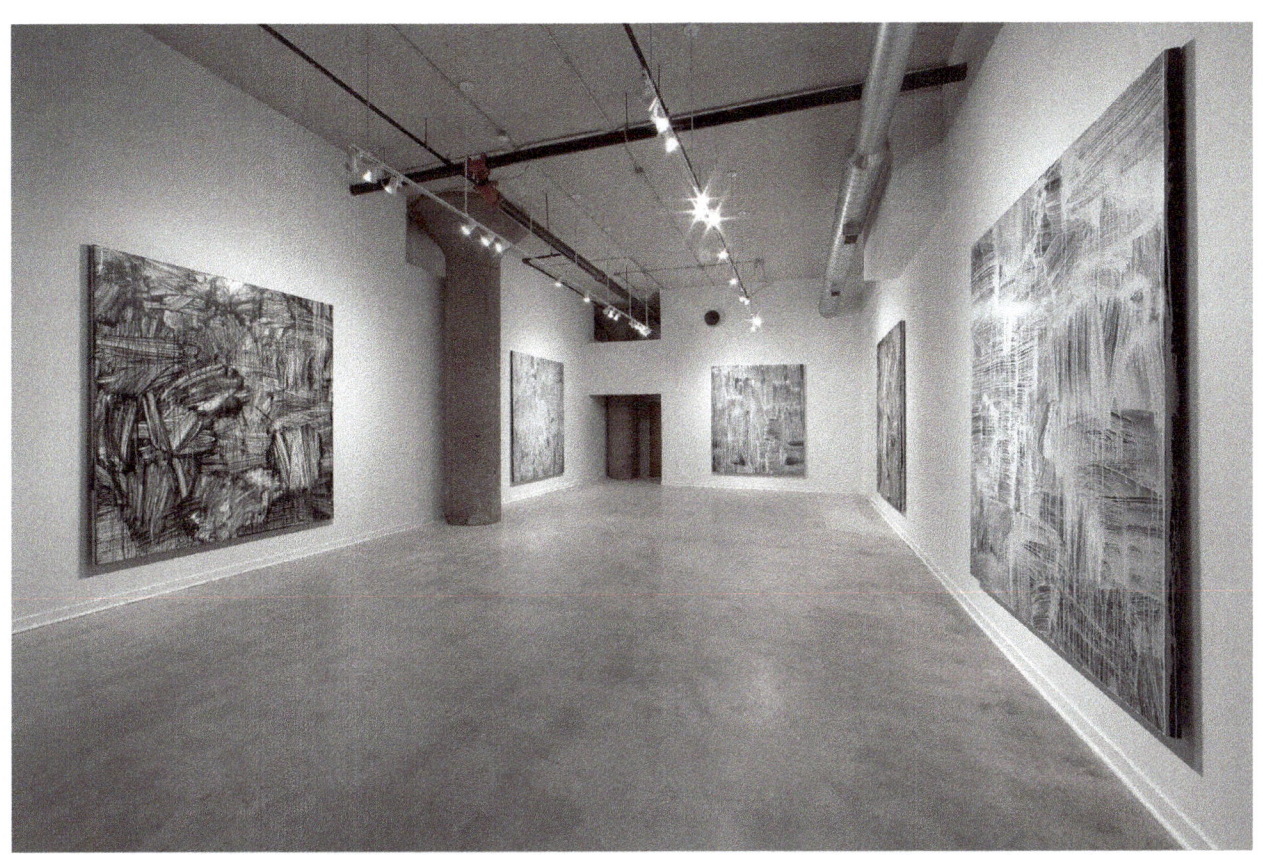

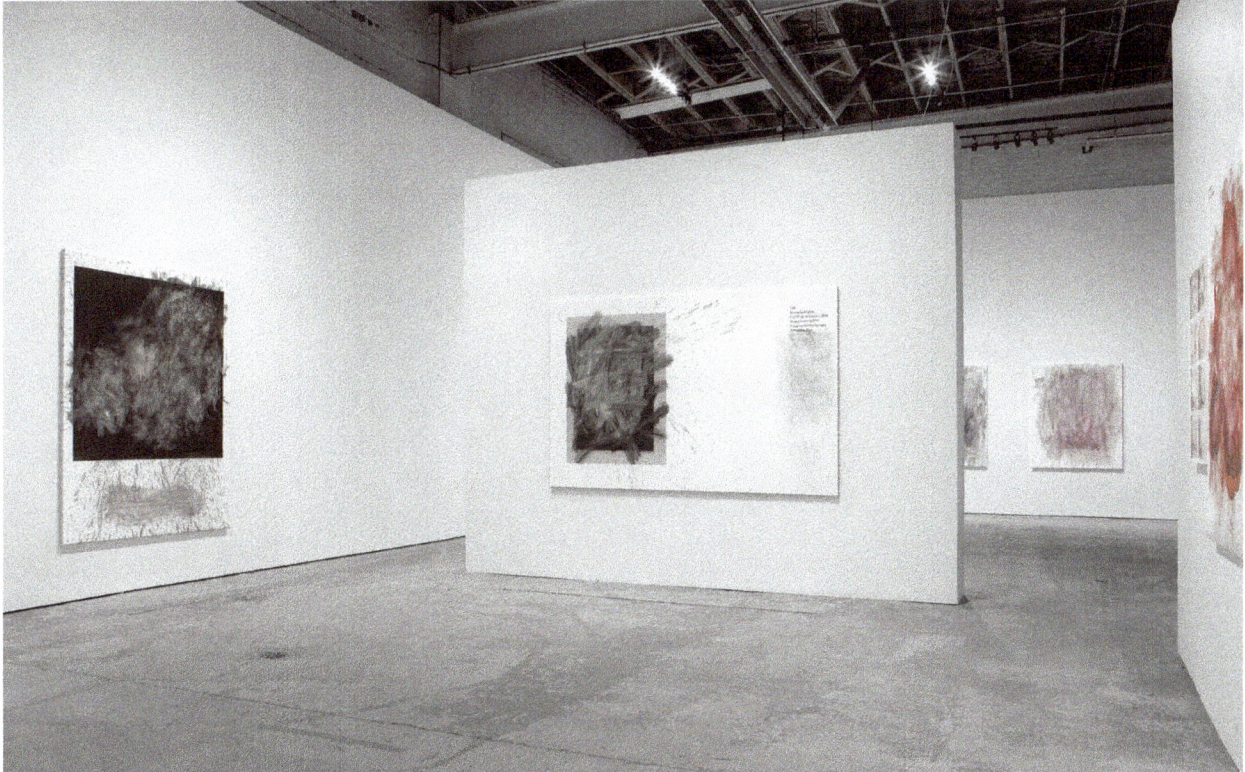

(Top) Nothingness (installation view). 2012.
(Bottom) Solo show, MOCAD (installation view). 2015.

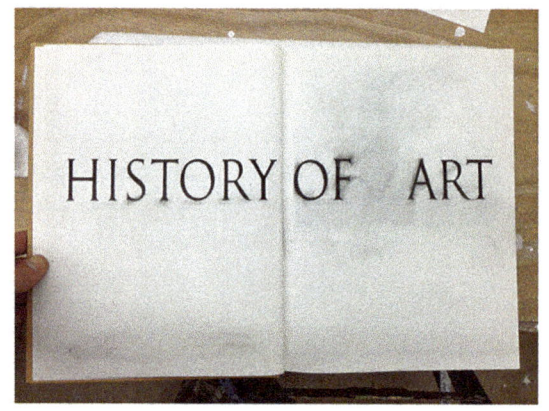
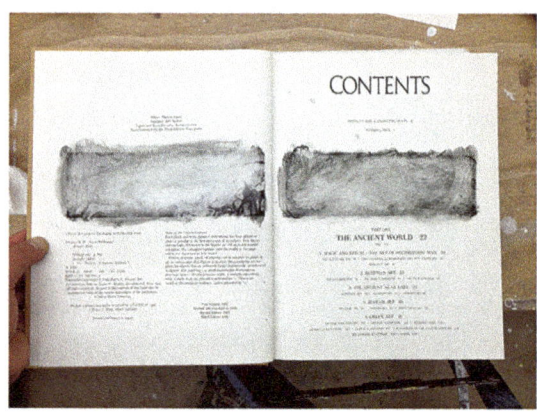

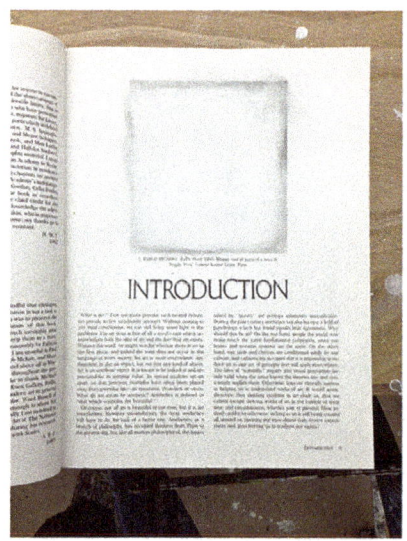
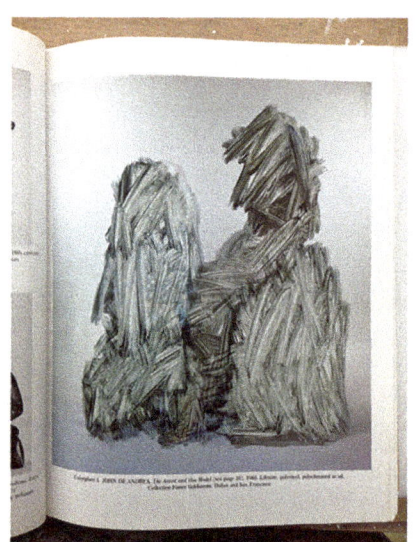

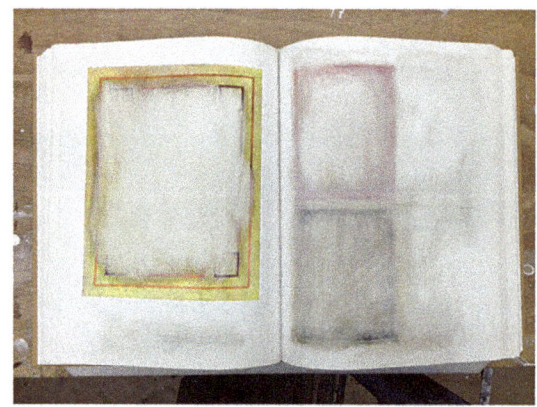
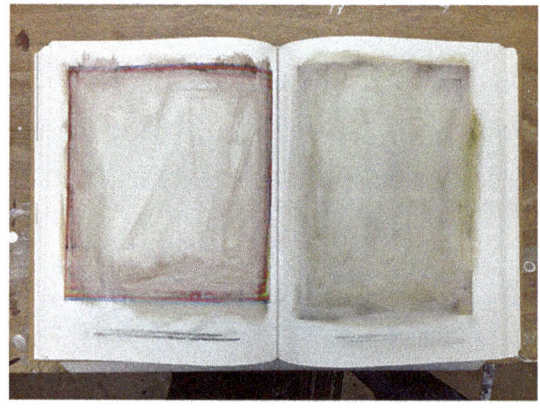

History of Art. 2013–present. H. W. Janson (third edition, hardcover) art history book altered by chemicals, 11 1/2 x 9 x 2 in. (824 pp).

The larger works, such as *Untitled (Dots)*, derived from a piece originally by Damien Hirst, come from initial explorations in alteration that Fadell made to the ***art history textbooks*** assigned to him in art school, and exemplify his pointed questioning of the hierarchy of value in the art world. Fadell is a complex character, and the uncompromising seriousness he invests in his work is mitigated by a playful detachment from the system that determines the success or failure of any given artist. Though he is quick to emphasize that the work must initially fulfill an inherent sense of purpose within him as a maker, it is also the price of entry into the wider system of the art market—one with which Fadell is driven to engage with the fervor of a day trader on the stock market. Art is his business, and he conducts it with focus that might be considered mercenary by those unaware of the role strategy plays in an artist's relative success.

But the art does come first—Fadell's work is composed primarily of ideas, and the processes he employs to refine objects in space hold value inasmuch as they present these ideas in a way that invites interaction. Fadell has not *forgotten* to paint the sides of his canvases—he has chosen to leave them as a keyhole into the laborious method by which, for example, he transformed what appears to be a thick buildup of paint, in the *Nothingness* series, into a very thin, smooth surface. In a sense, Fadell is an illusionist, but the effects of his tricks are slow dawning; the immediate impulse to dismiss a given body of work as simple gives way to an awareness of the effort, followed by wonder at exactly how it was accomplished. In this, Fadell's roots as a skater prone to long-form negotiation of streets and high half-pipes, rather than one-off tricks, show. His is a culture based on discipline, repetition, and practice, which make astonishingly hard things look easy, sometimes even effortless.

Fadell changes tactics and media with fluidity. His most recent show, *Agalma* (2015) derives its nomenclature from the Greek word for ornamentation left in sacrifice to the gods, and features decorative duct tape, meticulously applied to canvas and distressed. The care he has taken to account for the gallery's skylights and architectural details betrays Fadell's obsessive attention to the big picture, and the conceptual basis of the work combines accessible materials with Lacanian philosophy, and a sly poke at the "gods" of the art world, for good measure. Fadell has launched himself into an ambitious orbit, and spectators are watching to see if he can nail the landing.

SARAH ROSE SHARP,
DECEMBER 2015

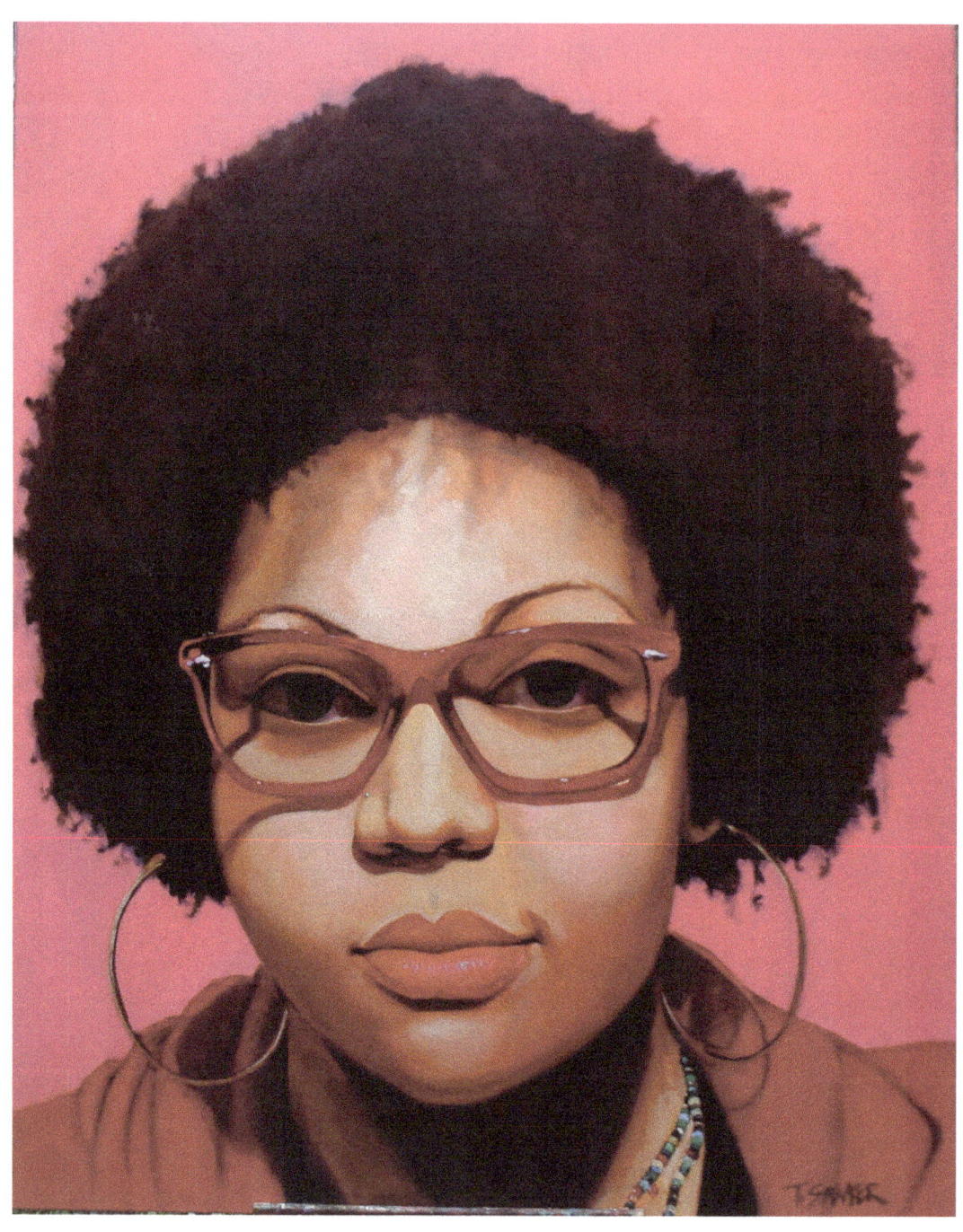

A Lady in Red . . . Not Jean Hill (Portrait of Whitney Syphax Walker). 2012. Oil on canvas, 60 x 48 in.

Born Detroit, 1976
BFA, Eastern Michigan University;
MFA, New York Academy of Art,
Graduate School of Figurative Art
Lives in Detroit

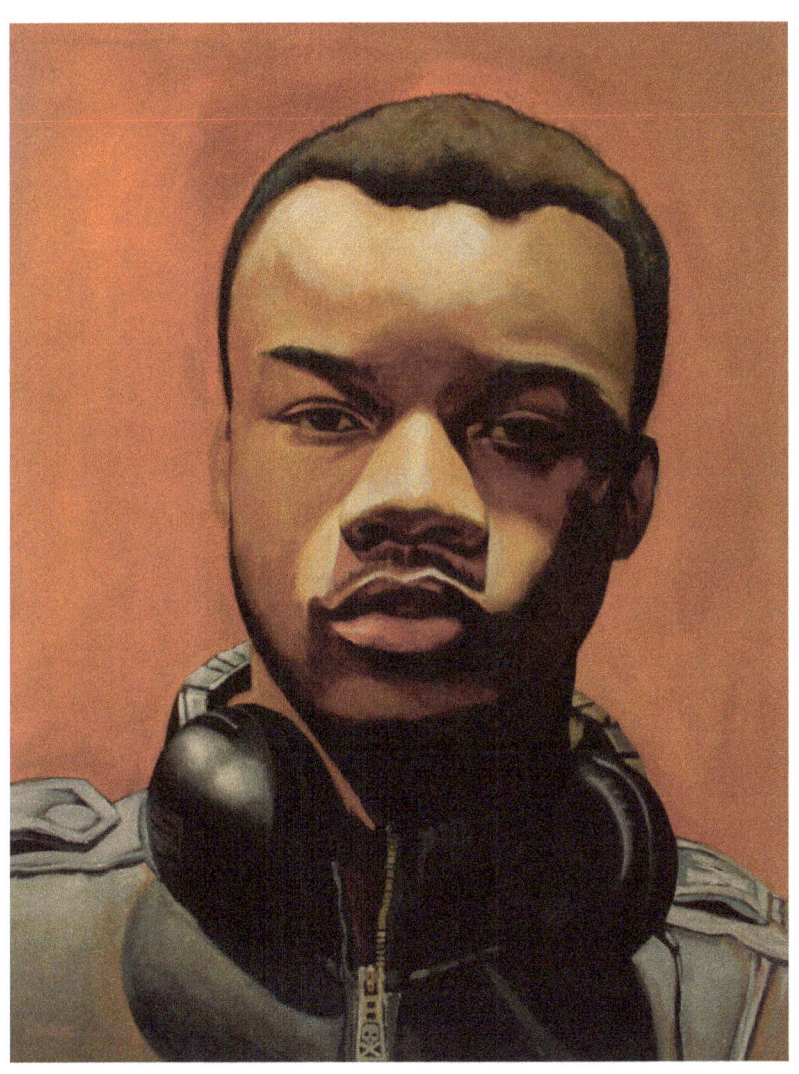

Visibility, accessibility, ambitious scale, and industrious zeal are some of the constituent hallmarks of Tylonn Sawyer's activist art and life. Such attributes are readily apparent in his very public, very large, Detroit-centric **Whole Foods Mural** of 2013. Drawing upon Marshall Fredericks's iconic *Spirit of Detroit* sculpture, Sawyer reinvents Fredericks's hero as a young African American lad with empty palms (freed of Fredericks's fusty totems of god and family) who, while awaiting new symbols to cross his palms, glances over a colorful, agricultural grid on the left, and a tidy, green, aerial urban view on the right. Such unconventional revisions of conventional tropes have been basic to Sawyer's vision

The Son (Sun). 2013. Oil on canvas, 42 x 30 in.

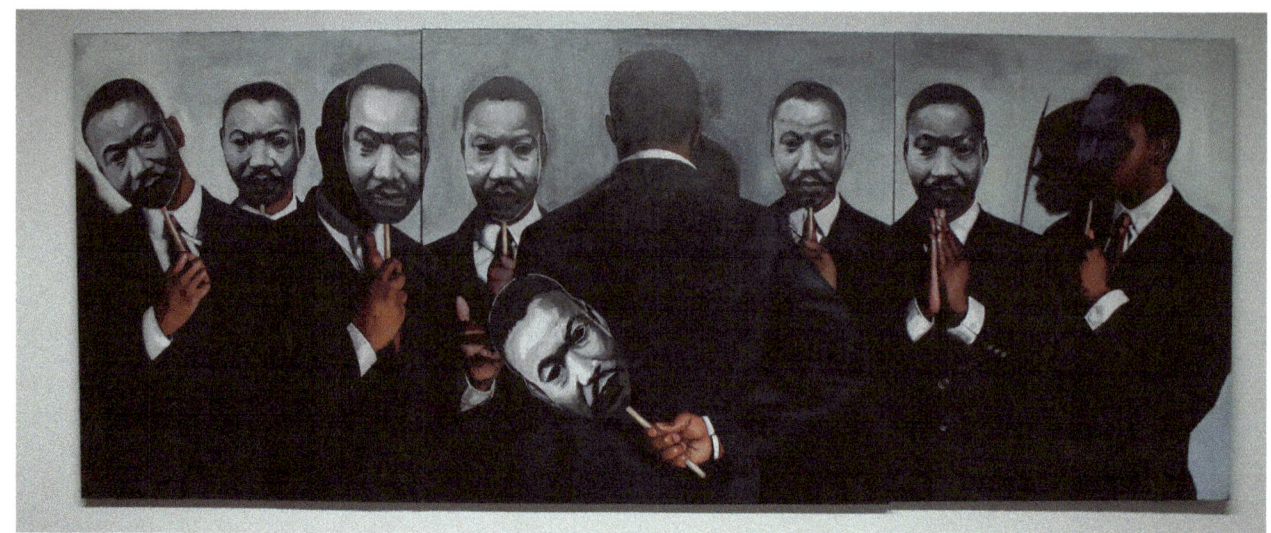

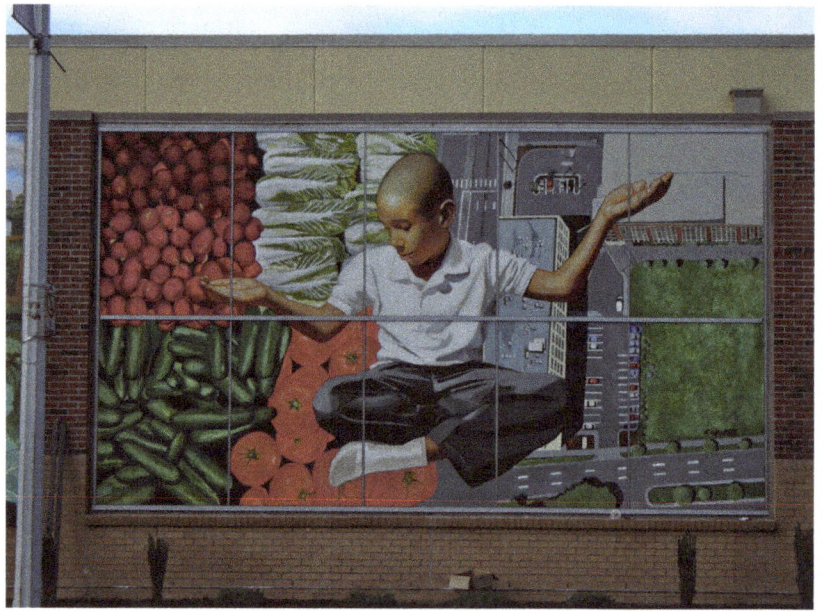

(Top) "Congregation" MLK. 2015. Oil on canvas, 48 x 120 in. *(Bottom) Whole Foods Mural.* 2013. Latex and oil on Mapes Corelite, 14 2/5 x 24 2/5 ft.

over the last several years. Here, it is a vulnerable, albeit perfectly balanced, adolescent who embodies a city's great expectations.

This envisioning of transformative progress on a muralist scale intersects with Sawyer's role in the Teen Council at the Museum of Contemporary Art Detroit, now

a two-dozen-member group that he founded in 2014 and continues to mentor. Its mission, to actively engage young people in the life of the museum, also introduces them to the dynamics of a life of dialogue, engagement, and activism. Sawyer's fervent commitment to arts education stems from his

belief that life opens outward both for oneself and to others when fostered within a social structure (home, institution, school).

For his own creative practice, Sawyer astutely primed himself for the production and goals of his art. Choosing what he describes as "an adamantly figurative" art school, he enrolled in the New York Academy of Art's Graduate School of Figurative Art to ensure the mastery of a highly accessible style and meticulous technique. He now teaches foundational courses at the College for Creative Studies, and in two recent bodies of work he has focused his ambition on emphatically frontal, large-scale portraits—*Faces*—and on masked individuals who hide their faces behind images of famous personages—*Black Masquerade*. In the latter, he has segued from his

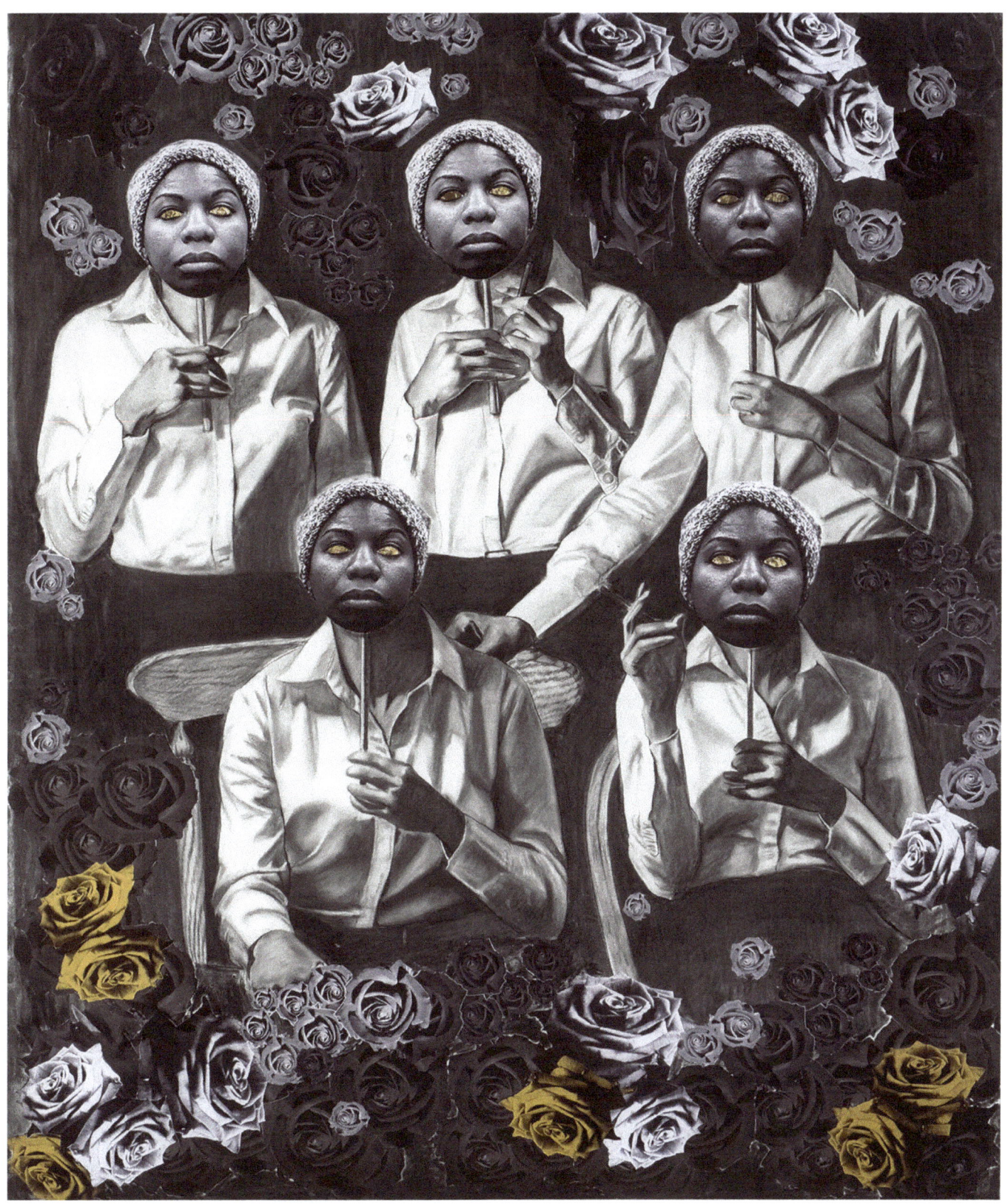

"Class Photo #1.5" Nina. 2016. Charcoal, collage, and gold leaf on paper, 5 x 4 ft.

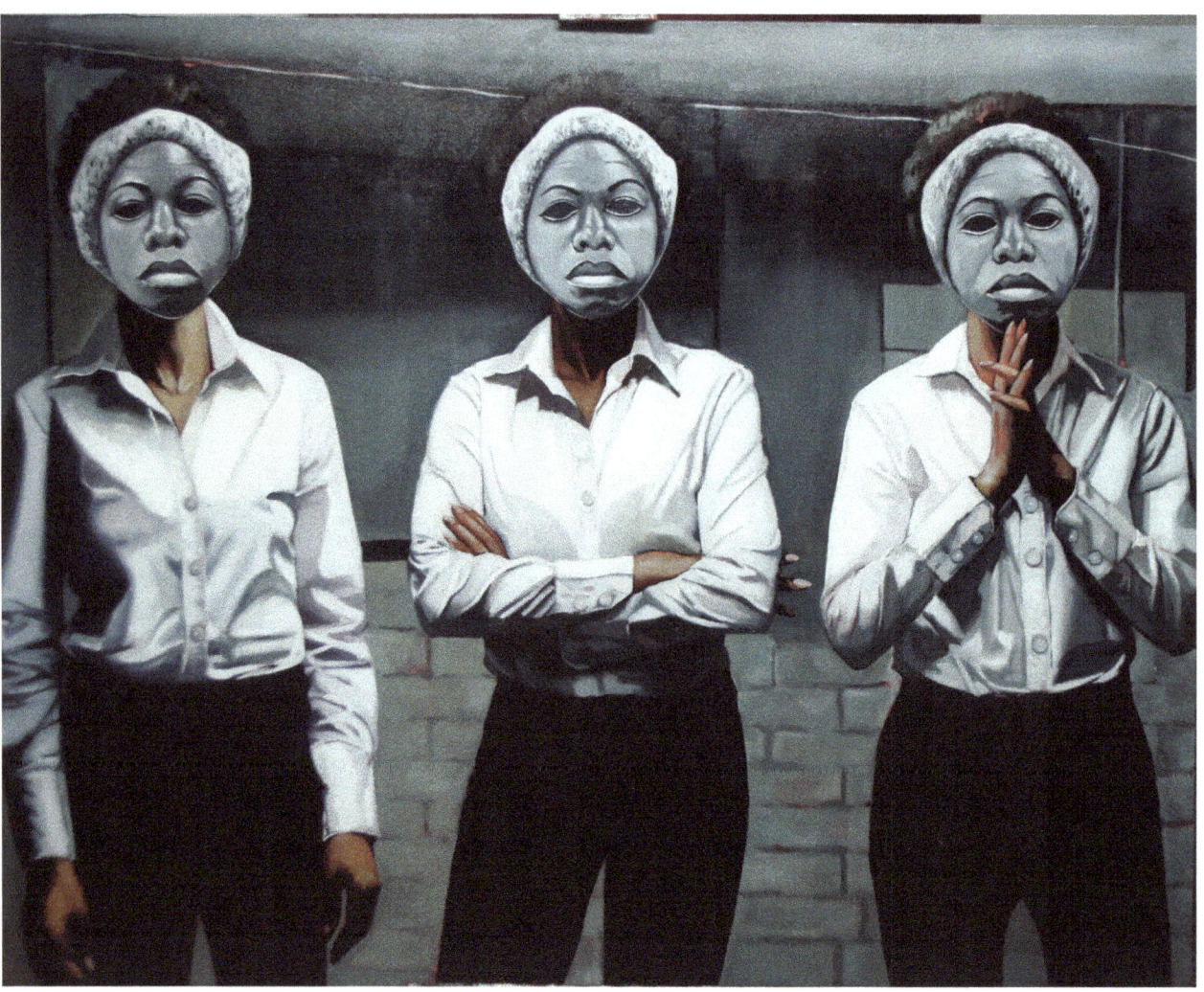

"3 Graces" Nina. 2015. Oil on canvas, 48 x 64 in.

earlier bust or waist-length single figures, as in *The Son (Sun)* (2013) and *A Lady in Red . . . Not Jean Hill* (2012) to dramatic, multifigural compositions like *"3 Graces" Nina* and the mural-scaled *"Congregation" MLK* (both 2015).

The shift from *Faces* to *Black Masquerade* is as interesting conceptually as aesthetically. The concentration in *Faces* on portraits of African Americans, Detroiters by and large, in a relatively sizable

scale (up to five by four feet) was intended to assert unmistakably their physical presence in the frame, on the wall, at a gallery, and in life. Subsequently, Sawyer began to think that their larger-than-life depictions, while arresting and boldly hued—reds, pinks, oranges, mustards—were insufficiently vocal for fraught times. Hence, the multifigural groupings, as in *"Congregation" MLK*, *"3 Graces" Nina*, and *"Class Photo*

#1.5" Nina, that mimic the format of group photographs of graduating classes, business officials, and miscellaneous awardees, but with a salient difference. Here, all raise masks depicting civil rights activists (Martin Luther King Jr., Nina Simone) to shield their faces, preferring, it would seem, to deny their own identities while hallowing their predecessors' hands-on, civil rights bona fides. Idols are endorsed and venerated,

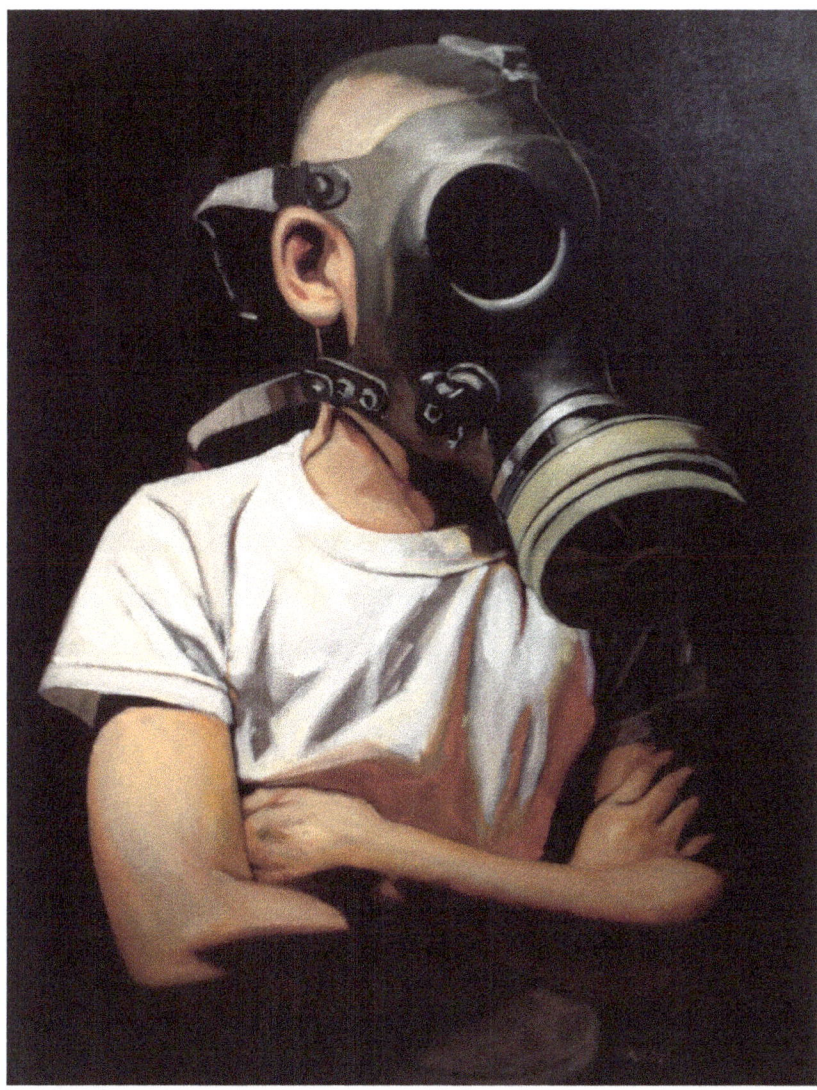

Precipice #1. 2013. Oil on canvas, 40 x 30 in.

against murky backgrounds heightens the portrayals of distress, while in the *Masquerade* canvases the gray, black, and bone-white chroma of *"3 Graces"* evokes a state of mind drained of robust color and action. In *Class Photo #1.5*, only the golden hue of a few of the ashen roses banking the figures evokes any sign of vitality. Sawyer's own vital, spirited immersion in teaching, mentoring, painting, and a broadly defined social practice, instead embraces Socrates's ageless mantra that "the unexamined [i.e., masked] life is not worth living."

DENNIS ALAN NAWROCKI,
DECEMBER 2015

but their rebellious, transgressive deeds are not, a paradox Sawyer reinforces by the stiff, static poses of his band of dissemblers.

A striking counterpoint to these masquerades is an earlier series of nightmarish figure studies, ominously christened *The Battle of Detroit*, in which the subjects—young men— donned grotesque gas masks, as in **Precipice #1** (2013). Here,

however, the impetus to do so was survivalist, since the figures were literally protecting themselves from a toxic environment and metaphorically from a world hostile to Black bodies.

The visceral and visual drama of Sawyer's art is enhanced by his vaunted, polished, academic skills as a painter. In *The Battle of Detroit* series, his deployment of a Caravaggesque play of light

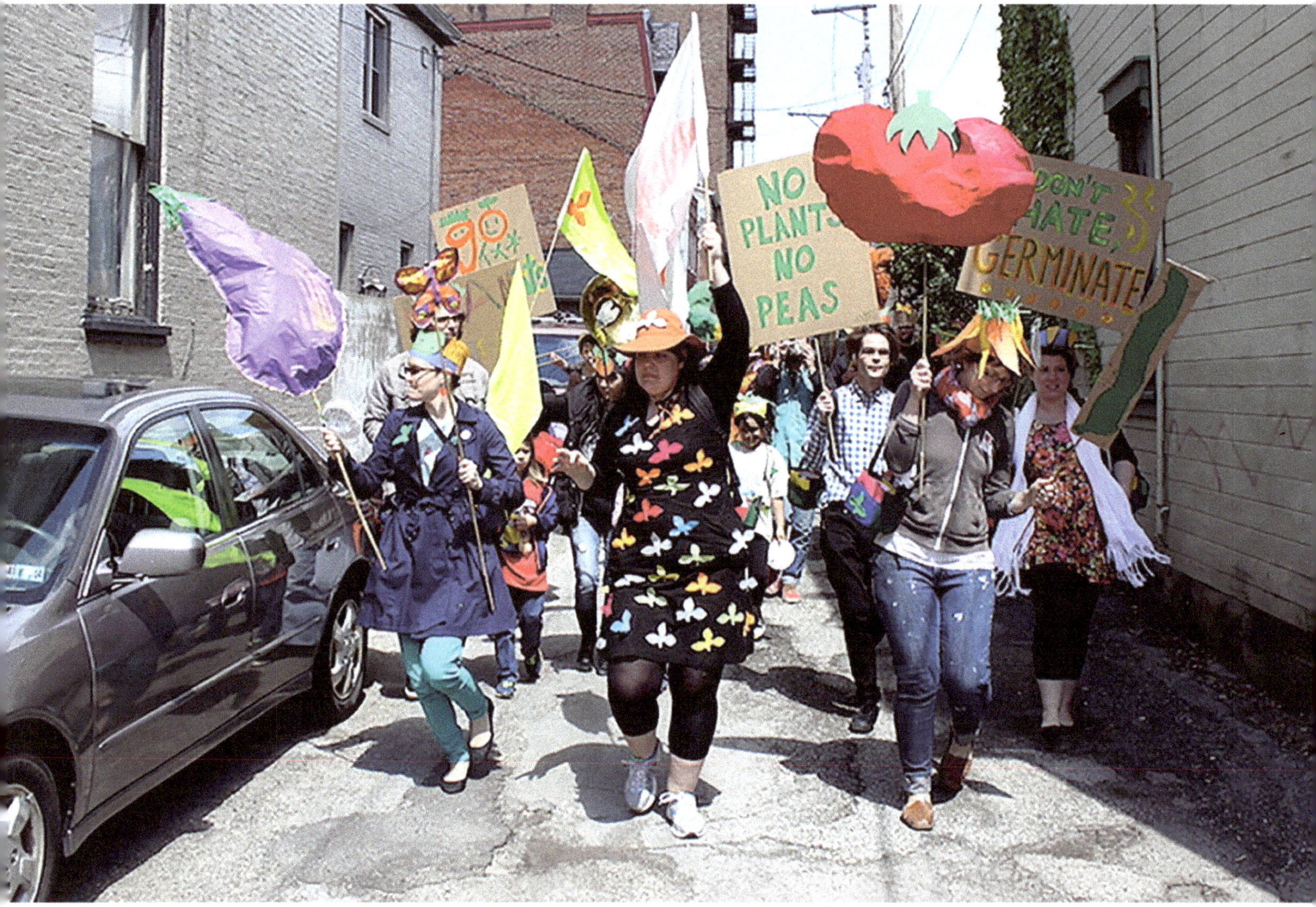

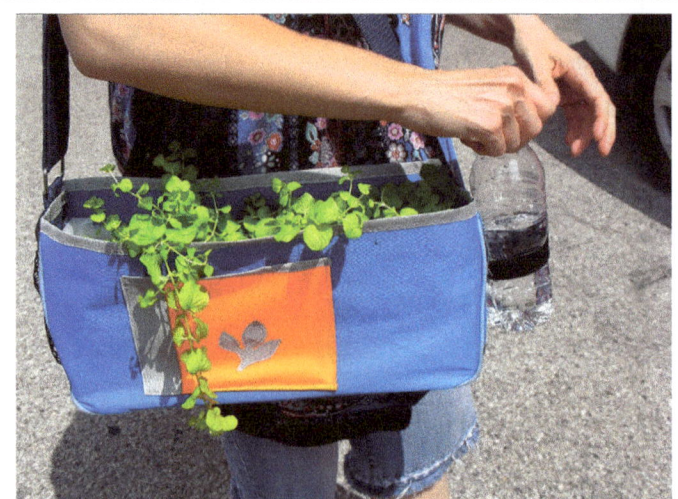

(Top) Germination Corps / Plant Parade.
2010–present. Mixed media and performance,
dimensions variable.
(Bottom) Germination Corps / Plant Backpacks.
2010–present. Mixed media and performance,
dimensions variable.

Born Bryn Mawr, Pennsylvania, 1980
BFA, Rhode Island School of Design;
MArch, Cranbrook Academy of Art
Lives in Hamtramck, Michigan

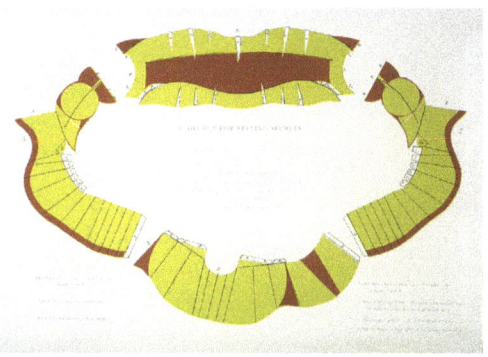

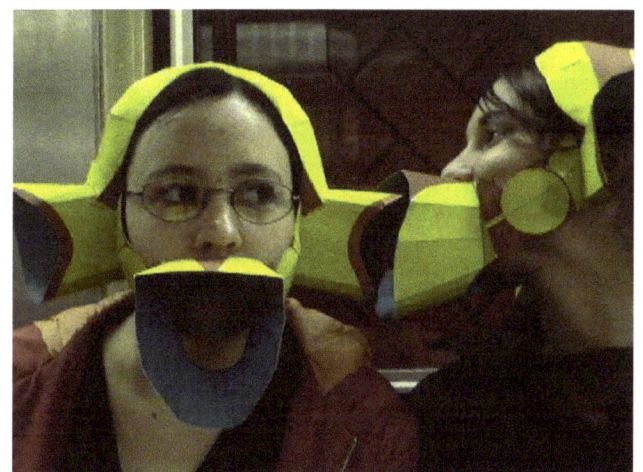

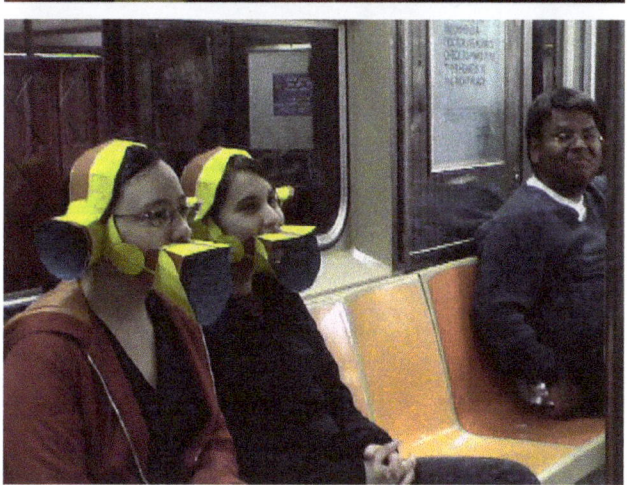

Art, it's been said, is often about taking something small and making a really big deal out of it. For Jessica Frelinghuysen, that initial seed is the minutiae of social interaction—the tiny events that individually are of little consequence, but that collectively make up the fabric of any society. Her concern is that, despite the increasingly impersonal nature of our modes of communication, and however personally awkward these microinteractions may be, we should continue to both value and question them.

Frelinghuysen's *Paper Helmet Series* (2002–present) focuses on somewhat unlikely "solutions" to everyday situations. For example,

(Top) Helmets for Telling Secrets. 2005. Constructable screenprint, dimensions variable.
(Middle & bottom) Helmets for Telling Secrets (video still), NYC subway. 2005. Constructable screenprint/performance. Performers: Angela Skeie and Heather Guidero.

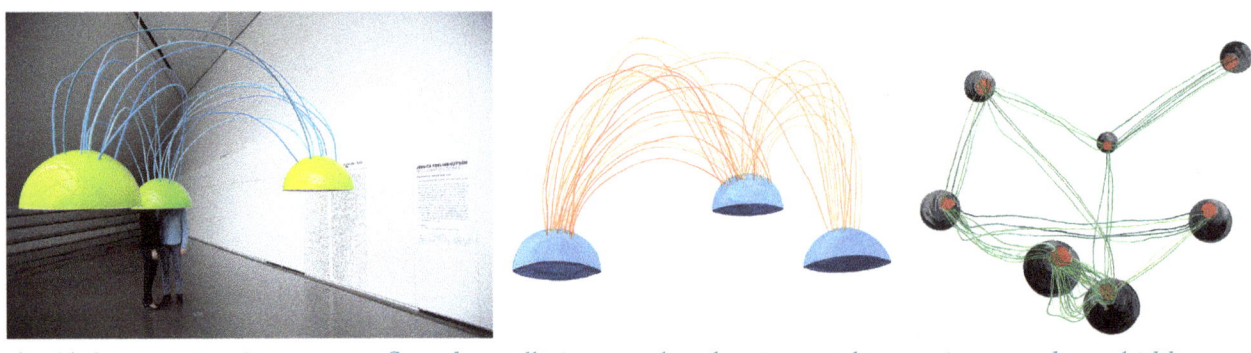

(Left) Conversation Domes. 2015. Sound installation, acrylic, aluminum tubing, voice recordings, hidden sound elements. Courtesy of Aaron Word, Eli and Edythe Broad Art Museum.
(Middle) No Words (Three-Way Thought Call). 2012. Gouache, 12 x 16 in.
(Right) Happy Hour. 2009. Gouache, 12 x 16 in.

her ***Helmet for Telling Secrets*** (2005) is a transportable device that allows pairs of wearers to create a temporary private space in a public location. Clearly, though, the device comes with its own social awkwardness, so one could argue that its real intent is not so much to solve the original problem as to transform it into a form of performance. There is certainly an element of absurdity in the work, but at their core, Frelinghuysen's objectives are serious; ultimately she envisions her projects as long-running experiments in which we can all participate, and that highlight something we might otherwise overlook.

The transformation of Frelinghuysen's *Paper Helmets* from flat printed sheets into sculptural microarchitecture is reflective of her own artistic trajectory. Her first degree is in printmaking, but a growing desire to take her work out of the gallery, and into participatory social situations, led to graduate study in architecture at the multidisciplinary, and historically design-focused, environment of Cranbrook. Much of Frelinghuysen's thinking still starts from "sketches," which may be mappings of the communication paths she sees around her (e.g., 2009's ***Happy Hour***) or concepts for hypothetical new projects (e.g., 2012's ***No Words (Three-Way Thought Call))***. If the concept sketches show the influence of Frelinghuysen's design/ architecture background on her two-dimensional work, the eventual three-dimensional implementations (e.g., 2015's ***Conversation Domes***), with their emphasis on shape, line, and color, show the continuing influence of her printmaking background. Frelinghuysen pays particular attention to color, and her selections are often informed by an awareness of psychology and the history of design.

As its name implies, the work of *Conversation Domes* is participatory. Standing under one of the stations, the visitor hears a disorderly soundtrack of various voices describing their difficulties in communication. The participant may either listen or join in. Frelinghuysen's objective is to "bring attention to roadblocks that compete with our attempts to listen, find meaning, and be understood," and hence "open a space for discovery, realization, and conversation." Clearly there is a paradox here; in order to encourage a deeper consideration of what may seem very natural, Frelinghuysen abstracts, aestheticizes, and conceptually remaps it into a highly artificial environment. The work's appearance is similarly contradictory—the sleek and shiny domes are connected by tubing that seems as much derived from the string between two tin cans as it does from fiber-optic cabling.

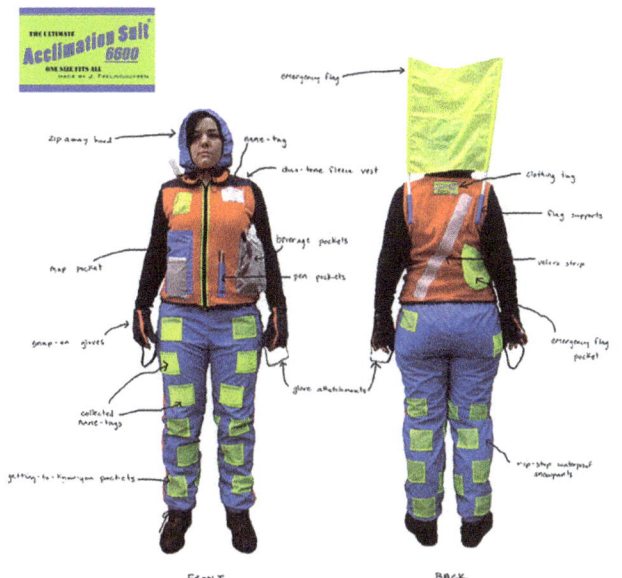
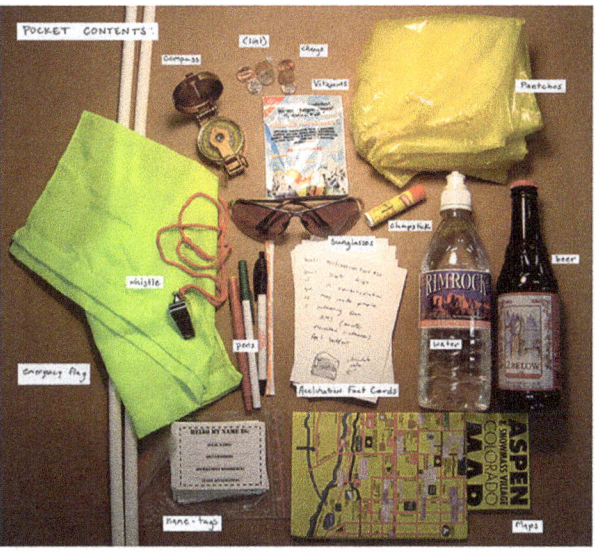

(Top) Acclimation Suit 6600 (for Aspen). 2006. Fabricated uniform, name tags, fact cards, "job," daily performance, dimensions variable.
(Bottom) Acclimation Suit 6600 (Emergency Flag). 2006. Fabricated uniform, name tags, fact cards, "job," daily performance, dimensions variable.

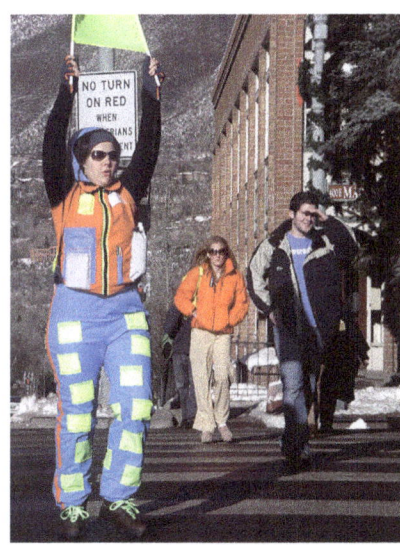

The overall effect, simultaneously impersonal and strangely folksy, is a defining characteristic of many of Frelinghuysen's projects. For example, her *Acclimation Suit 6600* (2006), which includes "everything to assimilate into the highly affluent and low oxygenated mountain environment (of Aspen)," is one of a series of *Task Uniforms* that concurrently embrace concepts of uniformity and vernacular personalization. Arguably, the contradictions that Frelinghuysen highlights are also a defining condition of our age, as we try to reconcile traditional, human-level interactions with a world of rapidly changing communication technology.

The Germination Corps (aka Plant Backpacks) project (2010–present) extends beyond consideration of the interpersonal to look at the relationship between people and nature. Project participants (typically children) are provided with a plant in a backpack that they are encouraged to carry with them and care for. The intention is to develop empathy for natural processes of growth through real-world experiences. The project has been performed in numerous locations, including Pittsburgh, rural North Carolina, Philadelphia, and Santa Fe. Often it culminates with Frelinghuysen—who by her own admission is naturally quite shy—leading an impressive parade. Each iteration of the project provides more insight into the work's educational potential and cultural nuances. As with all of Frelinghuysen's many activities, one thing that shines through clearly is her sincere and indefatigable desire to transform the world for the better—from the ground up.

STEVE PANTON, JANUARY 2016

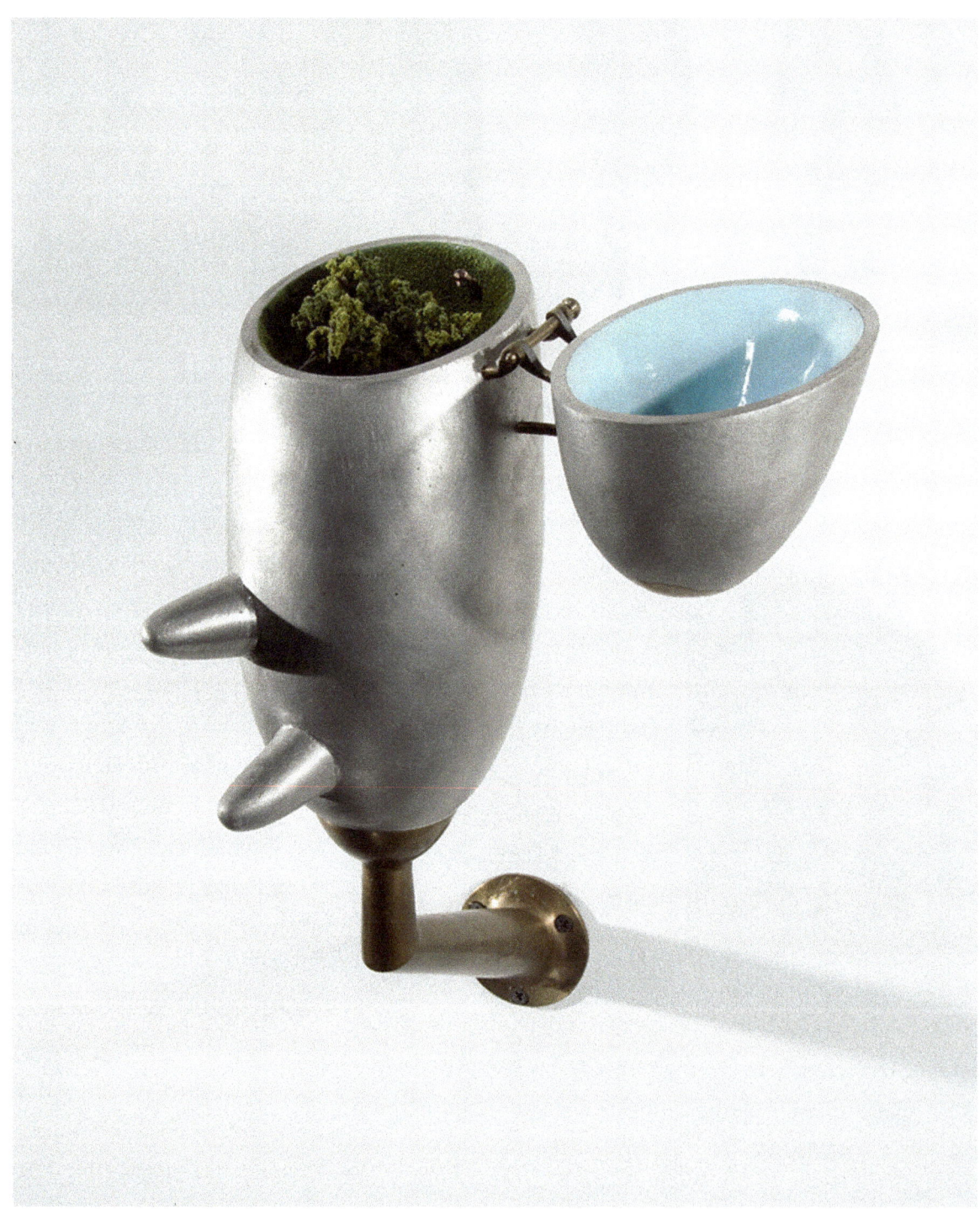

Camping with Gaia. 2008. Miniatures on cast aluminum, cast bronze.

43 // GRAEM WHYTE

Born Royal Oak, Michigan, 1970
Lives in Hamtramck, Michigan

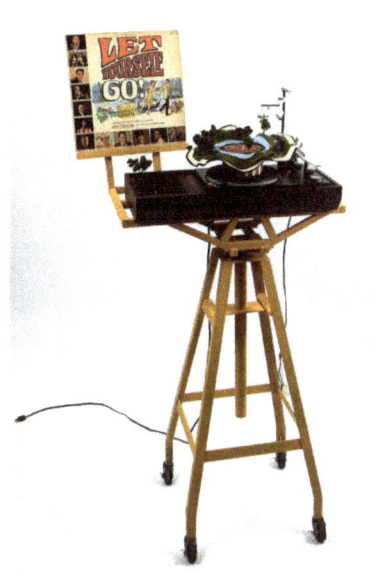

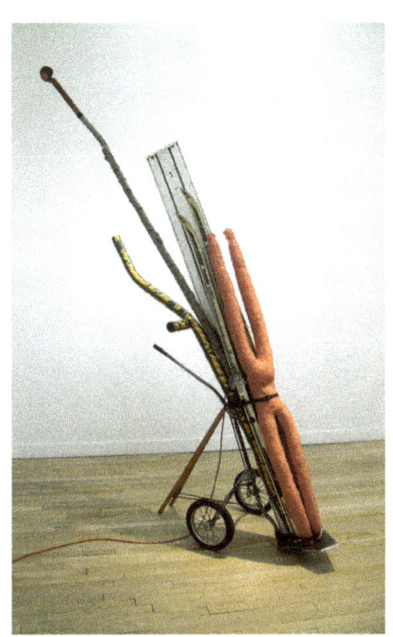

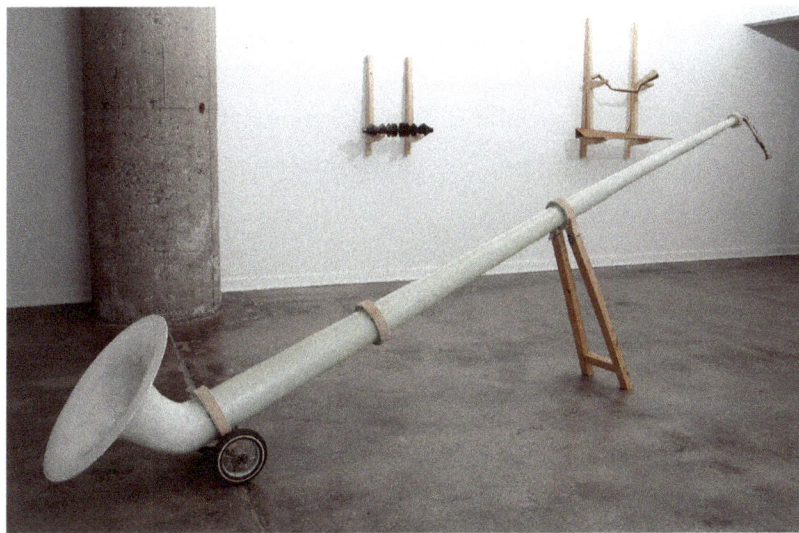

On the once-blighted northwest border of Hamtramck stands a well-lit building with a geometric pattern painted on its facade. This is Popps Packing. Graem Whyte and his wife, artist Faina Lerman, built Popps together. There is art in this building, and arguably Popps itself is an artistic undertaking. Since 2009, Whyte and Lerman have invested themselves in programming gallery events. They've built a sculpture garden and created a residency program, and they continue to activate their section of town by facilitating the work of artists from Detroit and overseas. This is about community. This is where Graem Whyte's work is rooted.

(Top, left) Let Yourself Go. 2007.
Miniatures on vinyl, record
player, wood.
(Top, right) United Rambler. 2010.
Golf bag cart, fluorescent light
fixture, wood, urethane rubber,
copper, steel.
(Bottom) Wishing for Mountains.
2013. Urethane resin, cherry,
found wheels, horn mouthpiece.

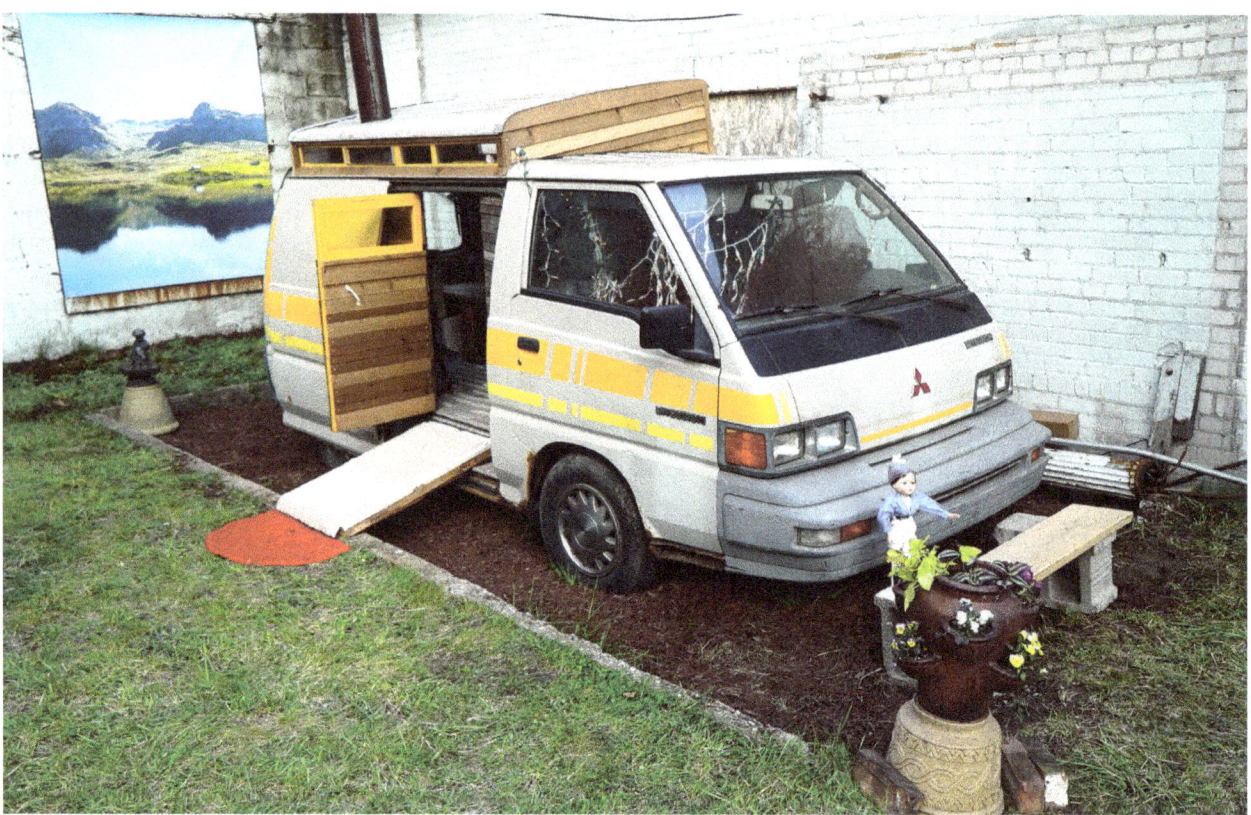

Popps Mobile Sauna (collaboration with Benny Henningsen). 2012. 1989 Mitsubishi van, cedar, steel, Christmas lights.

Whyte keeps his studio in the back of Popps. It's part woodshop, part material storage, part workspace for the artists on Popps's residency program. In the summer, bands play here and the dogs wander in and out of the open door, but in the winter cold, the space is less hospitable. The concrete walls, a good twenty feet high, are neatly arranged with shelves and crates holding tools, jars of fasteners, and casters of varied sizes. Large racks hold plywood and door slabs. Most of this stuff is pulled out of the alley or given to Whyte. It's waiting to be repurposed. "That's mostly what I do now," Whyte says. "I manage materials. I reassign use." He didn't always work this way.

Some of Whyte's earlier sculptures are studies of possible worlds. They begin with a common object like a record player and reimagine it as a scale chunk of the world. In *Let Yourself Go* (2007), a wildly warped record, felted with grass and dotted with little human and animal figurines, suggests that something weird or wonderful has happened there. In *Camping with Gaia* (2008), the interior of a polished aluminum pod splits open to expose small trees, a park maybe. It's a place of peace amid an otherwise inhospitable vessel.

"I'm not interested in commodification as it relates to art. My work is more about spiritual, ancestral, and community value. Check it out." Whyte points to a twelve-foot horn on wheels that he fabricated from fiberglass. He carries it down the ladder, inserts the mouthpiece, and blows. "I think it's in G sharp," he says. "That was unintentional, but that's how it turned out." The piece, *Wishing for Mountains* (2013),

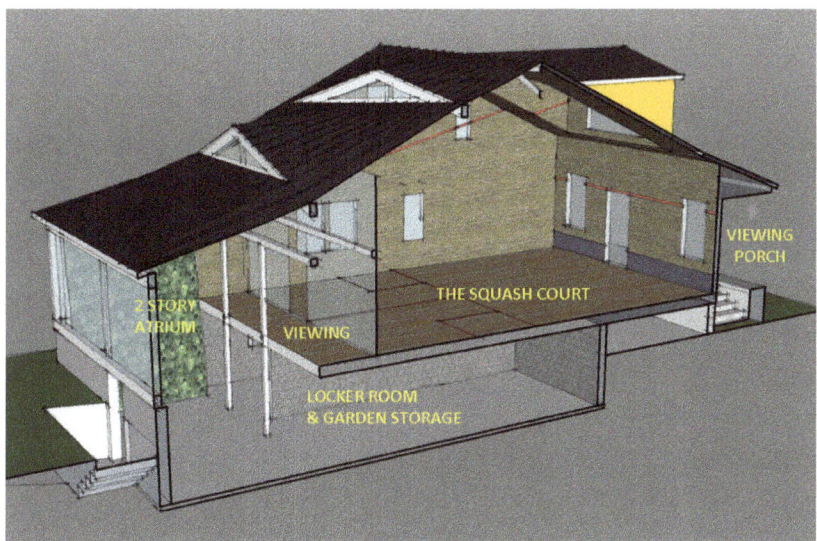

Squash House rendering. 2011. SketchUp model.

puts out a call like a dinner bell. It lets people know that something is happening in the neighborhood. It's inviting them to participate.

In the piece **United Rambler** (2010), also on wheels, a giant chromosome stands alongside an eight-foot fluorescent tube light. Here a microscopic component of cellular life is made giant and leaned on a dolly for easy transportation. "One of my main philosophies is to put everything on wheels. Makes it easy to move. Makes it more versatile." He points to *Lighthenge v.2* (2012). Standing ten feet tall, it currently includes three towers of fluorescent tube fixtures salvaged from a drop-ceiling tear out. They too are mounted on dollies, and utilized for events at Popps such as lighting the track of the biennial summer fundraiser, *The Pinewood Derby* (2011–present).

Besides programming Popps, the focus of Whyte's recent work is scaled for human use. *The Squash House* (2011–present), a collaboration with Power House Productions, transforms a burned-out house in Banglatown to create a squash court. "In fact," Whyte says, "I've heard one of the neighbor's sons is a squash champ. I'm looking forward to taking him on. Fact is, the neighborhood needs more space and more opportunities for play. Food is important too. So we're going to grow squash out back as well." Over the course of three years, Whyte and a team of artists and contractors has reconfigured the building, opening it up completely, adding a series of metal beams, and

soon will be applying plywood to the walls and striping the floors.

"My work often begins like this: I think about what will add to our quality of life. Then I look at what I have, like my old Mitsubishi van. It's not running so good. Well, a sauna would be nice." Whyte, with the help of Danish artist Benny Henningsen, covered the interior walls of the van with cedar and installed a stove, which provides heat for the rocks. "You can sit in here and have some beers and sweat out your toxins. It makes us healthier." It's **Popps Mobile Sauna** (2012), right in the sculpture garden. "It's there to be used," Whyte says. "Come over sometime. We'll fire it up."

STEVE HUGHES, FEBRUARY 2016

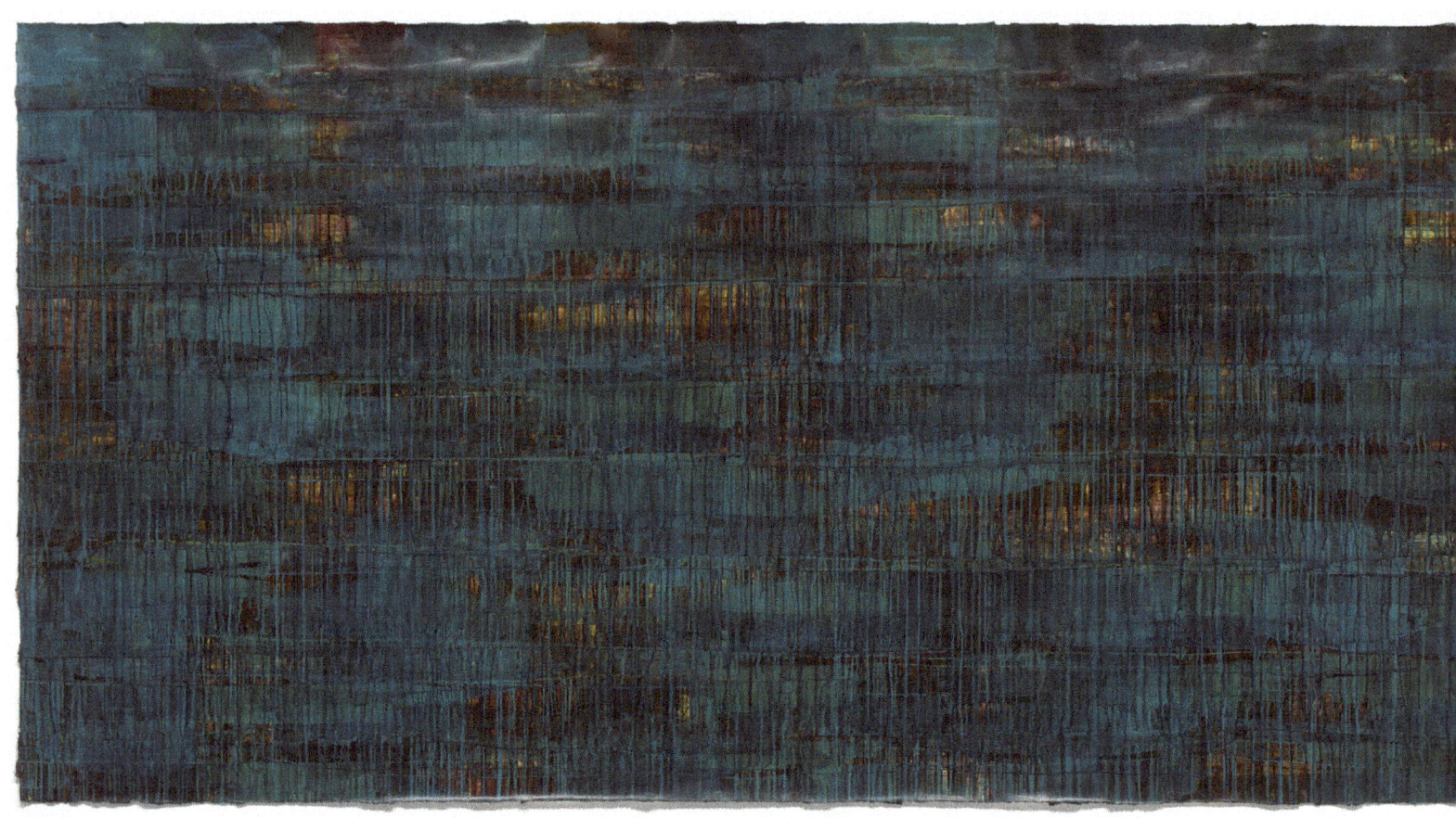

The Hanging Gardens 3: Sea Red. 2013. Acrylic, ink collage on gessoed paper mounted on linen, 55 x 105 in. Photography by Tim Thayer.

44 // ADDIE LANGFORD

Born Louisville, Kentucky, 1974
BFA, Rhode Island School of Design;
MFA, Cranbrook Academy of Art
Lives in Detroit

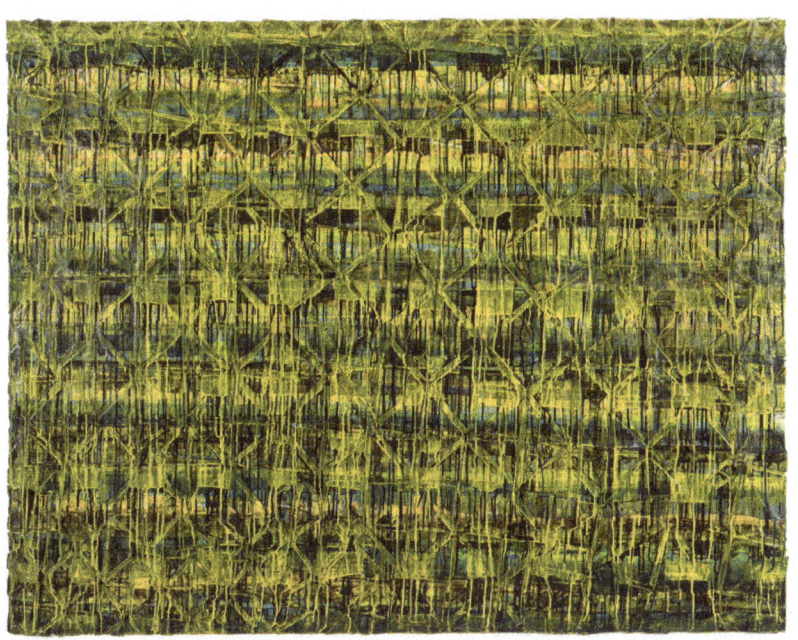

Four years into an architectural program at RISD, Addie Langford found herself confronting a hard truth: she missed making things. All the theoretical design emphasis in her formal studies could not replace the importance of the hands-on process of creation that had always been a fundamental part of her practice.

Retreating from architecture into an all-encompassing two-year stint of architectural tile-making, under the tutelage of well-known Russian ceramics artist Sergei Isupov and his then-wife, Dana Major, Langford used that time in her native Kentucky to recalibrate. Her next move was a master's study of ceramics, which included fiber and a Fulbright

The Hanging Gardens: Blue/Green/Yellow. 2014. Acrylic and mixed media on gessoed paper mounted on linen, 55 1/2 x 70 1/2 in. Courtesy of the N'Namdi Contemporary, Miami.

65

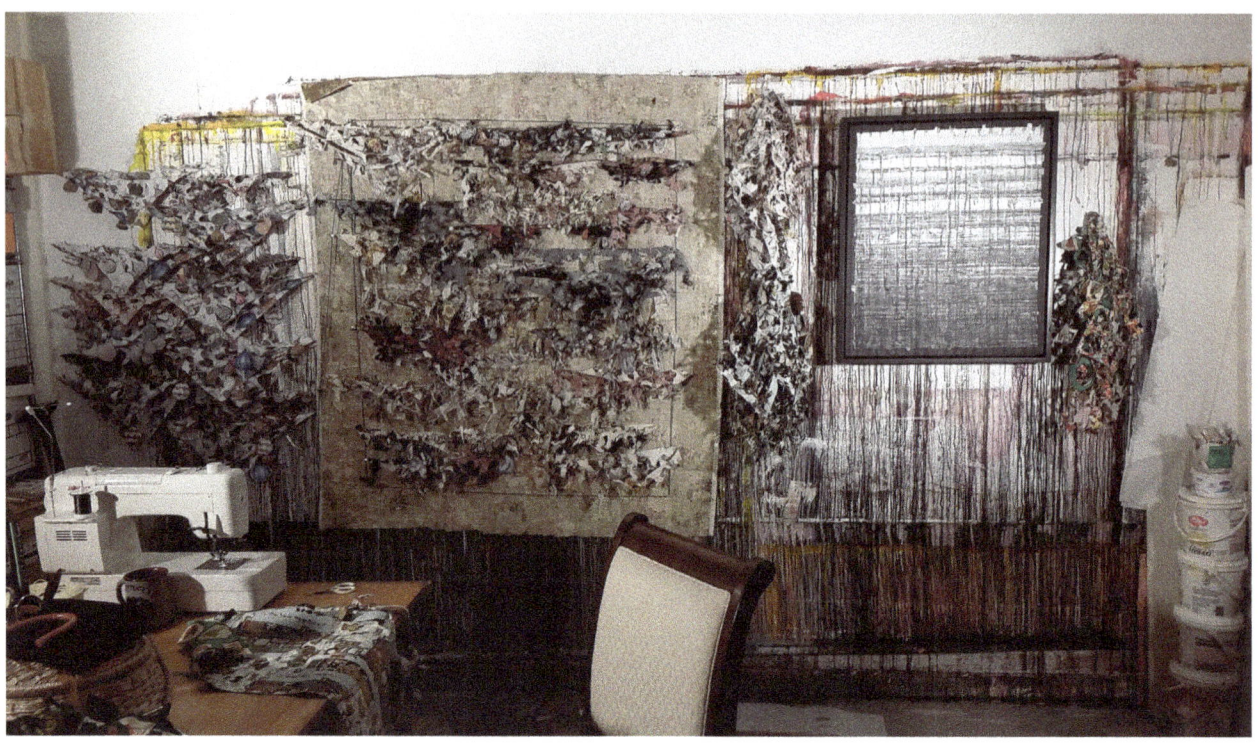

Studio detail, works in progress. 2016.

Fellowship that took her to Madrid to research "Renaissance Tapestry as a Harbinger of Contemporary Collage." However, Langford has not truly abandoned architecture, and her subsequent explorations in ceramics, painting, and textiles all pay deep attention to the indispensable architectural factor of structure.

This consideration may manifest as a rigorous testing process; in ceramics and painting, Langford is interested in the limits of her materials, pushing the porosity and structural integrity of clay and paper. In her works on paper, she piles layered washes of watercolor or acrylic atop a mixed-media matrix of collage, strengthened with a backing layer of gesso. The collective density of these materials defies the paper base to hold together; each piece can absorb as much as five gallons of water by the end of the process. These large-scale works balance repetitious horizontal geometrics, established in the collage layer, with the chaotic overlay of vertical drips, forming colorful abstractions. The more strongly geometric works, such as **Blue/Yellow/ Green** (2014) could pass for textile designs; the looser works, such as **Hanging Gardens: Sea Red** (2013) seem to be landscapes, as viewed through an obscuring mist. In ceramics, these explorations include the 2010 **Soft Compression** series—a compressive stress-testing of porcelain, creating forms that Langford characterizes as, "bodily, without being figurative." As installed, these lumpen and partially glazed vessels were surrounded by fabric in dense, padded piles, almost as though offering comfort or ease to the pressurized porcelain. This work is perhaps an extended abstraction of her 2006 series **Seven Breaks**, which contains sculptures like **Bone** (2006) and **Wheel** (2006)

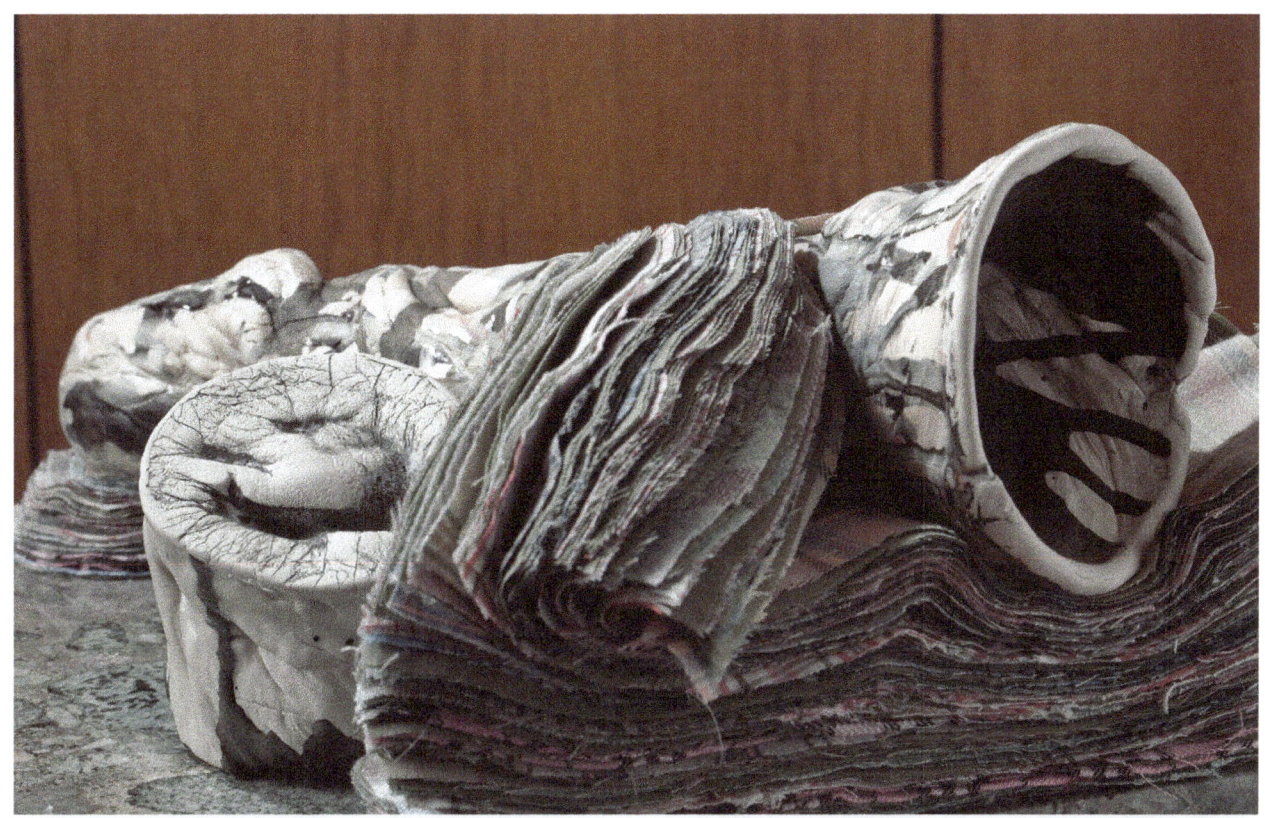

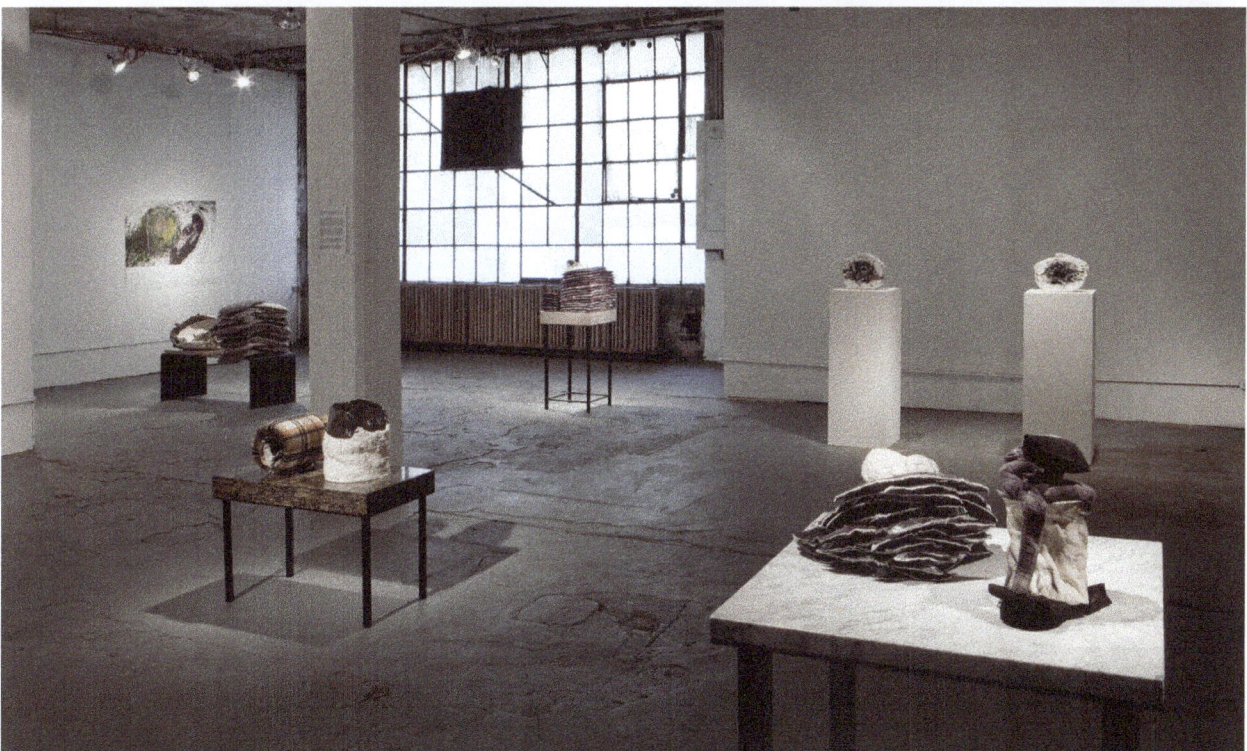

(Top) Soft Compression: Green (detail). 2014. Acrylic and mixed media on gessoed paper mounted on linen, 60 x 30 x 30 in. Photography by Tim Thayer.
(Bottom) Soft Compression series (installation view). 2010. Photography by Tim Thayer.

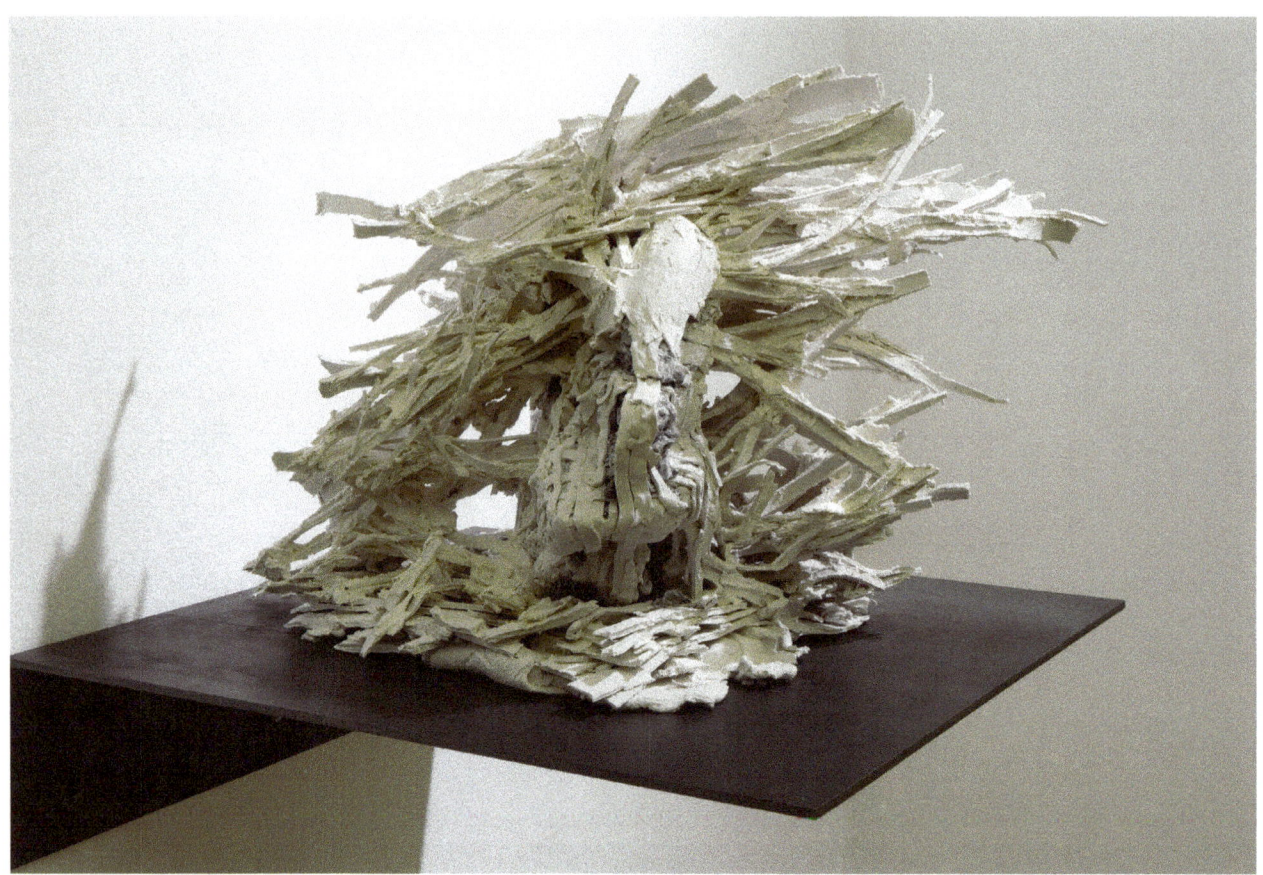

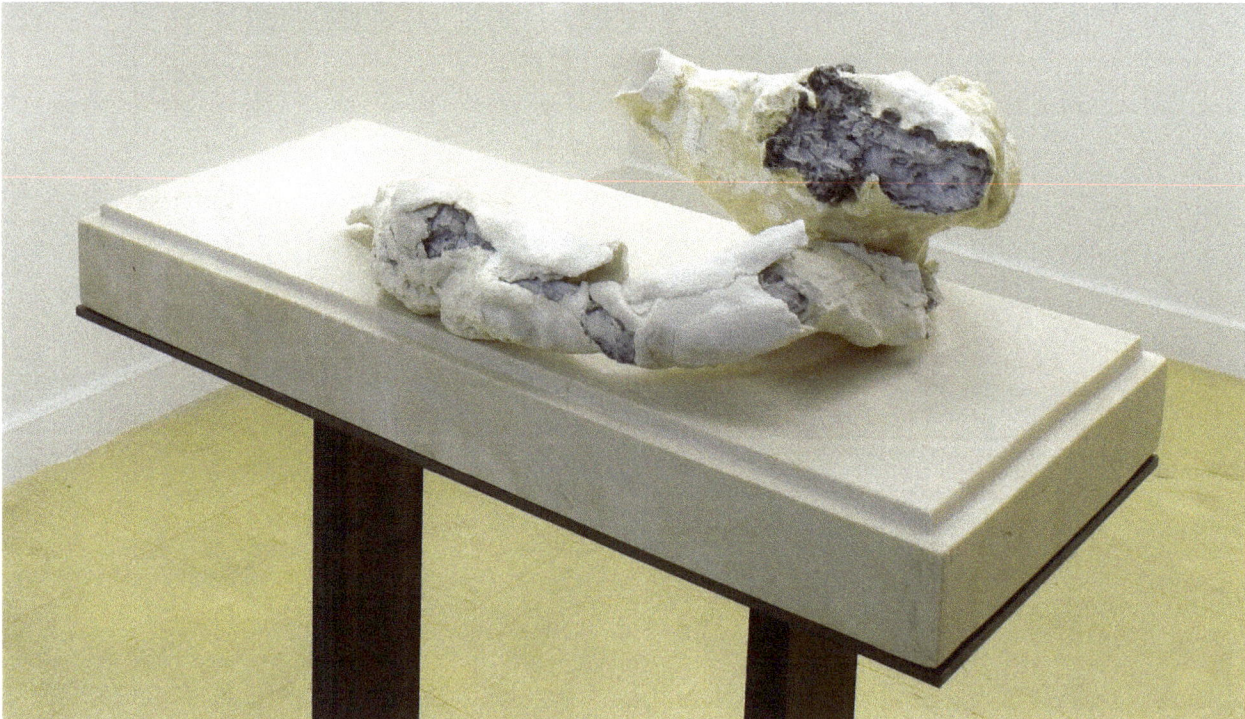

(Top) Seven Breaks: Wheel. 2006. Porcelain, paper clay, and mixed media, 19 x 29 x 24 in. Photography by Tim Thayer.
(Bottom) Seven Breaks: Bone (detail). 2006. Porcelain, paper clay, steel, and mixed media, 7 x 9 x 24 in. Photography by Tim Thayer.

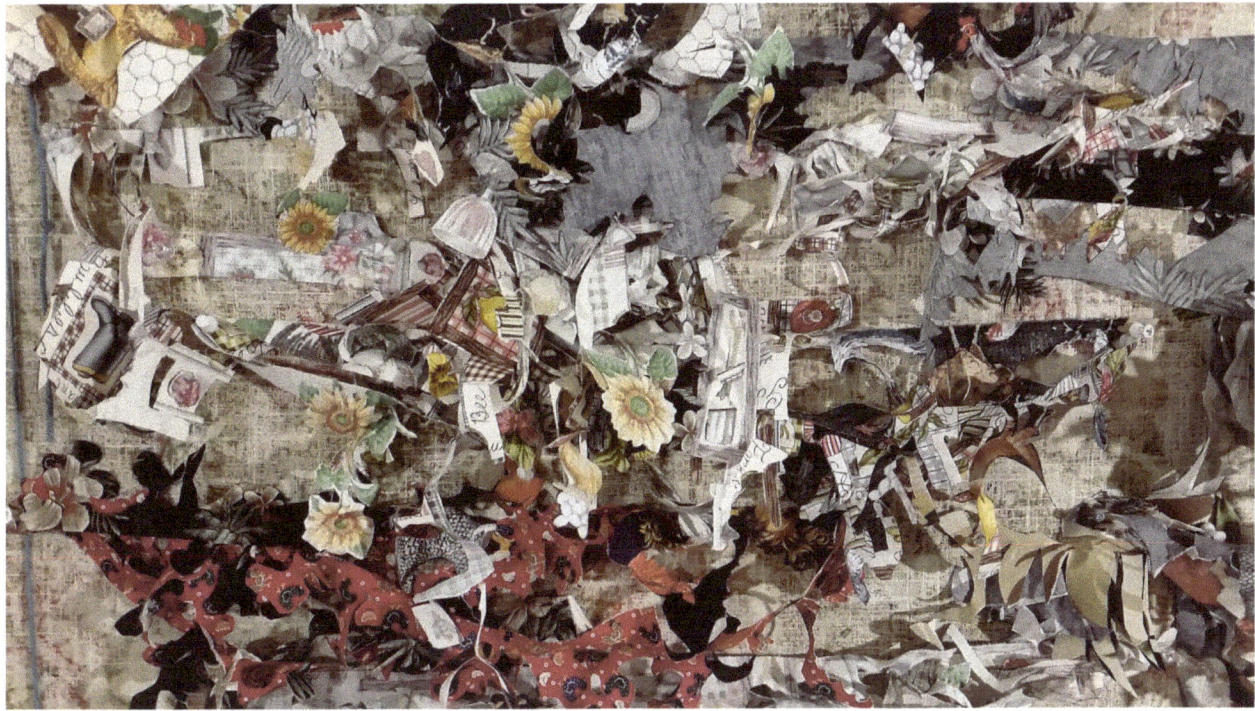

Studio detail, work in progress. 2016.

that, in their viciously desiccated skeletal armature, more literally suggest a violent collapse of bodily or mechanical structure.

"There's very rarely a moment of rest in being an adult," Langford says, somewhat wistfully, in terms of her attraction to bearing down hard on her materials. Her work is quite emotional, but the dramatic, underlying feelings are channeled through a deep layer of abstraction, leaving little trace of self-portraiture. If the tendency of her works on paper to be overwhelmed with content, or her ceramics to be vulnerable and in need of material comfort, is indeed a reflection of Langford's interior existence, one must know the artist well to see it—the face she presents to the world is smooth as porcelain (certainly smoother than the porcelain rendered by her hand).

Steeped in art history, Langford cites Simon Hantaï, François Rouan, and Richard Tuttle as influential to her process, but is also swift to credit influences as close to home as her mother's domestic quilt-making. For her part, Langford is relentless in her pursuit of more perfect expression, and exceptionally exacting in her definition of accomplishment—most recently in her preparation of *large-scale accretions of fiber on canvas* that will be included in a solo show at Simone DeSousa Gallery. There is something chimera-like about Langford's forms enabling them to encompass divergent sources, occupying a space between rigid formalism and raw emotion, architecture and art history—all held in a tense conglomerate of materials pushed to their breaking point.

SARAH ROSE SHARP,
FEBRUARY 2016

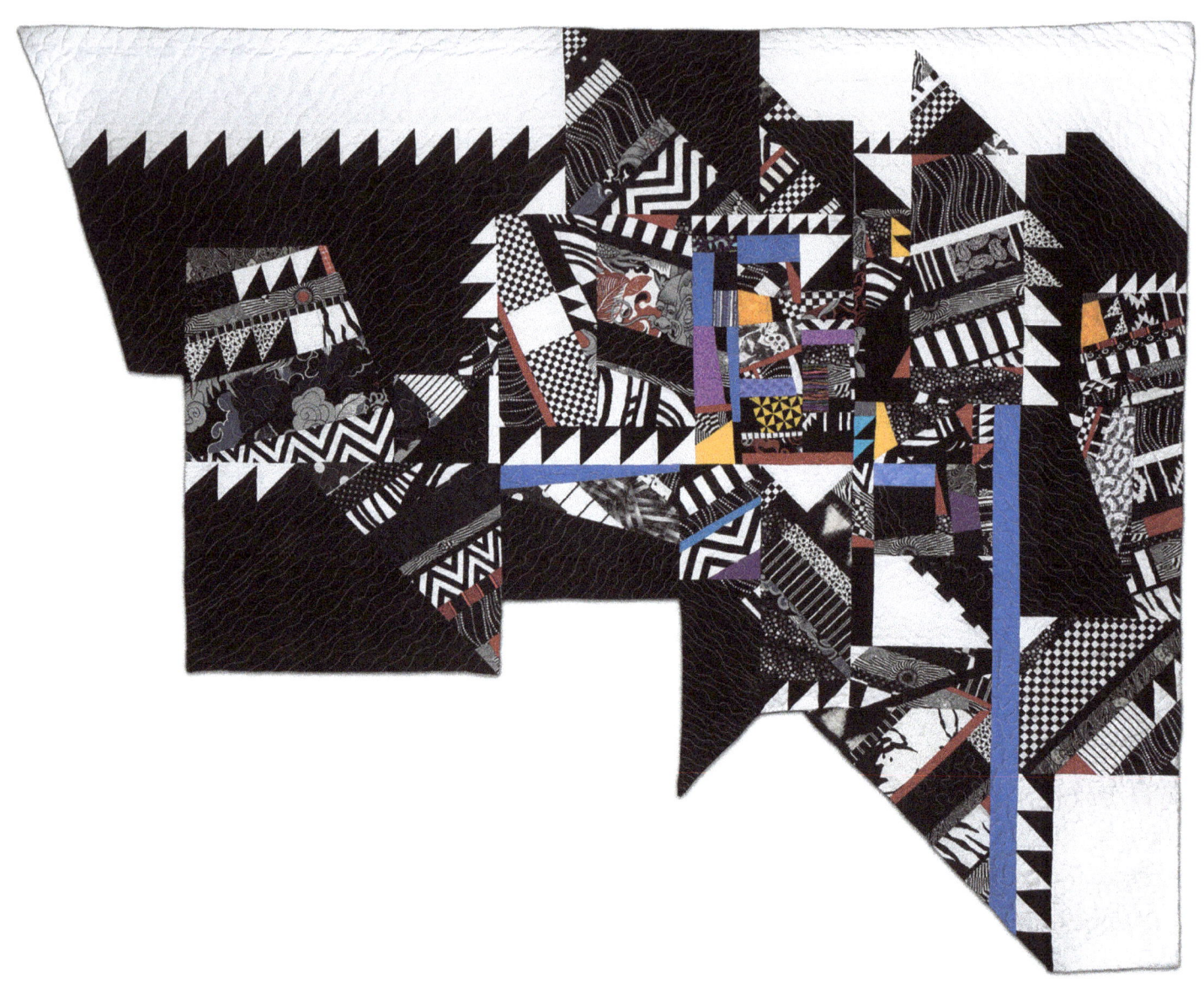

Blues and the Abstract Truth. 2014. Printed cottons, cotton batting, machine pieced and quilted, 50 1/2 x 64 in.

45 // CAROLE HARRIS

Born Detroit, 1943
BFA, Wayne State University
Lives in Detroit

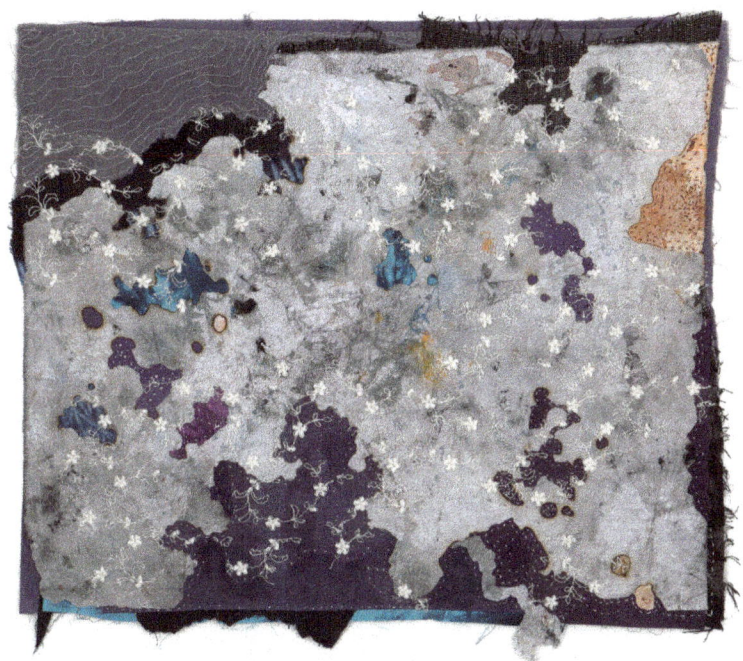

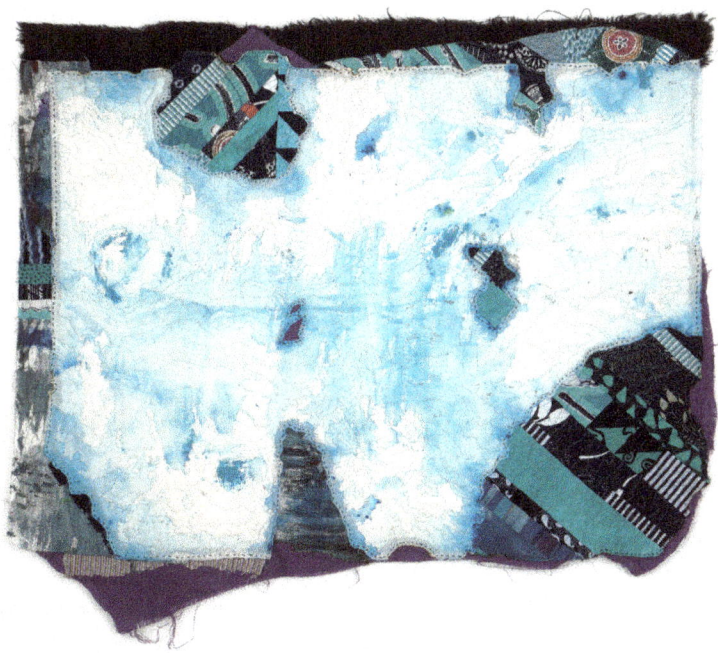

Carole Harris modestly describes her art practice as "that of a fiber artist working primarily in the art quilt tradition." Yet very few of her quilts are "traditional," four cornered, or intended to swaddle, wrap, or warm one on a cold winter's night. Rather, they are wall hangings, even "constructions" or assemblages—albeit crafted of soft, supple materials—often of a strikingly eccentric outline far from the standard rectilinear form.

Think, for example, of Frank Stella or any of a number of aesthetic shape-shifters of the 1960s who introduced such innovative

(Top) Winter Etude. 2015. Printed cottons, linen, lace, acrylic on muslin, cotton batting, burning, hand stitched, machine quilted, 20 x 22 1/2 in.
(Bottom) *Ice Music.* 2013. Printed cottons, linen, acrylic on muslin, cotton batting, machine pieced, hand stitched, machine quilted, 26 1/2 x 30 in.

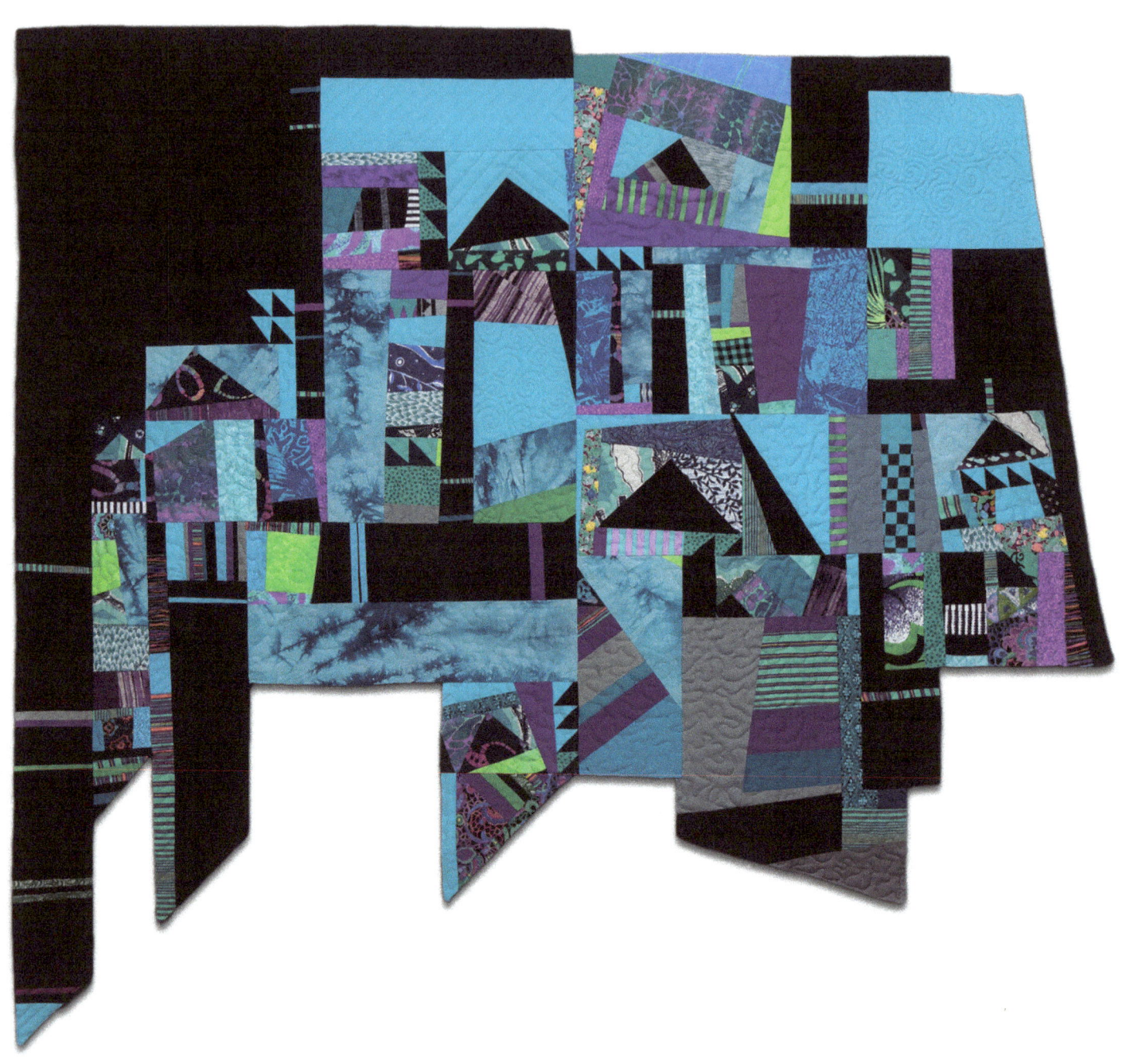

Blues in the Night. 2010. Printed cottons, cotton batting, machine pieced and quilted, 42 x 45 1/2 in.

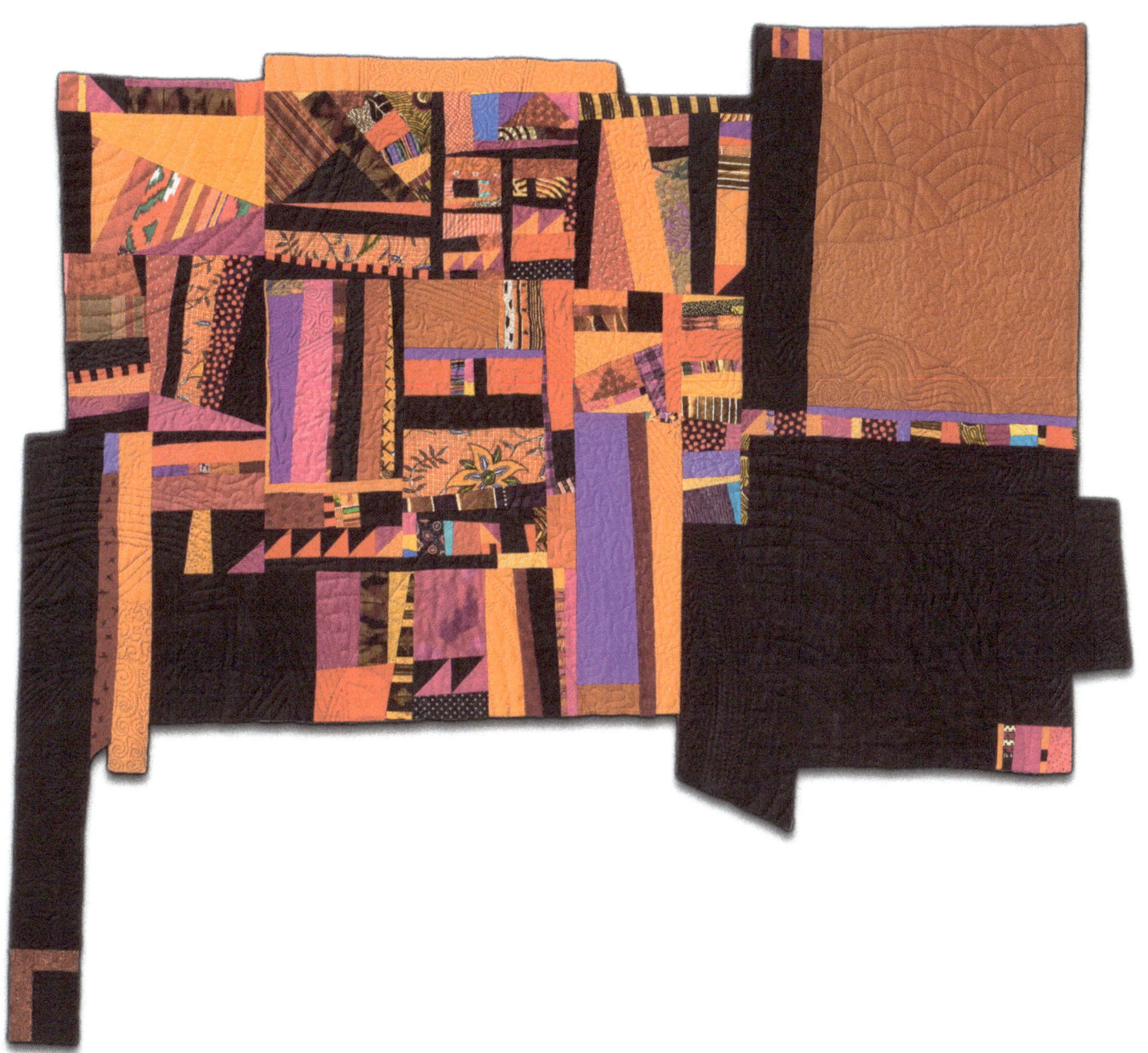

Before the Freeway. 2008. Printed cottons, cotton batting, machine pieced and quilted, 55 x 61 in.

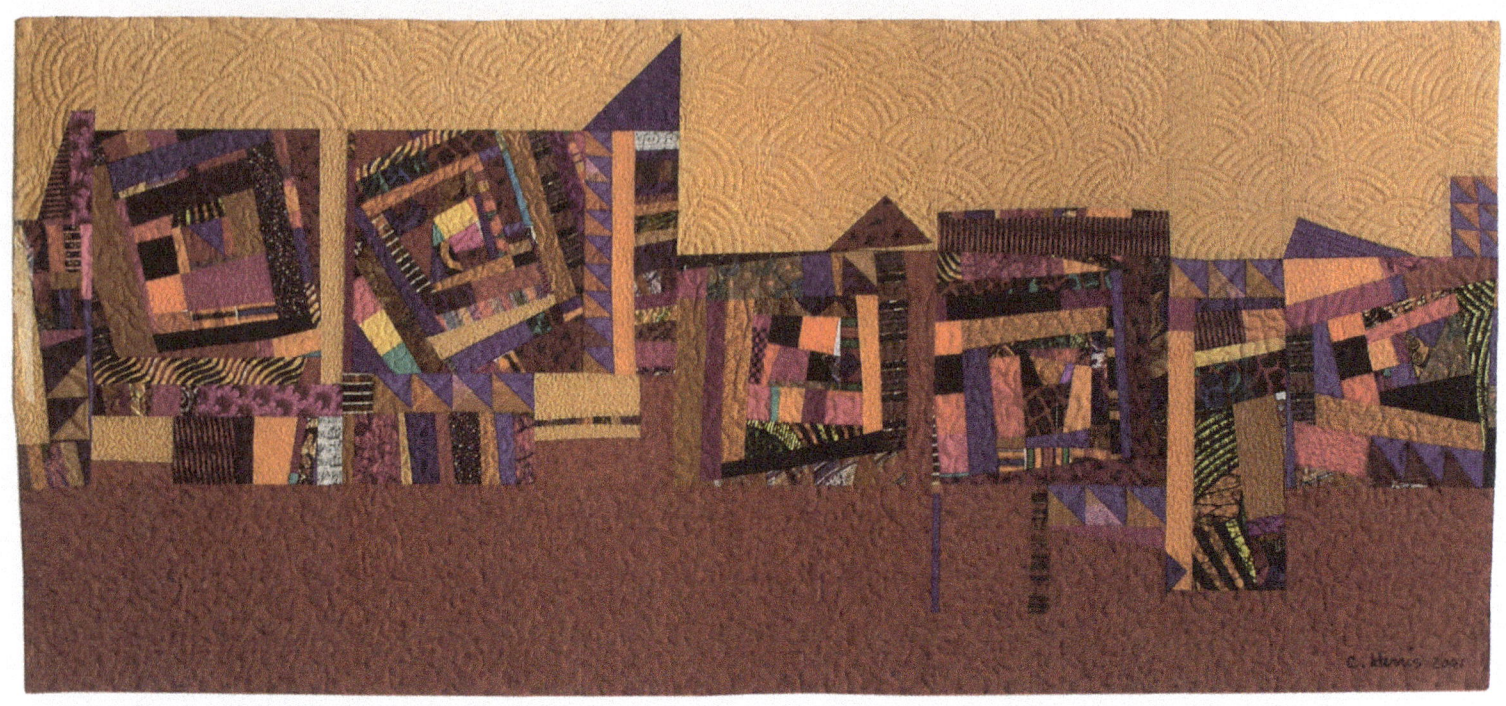

City Rhythms. 2001. Printed cottons, cotton batting, machine pieced and quilted, 32 x 71 in.

pictorial formats as the shaped canvas. Likewise, Harris's artful, asymmetrically contoured quilts often subvert the hidebound designs and prevailing expectations that linger in the firmament of quilts and quilting.

Yet pieced quilts they are, Harris employing that discipline's cutting, piecing, stitching, and improvisatory abutting of triangles, polygons, and squares of cloth in an overall design, often calling to mind the crazy quilt motifs of the late nineteenth century. Her use of old and new fabrics, off-the-bolt cottons and fancy silks, painted, hand-dyed, or commercially printed textiles,

and contrasting or harmonizing textures, yield dazzling, revved-up compositions. Nor are her subjects rural or folkish, but draw their inspiration from urban environs, often the hustle and jostle of Detroit, its temperament, rhythms, and bluesy, cacophonous sounds. A quilt maker since 1966, Harris studied at Wayne State University before founding the interior design firm that she headed from 1976 until 2009. Since then, she has focused on her studio practice, earning a Kresge artist fellowship in 2015.

An eye-catching, relatively early, large-scale example of her oeuvre, **City Rhythms**,

commissioned for Detroit Receiving Hospital in 2001, highlights many of the elements that figure in Harris's wall hangings. In this elongated, classical-frieze-like urbanscape, hundreds of pieced, faceted forms and bold, clashing colors gambol edge to edge across its six-foot width, its *joie de vivre* palpable and contagious. **Before the Freeway**, a design of 2008, sounds a different note, both in content and pictorial impact. The colorful riot of hues and densely packed forms on the left side of this idiosyncratically shaped "quilt" implies an animated urban grid counterpointed by the blank, weighty, rust and black boxes on the right. This somber, abstract image invokes the bustling Paradise Valley district of Detroit infamously bulldozed for the I-75 expressway—or, more resonantly, the demolition of neighborhoods that grow organically, if haphazardly, over the years, and inevitably run counter to someone else's "master plan."

In Harris's own categorization of her several bodies of work, *City Rhythms* and *Before the Freeway* are identified as examples of her *Cityscapes*. Another group, dubbed *Singing and Dancing and All that Jazz*, includes such active, vivacious titles as *Dancing in the Streets*, *Something Like a Jitterbug*, and *Fire Music*. **Blues in the Night** (2010), however, with its haunting, velvety hues of black and blue, angled shapes, and hard-edged diagonals defining the bottom of the composition, embodies something of the sadness and harshness of the blues. Ominously, a sizable, looming black patch of fabric at upper left seems to be gliding inexorably, like a lunar eclipse, over the darkling scene. One of Harris's last pieced designs from the series, an exhilarating encounter between equally matched conceits, is the striking black-and-white **Blues and the Abstract Truth** of 2014.

Of late, Harris's imagery and technique reveal a decided swerve down a road not heretofore taken. Gathered under the rubric *Mapping in Time and Place*, evocative titles—*Wall Series: Amalfi* and *Yesterdays*, for example—reference such sources as ancient, eroding walls, weathered objects, tactile, textured strata, and etudes (i.e., studies, as opposed to perfected, completed works). **Ice Music** (2013) and **Winter Etude** (2015) manifest Harris's fresh, less-is-more aesthetic. Instead of looking out, she looks within: jewel tones are replaced by intimate, muted hues; execution by scissors and thread is replaced by draping; single unitary compositions banish commingling fragments; and the elemental replaces the topical. Soft, frayed edges, and vintage, torn (or even burned) fabrics form palpable, multilayered compositions. Visible lengths of material, rather than sewn flat and edge to edge, become loose, informally arrayed elements. A viewer might even be sorely tempted to lift and separate the panels of fabric—gently, of course—to see what lurks underneath. No wonder then that about this new tack, Harris quietly notes: "Fabric has memory. It holds onto time." And indeed it does.

DENNIS ALAN NAWROCKI, FEBRUARY 2016

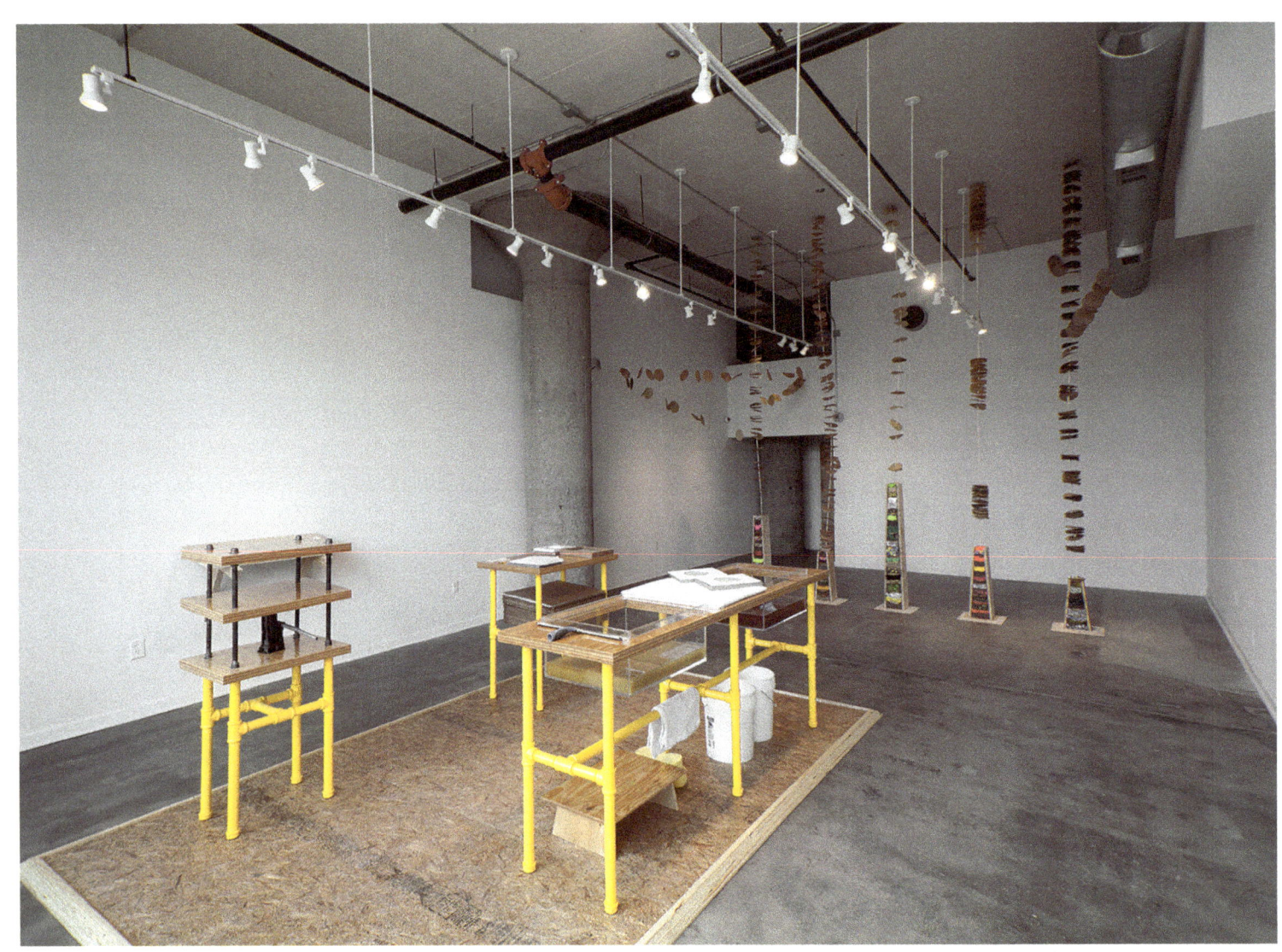

The More We Get Together. 2015. Handmade paper with non-native plants, Detroitus totems, paper-making stations. Photography by Eric Wheeler.

Born Battle Creek, Michigan, 1979
BA, University of Michigan; MFA,
Cranbrook Academy of Art
Lives in Detroit

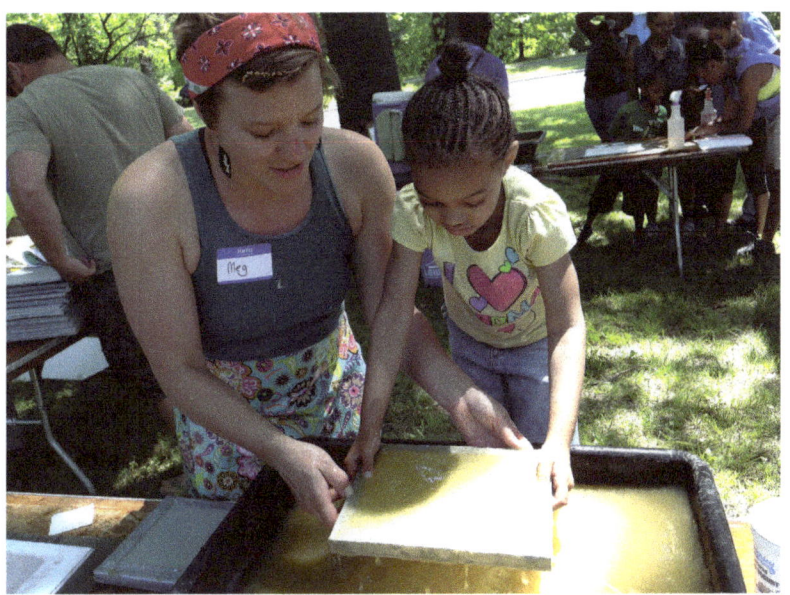

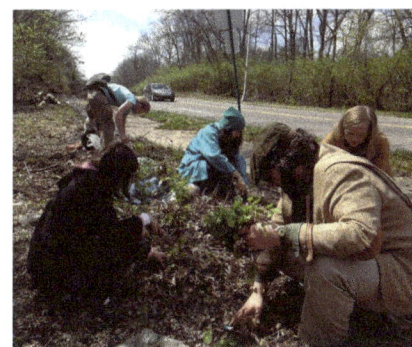

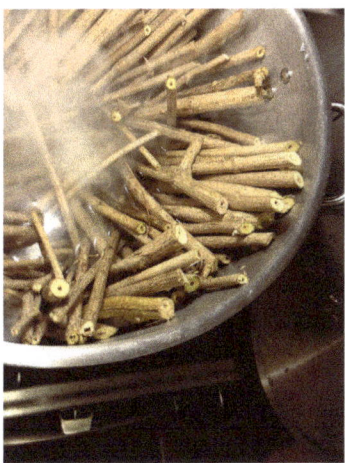

Megan Heeres's ***Invasive Paper Project*** (2014) is, in principle, quite simple: participants take vegetable matter from invasive plants, such as phragmites, honeysuckle, and garlic mustard, and use it to create paper. Along the way they may learn something about paper making and also about the environmental impact of invasive plant life on local ecosystems. While developing the project, Heeres has had to learn, through trial and error, about the paper-making properties of the plant materials and, since she does not want to further propagate invasive species, develop a way to dispose

(Top) Invasive Paper Project—Making Honeysuckle Sheets. A paper-making workshop with invasives at a park in Detroit. 2014.
(Bottom, left) Invasive Paper Project—Harvesting Garlic Mustard. 2014.
(Bottom, right) Invasive Paper Project—Cooking Amur Honeysuckle. 2014.

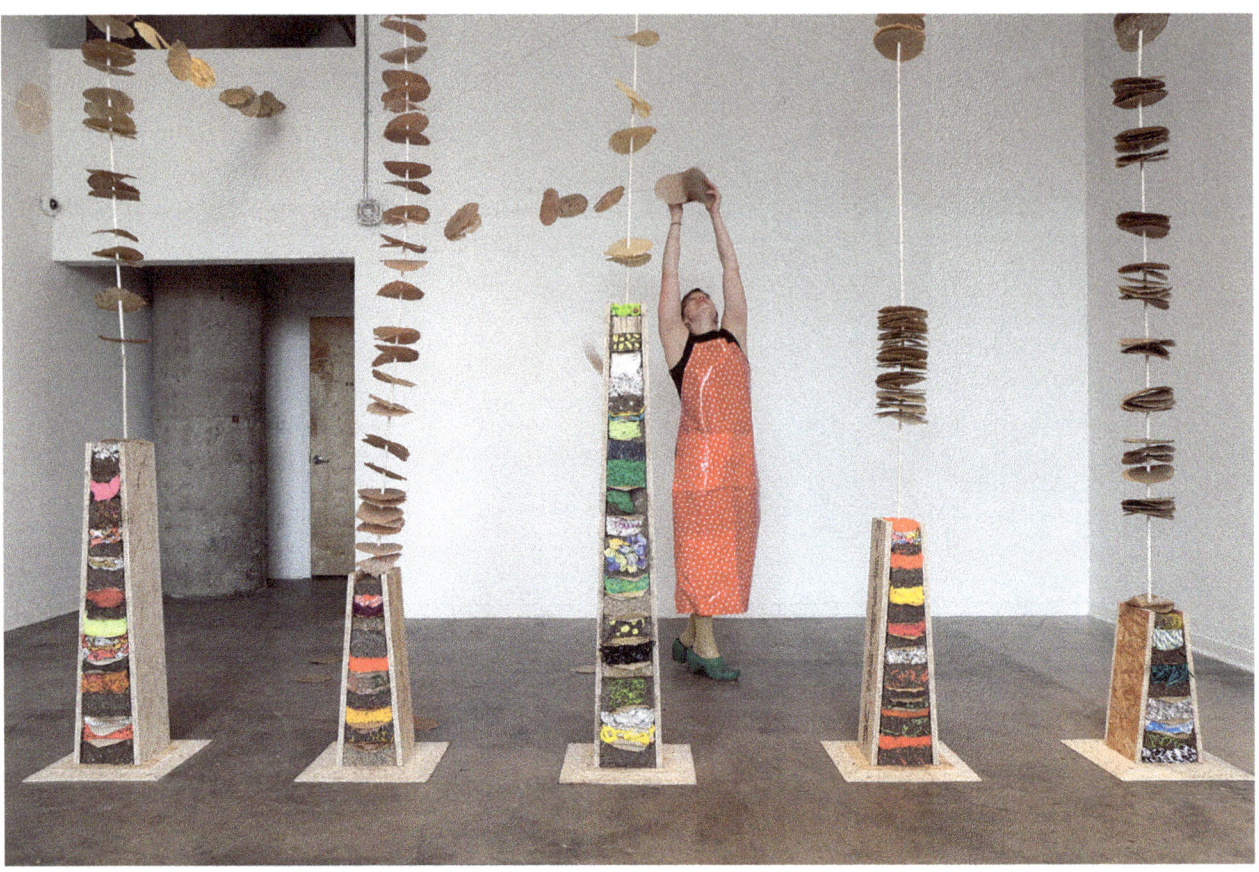

Detroitus totems from *The More We Get Together*. 2015. Plywood with soil, trash collected from lots and neighborhoods in Detroit. Photography by Eric Wheeler.

of the remaining vegetable matter in an environmentally responsible manner. In configuring the work for a gallery setting (2015's ***The More We Get Together*** at Detroit's Simone DeSousa Gallery) Heeres has gone to great lengths to create an environment that harmonizes the physical and emotional comfort of project participants with more traditional formal and aesthetic concerns; nothing seems unresolved. Whereas much participatory art creates the impression that visitors are simply actors in

a theater of the artist's construction, Heeres's installation seems to genuinely project an atmosphere of thoughtful inclusivity. It goes without saying that all artists care about their art; Heeres has made an art out of caring. Tellingly, Heeres chose her first degree in health studies and art because she wanted to investigate art's potential for allowing people to heal themselves.

At first sight, the work ***Home. HomeGrown.*** (2012) seems very different. Ink solution cascades

through a series of twelve approximately conical cups onto a panel mounted horizontally below. "Completed" panels are displayed on the wall alongside. This is art that generates art. By unmasking the process behind the panels' creation, Heeres's intent is to reduce the psychological divide between the viewer and the artist. The slow dripping cadence, and the soft hum of the pump, create a meditative experience that Heeres perfects in her studio. She considers the work to be a type

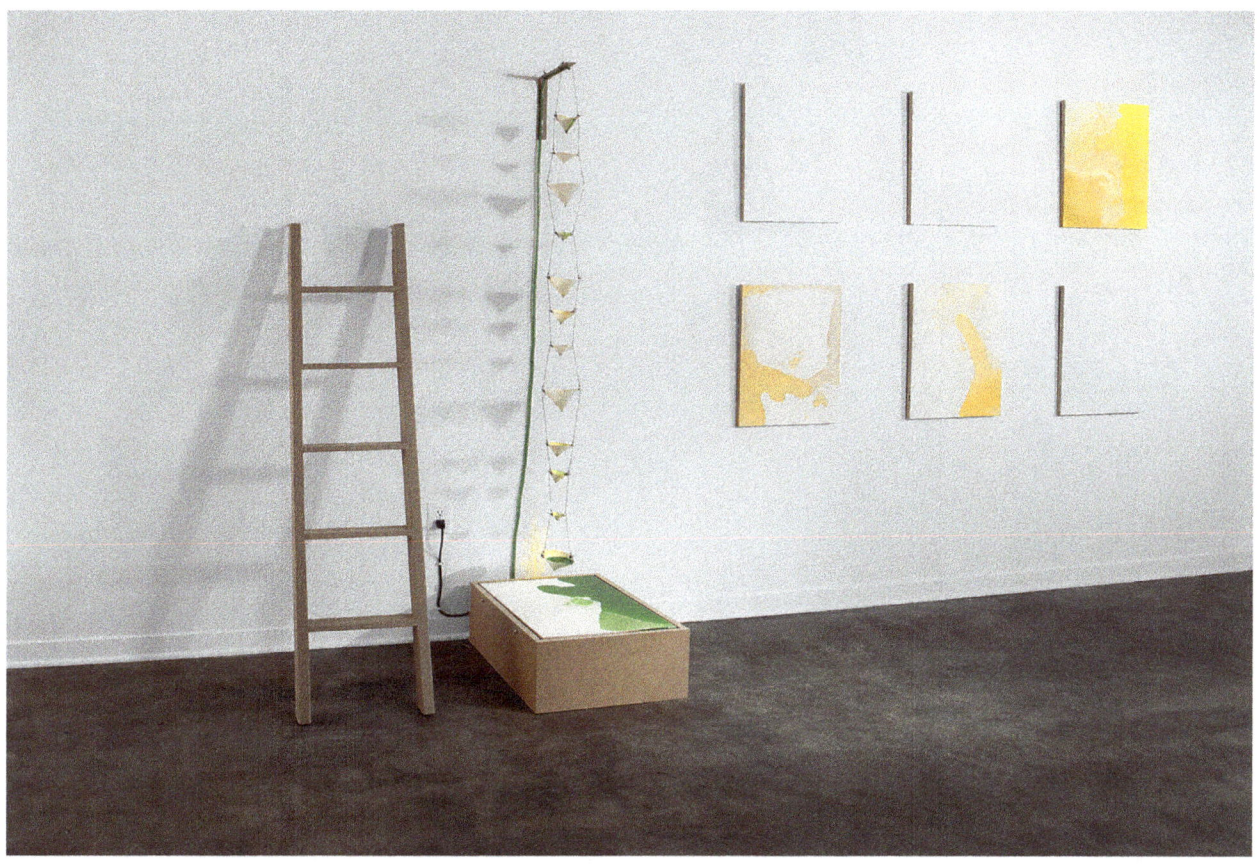

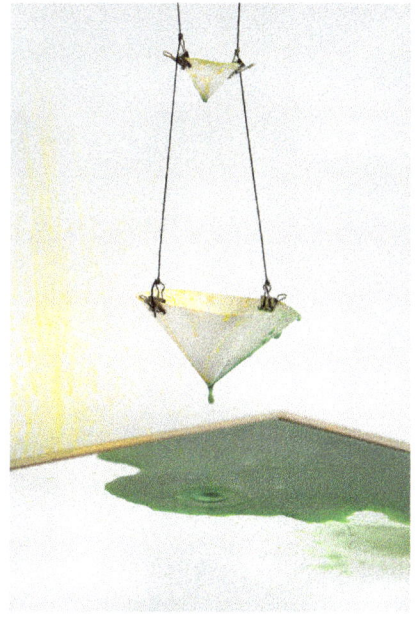

of clock, differentiating between her extrastudio life, in which she never seems to have enough

time, and the relative sanctuary of her studio. By reproducing it in the gallery, she includes the visitor in this subliminal experience. Natural processes are rarely far from Heeres's thoughts; the most obvious one in *Home. HomeGrown.* is gravity, but more subtly, the work relies on alginate, a natural seaweed-derived thickening agent, to maintain the required ink viscosity.

The process for "painting" the panels is inherently very sensitive to variation. Heeres describes the compositions that emerge as being "dependent upon efficiency of the pumping mechanism, the viscosity and color of the ink solution, the temperature/humidity of the space, the caretakers tending to the piece, and the amount of time the solution dripped upon the surface." It is perhaps not coincidental that this sounds more like the conclusion of a scientific paper than a traditional artist's statement; Heeres is that rare artist who instinctively, but consciously, develops her work

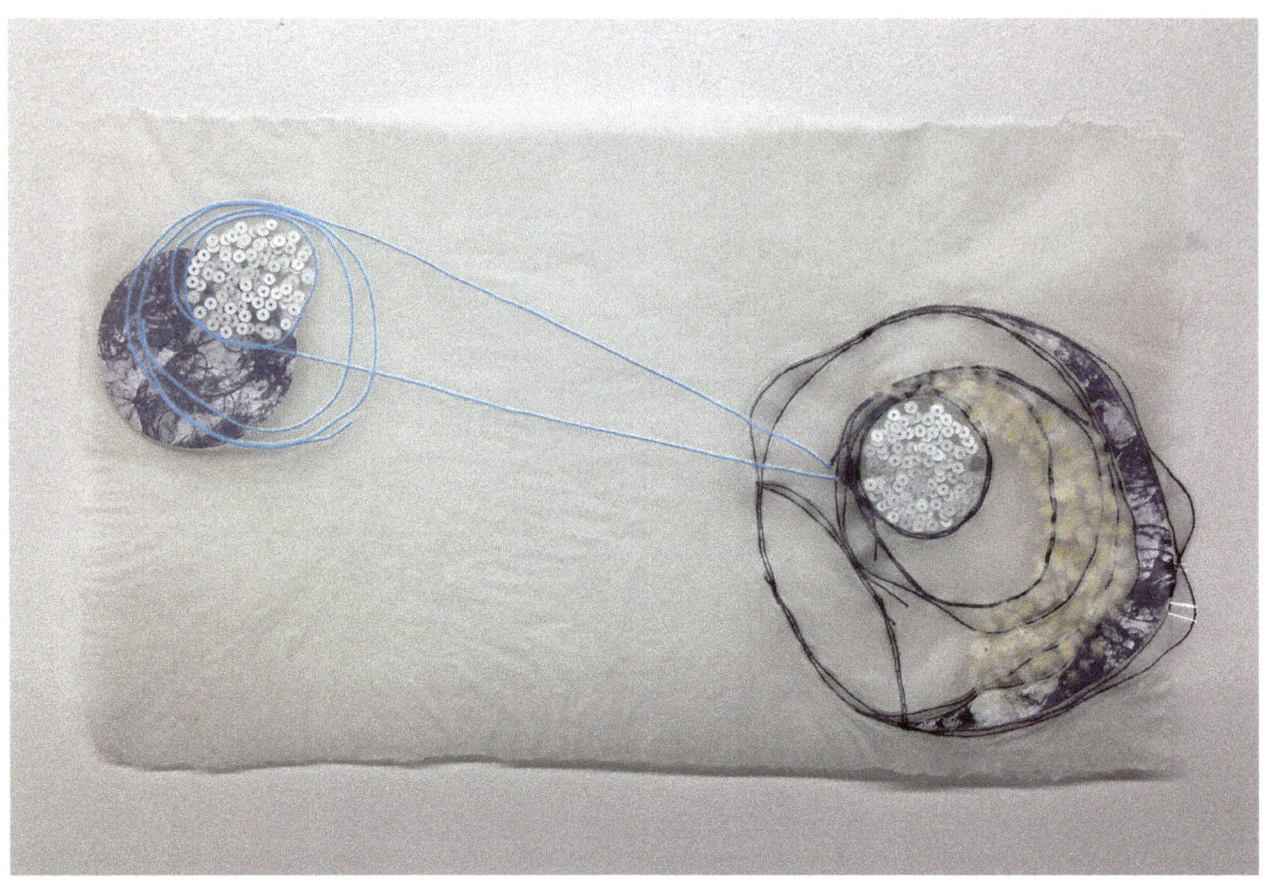

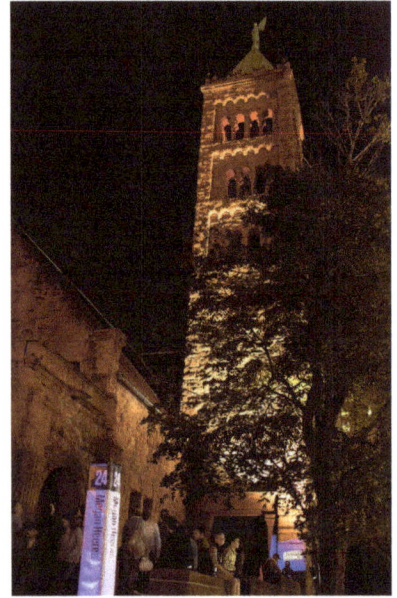

(Top) *Blue Reach.* 2016. Mixed media embedded in handmade paper.
(Bottom) *Beacon.* 2014. Sound-responsive lighting and sound, community interaction. Photography by Tim Thayer.

within a far larger conceptual, and social, framework. Currently she is working on a series of works (e.g., 2016's ***Blue Reach***)

inspired by a collaboration with eye surgeon Dr. Alon Kahana, and more specifically by discussions surrounding his research on neural crests and their potential for regenerative medicine. Kahana says of their collaboration, "Megan likes to think in big-picture terms before figuring out details. As such, she and I are very much alike. Many artists I am familiar with are focused on the details—shape, color, texture,

etc. Megan's work is more experimental. . . . I really like that!"

Heeres's work ***Beacon*** (2014) is an ambitious collaborative project that was installed in Detroit's First Congregational, a historically important church noteworthy for its involvement in the Underground Railroad. The installation's central concept was to reconfigure the building into an "instrument" for translating movement from participants at ground level into

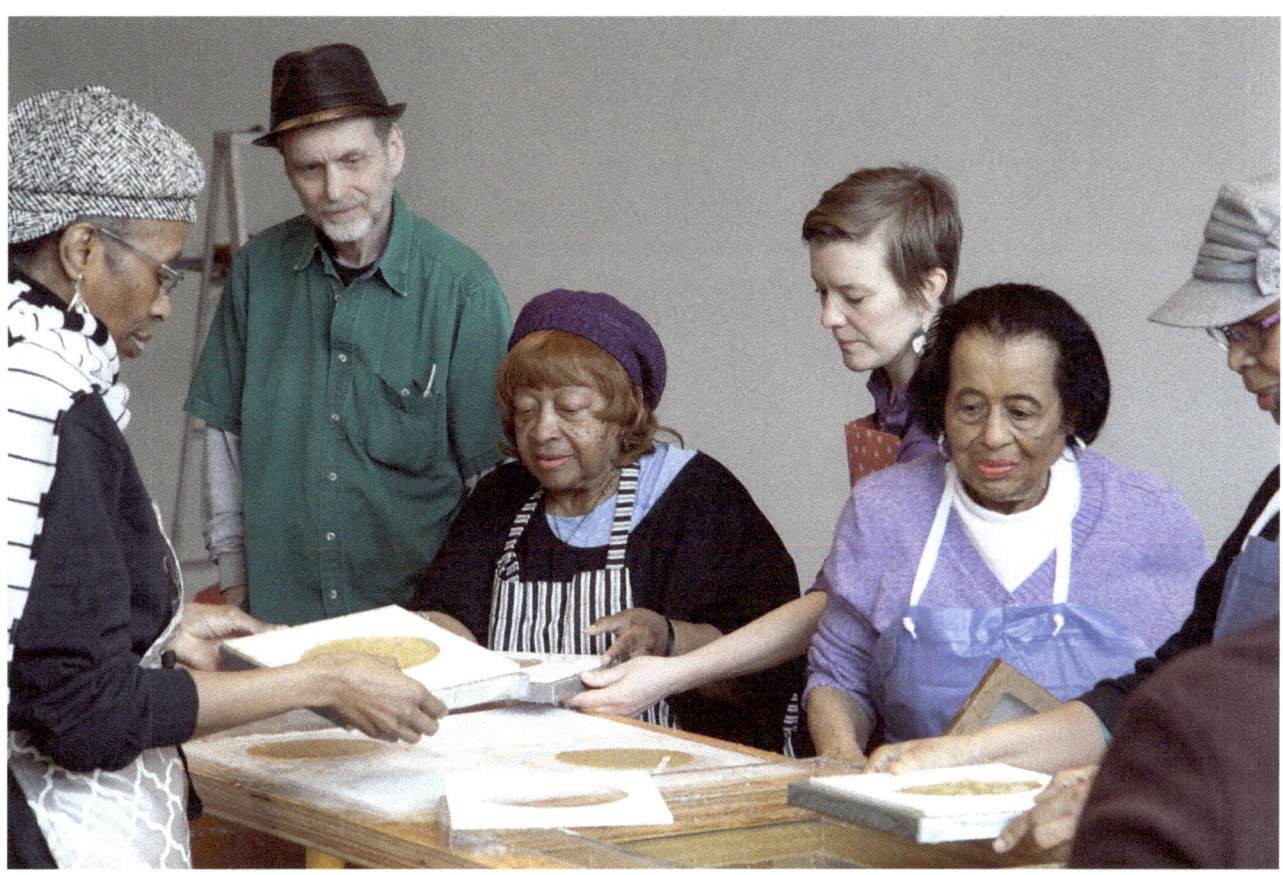

Hannan House visits *The More We Get Together*. 2015. Photography by P. D. Rearick.

sound and light emanating to the street from the bell tower. The work served as a metaphor for Heeres's belief in the capacity of communities to collectively generate transcendental experiences, and was inspired both by its location in a city where faith-based social structures are still very strong and by recollections of her childhood involvement in the ELCA Lutheran church. She regards the social relationships created around the project, most notably the involvement of the initially suspicious church members, to be an important aspect of the work. In a way, this is the central strand of Heeres's art—inclusion, not as a gift to be bestowed by the artist, but as a process of finding common ground.

STEVE PANTON, MARCH 2016

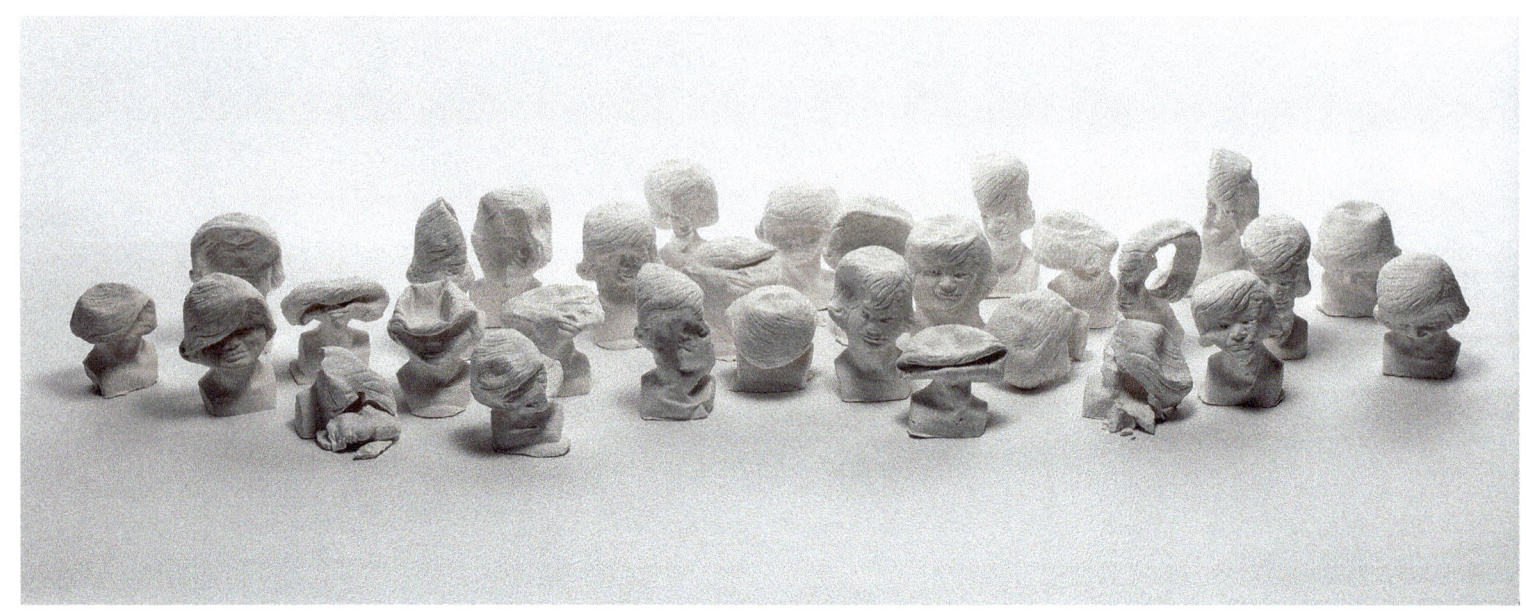

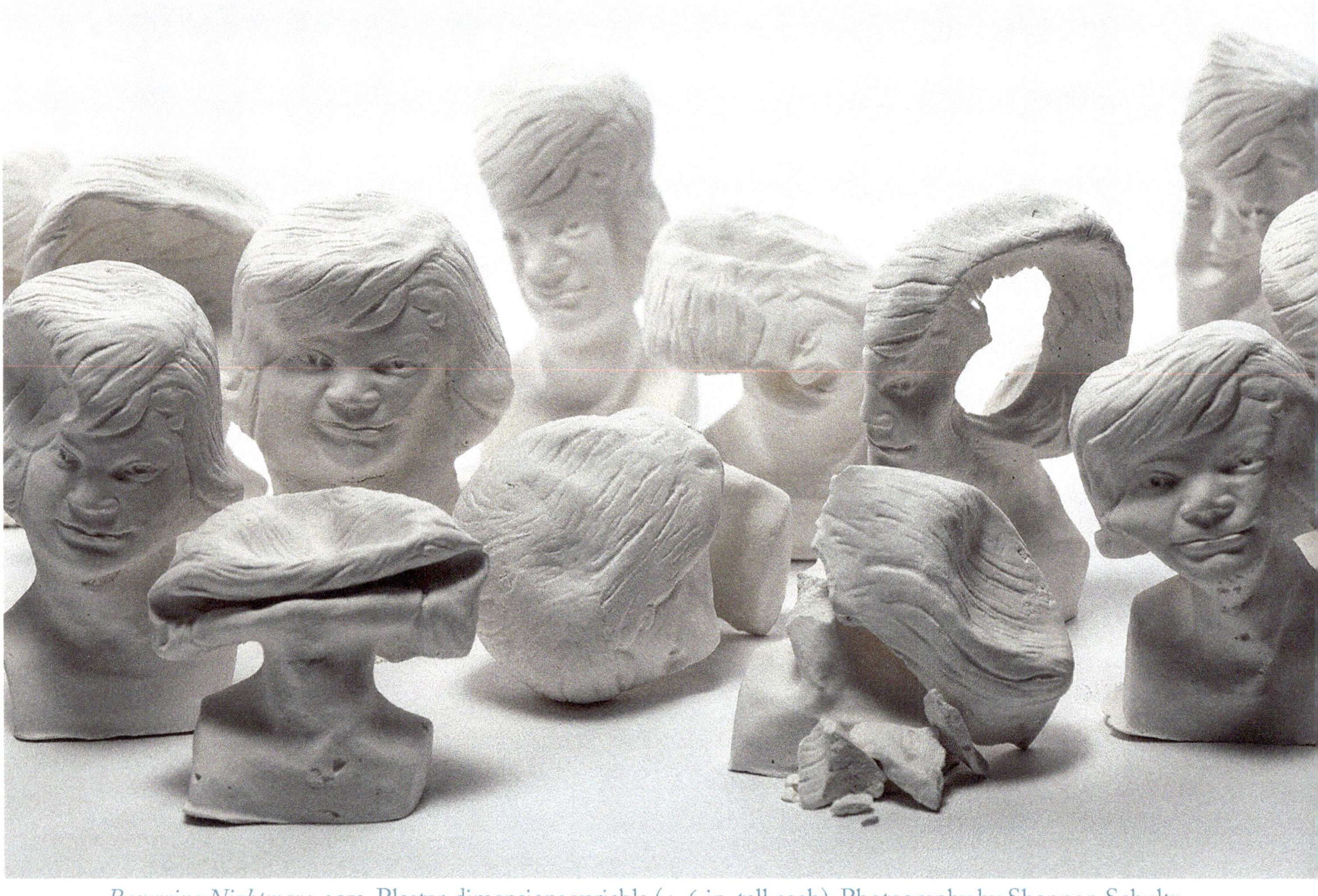

Recurring Nightmare. 2013. Plaster, dimensions variable (4–6 in. tall each). Photography by Shannon Schultz.

47 // SCOTT NORTHRUP

Born Dearborn, Michigan, 1969
BFA, College for Creative Studies; MA
(Media Studies), New School
University, New York
Lives in Detroit

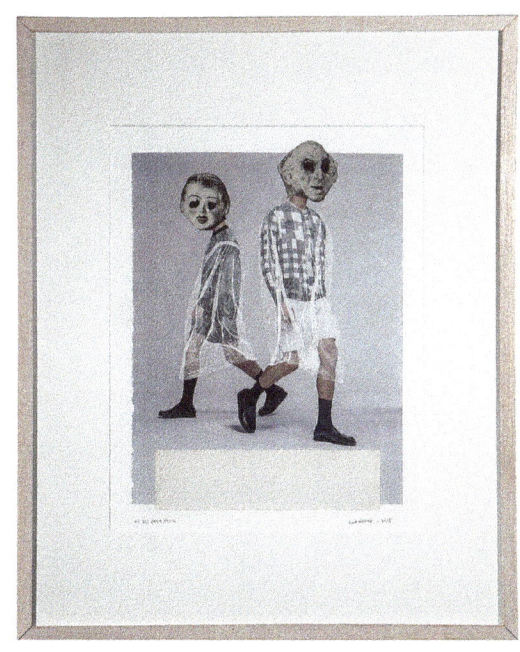

Scott Northrup's recent temporary installation ***Hämeenkyrö,
Mon Amour*** (2015) was comprised
of text projected onto the landscape near the town of Hämeenkyrö, Finland, at sundown. For
about thirty minutes, excerpts
of scripted dialogue from Alain
Resnais's *Hiroshima, Mon Amour*
and several movies by Finnish
filmmaker Aki Kaurismäki, as
well as Northrup's own writing,
crawled across the vast, dark-
ening plain in what the artist
refers to as a "love letter" to the
beautiful, welcoming place he'd
come to know after a month-
long residency there. If the scale
of *Hämeenkyrö, Mon Amour* is
notably ambitious, its sense of
near-boundlessness is fitting for a

*(Top) Hämeenkyrö, Mon Amour.
2015.* Thirty-three-minute textual
film projected on the Finnish
landscape at sundown. Photography by Julia Martin.
(Bottom) We See Each Other. 2015.
Magazines and tissue paper, 16 x
20 in.

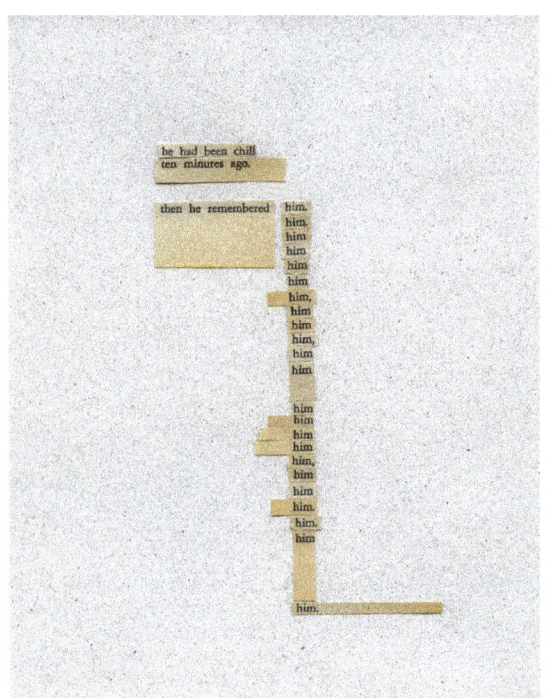
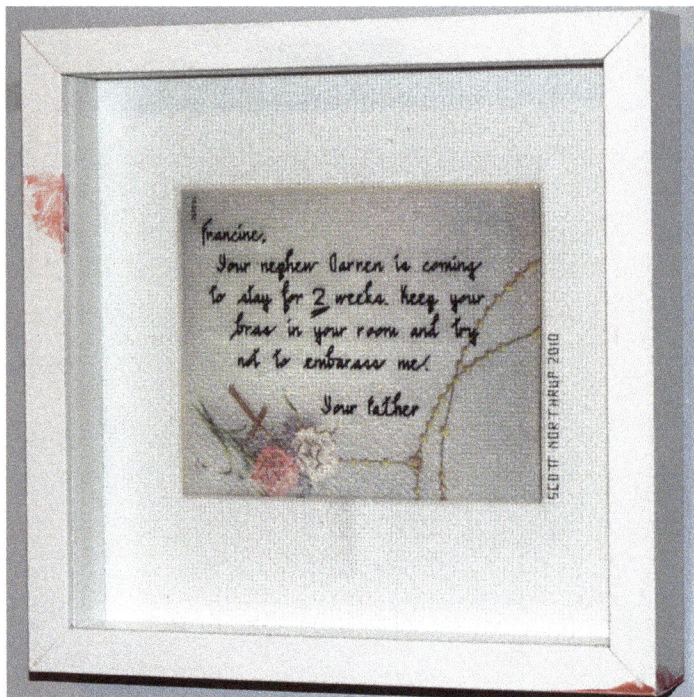

(Left) From *Alone.* 2015. Cut-up poetry zine.
(Right) A Father's Love (greeting card). 2010. Cross-stitch, lipstick, frame, 10 x 10 x 2 in.

conceptual artist whose work will be confined to no medium. And in its public display of intimacy, its deep roots in both personal experience and popular culture, and its tightrope dance between immateriality and physicality, it is classic Northrup, scaled up.

Other works that Northrup produced during the residency—which was for English-speaking poets, writers, and text-based artists—are more modest in size but no less beguiling. Consider, for example, *Alone.* (2015), a book of poems assembled from the text of an American war novel that Northrup found at a Finnish recycling center and later cut up. (He'd brought with him only his

smartphone and laptop, determined to work, as he so often does, with whatever materials serendipity sent his way.) In these poems, Northrup is revealed to be both a masterful miner and maker of texts, as well as a pithy and powerful storyteller. But as with his many earlier text-based works, including the 2010 cross-stitch piece *A Father's Love (greeting card)*, this is accomplished visual art, too. Note, in the poem beginning "he had been chill," how the negative space beneath the words "then he remembered" evokes the immensity and weight of memory, how the obsessive repetition of the word "him" beats a syncopated, insistently

sexual tattoo, and how the last two long spaces before and after the final "him," one vertical and the next horizontal, represent a release that is both carnal and formal, fluidly leading the eye off one page and toward the next.

Alone., along with other recently produced zines like *MEN* and *I Think We're Alone Now* (both 2015), is replete with references to male desire for men. While Northrup's work has for years employed a queer or camp sensibility that accounts for much of its playfulness, drama, and bite (see, for instance, the ***Grey Gardens Board Game***, 2005), it has only recently become more overtly homoerotic. Nowhere

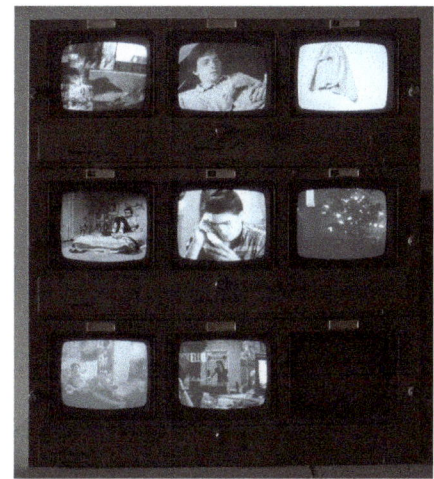

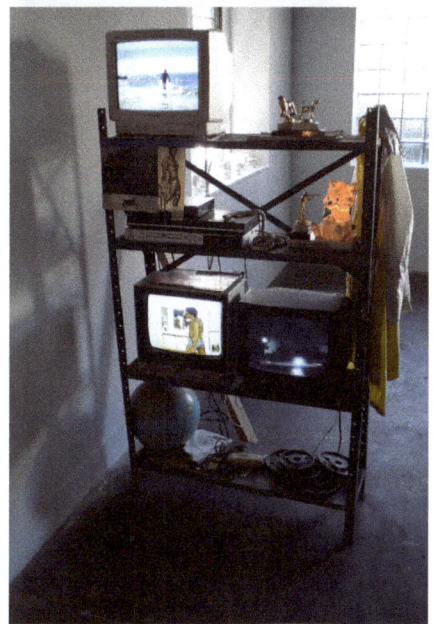

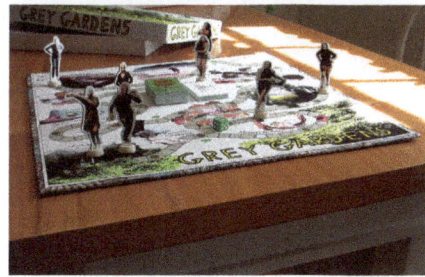

(Top) Where the Boys Are. 2015.
Video sculpture, 22 x 18 x 9 in.
(Middle) Be (with) Him. 2015.
Video sculpture, found objects, 78
x 40 x 18 in.
*(Bottom) Grey Gardens Board
Game* (gameplay view). 2005.
Paper, ink, chipboard, Sculpey, 24
x 24 x 5 in.

is this emergent tendency more evocatively and sensitively explored than in two sculptural/ video works from 2015, ***Where the Boys Are*** and ***Be (with) Him***, each including found footage from Hollywood movies that has been recut, looped, and recontextualized to emphasize male sexuality and desire. Northrup, who went to Catholic school for twelve years and was an altar boy for eight, avows to certain "devotional" impulses, and he considers the former work, an assemblage of nine closed-circuit TV monitors, to be a kind of altar to romantic male longing. The latter, a "Buddhist shrine," is a shelving unit stocked with both monitors and talismanic objects that evoke the transition from boyhood to manhood, as well as the complex vacillation between identification and objectification that is part and parcel of budding gay sexuality.

Northrup attests to an increased interest, in recent years, in creating work that is rooted in "the performance of the self," but no matter how specifically personal his works are at their inception, or how "impulsively" he creates, his universe is a fundamentally expansive and inclusive one. A viewer does not need to

know, for instance, that the 2015 collage ***We See Each Other*** was inspired by the end of a relationship to be absorbed by its mystery and formal elegance. "I think very emotionally," he says, and by dwelling in a space where secrets are made public, his work has wide-ranging reverberations.

2013's ***Recurring Nightmare***, a collection of thirty small, variously deformed plaster busts of Jackie Kennedy, was made in response to a traumatic event in his childhood, a violent assault on his young mother. He hesitated to show it publicly because "it felt too private," but this disturbing, quietly monumental work stands on its own as a nonetheless profound and humane vision of universal deformity. It magnanimously affirms—as does so much of Northrup's evolving oeuvre, with its remarkable variety and dazzling multimedia fluency—that famous dictum of Kant's, that "out of the crooked timber of humanity, no straight thing was ever made."

MATTHEW PIPER, MARCH 2016

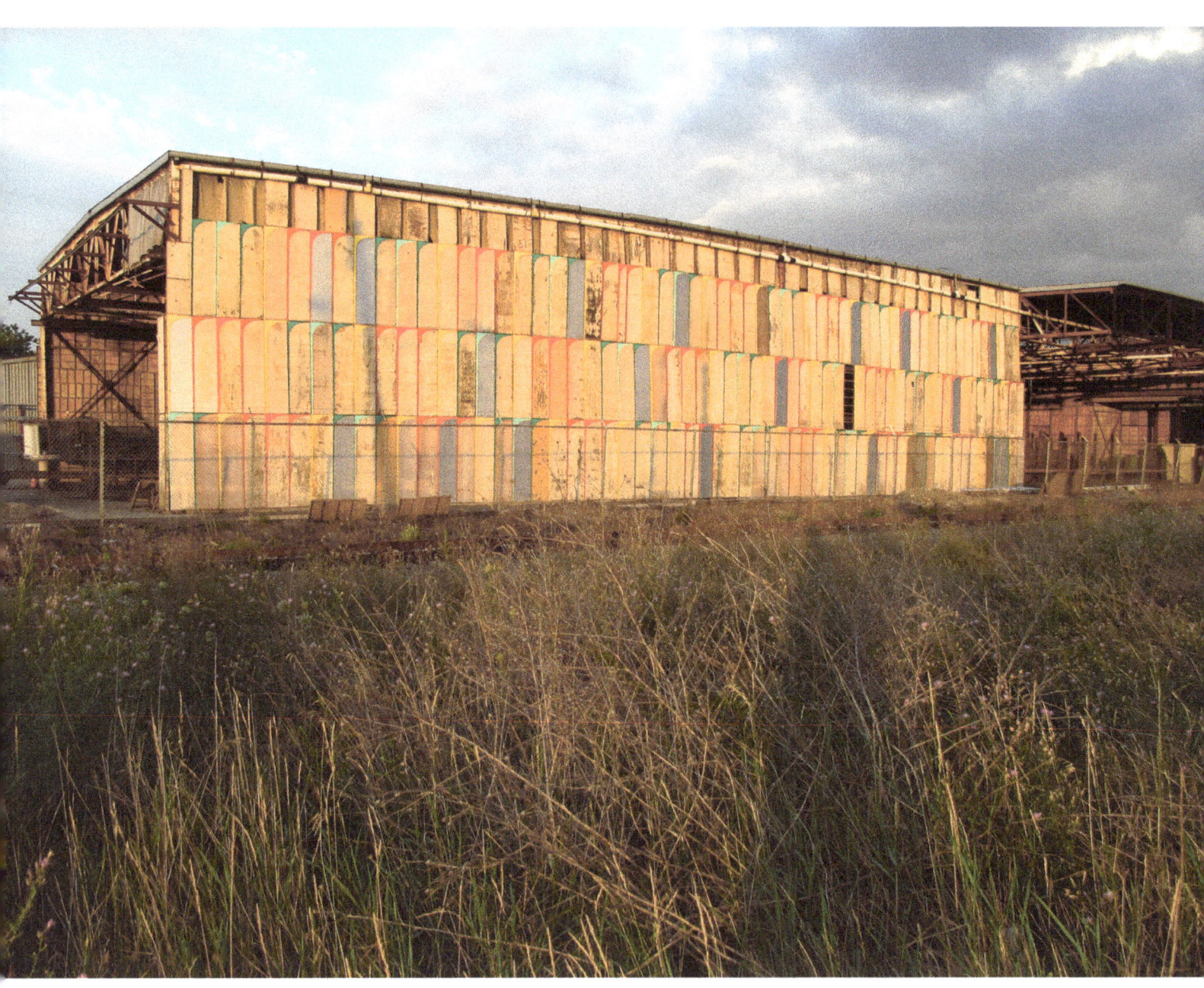

Boomer. 2011. Enamel on concrete molding, 24 x 180 ft.

Born Detroit, 1976
BA, Bennington College, Vermont;
MFA, Columbia University, New York
Lives in Hamtramck, Michigan

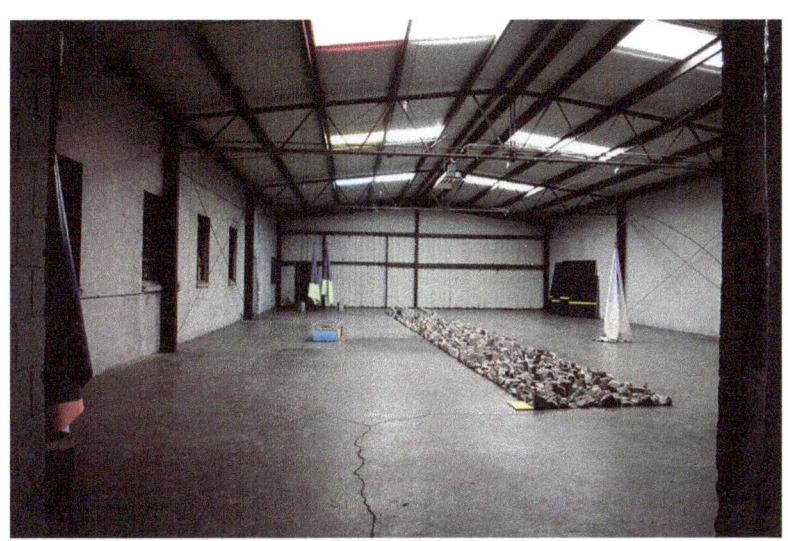

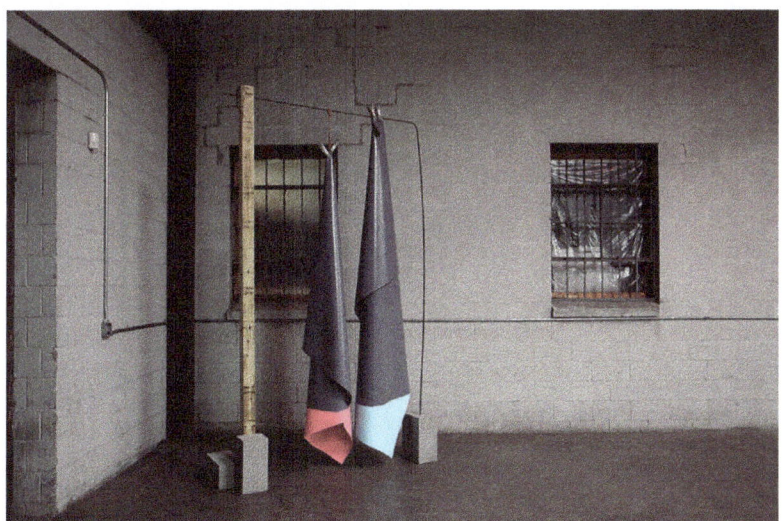

There is a chrysalis-like flux in the recent artworks of Jason Murphy. You feel it in the roughness of his constructions, as if we've interrupted a process, caught something between stages, or found artwork paused midconstruction. You find it in the vacillation of materials, a bit precarious and unstable, with histories and symbolism referencing building, but also breakdown, negligence, and accident. This is artwork precise and unstable, beautiful but a bit unsettling.

Murphy's practice is difficult to position. You might call him a sculptor, for his work is materially based, but the classification does not quite fit. He began as a painter and his practice is still engaged with formalist

(Top) Field Guide. 2015. Reclaimed concrete, brick, and asphalt, 6 x 115 ft.
(Bottom) Superman. 2015. Concrete, rebar, Oatey's, paint, 12 x 4 3/4 x 2 ft.

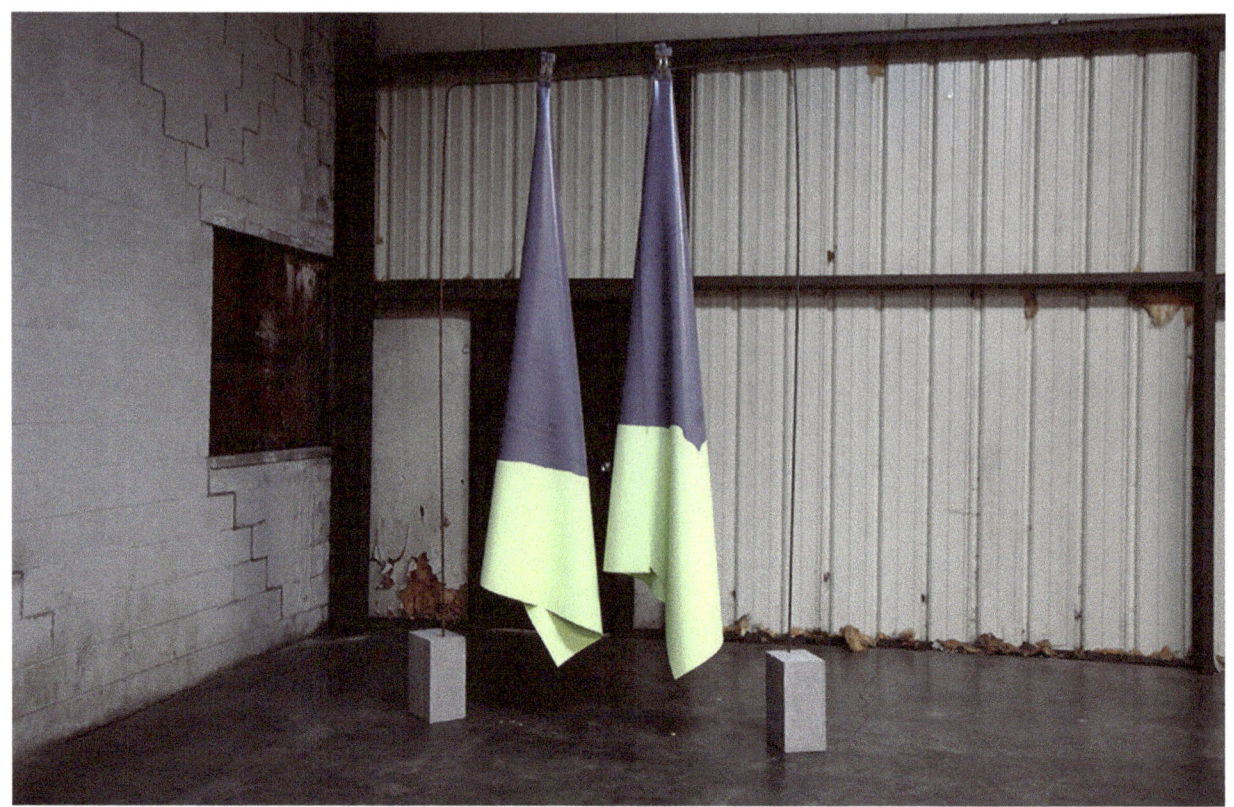

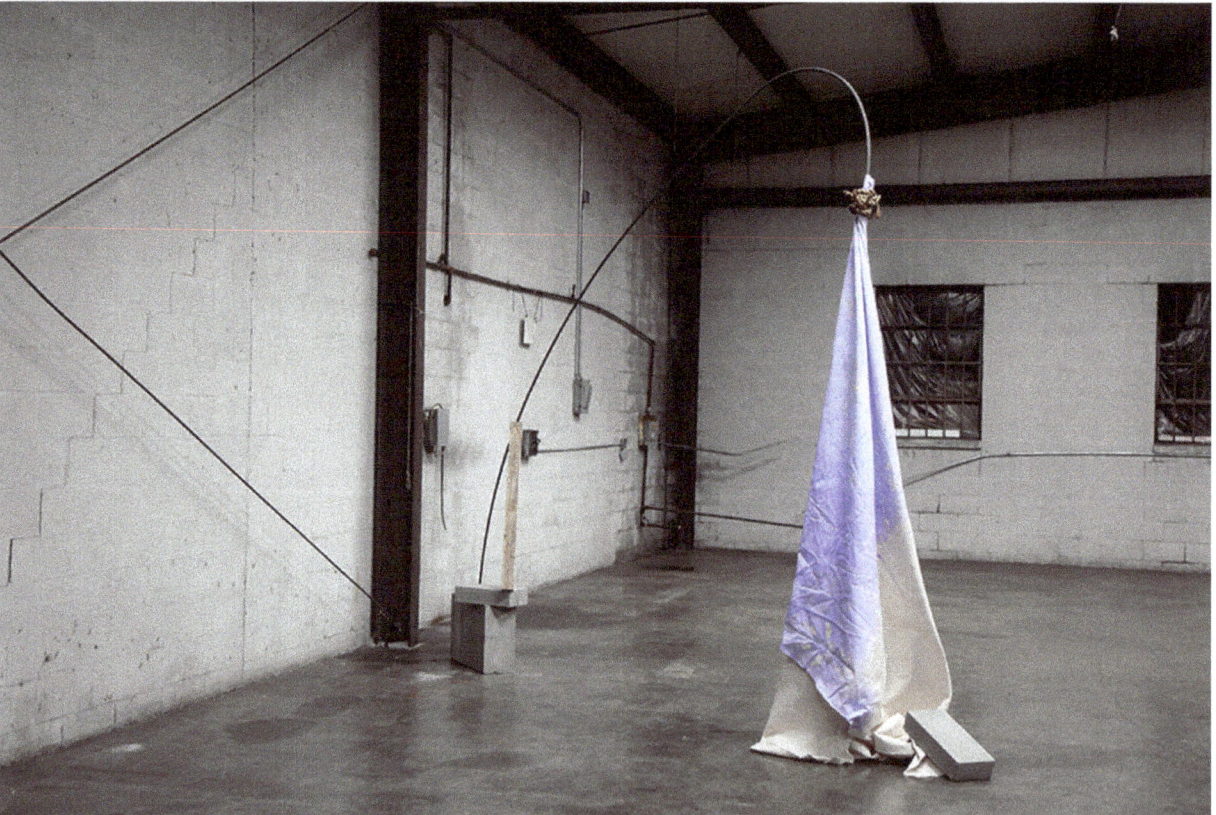

(Top) For Tony Gwynn. 2015. Concrete, rebar, Oatey's, paint, 12 x 4 1/2 x 2 ft.
(Bottom) Manatee. 2015. Canvas, rebar, concrete, paint, water, 17 x 4 x 8 1/2 ft.

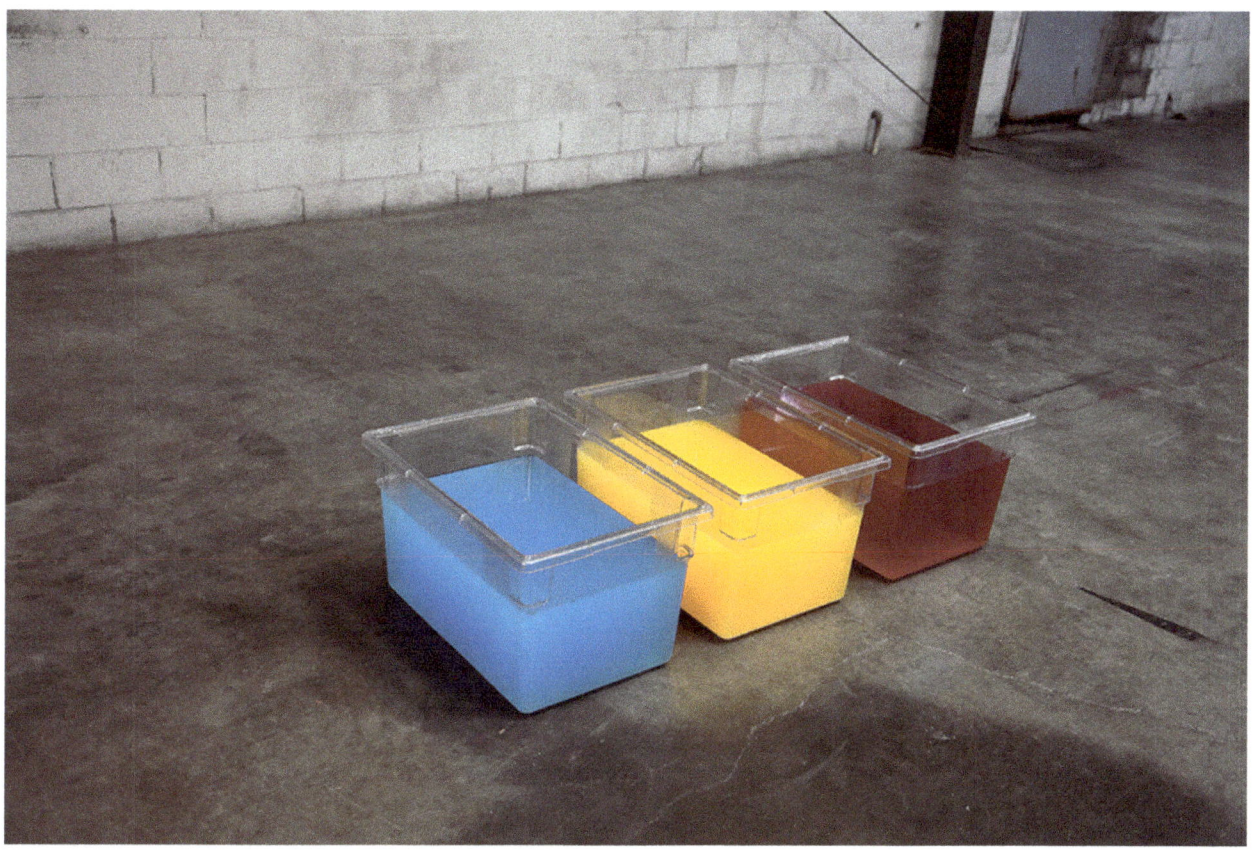

Huachipato. 2015. Cambro's water and Kool-Aid, 2 x 8 x 2 ft.

painting; there are strong elements of color, line, shape, and texture. But his artworks are not paintings; they are definitely things. They have a presence and must be negotiated with.

His move toward sculpture may be a reaction to the fixity of painting, a medium that seems already resolved, the stretcher providing a frame, definition, and a destination: the wall, the domestic. Or perhaps it is painting's commodity status, its salability and confident presence in the art market, the standing and attitude

of contemporary painting seeming so at odds with the daily lives and struggles of people in Detroit, where Murphy lives. Yet ultimately these concerns are probably secondary to his interest in the elegance of common materials. Born and bred in Detroit, Jason was/is surrounded by construction materials, the leftovers from departed factories and houses, and new construction projects ongoing. There is raw beauty to these objects of labor, blue-collar things that become amplified in his artworks. Ultimately it is the history

and sociopolitical resonance of materials that dominates, rather than what happens on the surface.

These interests are apparent in the last five years of his practice. You find them in his experiments painting on nonart surfaces, such as ***A Spanish Father and an Italian Mother #2*** (2012), where he has painted a series of colored horizontal stripes on a moving blanket, or in ***Boomer*** (2011), where he negotiated with a Detroit construction company to magnify the patterned exterior of a warehouse by adding

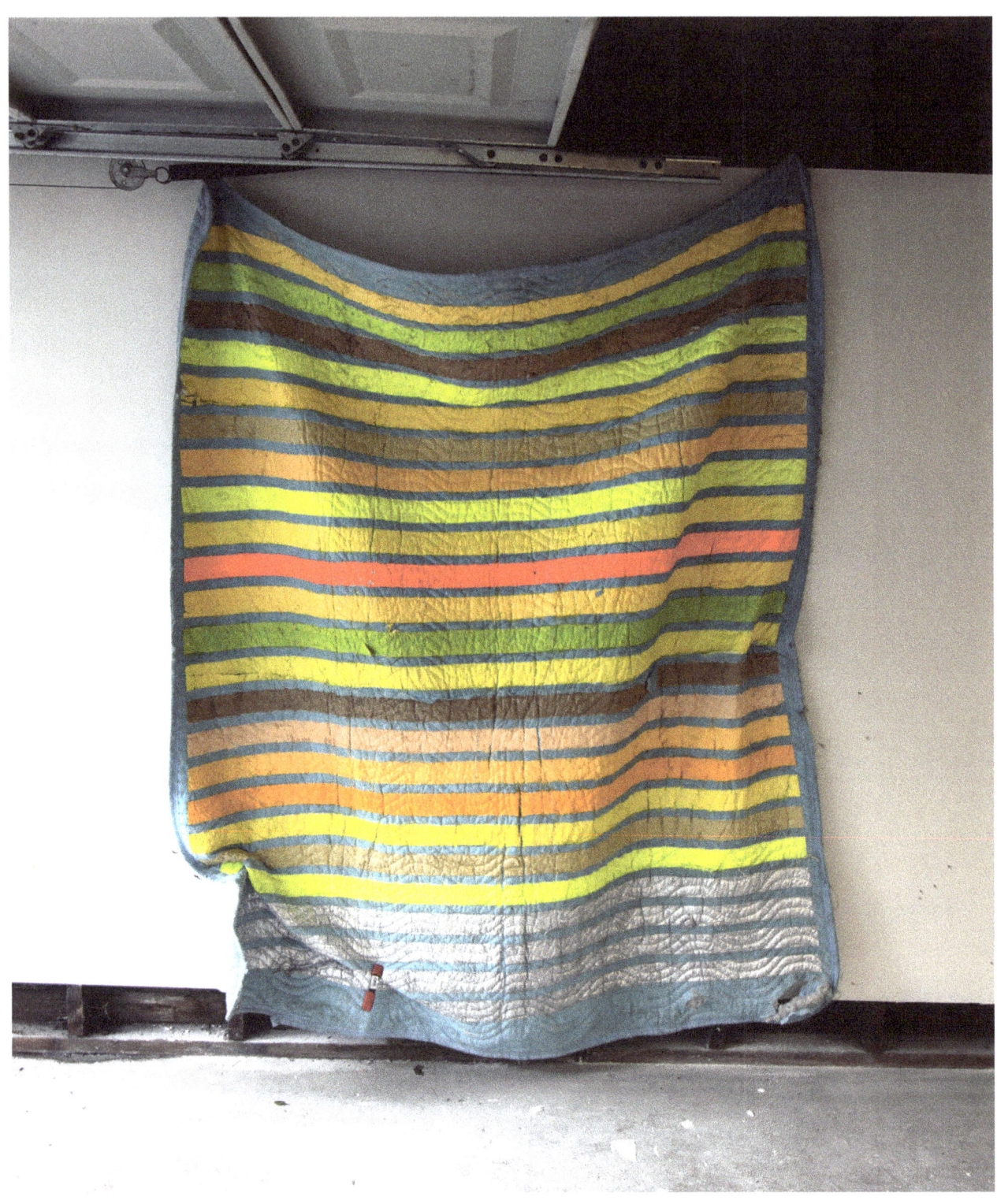

A Spanish Father and an Italian Mother #2. 2012. Enamel on moving blanket with spring clips, 74 1/2 x 67 1/2 in.

enamel colors. Yet in his 2015 show at Young World, these concerns are most evident. Here, his materials are carefully selected, their interactions planned, and his operations carried out with rehearsed precision. These deliberately blunt actions evoke factory systems, amplifying objectness. The experience is almost like visiting a painter deconstructing his artworks, where all elements take on a physicality, transforming from planes into objects. The canvas a clump of cloth, the stretcher an apparatus, and the fasteners, ropes, and clamps in place of staples, devices no longer hidden.

In *Superman* (2015) and *For Tony Gwynn* (2015), large industrial rubber sheets have been dipped in neon paint, hung from their corners by metal clips attached to steel armatures anchored into concrete blocks. The wrinkled rubber is left to drip-dry, while on the floor the paint's remains show evidence of the process. In *Manatee* (2015) a piece of canvas is similarly treated, stained with blue paint and tied to a length of steel, bent back like a catapult, held taut by a concrete anchor.

As the constituent elements emerge, so too does the importance of each object's socioeconomic properties. We are drawn to consider the material's history and significance, the role it plays, and how it is viewed by society. In *Huachipato* (2015), Murphy presents three clear plastic, five-gallon food storage tubs containing bright pools of saccharine color, a cool icy blue, a yellowy orange, and shimmering wine red. On closer inspection they are revealed to be Kool-Aid—cherry, pineapple, and twist berry blue—the beverage a cultural signifier of childhood, home, and lower socioeconomic class. Murphy has left the bins open, letting Kool-Aid mingle with airborne debris, dust and insects settling, mold slowly growing. Pleasurable childhood associations turn toward dereliction. *Field Guide* (2015), a carefully arranged taxonomy comprising hundreds of broken stones and reclaimed concrete, brick, and asphalt, evokes similar associations. Here, he has given each object a color name listed in the galley handout, creating a language from the abandoned and ignored.

Even in these sometimes eviscerating reactions to formalism, there remains remarkable care and compassion. Murphy has logged many hours selecting materials, both the discarded and the common. He has cleaned, prepared, and arranged them with objects that will complement their qualities. And he has taken things that were formerly overlooked and resurrected them into new relations and new representations.

ANTHONY MARCELLINI,
MARCH 2016

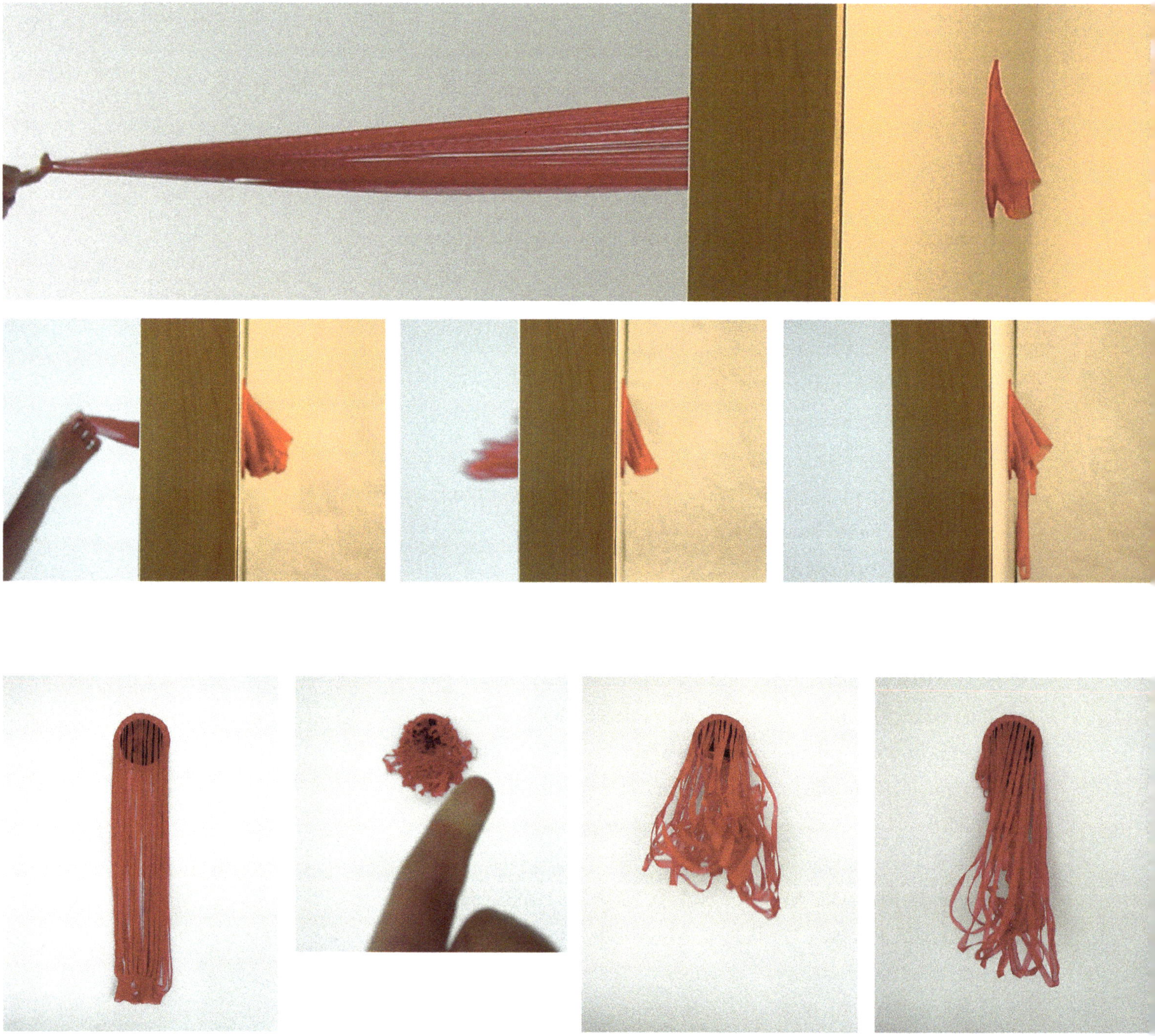

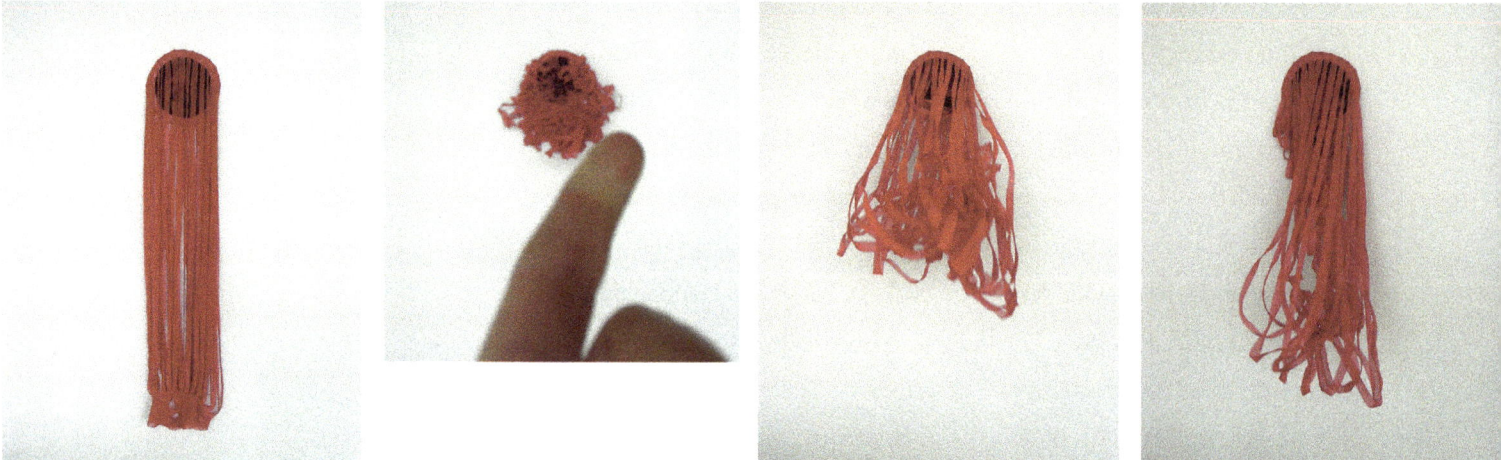

Snap! (installation view). 2003. Two-way stretch netting, tacks, dimensions variable.

49 // MARCELYN BENNETT-CARPENTER

Born Grand Rapids, Michigan, 1971
BA, Wheaton College, Illinois; BFA,
University of Colorado at Denver;
MFA, Cranbrook Academy of Art
Lives in Bloomfield Hills, Michigan

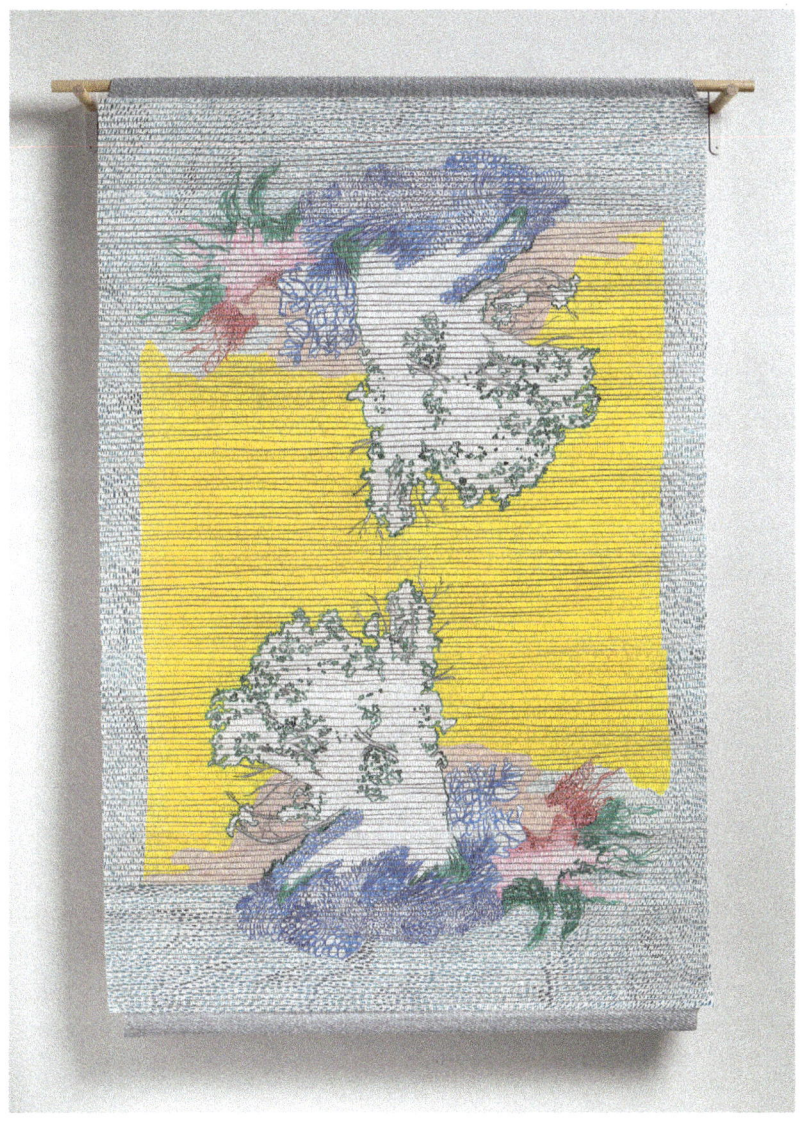

Marcelyn Bennett-Carpenter would like for you, the viewer, to be involved. Engagement with her work, ideally, goes beyond aesthetic appreciation; her pieces are designed for physical interaction: wearing, blowing, navigating, and especially stretching. Tension is the fundamental quality of weaving; as a fiber artist, accomplished weaver, and instructor at Cranbrook's Kingswood Weaving and Fiber Art Studio, Bennett-Carpenter's work is fraught with a baseline tension that is belied at first blush by soft palettes and inviting surfaces.

In many ways, Bennett-Carpenter is the consummate fiber artist—a cohort prone to obsession with materials and the desire to synthesize radically different points of inspiration. The ability to tie together disparate strands is, again, critical

Tamarack. 2015. Handwoven drawing, 4 x 6 ft.

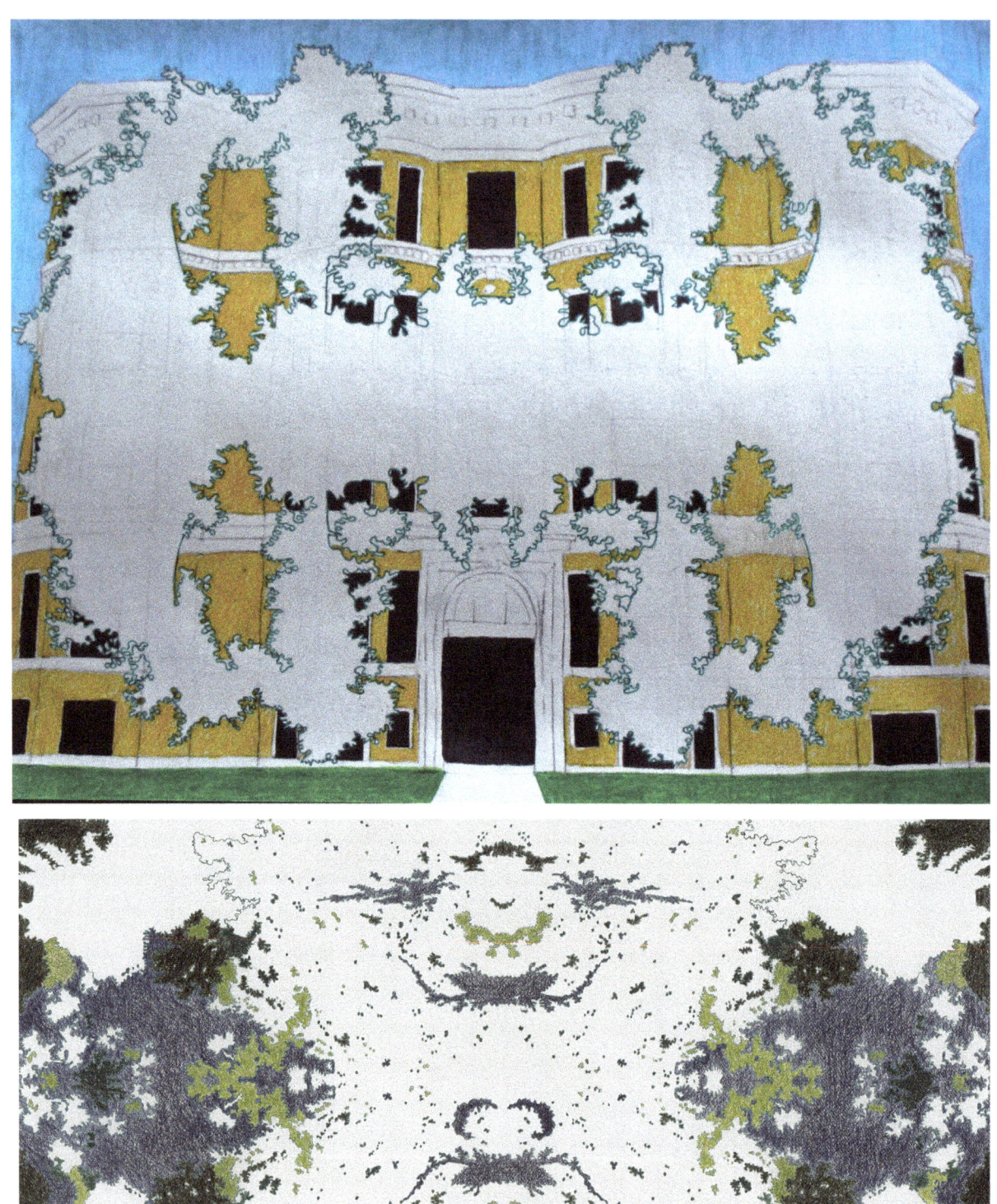

(Top) Abandon: 14th Street. 2016. Pencil and ink, 11 x 13 1/2 in.
(Bottom) Abandon: Institute Way. 2014. Pencil and ink, 30 x 24 in. Photography by Tim Thayer.

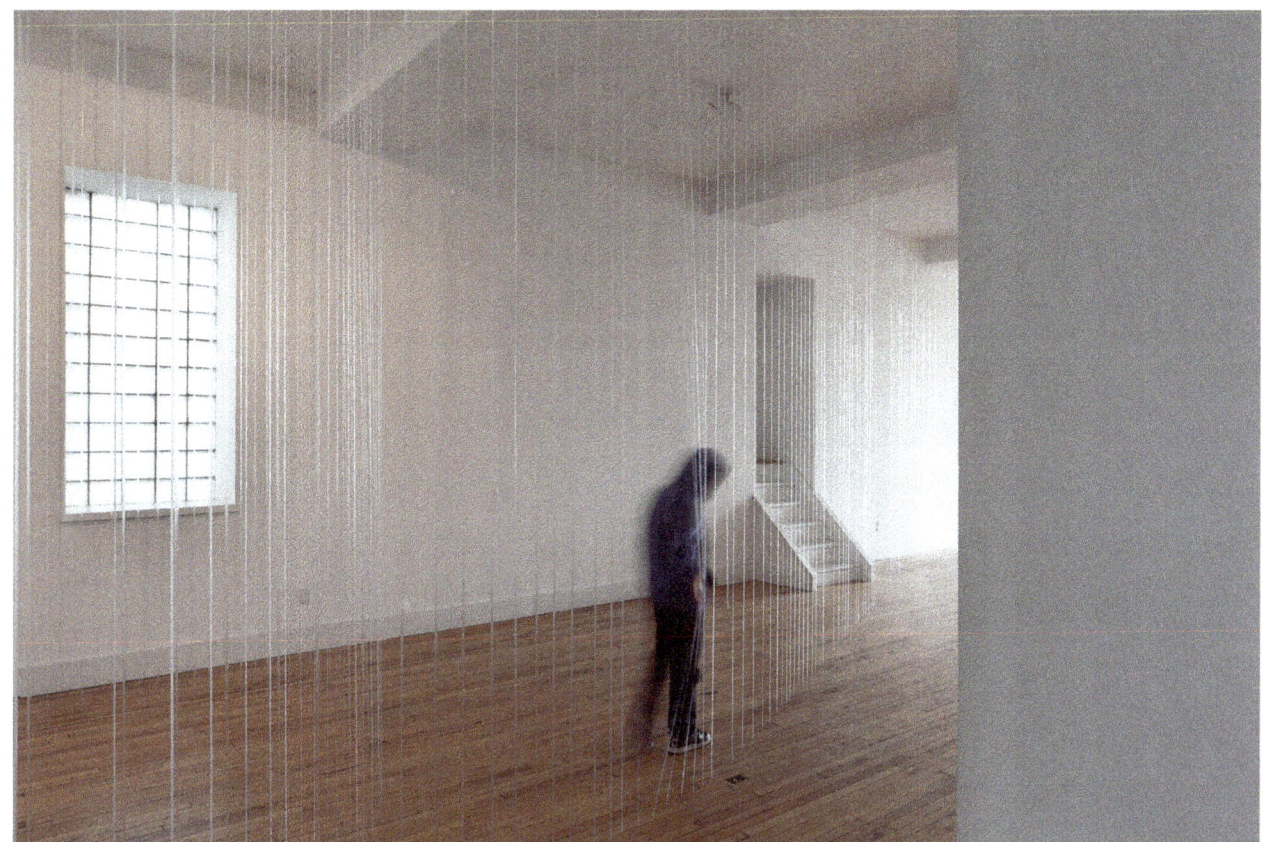

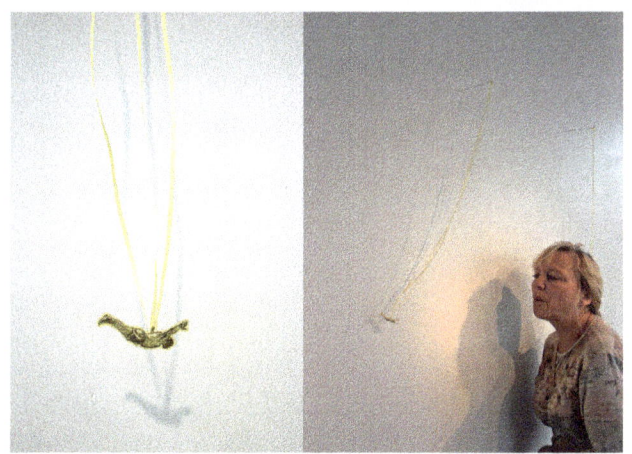
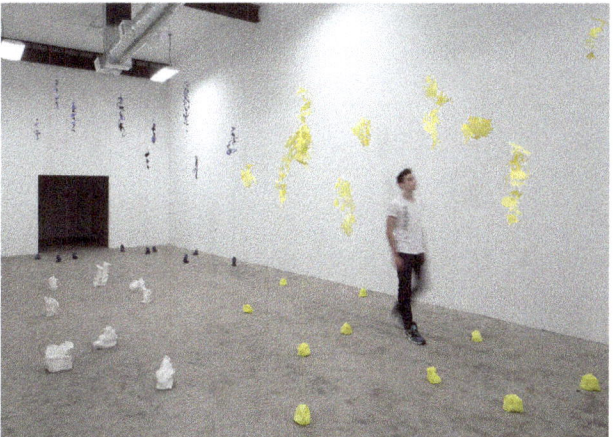

(Top) Turn. 2011. Elastic, 13 x 60 x 24 ft. Photography by Shell Hensleigh.
(Bottom, left) Dive (from *Flyers*). 2007. Paper and graphite, dimensions variable.
(Bottom, right) Tensions: Yellow, Red, Blue. 2016. Elastic, paper, porcelain, felt, cotton, lead, 60 x 20 x 20 ft.
Photography by P. D. Rearick.

to the process of weaving, and one supposes that more than a decade of training and practice with this art has left Bennett-Carpenter in a state of constant and reflexive incorporation of new ideas with old. An ongoing series of house drawings that feature pencil and ink sketches of architectural subjects from around the Cranbrook campus (***Abandon: Institute Way***, 2014) and the city of Detroit (***Abandon: 14th Street***, 2016), obscured by Rorschach-like blots of negative-space vegetation, demonstrates Bennett-Carpenter's focus on the immediate, the domestic. Not only do these meditations on space, nature, and architecture translate directly to her woven pieces, the

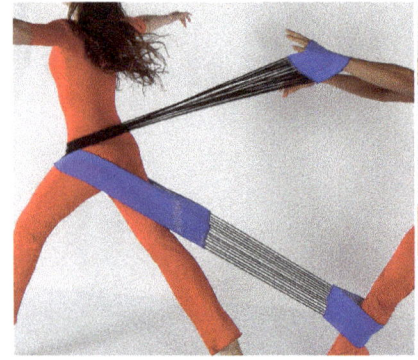
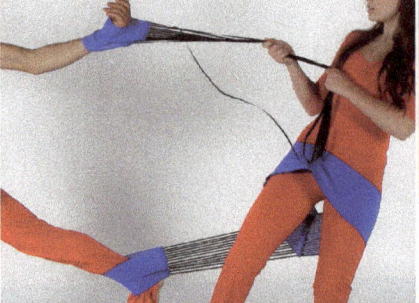
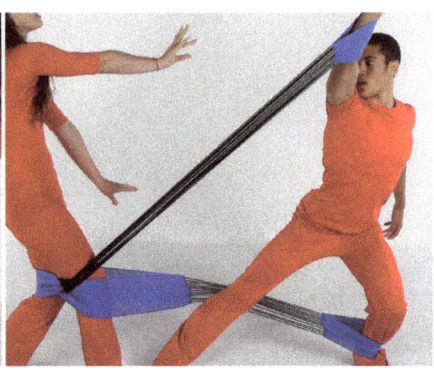

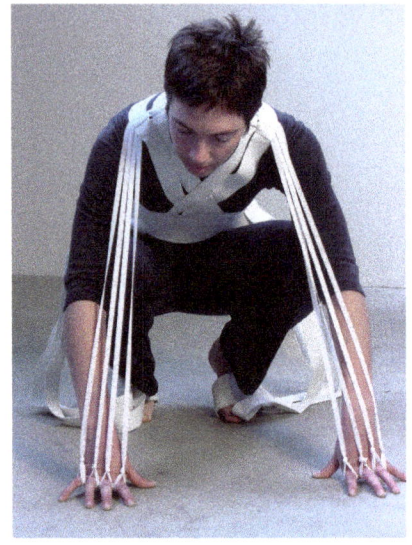

(Top) Fitting: Blue and Black. 2009. Elastic, dimensions variable.
(Left) Experiment: Fingers to Toes. 2003. Elastic, dimensions variable.

center-reflected nature of the drawings suggests the two-sided process that makes all weavings inherently dual (reverse-relief) images. Many of her drawn and woven pieces resemble interior design; Bennett-Carpenter recalls the example set by her mother's determination, throughout a childhood punctuated by frequent moves, to painstakingly decorate each new home. A series of panels, such as **Toward the Left** (2011), deals very directly with these ideas of interior and decorative spaces, overlaying Diane

Simpson–esque fields of wallpaper and Mylar with tight, delicate constellations of thread on pins— modeling an appealing domestic tableau that is subtly fraught with quiet tension, as so many are.

Bennett-Carpenter further deconstructs weaving in a series of focused explorations: **Flyers** (2007), a series of suspended drawings and streamers animated by viewers blowing on them; **Snap!** (2003), which presents interactive sculptures in two-way stretch netting, pulled and released through a hole in the gallery wall to create kinetic flashes of line and motion; **wearable elastic structures**, some of Bennett-Carpenter's only work that ties into a figurative form, lacing human subjects with flexible contraptions that add resistance and tension to their very movements; and floor-to-ceiling installations of stretchy elastic lines, sometimes

plain and densely strung, as with **Turn** (2011), sometimes sparse and adorned with paper embellishments, recalling her drawings of vegetation, or anchored by ceramic bases, as with **Tensions: Yellow, Red, Blue** (2016)—all of which draw the viewer to play and experiment physically inside the warp of weaving.

But this disparate examination of form seems to be culminating, of late, into the blessed synthesis that creates whole cloth. Bennett-Carpenter's most recent works are "woven drawings"—for example, **Tamarack** (2015)—that combine many of the elements upon which she has focused so intently. An abstract biota, rendered in bright, playful colors, is drawn onto thin wooden slats, which are subsequently hand-cut into thin horizontal strips. These images are reconstructed through a woven matrix, much like a roll-down wooden window shade, and work in progress shows some of them featuring additional layers of drawn collage elements that have begun to appear on the surface of the weaving. After so much work that isolates the singular dimensions of her craft, it is exhilarating to see Bennett-Carpenter combine these aspects so richly, leveraging the tension of viewer expectation through the process of slow buildup.

It is easy to notice bombast, drama, shock-and-awe. Often the loudest voices are those that draw the most notice, and a call to action is easier to hear than a whisper. Knowing, as we do, Bennett-Carpenter's interest in the viewer, her quietness as an artist and a person is somewhat counterintuitive. But to look at her work is to understand the power of quietness to make the avid listener lean in—and to do so is to make the surprising discovery that something that looked rigid and tense is, in reality, ready to lean with you.

SARAH ROSE SHARP,
FEBRUARY 2016

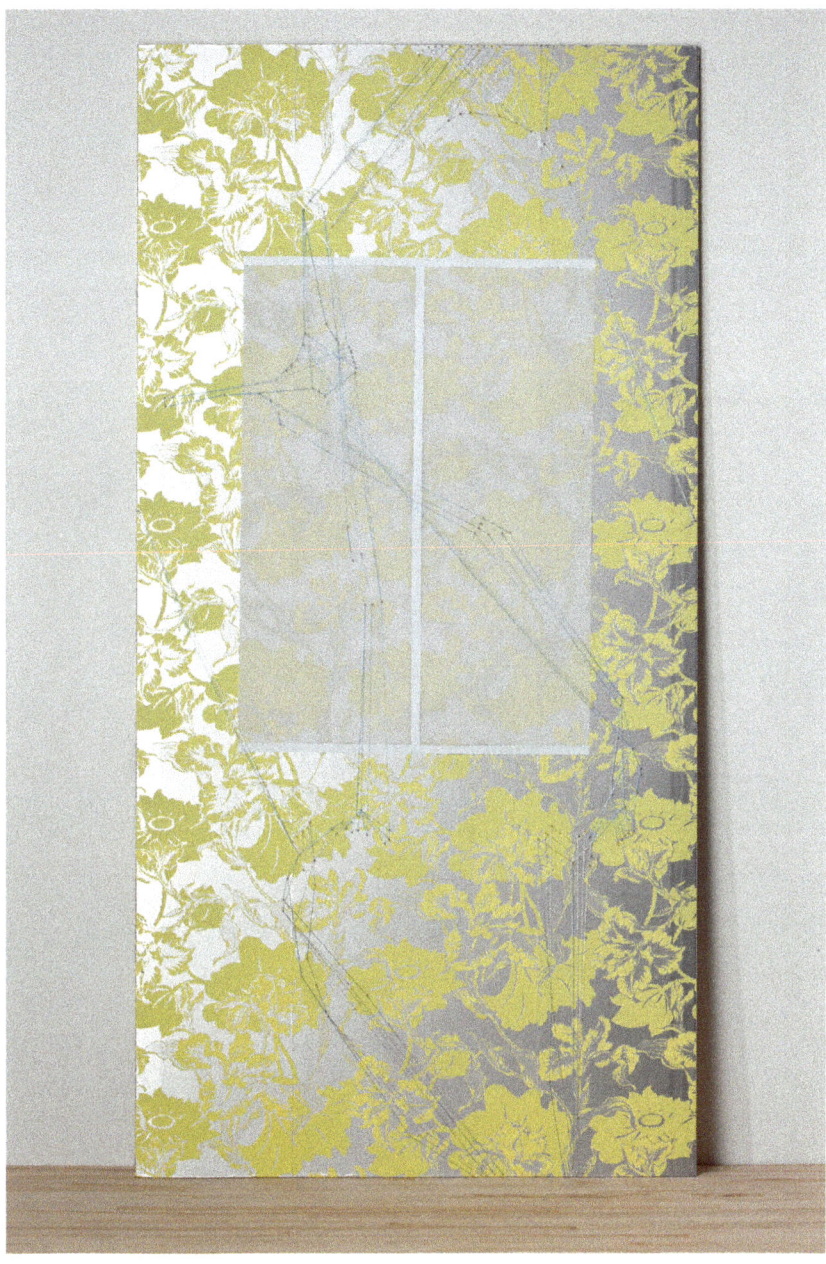

Toward the Left. 2011. Panel, wallpaper, Mylar, paint, thread, pins, 8 x 4 in. Photography by Tim Thayer.

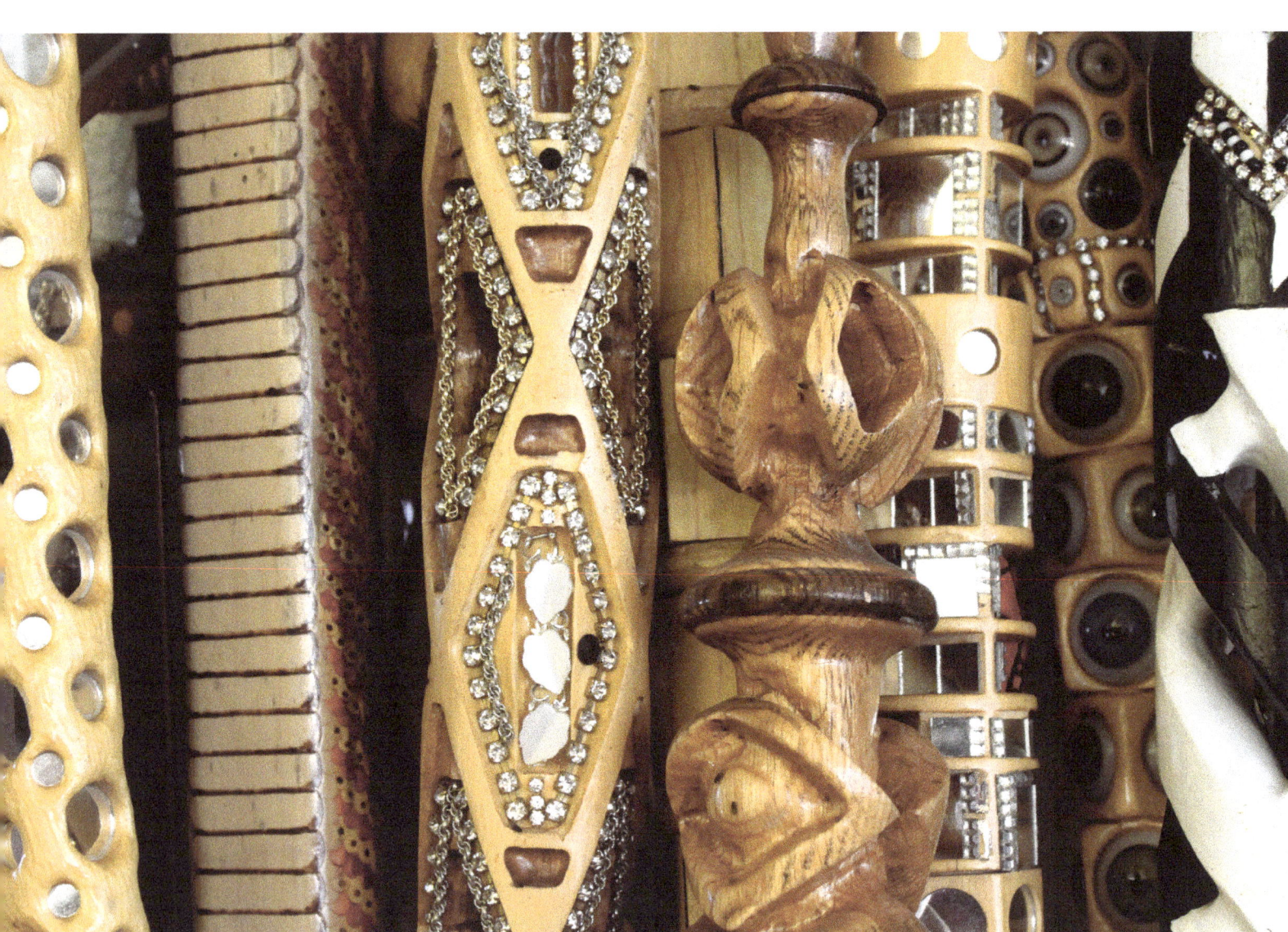

Staffs (detail). Wood, mixed media. Photography by Matthew Piper.

Born Chicago, Illinois, 1940
Lives in Detroit

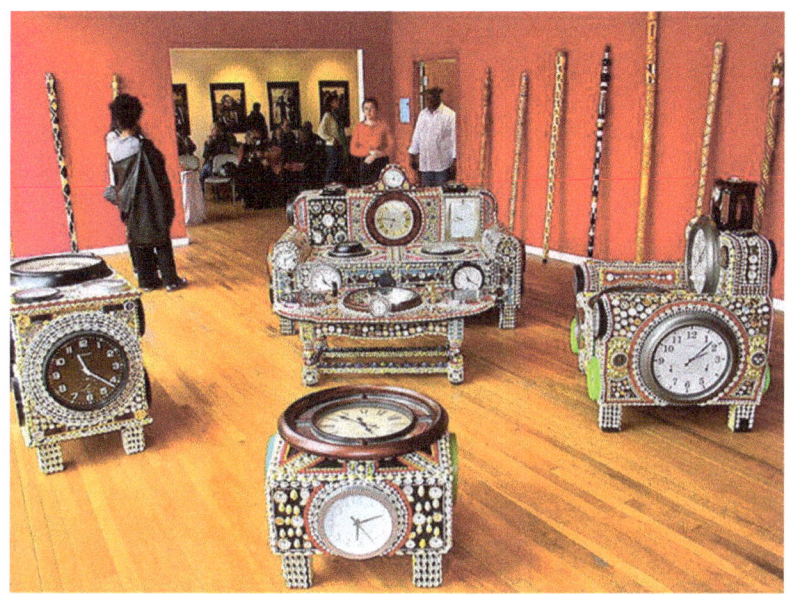

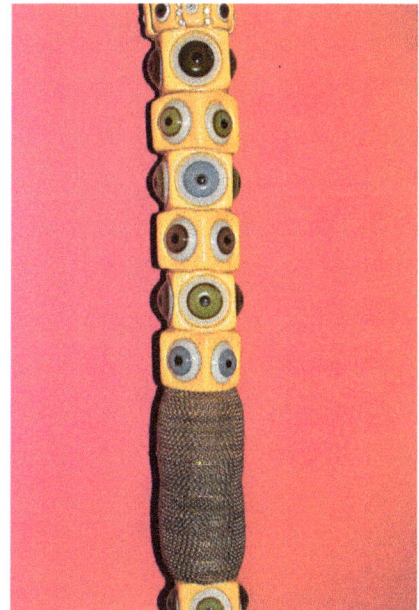
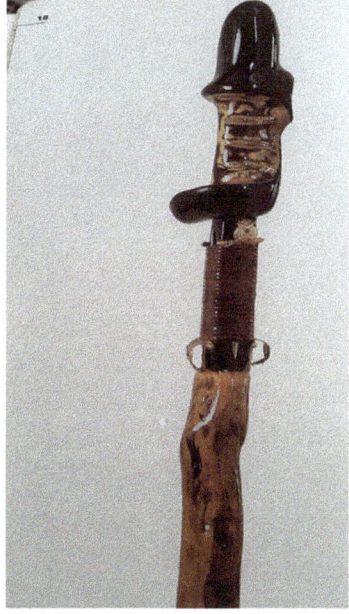

David Philpot is an antenna, finely tuned to subtle frequencies. He listens carefully, receiving transmissions from as far away as West Africa, and from as nearby as God or the wood in his hands. His primary medium, fittingly, is the *staff*, an energizing rod that joins the earth to the sky via the human being who wields it.

Long before he ever considered himself an artist, the then-thirty-year-old Philpot heard a voice call his name, leading him, amazed, to an oasis: a grove of trees in a Chicago housing project. A week later, Philpot, who had never abandoned his childhood habit of gathering and carrying sticks, and who had recently admired Charlton Heston's staff in *The Ten Commandments*, woke

(Top) Time. 2013. Mixed-media installation.
(Bottom, left) Eyes of God (detail). 2015. Wood, mixed media, 6 ft. x 3 in.
(Bottom, right) Genesis (detail). 1971. Wood, mixed media, 4 ft. x 2 in.

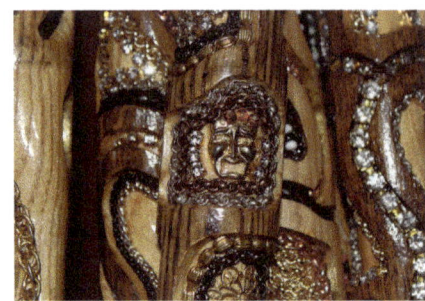

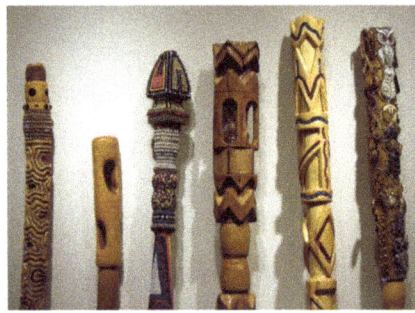

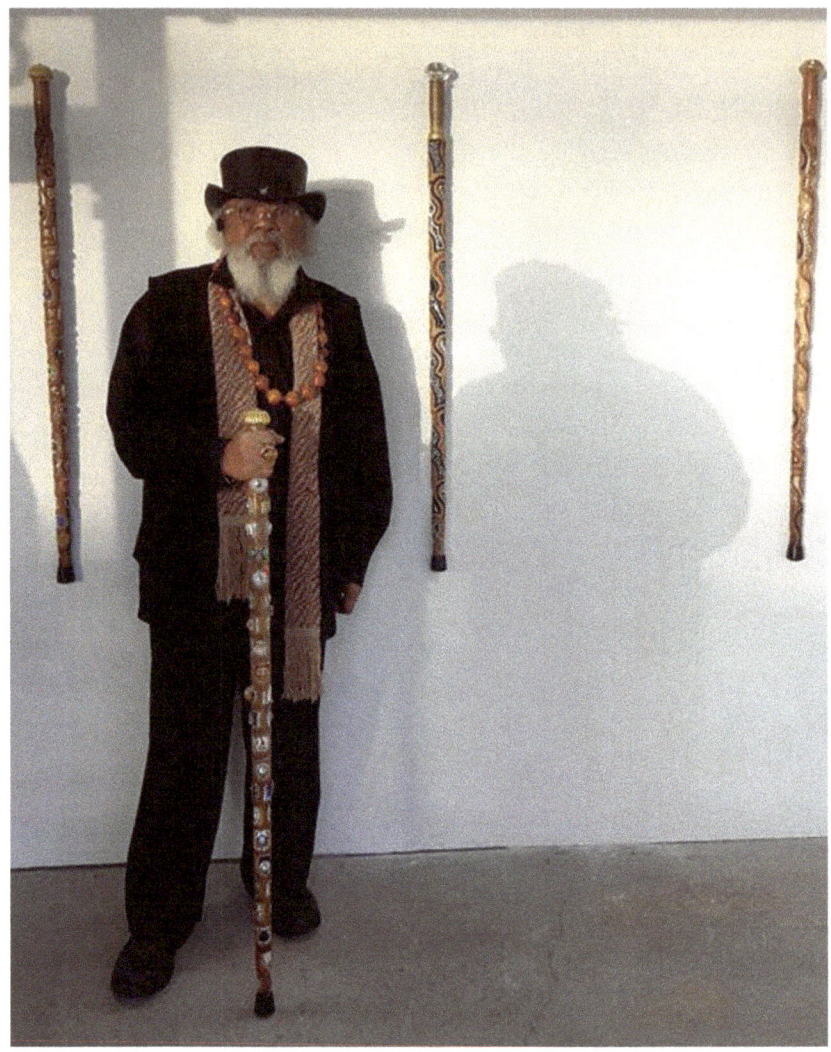

in the night with a mission: to chop down one of those trees and make from it a staff of his own. When it was done, he called it **Genesis** (1971), an apt title for the first of more than 350 staffs he has made in the forty-five years since.

Philpot, who has no formal art training, says that he felt "satisfied" for three or four months after the completion of *Genesis*, but soon began to feel the need to make another staff, and after that, another. For years, he could be seen traversing his urban environs, cutting down *Ailanthus altissima*, also known as ghetto palms or trees of heaven, and carrying them home, where he meticulously carved them into staffs, embellished them, and then set them aside. This was just a hobby, he says, a getaway from a world that

(Top, left) Canes (detail). Wood, mixed media. Photography by Matthew Piper.
(Bottom, left) Staffs (detail). Wood, mixed media.
(Right) David Philpot with canes. 2016. Photography by Marsha Battle Philpot.

could be cruel to a "big, raggedy-looking Negro" with a stammer. But when he began to show the work, it was met with enthusiasm, and Philpot was nonplussed to hear himself described as a talented "African-style artist." The following years were marked by a succession of laurels, including invitations to exhibit his work at

African embassies, the DuSable Museum of African American History, and, in 1989, the Dallas Museum of Art, as part of its landmark exhibition exploring the "African impulse" in the work of fifty American artists.

Nonetheless, the idea that his hobby was related in any meaningful way to the art of Africa

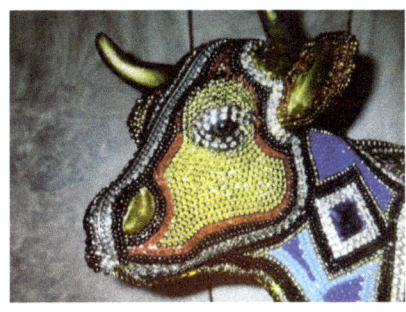

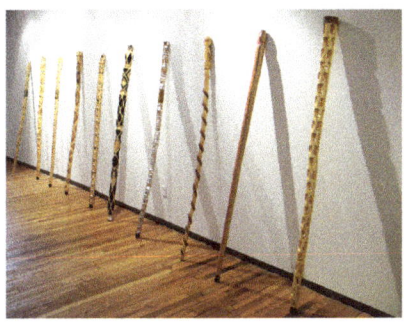

(Top) Cow (detail). 1999. Mixed media.
(Bottom) Staffs. Wood, mixed media. Photography by Matthew Piper.

was one that took Philpot years to accept. He labored with no practical knowledge of African staff-making traditions until 1997, when he took a research trip to West Africa. In Ghana, he gifted a staff to a tribal king, who installed it near his throne, and he met with fellow staff makers, who illuminated his own practice with their learned explications of his work. It was there that Philpot finally accepted that he was indeed an artist, and that his intuitive creations were his "ancestral legacy," reaching out to him in the form of the staff.

Philpot's staffs are typically six to eight feet tall. Each is an intricate, self-contained world. They are sinuous or geometric, painted or uncolored, elaborate or plain. They are unadorned or embellished with found objects, including rocks, jewels, coins, and mirrors. They take shape slowly, telling Philpot while he works how they want to be carved and with what materials they would prefer to be adorned. They are often untitled; Philpot says he is not always privy to their names, which should ideally be given by "whoever raises them up."

For many years, Philpot restricted his creative output to these staffs or his smaller *canes*. But his participation in several civic art initiatives in Chicago took him on a notable creative detour that found him transforming existing objects via the application of found materials—see, for example, *Cow* (1999) and *Time* (2013). Because these fantastic, bewitching works do not involve the artist's masterful carving, they bring into starker relief his gifts as a mosaic maker, including his sensitive consideration of material and proportion, and his painstaking application and arrangement of objects like beads, shells, clocks, and glass eyes.

Five years ago, Philpot became a Detroiter. He'd been invited to exhibit at the N'Namdi Gallery here, and when a voice in the night told him to come, he listened, arriving as a well-known elder statesman of African American folk art. (The Heidelberg Project's Tyree Guyton, a longtime admirer, greeted Philpot on his knees.) He's been here ever since, and says he feels, for the first time, a growing connection to a wider art world. Now that he's put down roots here, he's picking up transmissions from the local scene and gathering ideas for his work: "I have entered this new universe," he says, "and now I have to let it guide me."

MATTHEW PIPER, APRIL 2016

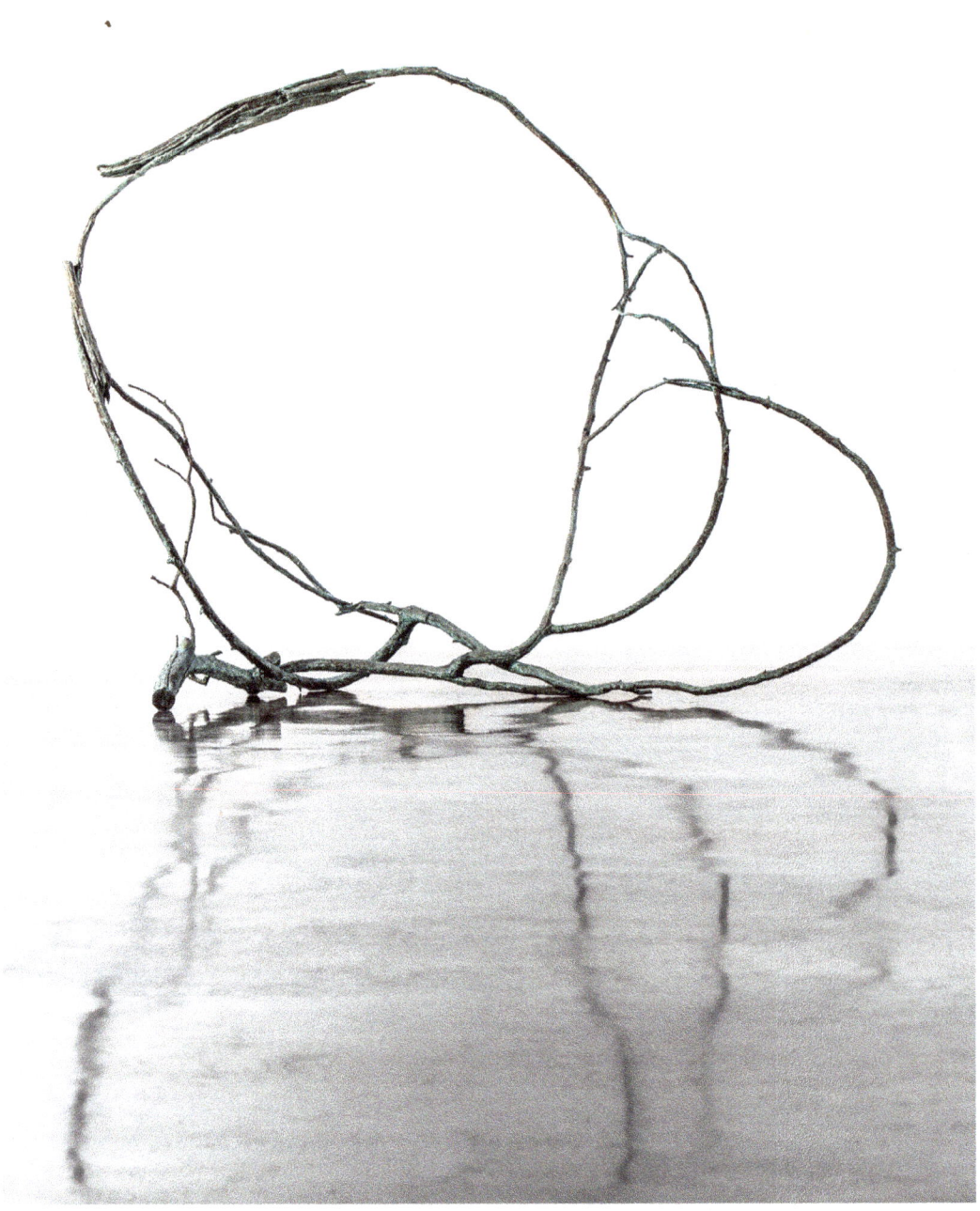

Hold Free River. 2013. Cast bronze, 61 x 81 x 52 in.

Born Lansing, MI, 1959
BA, Hope College, Holland, MI; MFA,
Cranbrook Academy of Art,
Bloomfield Hills, MI
Lives in Farmington Hills, MI

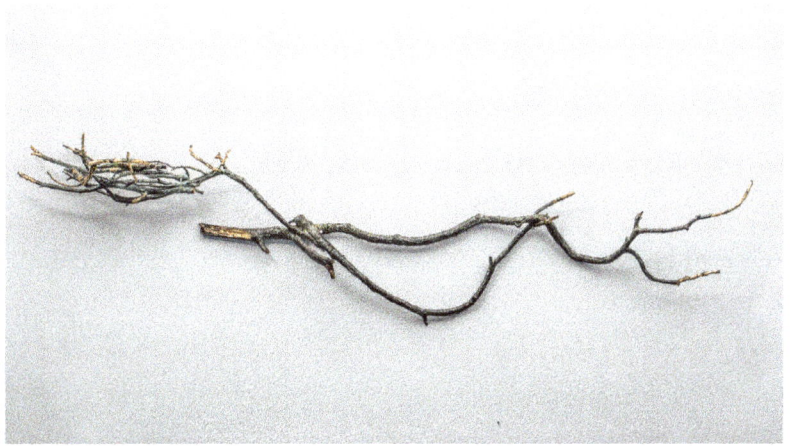

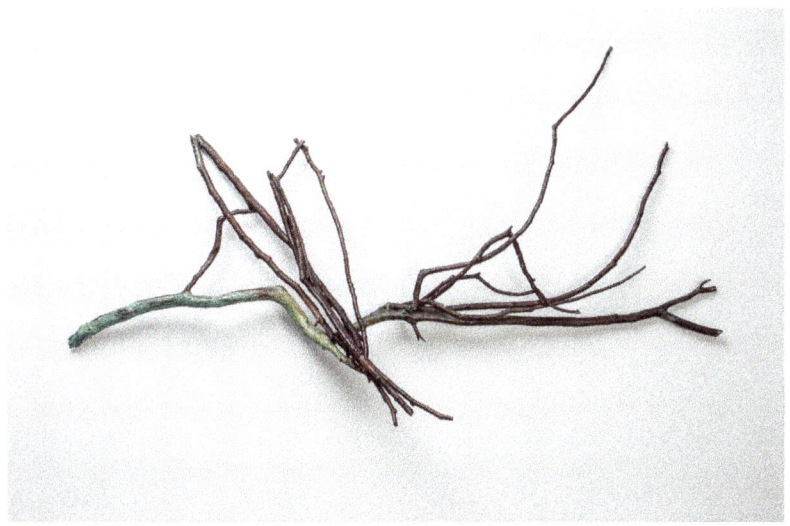

Todd Erickson's recent sculptures, the *River Series* of 2009–2016, treat the eye to a richly inventive array of looping, interlacing ovals and circles. Each sinuous variant, however, also harbors singular details and idiosyncratic extrusions that further animate these "bronze rivers." They range from an occasional thickening of the slender, linear outlines to projecting "growths," intent, it seems, on springing free of the governing rings and hoops. Cast in bronze from branches and twigs gathered by the artist, these restless rivers twist and turn, swerve and whipsaw as the eye flows around their final form.

In **Betsie River II** (2015) the vertical oval at right is counterweighted by the tall, bending branch at the left that sports half a dozen thin, upward-swerving

(Top) Nesting River. 2015. Cast bronze, 15 x 56 x 8 in.
(Bottom) Blue Line River. 2012. Cast bronze, 36 x 58 x 11 in.

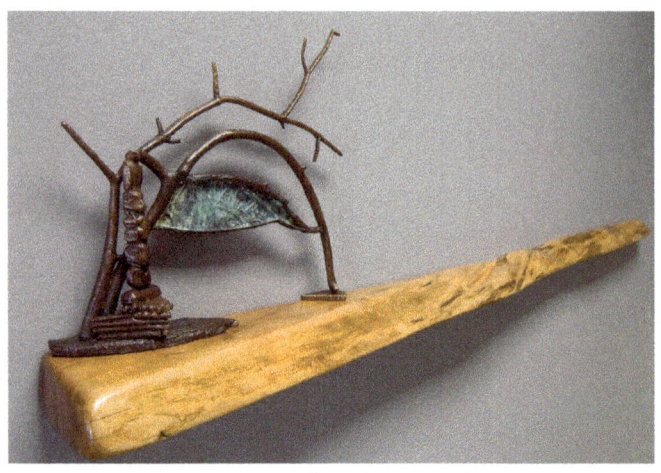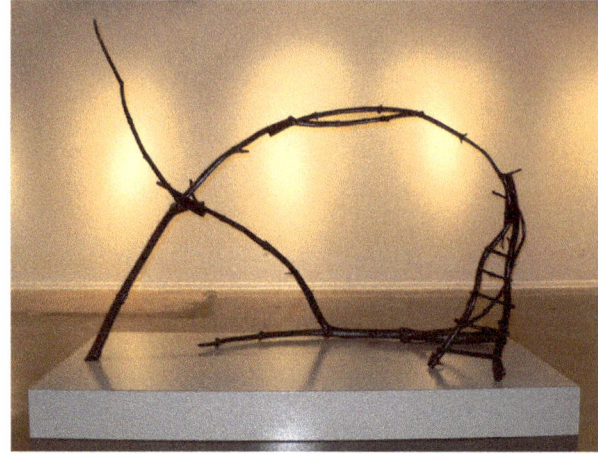

(Left) Trading Post. 2008. Cast bronze, cherry, 14 1/2 x 58 x 6 in.
(Right) Paradise Ascension. 2009. Cast bronze, 6 x 9 x 3 ft.

limbs that break free of this stabilizing element. Such rogue appendages are endemic to Erickson's meandering sculptures and akin to the networks of streams, creeks, and rivulets that glide toward or away from a waterway's main branch. As Erickson sees it, "Much like humans, rivers are programmed to let go at a certain point. They are geographically prone to allow the water to flow into the next channel, lake, or tributary. . . . Letting go is what protects and keeps them alive [while hanging on] to certain aspects of their aquatic systems." This "story of the river" is, for him, germane to the enduring human conversation about constancy and change, stasis and flux.

"Letting go" and "hanging on" are invoked in the aptly titled **Hold Free River** of 2013. Its broad, central, head-like form— five feet tall—and overlapping

half circles at right give rise to fragile, nascent outgrowths that gingerly parallel the dominant branch. Wall reliefs are another often essayed format. Some, such as **Blue Line River** (2012) and **Nesting River** (2015), approach five feet in width and course along horizon lines from which jut numerous extensions: angled, bundled, highlighted in color as in the former; swaged, nested, and gold-tipped in the latter.

The meticulously detailed and subtly patinated bronze "branches" (ranging from mossy greens to variegated browns) of Erickson's river pieces are due in large part to his self-described "plein air" practice. Often harvesting branches from the meadows, forests, and beaches of a family retreat near Crystal Lake in northwestern Michigan, he builds a full-scale model out of doors—with twist ties!—that he subsequently

transports to his urban studio. There he casts, then seamlessly and invisibly welds, multiple lengths of bronze boughs—anywhere from eighteen to thirty-plus units in the largest works—to faithfully recreate his original design. This comprehensive expertise serves him well at the College for Creative Studies, where he teaches sculpture and oversees the foundry and exhibition services.

Interestingly, Erickson's portage to his current, aqueous-imbued bronzes opened with such bold and hunky steel objects as **Rolling Home** (1992) and **Beverly's Song** (1990). Both employ wheels, the first suggestive of a winged wheel that actually rolls, and the second indicative of some vaguely functional (or dysfunctional) artifact. Its wheel turns while the sphere spins, the curved, mini–Richard Serra steel plate scraping along in its wake. The branches

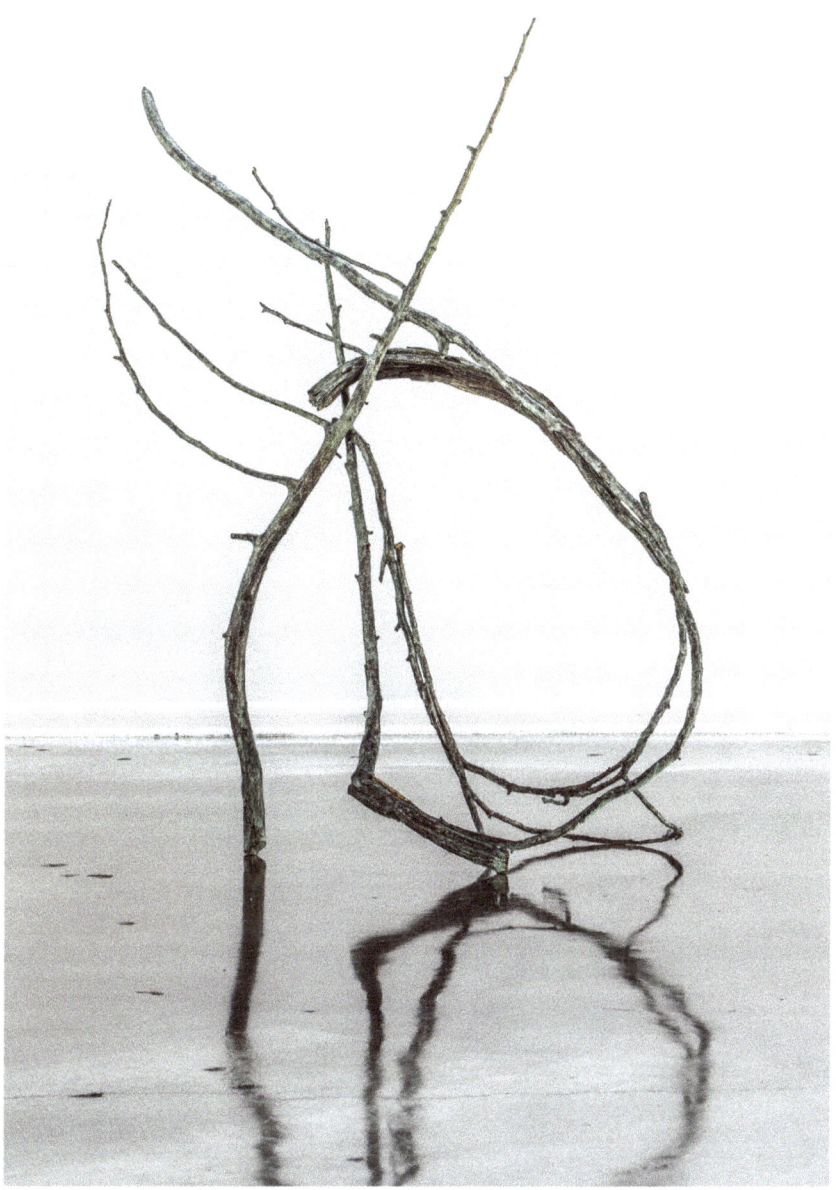

Betsie River II. 2015. Cast bronze, 65 x 52 x 32 in.

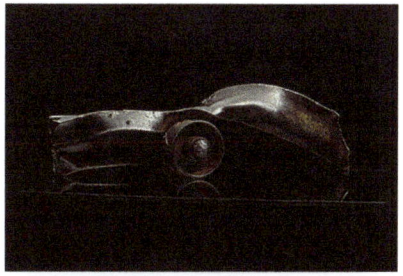
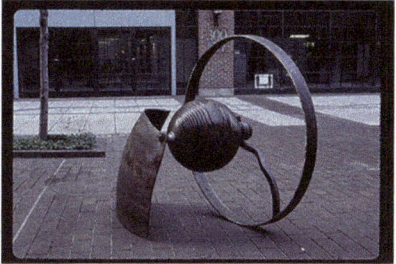

and arcs emerged in miniwoodland scenes like 2008's **Trading Post**, a wall-mounted relief of bronze and wood intended as a critique of the commercialization of national parks, historical sites, and highway rest stops (note the ubiquitous McDonald's arches).

Other early works featured ladders as prominent totems, an armature that appears in one of the earliest of Erickson's faux-branch sculptures: **Paradise Ascension** of 2009. Its title refers to the historically Black business district of Paradise Valley, largely demolished by the routing of I-75. Commissioned by the Virgil H. Carr Cultural Arts Center in Detroit, it resides in the foyer of the center to greet arriving guests. Fully six feet tall and nine feet in width, its thin, linear silhouette resembles both a striding animal and a domed structure. Two points of access draw the eye to its arching, aspirational form, the ladder to the right and the tall S-shaped branch on the left that extends above and beyond the arching "back" up into the sky via its searching, upthrust "neck." Boding renewal and hope for a city in transition, it embodies as well an early example of the aesthetic sensibility Erickson has continued to evolve.

DENNIS ALAN NAWROCKI,
APRIL 2016

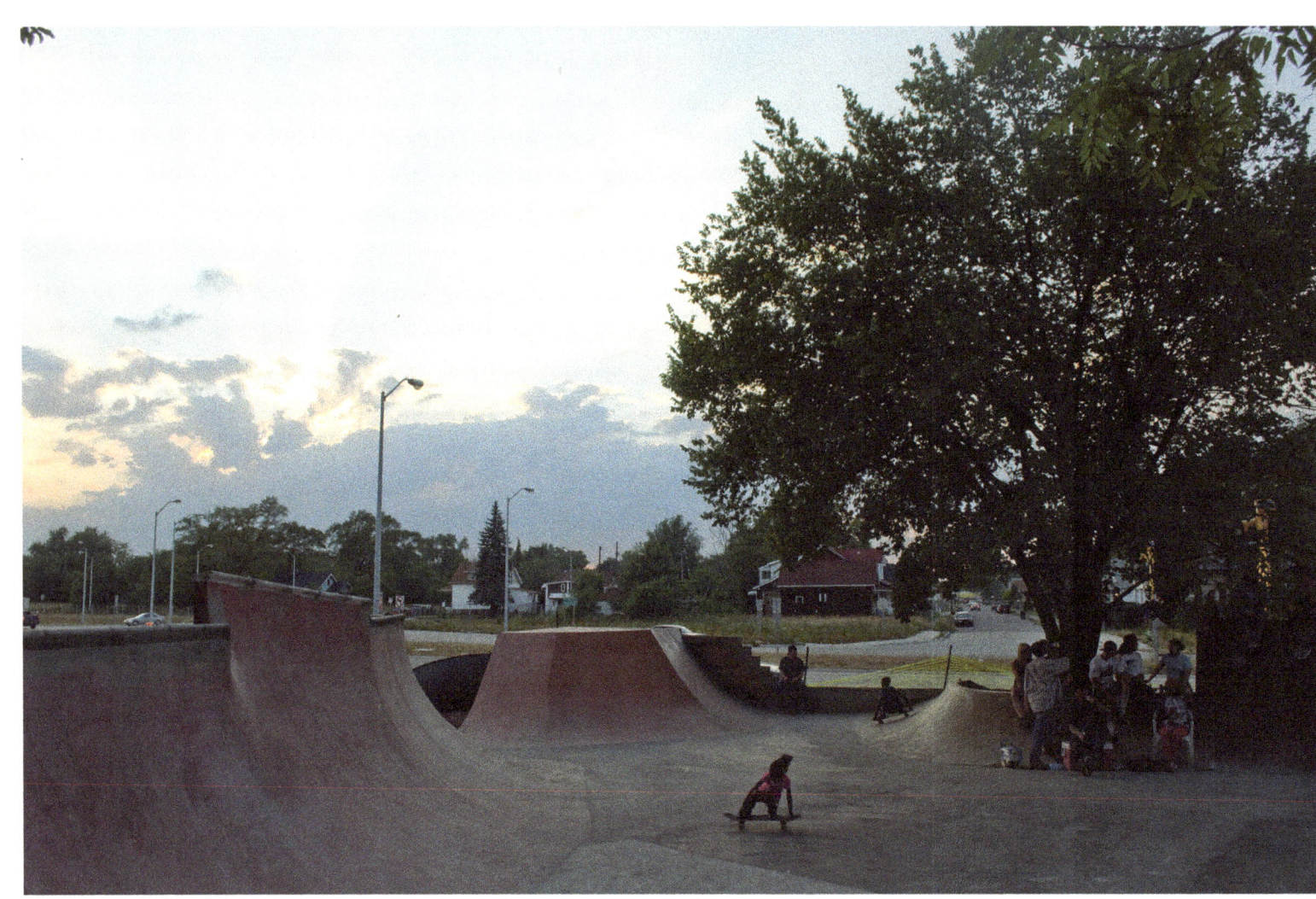

Ride It Sculpture Park. 2012–present. Photography by Mitch Cope.

Gina Reichert, born Cincinnati, OH, 1974
BArch, Tulane University; MArch,
Cranbrook Academy of Art
Lives in Detroit

Mitch Cope, born Detroit, 1973
BA, Center for Creative Studies; MFA,
Washington State University
Lives in Detroit

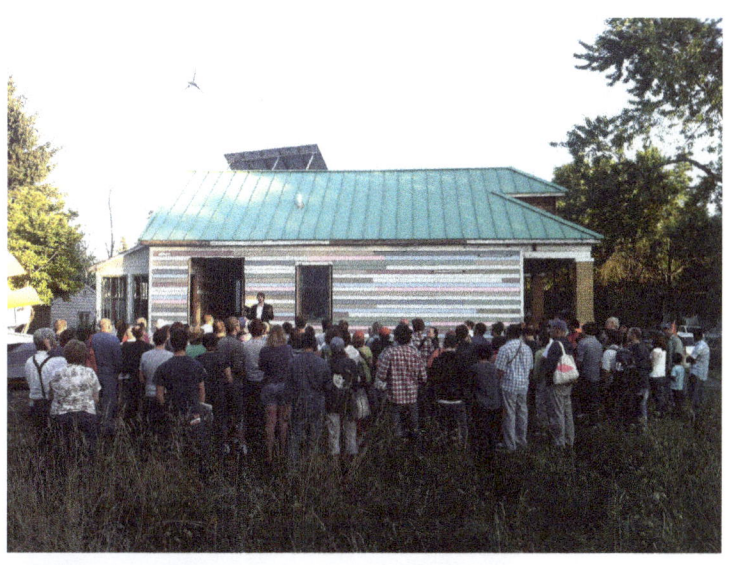

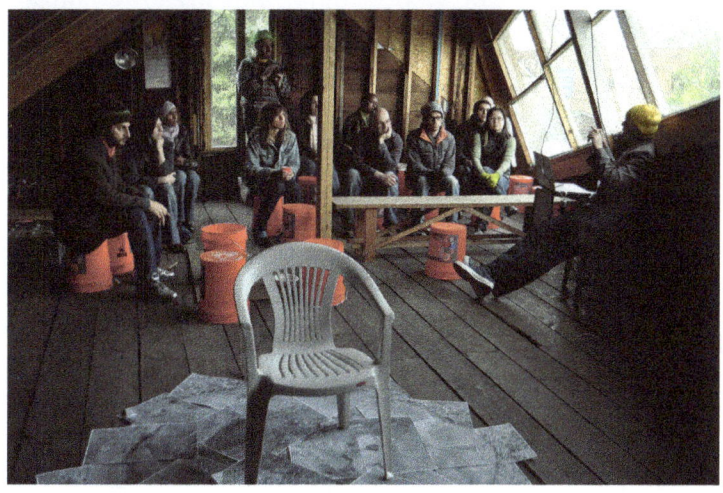

There are effectively two periods in the recent history of Detroit art: before and after the publication of "For Sale: The $100 House," the now infamous 2009 *New York Times* article that extolled the creative possibilities of minimally priced Detroit real estate by relating the experiences of Gina Reichert and Mitch Cope, the couple behind art/ architecture practice Design 99, and the artist-run, neighborhood-based nonprofit Power House Productions. After the article was published, the pair was deluged with interview requests, and with e-mails from artists around the world requesting information on how to move to Detroit and participate. They decided that for a period of two months they

(Top) The Power House (exterior). 2008–present. Photography by Gina Reichert.
(Bottom) The Power House (interior). 2008–present. Photography by Gina Reichert.

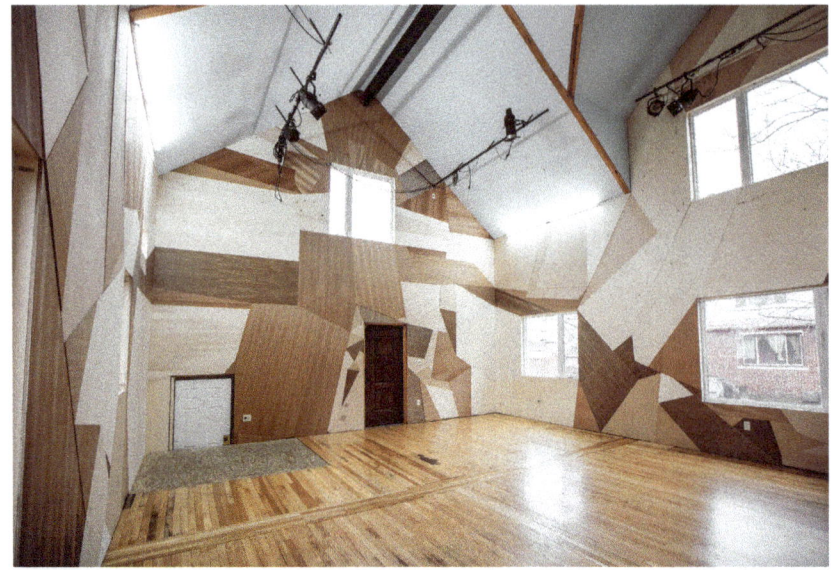

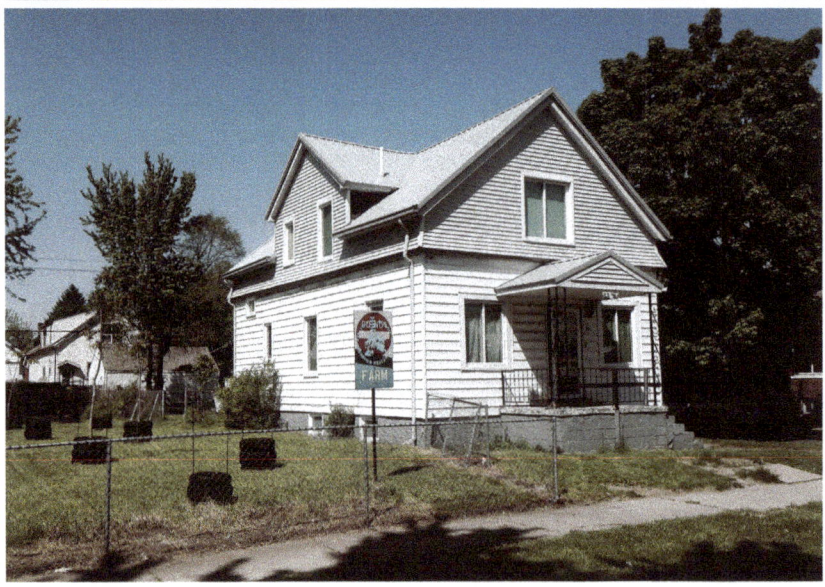

(Top) Play House (interior) (in collaboration with the Hinterlands).
2012–present. Photography by Michelle Gerard.
(Bottom) Play House (exterior) (in collaboration with the Hinterlands).
2012–present. Photography by Mitch Cope.

distinctive exterior paint scheme, and that was ultimately intended to service a small local grid through solar and wind energy. The title of the work was a statement of intent, the word "Power" referring to both the creation of renewable energy and also to a process of empowerment through highly localized acts of creative agency. If Reichert and Cope have a philosophy, it is expressed through this combination of tangible and symbolic objectives.

After *The Power House*, things moved quickly. In short order, local properties were repurposed into **Play House**, a space for performance-based work operated in partnership with The Hinterlands, *Sound House*, an experimental sound studio, and *Jar House*, an office, library, and local gathering space. This expansive project was the beneficiary of *Juxtapoz* magazine's fifteenth-anniversary auction, providing funds for working visits by notable artists such as Swoon that resulted in a significant collection of site-specific art throughout the properties. **Ride It Sculpture Park**, a neighborhood skate park, was begun in 2012, and the conversion of the *Squash House*—a small community space intended to

would try to answer every media approach they received. At the end of that period their lives were irreversibly changed, and if the truth be told, so was the narrative of Detroit art.

Ironically, their vision, to stabilize the Detroit neighborhood

they had recently moved to via a loose network of art/architectural interventions, was at that stage little more than an idea. The one component somewhat in place was *The Power House*, a compact wood-frame house typical of the area to which they had given a

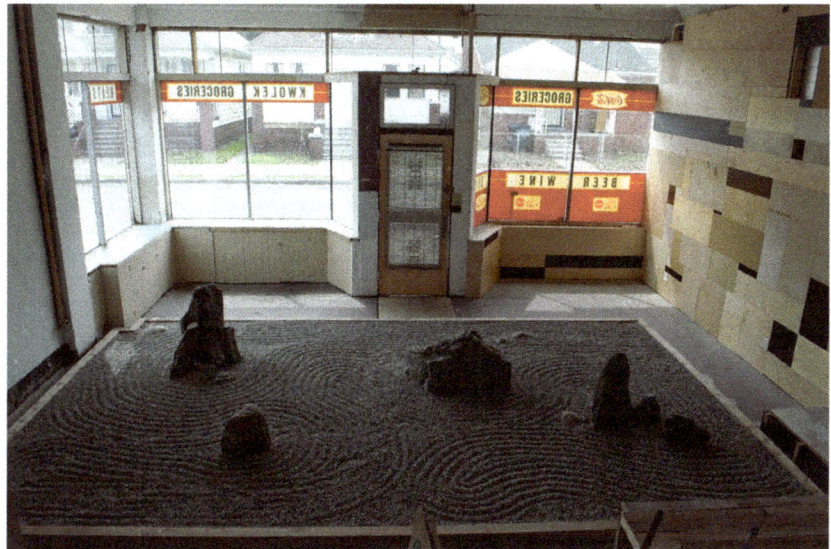

Corner Store. 2013. Rock garden installation at the home of the artists.

combine the playing of squash, the sport, and the growing of squash, the vegetable—in 2011. The result of all this effort was a remarkable collection of art/architecture projects, drawing both local and international visitors.

Alongside the development of the physical structures, another aspect of Reichert and Cope's vision began to evolve. The area already had a substantial, and stable, Bangladeshi population—it was part of the reason that the pair first purchased a home there. As word of the area spread, a significant number of artists started to purchase homes there, some collaborating directly with Reichert and Cope, others pursuing their own projects, yet others moving simply to become part of the local community. The publicity

that the area's artistic activity generated created a broader awareness of the neighborhood, and increasingly this formerly anonymous area became known as "Banglatown." Heavy support from philanthropic foundations allowed a number of neighborhood events and festivals to take place, attended by large and diverse audiences. The net result? According to Cope, the area's population is growing, and there is a steady demand for properties.

Ultimately, many of the questions that the couple's work raises are about agency and our ability to transform our surroundings. Charles Esche, the massively influential director of the Van Abbemuseum in Eindhoven, and an early collaborator with the pair, believes that they are

developing a "new kind of artistic agency," one that is "more modest, less openly artistic, crossing disciplines and often just about being in the world in this place and time." He may be right. But can an artistic project that has generated as much media interest as this ever again "just be"? To a certain extent, Reichert and Cope are victims of their own success. As Cope puts it, "We've only ever put out one press release, we've stopped answering requests for interviews, we've stopped publicizing events because we want to keep them to the neighborhood . . . but still they come." In the end, this too may serve Reichert and Cope's overarching project—of changing perceptions, both at the local level, and in the broader sense, of the role of the artist.

STEVE PANTON, MAY 2016

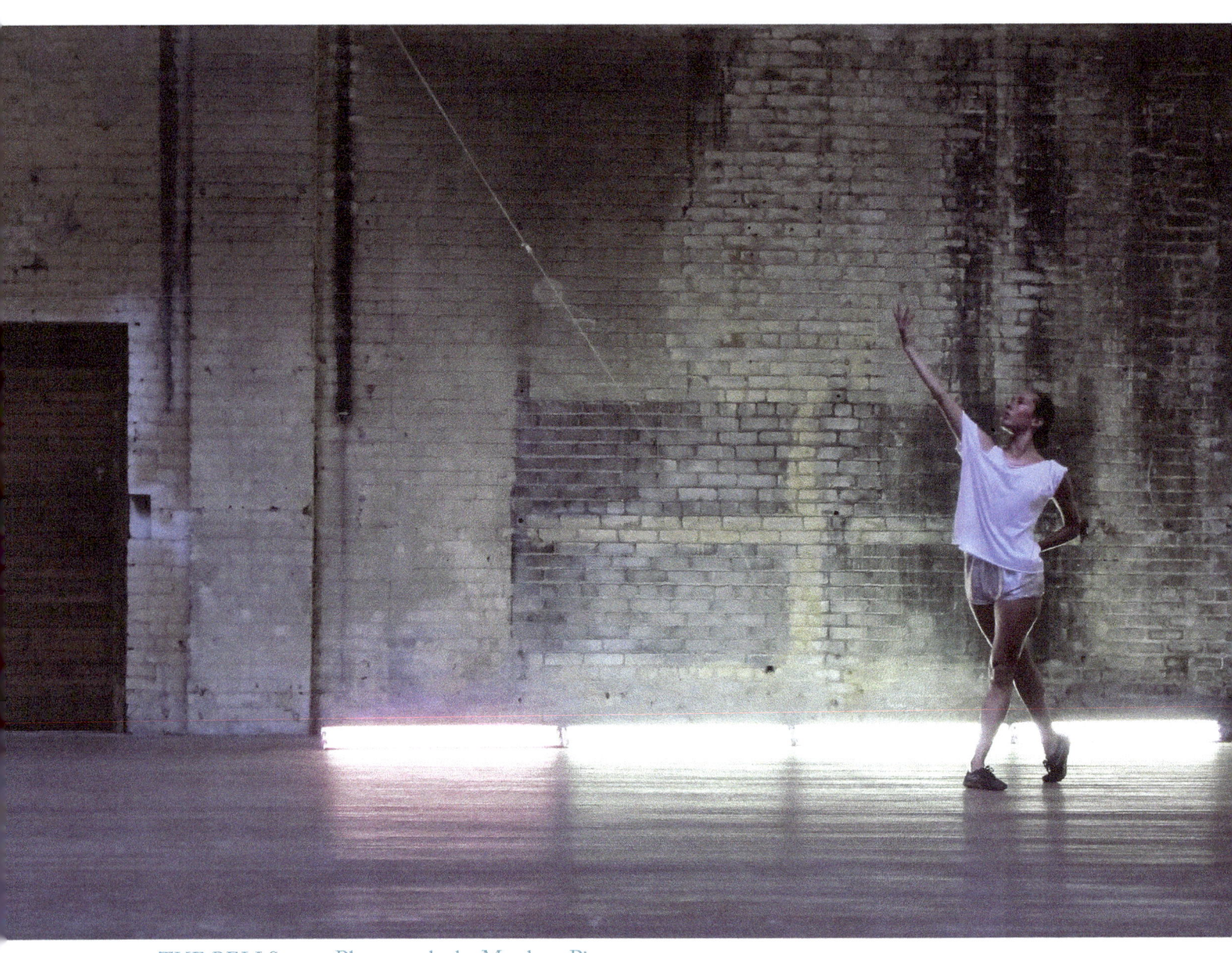

THE BELLS. 2012. Photography by Matthew Piper.

Born Sebastopol, CA, 1976
BA, University of California Santa
Cruz; MA and PhD (Performance
Studies), New York University
Lives in Detroit

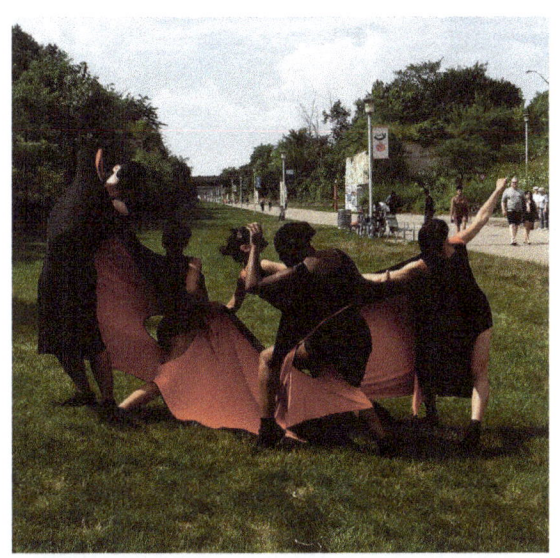

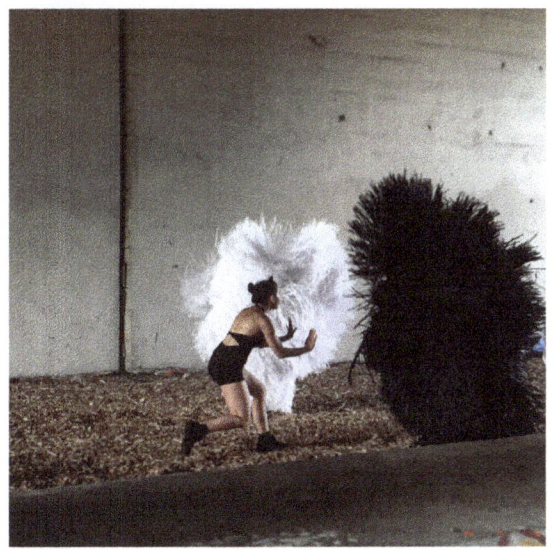

On a sunny Sunday afternoon last July, several hundred people crowded the Dequindre Cut, a popular recreation path in Detroit, to watch a dance. The performance, one of three public **dance labs** programmed to accompany *Here Hear*, the Cranbrook Art Museum's celebrated exhibition of Nick Cave soundsuits, included music by Frank Pahl and choreography by Biba Bell. There is no telling what, exactly, the audience expected. What they witnessed was a distributed dance, a decentered performance event, in which any vantage point along the Cut's long, linear footprint offered a different view of different groups of dancers, some of whom slinked by in sinuous silence, while others posed, elegant and remote, above the crowd. Others danced a

(Top) Nick Cave Dance Lab. 2015. Photography by Sarah Szurpicki. (Bottom) Nick Cave Dance Lab. 2015. Photography by Stephan Bobalik.

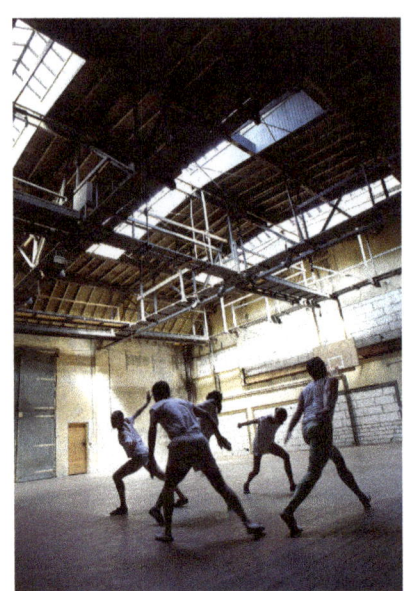

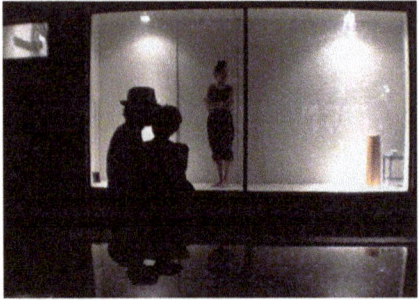

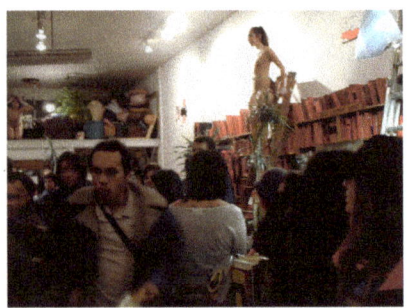

(Left) THE BELLS. 2012. Photography by Michelle Andonian.
(Middle) *Who Me House.* 2004.
(Right) Peacocks. 2005.

mannered duet involving the ritualistic exchange of their black or white soundsuit costumes, and the rest, by the end, were dancing in furious, ecstatic unison. When all was said and done, no one present had seen a complete dance, or the same dance. Everyone, however, had seen a dance by Biba Bell, an artist who specializes in the unexpected.

Because Bell is such an urgent, accomplished, and prolific dancer and choreographer, it is perhaps surprising to learn that at one time, she considered another career entirely. As an undergraduate at UC Santa Cruz in the late 1990s, Bell was studying glacial geology when she encountered a dance performance that completely altered her professional trajectory. She'd

grown up training in ballet, but ultimately just "didn't have the body" for a career as a ballerina, and so had largely moved on to science. Then she saw a performance by Mel Wong—a one-time member of the Merce Cunningham Company—which she recalls as sprawling, beautiful, and campy. At once deeply personal and tinged by science fiction, it involved dancers both nude and elaborately costumed, and took place both inside a dining hall and outside of it, on a hill leading down to the Pacific. "This," Bell remembers asking, "is *dance*?" In short order, she'd switched majors and begun studying under Wong, whose influence has proved profound.

As Wong's pupil, Bell is a direct descendent of Cunningham—in whose long, lithe shadow contemporary dance still, to some degree, labors—and she

has undoubtedly inherited the penchant for boundary blurring that is the legacy of her ancestor and his illustrious coterie (Cage, Johns, Rauschenberg). It is somehow incomplete to call Bell a dancer or choreographer, merely, as she has long worked within multidisciplinary artist communities. She is that rare choreographer who moves with ease between the typically demarcated territories of Art and Dance.

A formative period was her association with the tail end of the Mission School in San Francisco in the early 2000s, where a largely visual art scene concerned with amateurism, street art, and rawness of material had burgeoned after the first tech bubble burst. It was in this milieu that Bell staged her first solo work, *Who Me House* (2004), during which she occupied a storefront window for one hour every night

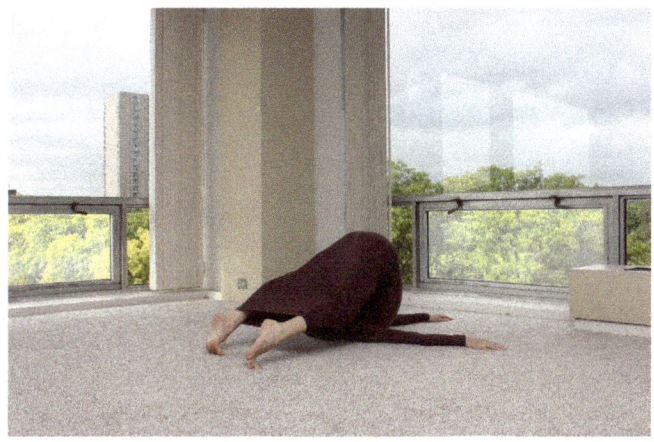

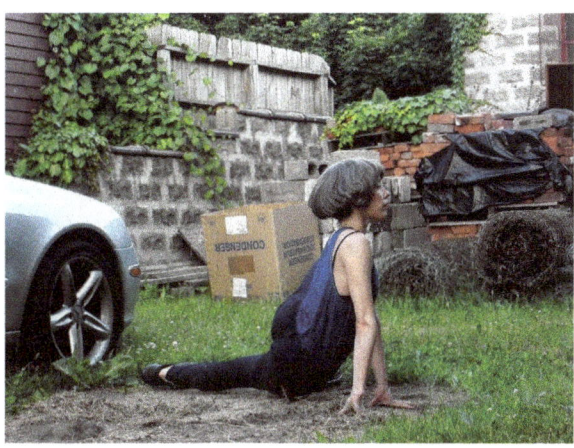

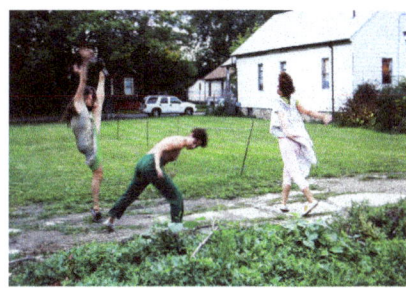

(Top, left) It Never Really Happened, Part 1. 2015. Photography by Christine Hucal.
(Top, right) (Cont.). 2014. Photography by Corrie Baldauf.
(Bottom, left) MGM Grand performing in Detroit. 2009.

for fifteen nights, performing various domestic acts. Shortly thereafter came **Peacocks** (2005), a dance for six that was staged in Adobe Books, a locus of the Mission School art community, and inspired by its colorful denizens.

Peacocks points to a fundamental concern of Bell's, something she calls dance's "promiscuity"—that is, its ability to happen anywhere, anytime that bodies are present. While she has worked in institutional contexts, audiences are more likely to witness her dancing outside of them, "in the world." She explored this infiltrating tendency with vigor during her time with **MGM Grand**, a performance trio she cofounded

in 2005 that toured original dances across the country, like a band, and performed "everywhere"—in "spas, backyards, gardens, people's homes, gift shops, bars, a llama barn, the beach. . . ."

It was with MGM Grand that Bell first came to Detroit, in 2008 and again in 2009. By 2011, the year MGM made and toured *Nut*, their last piece together, Bell had been living in Detroit for a year. Since then, she has brought her own inimitable choreography— charged and visceral, formidable and fractured—to a variety of Detroit spaces, including the Jam Handy Building (**THE BELLS**, 2012), a Corktown backyard (**(Cont.)**, 2014), her Lafayette Park

apartment (**It Never Really Happened, Part 1**, 2015), the Cranbrook Art Museum, MOCAD, and the DIA, among others. In Detroit, working within another diverse artist community, she has begun to excavate a new interest that foreshadows intriguing work to come: "What is the boundary between the highly trained concert dancer and everybody else just getting up and dancing?" she wonders. "There's an edge there, a periphery, that becomes an interesting pathway for choreography to happen."

MATTHEW PIPER, JUNE 2016

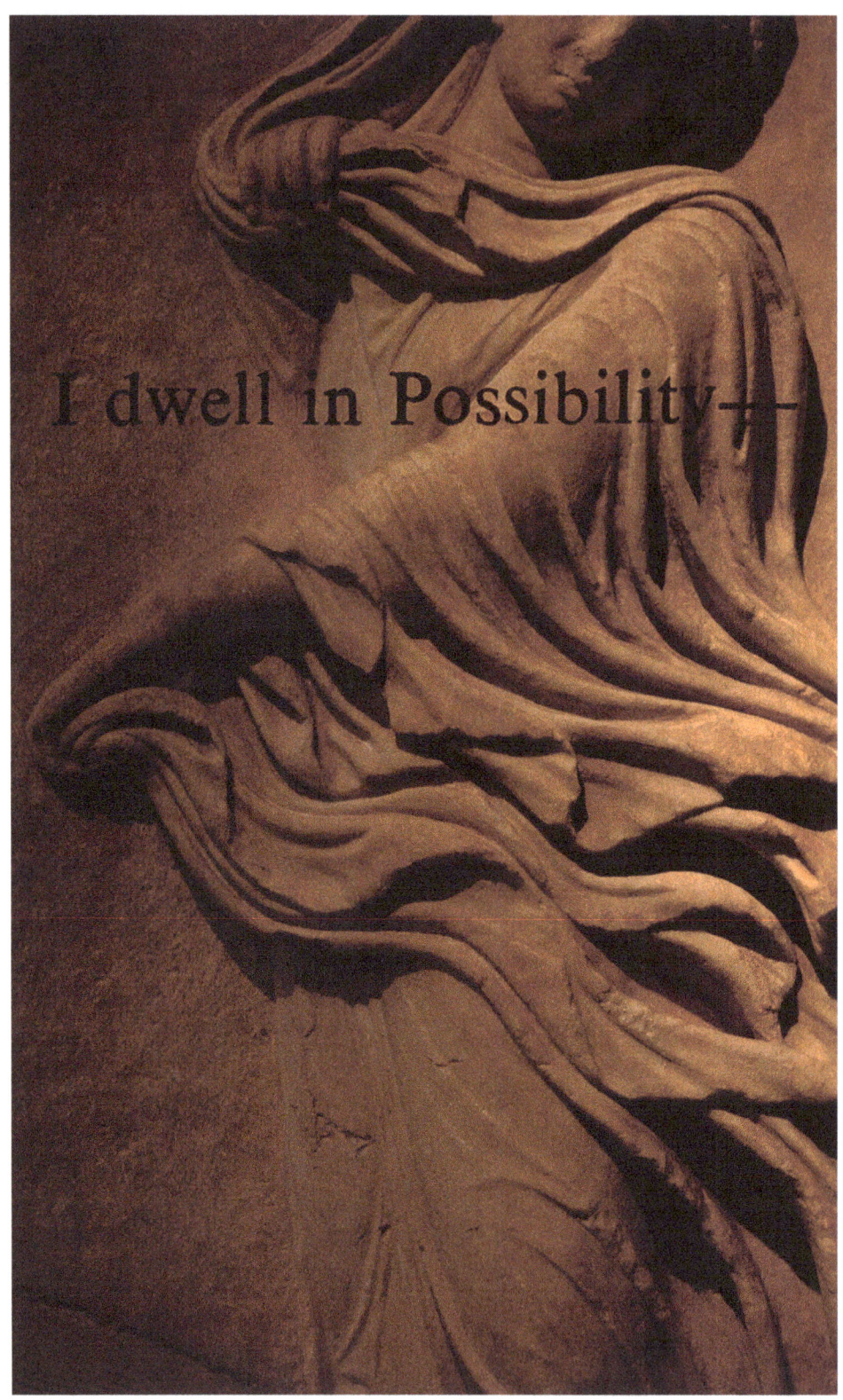

I dwell in Possibility— (Emily Dickinson). 2006/2008. Dye sublimation print on chiffon, 47 x 23 in.

Born New York, New York, 1952
BA, Beloit College, Wisconsin; BFA,
Minneapolis College of Art and Design;
MFA, Cranbrook Academy of Art
Lives in Royal Oak, Michigan

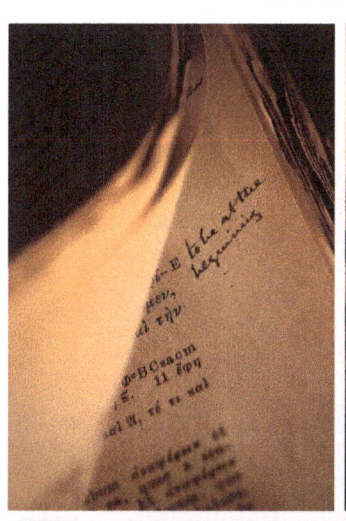
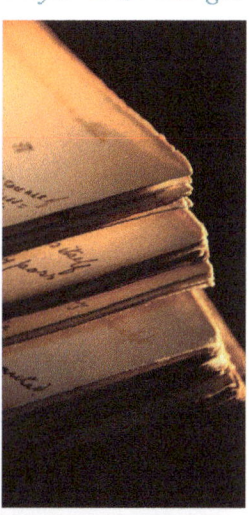
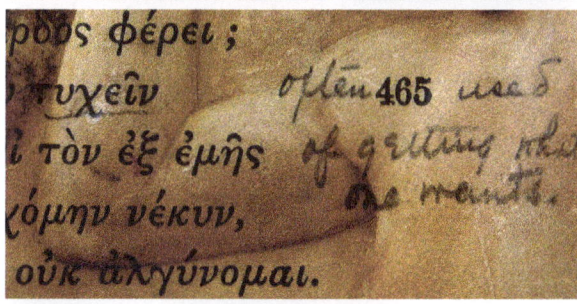
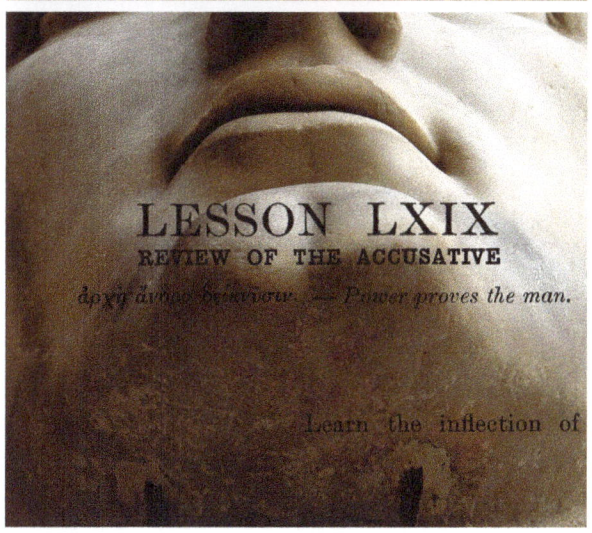

With a virtual wave of the hand, Andrea Eis beckons all seekers of enlightenment to traverse an enfilade of tall columns for a consultation with the **Oracle of Delphi**. In this 1992 installation, a large, impassive visage of the priestess awaits the curious visitor at the end of the processional way. Once in her presence, red vinyl letters affixed to the photograph announce: SHE SPOKE HER MIND. Simultaneously, the truth seeker notes that at her feet, embedded in rocks on the floor, another phrase claims: THEY HEARD HIS. This startling

(Top, left) To be at the beginning (Plato's *Phaedo*; Leipzig: B. G. Teubneri). 2016. Archival pigment print, 22 x 15 in.
(Top, right) Edge Light (Plato's *Phaedo*; Leipzig: B. G. Teubneri, 1875). 2015. Ink jet on fabric, 60 x 30 in.
(Middle) Getting what one wants (Sophocles, *Antigone;* American Book Co., 1891). 2008/2012. Archival pigment print, 20 x 40 in.
(Bottom) Power proves. 2006. Archival pigment print, 35 x 38 in.

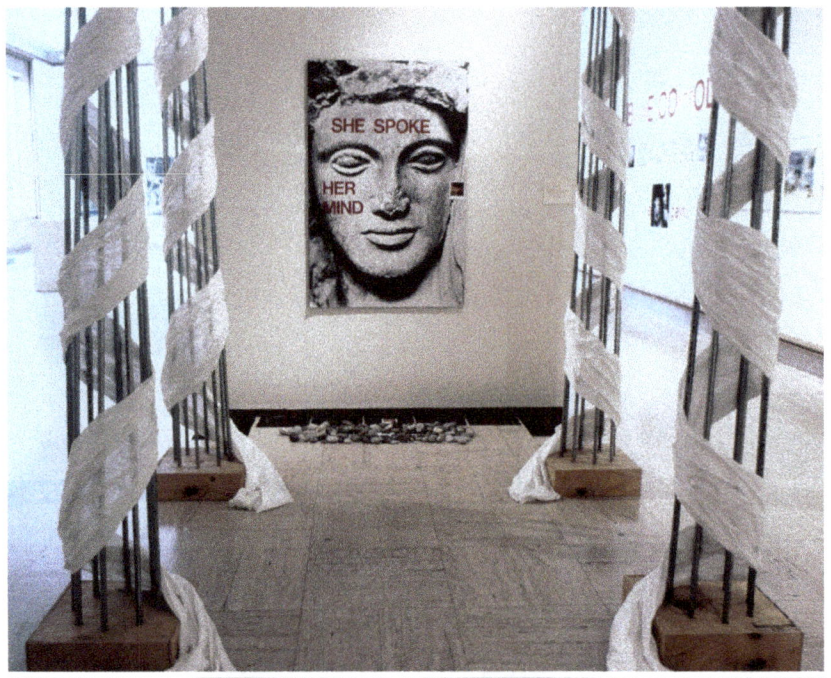

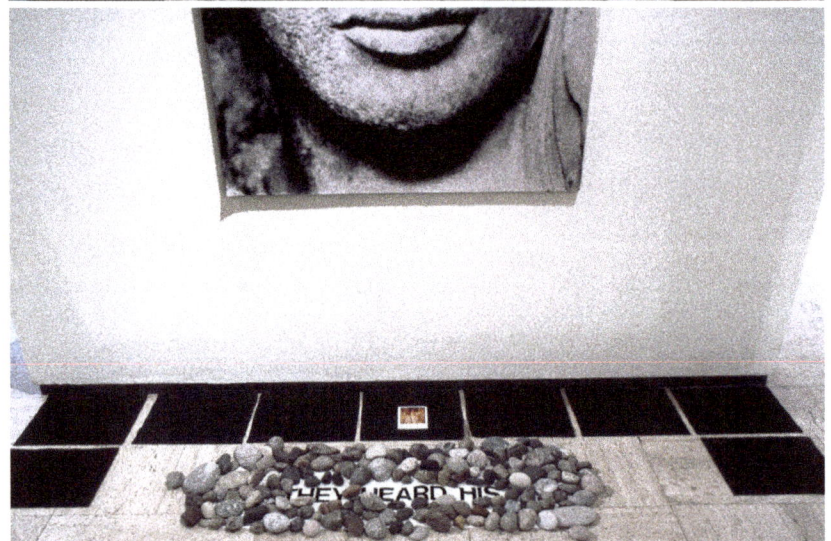

(Top) Oracle of Delphi. 1992. Silver print, SX70s, vinyl letters, wood, fabric, metal, stones, 12 x 6 x 8 ft. *(Bottom) Oracle of Delphi (detail). 1992. Silver print, SX70s, vinyl letters, wood, fabric, metal, stones, 12 x 6 x 8 ft.*

Oakland University in Rochester, Michigan, saw her move from art and art history teacher to professor of cinema studies in the department of English. Her art practice has ranged as well, from photography to film to installation to graphic design.

The publication of *Ancient Finds* in 1993, devoted to images in which Eis combined cropped photographs and laconic texts, set forth her revelatory explorations of consonances between ancient and modern mores. In **Persephone's Mother** (1993), one of several diptychs in the book, a mother, Demeter, is torn by the double bind of neither being able to release nor hold onto her daughter Persephone. The fragmentary figures, here and in subsequent series, were shot from Greek or Roman sculptures at sites stretching from Detroit and Chicago to numerous European settings.

In the *Selective Memory* series, begun in 2002, Eis lasers in on her marmoreal subjects, capturing telling details—a close-up of a smile, the arch of a foot, the motion of a hand. The preternaturally white hue of hand and drapery in **She left it all behind** (2003)

contradiction, like a wallop to the head, swiftly apprises the visitor of the phallocentric dynamic between genders—then and now. As Eis asserts: "From Antigone's battle with her conscience and her sense of moral duty, to Demeter's conflict over separation from her daughter, mythic people struggled with dilemmas we still encounter."

As an undergraduate, Eis focused on learning ancient Greek and translating the classics before segueing to photography, film, and video in the late seventies. Her long association (since 1983) with

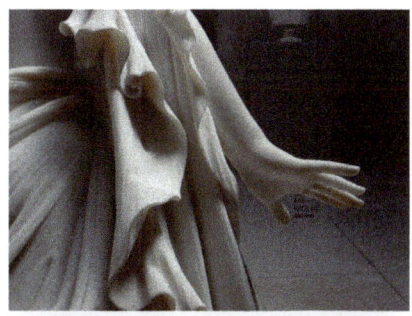

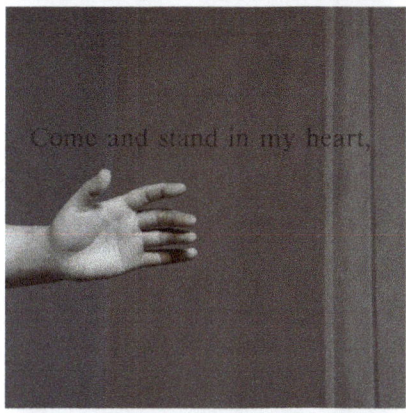

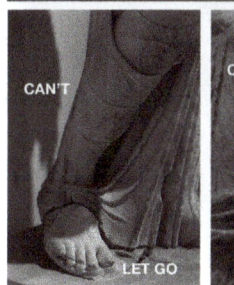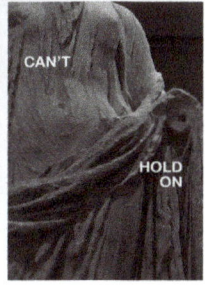

(Top) She left it all behind. 2003. Archival pigment print, 12 1/2 x 16 1/2 in.
(Middle) Stand (Eudora Welty). 2006. Archival pigment print, 17 x 17 in.
(Bottom) Persephone's Mother. 1993. Silver gelatin print, 16 x 20 in.

captures the decisive, dismissive gesture of a person's hand. Perhaps one thinks of Lot's wife, or Ibsen's protagonists Hedda and Nora who so decisively take charge of their destinies by play's end.

Writers also wend their way into Eis's oeuvre in 2006, among them Emily Dickinson, D. H. Lawrence, and Par Lagerkvist. Her *I dwell in possibility—* (2006/2008) links Dickinson's poem about the heady, wide-ranging possibilities of poetry with the flowing, fluid drapery of a chiton-clad woman. Printed on chiffon, the warm, burnt-orange hue attests to the boundless fervor of inspiration. Conversely, the stark simplicity and pale-gray palette of *Stand* (2006) poignantly highlight a welcoming, open-palmed, androgynous hand seeking emotional attachment.

Words, in frame-filling compositions, emerged in two subsequent series: *Marginalia* (initiated 2008) and *Greek Grammar* (begun 2006). The former originated when Eis unearthed a bevy of early twentieth-century tomes replete with marginal notations by Meta Glass, classicist and long-time college president. Here Eis could layer Greek text, notations by Glass, sculptural details, and her own thematic embrace of human connection across centuries. In *Getting what one wants* (2008/2012), Glass's handwritten note, appended to Sophocles's *Antigone*, is superimposed across the marble bicep of a muscular male figure. Alpha

arrogance figures in the *Greek Grammar* compositions as well: *Power proves* (2006), a sizable print (thirty-five by thirty-eight inches), associates the accusative case with the imposing, colossal head of emperor Constantine.

Recently, Eis has embarked on a cycle, titled *Palpable Knowledge* (2015), which might be described as images of books qua books. These sensual, dramatically lit compositions home in on the bindings, edges, and pages of various texts collected by the artist. While print, and marginalia, may be discernible in some of them, it is BOOK as resplendent icon that is foregrounded, its significance heightened by amplified proportions and golden, Rembrandt-like illumination, as in the five-foot-tall *Edge Light* (2015). The title of a modestly scaled example from the series, *To be at the beginning* (2016), signals Eis's perennial, anticipatory thrill upon cracking open a new book, however aged it may be. Or, especially because, despite its antiquity, it pulses with reverberations for contemporary life.

DENNIS ALAN NAWROCKI,
JUNE 2016

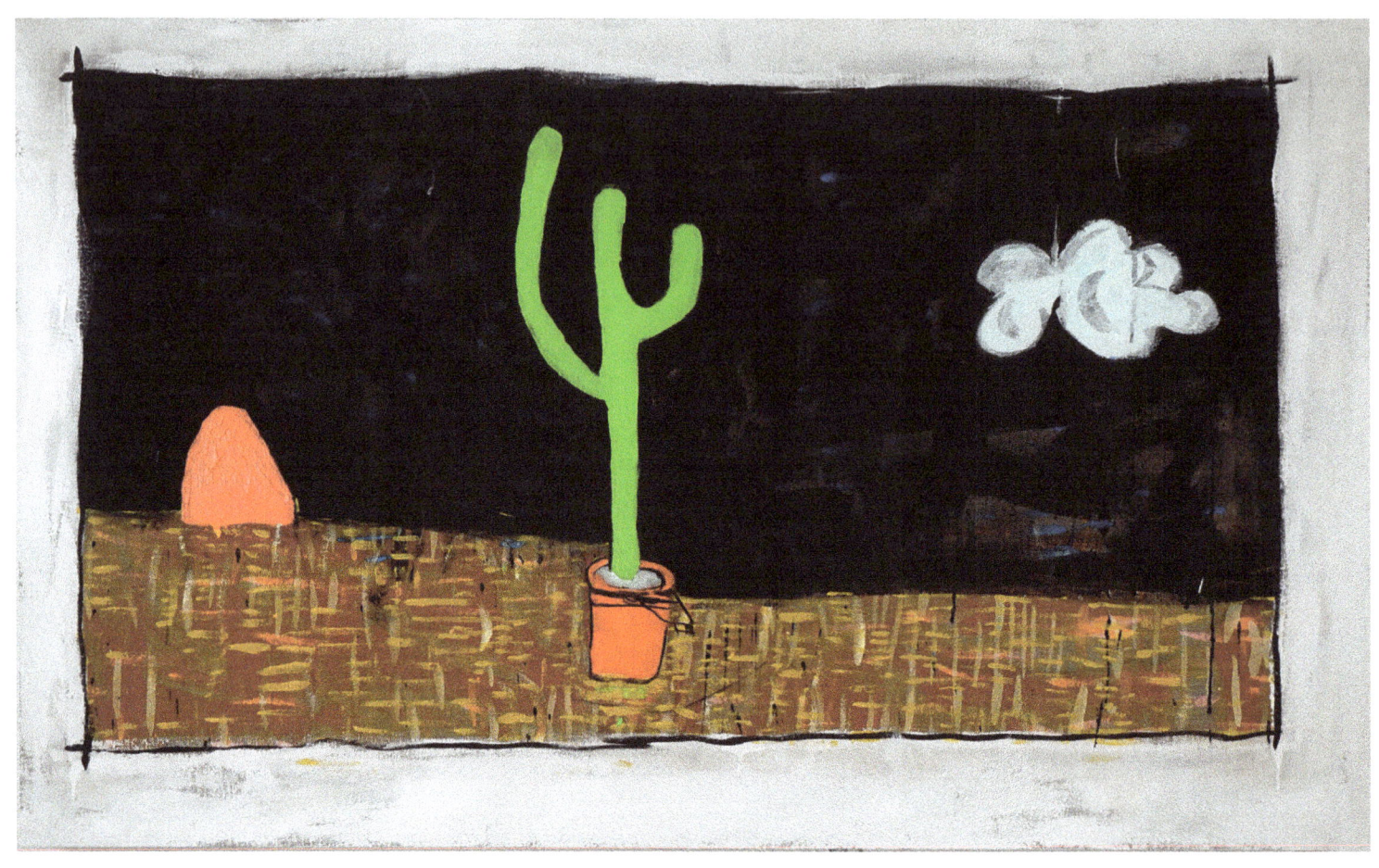

Lonesome Nights. 2016. Acrylic, crayon, ink on raw linen, 56 1/2 x 35 in.

55 // ALEX BUZZALINI

Born Warren, Michigan, 1990
BFA, Wayne State University
Lives in Hamtramck, MI

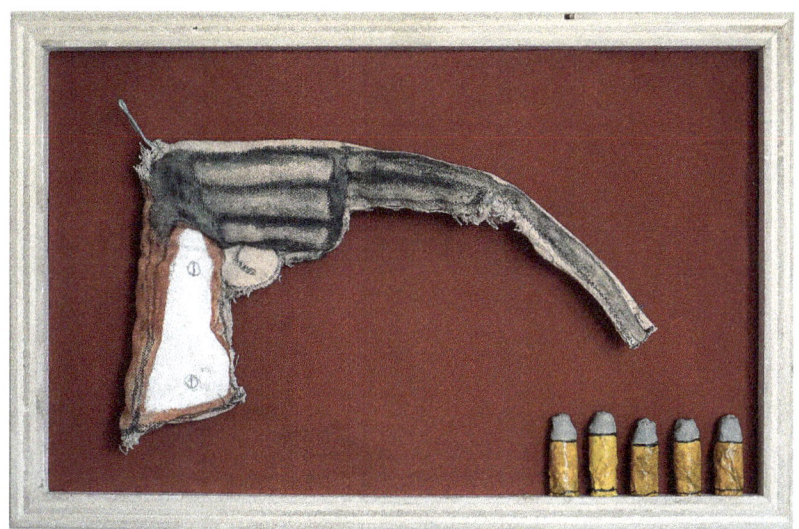

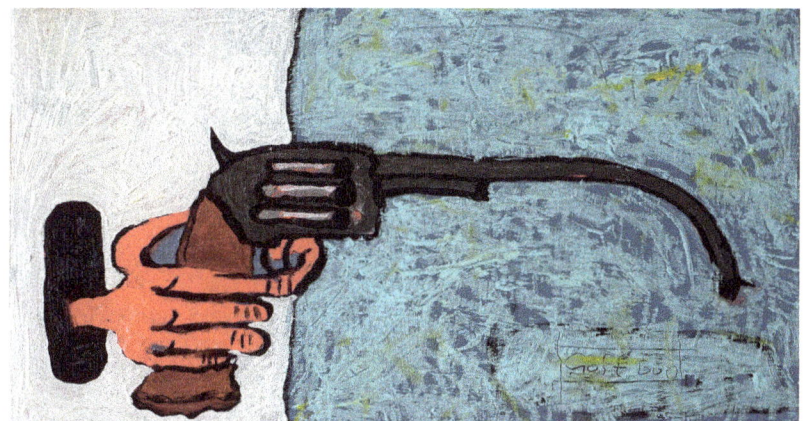

Alex Buzzalini stands in the carpeted living room/art studio of his Hamtramck flat. The walls are covered with his paintings, some on paper, some on canvas. Shelves hold an array of his sculptural work: a pointy **Red Cowboy Boot** (2015) made of duct tape, a brick transformed into a fruitcake. With a can of Stroh's in his hand, he explains that to get a really good look at anything, he has to back up into the other room. He keeps an old Herman Miller chair in the entry hall, an ashtray as well, and a book he's been reading about the American West, all for the purpose of looking and contemplating.

Buzzalini started as a printmaker, but without access to a press, he turned to painting. "This

(Top) Soft Gun. 2015. Canvas, acrylic, metal wire, velvet, water putty, 17 1/2 x 11 1/2 x 3 in.
(Bottom) Soft Gun. 2016. Oil paint on wood, 8 x 16 in.

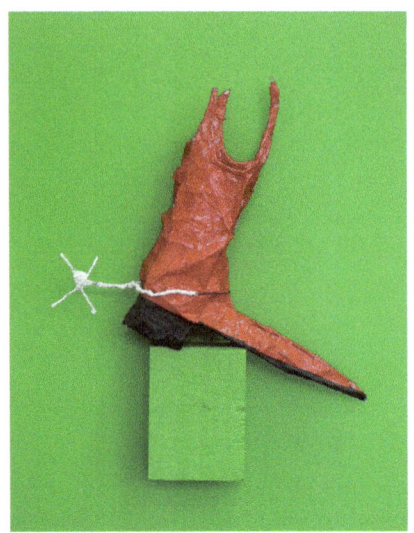

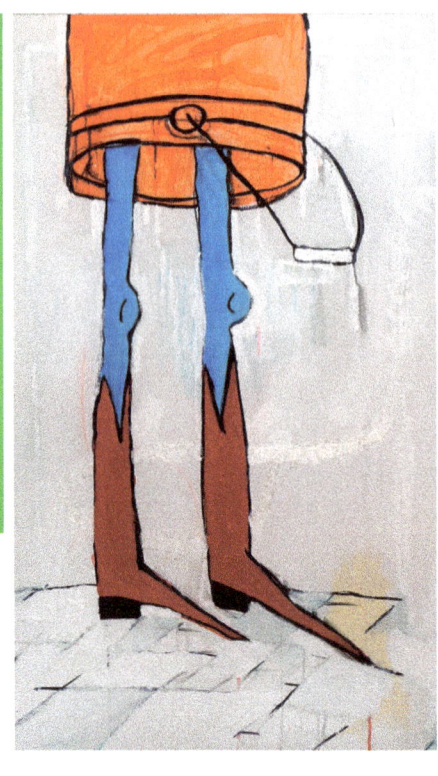

(Left) Red Cowboy Boot. 2015. Wire, duct tape, gaffer's tape, white oak, 20 x 17 x 4 in.
(Right) Cowboy John. 2016. Acrylic, ink, crayon on canvas, 26 x 42 in.

is just one quick hit," he says of his current piece, ***Lonesome Nights*** (2016). The canvas depicts a saguaro cactus that's planted in an orange Home Depot bucket, a brushy blue sky, a pink teepee, and a puffy cloud that dangles from a rope. In this, like many of his Western scenes, the elements of staging are exposed. The rope that the cloud hangs from suggests that it's not just a watery mist, but that it's actually heavy and fake. The rest of the elements feel like they might be stage props too.

"One time," Buzzalini says, "I was hiking with my uncle in the Colorado mountains and he tells me to look at this huge rock that we were passing. So I

walked around to the other side and see there's all this exposed chicken wire and you can see where the plaster had broken off. Apparently the boulder was constructed for a scene in a John Wayne movie. I find that idea really kind of interesting. They're in the middle of Colorado and surrounded by boulders, but that's not good enough. They have to construct their own. They can't just use the natural landscape. It has to be fabricated."

Buzzalini is well read. He produces this quote by author Larry McMurtry: "For the lies about the West are more powerful than the truth about the West—so much more powerful that, in a sense,

lies about the West are the truths about the West—the West, at least, of the imagination." Buzzalini continues: "So what is fabricated and what is told becomes more true over time than what actually happened. And what actually happened doesn't always really matter." So maybe rocks are not rocks. Cacti might be molded from plaster and shipped in by truck in concrete-filled buckets. The heroes of the American West, the cowboys, might not be horse-riding, Marlboro-smoking, masculine go-getters, but might just wear red boots made of duct tape and carry bent guns, with broken bullets. These might just be men with no mettle whatsoever. That's at least how Buzzalini depicts them, as a sorry lot of failures in fake landscape where even the clouds hang from rope—for example, ***Cowboy John*** (2016).

Make no mistake, Buzzalini is not mocking the idea of the West or the cowboy. He's earnest about his disillusionment. One of Buzzalini's most striking pieces is ***Soft Gun*** (2015). Cut from canvas in the shape of a long-barrel revolver, it's loosely packed with poly-fill, then hand-sewn with metal wire and painted. Its eight-inch muzzle sports a

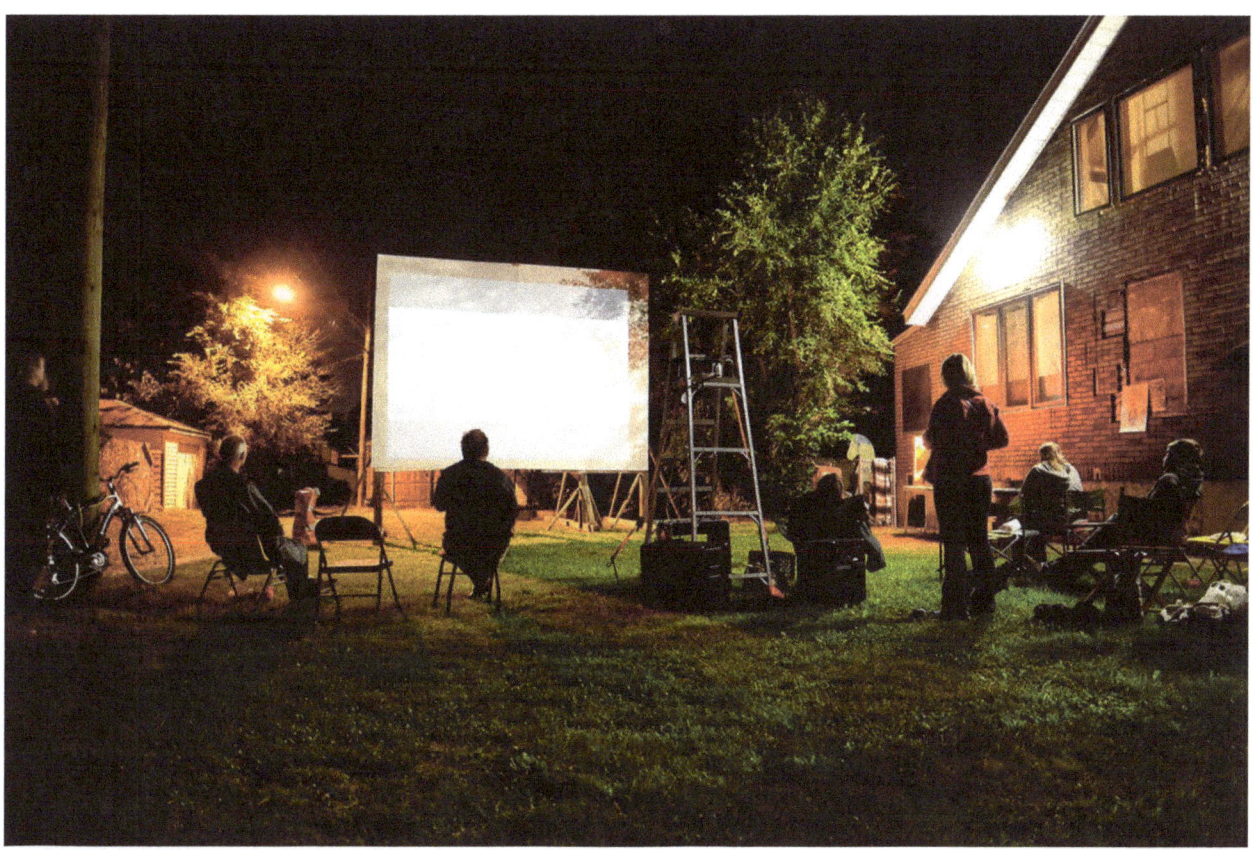

Ride'n Movie. 2014. Photography by Alex Tsocanos.

pathetic droop. It comes with six oversize bullets cast in water putty. The gun is held loosely in a frame with high sides. More than anything, *Soft Gun* speaks of masculine failure. It can fire no bullets. In the event of a bank robbery, *Soft Gun* will not save the day, nor will it force anyone to do anything. "Stick 'em up" is not a phrase associated with this sort of limpness. It is only a mechanism of comic disappointment and masculine embarrassment.

Besides paintings and sculptures, Buzzalini invented the **Ride 'n Movie** (2014). The project is a collaboration with his roommate, artist Matt Hunt. Disappointed that there is no movie theater in Hamtramck, they decided to build their own screen in an empty lot on the north side of town and started showing movies. "We tried to create something uniquely Hamtramck but with a cowboy spin. So the idea was, you ride up on your bike. There's always popcorn and beer. And we watch my favorite cowboy films." Ride 'n Movie had a two-night showing at last year's Porous Borders festival. "One night we showed *The Good, the Bad, and the Ugly*, the other night we showed a Czecho-slovakian film, *Lemonade Joe*, which was a spoof on the silent film Western. People loved it."

STEVE HUGHES, JULY 2016

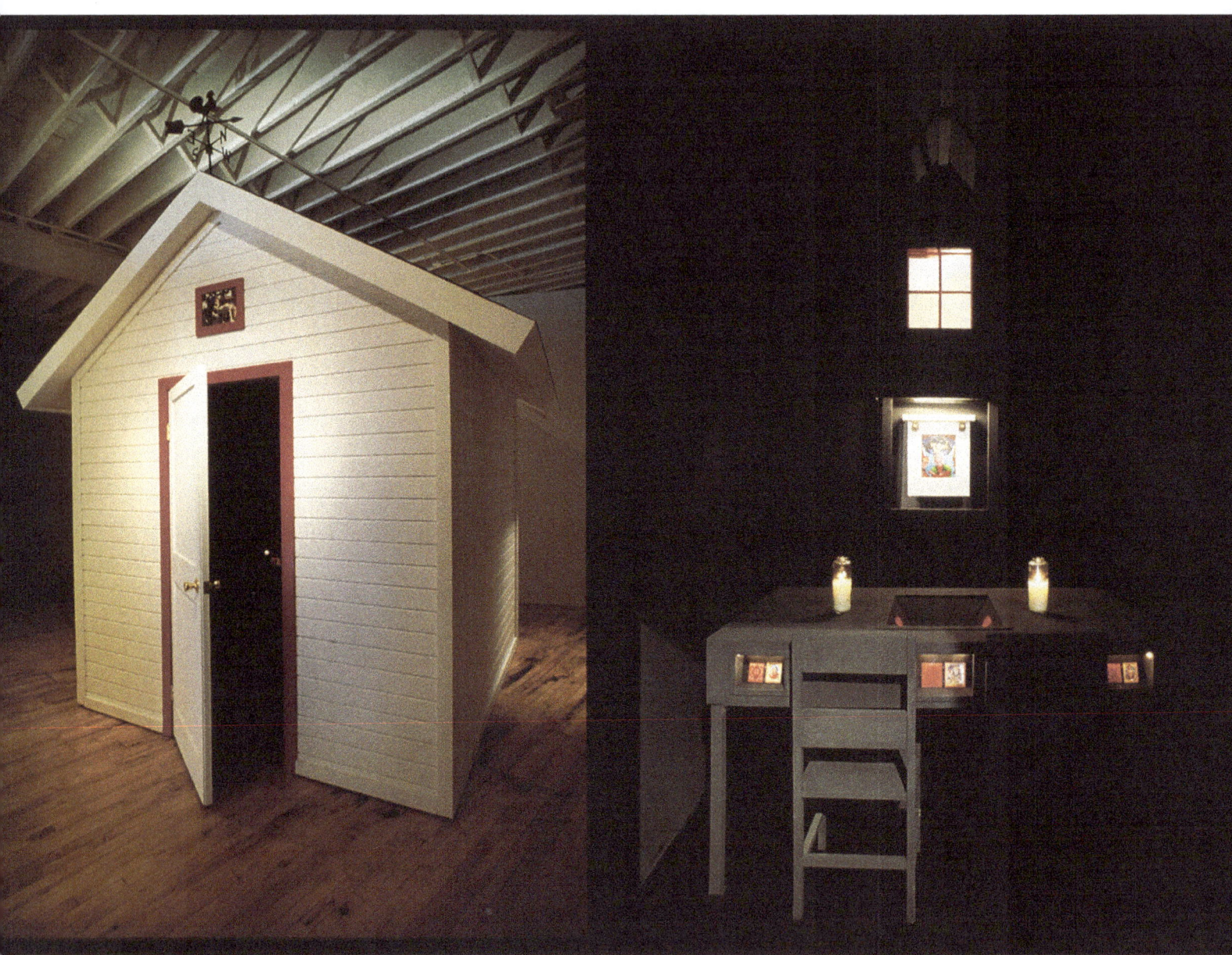

Little White House, Revolution—A Gallery Project. 1993. Wood, shingles, paint, glass, lights, 11 x 8 x 9 ft.

56 // CARL DEMEULENAERE

Born Detroit, 1956
BFA, Wayne State University
Lives in Grosse Pointe, Michigan

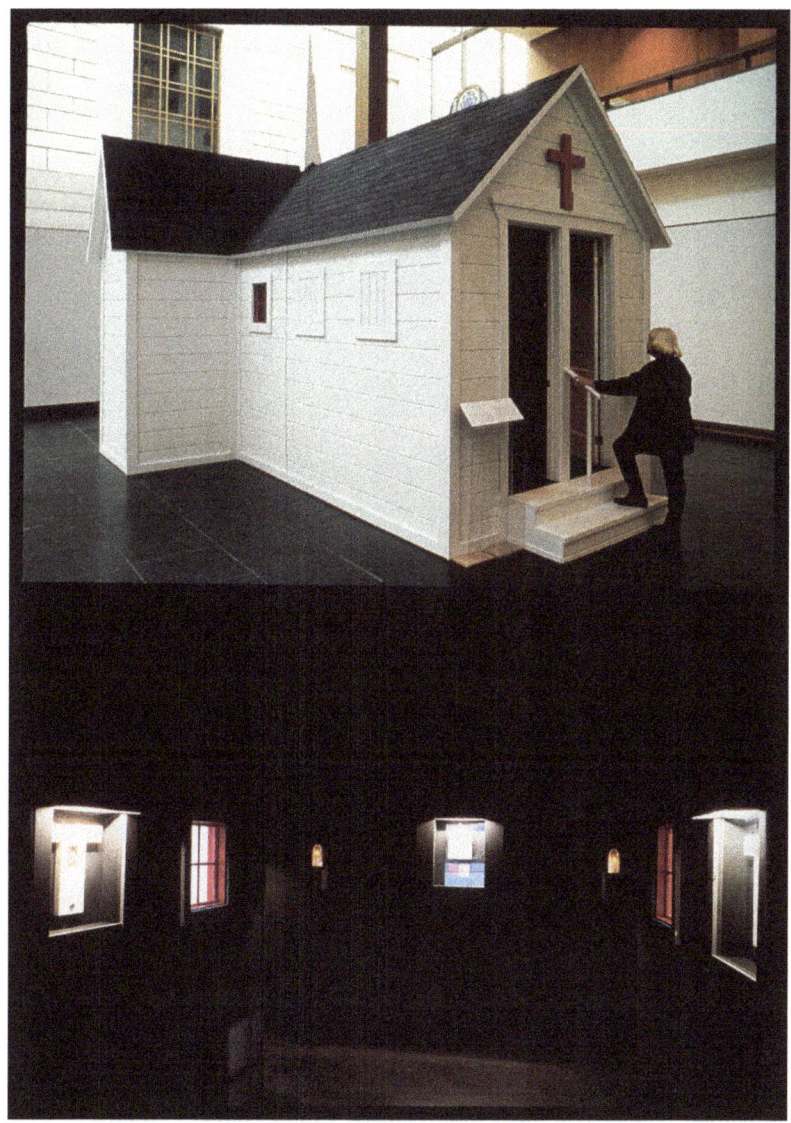

To understand Carl Demeulenaere, it is best to approach his art from the perspective of technique, but also to remain conscious that the resulting work originates from a place of deep-rooted anger. Demeulenaere sets out to seduce you with color and craft. He sees himself as a "contemporary pre-Raphaelite," seeking to emulate the nineteenth-century English "brotherhood," who themselves sought a return to the detail and intense coloring of fifteenth-century Italian art. The pre-Raphaelites famously created vibrant colors by applying successive thin layers of bright paint. Demeulenaere does something similar, except he uses a self-developed process of meticulously applying tiny marks with a sequence of colored pencils. It is painstaking work, performed

Sanctuary, Detroit Institute of Arts. 1993. Wood, shingles, paint, glass, lights, 18 x 16 x 16 ft.

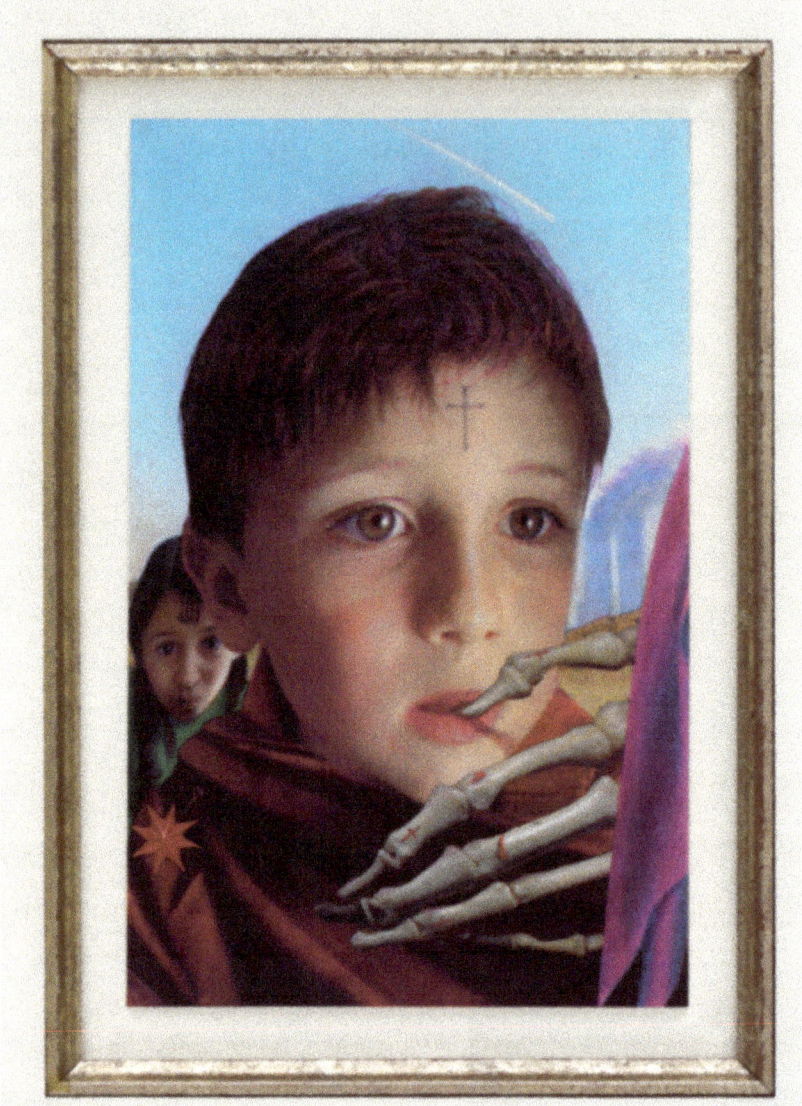

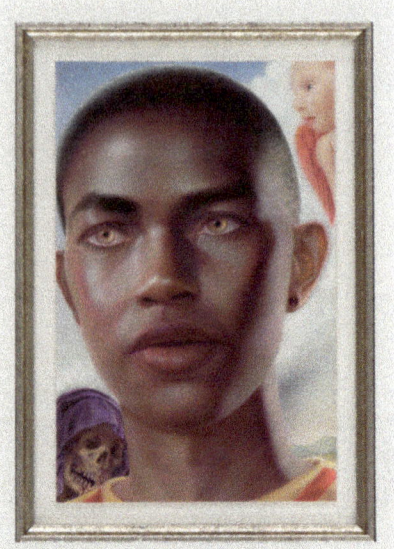

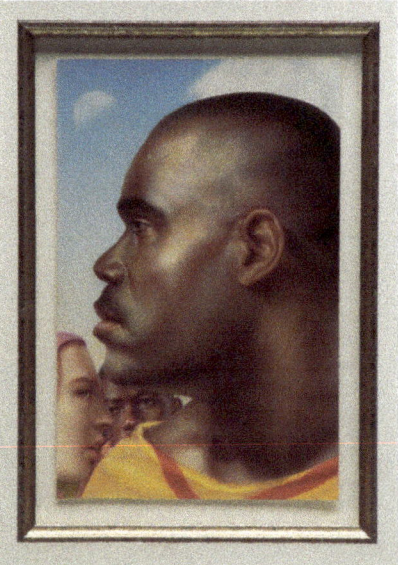

(Left) Bistre and Ash and a Boy, part of *Arcada Triptych* (left side). 2010–13. Colored pencil, linen paper, blood, 5 1/2 x 3 1/2 in.
(Top, right) Witch, Ambers, Garnet, part of *Arcada Triptych* (middle). 2010–13. Colored pencil, garnet, 5 1/2 x 3 1/2 in.
(Bottom, right) Requiem Prayer for a Muslim, part of *Arcada Triptych* (right side). 2010–13. Colored pencil, 5 1/2 x 3 1/2 in.

under a consistent incandescent light, and on surfaces that are often smaller than the size of a postcard. By using pencil, rather than paint, Demeulenaere greatly increases the effort involved but achieves a unique effect that pulls viewers in while simultaneously keeping them slightly off balance. Crucially, Demeulenaere also believes that artworks are stronger when the "heaviness" of their subject matter is reflected in the labor involved.

Demeulenaere sees his drawings, paintings, and installation work as addressing conflicts that arise from history, religion, sexuality, race, and prejudice. His formative years were not easy. As he puts it, "Growing up a

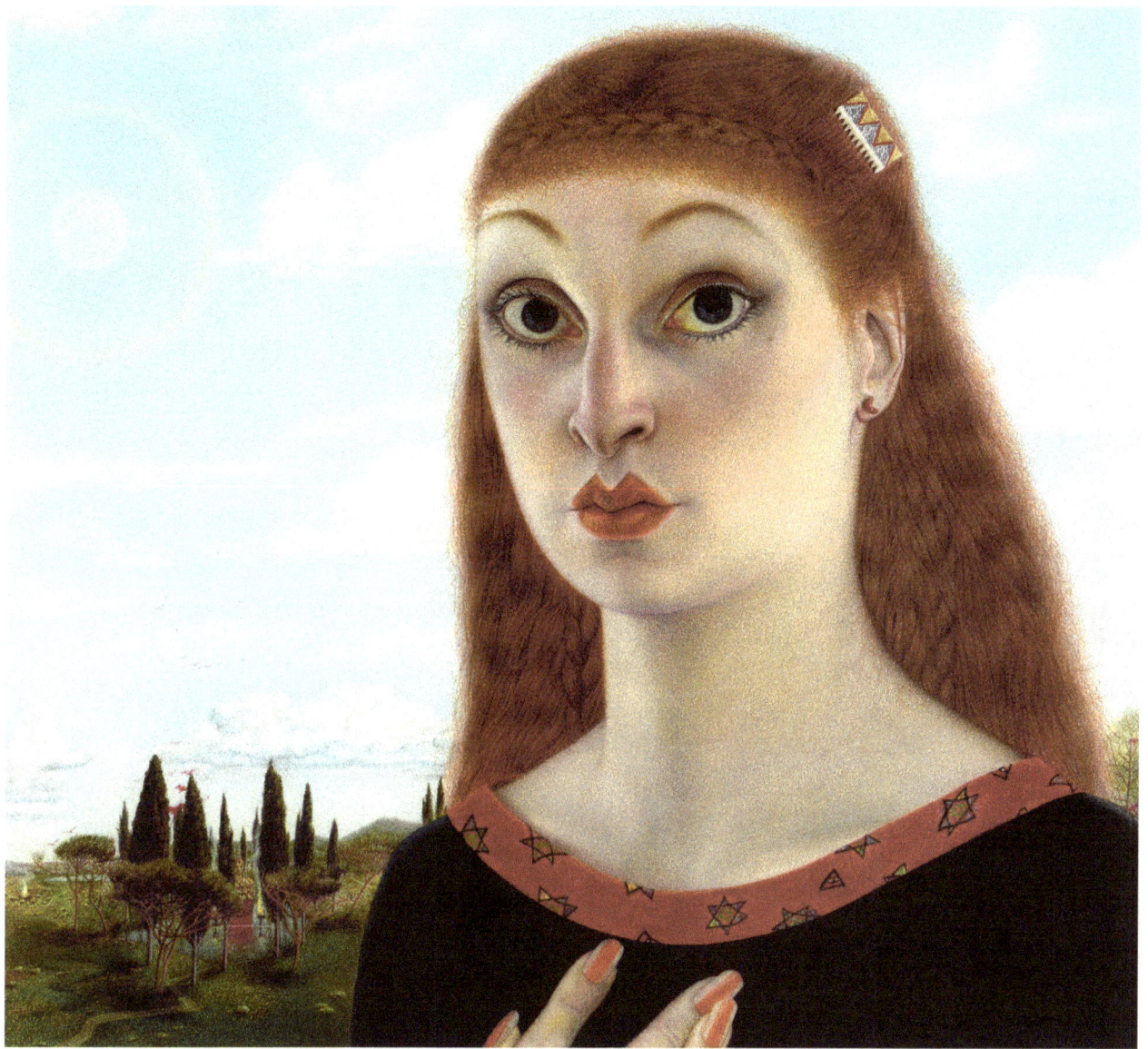

The Past in Myth. 1980. Colored pencil, acrylic, gold and aluminum leaf, 8 x 9 x 1/8 in.

gay Catholic in a racially mixed, eastside Detroit neighborhood, my schoolbooks negated homosexuality, my church prayed to heal me, acting on sexual impulse condemned me, and prejudice was directed toward me. I was often bullied." Demeulenaere also talks about a dark period between 1980 and 1987, when a series of personal crises led him to psychiatric help and regression therapy. In 1987, he started coming out to friends, and in 1989, he came out to his parents, a watershed moment. The following years were hugely productive and resulted in major installations, Demeulenaere's first openly gay-themed works, and a growing politicization as he attended increasing numbers

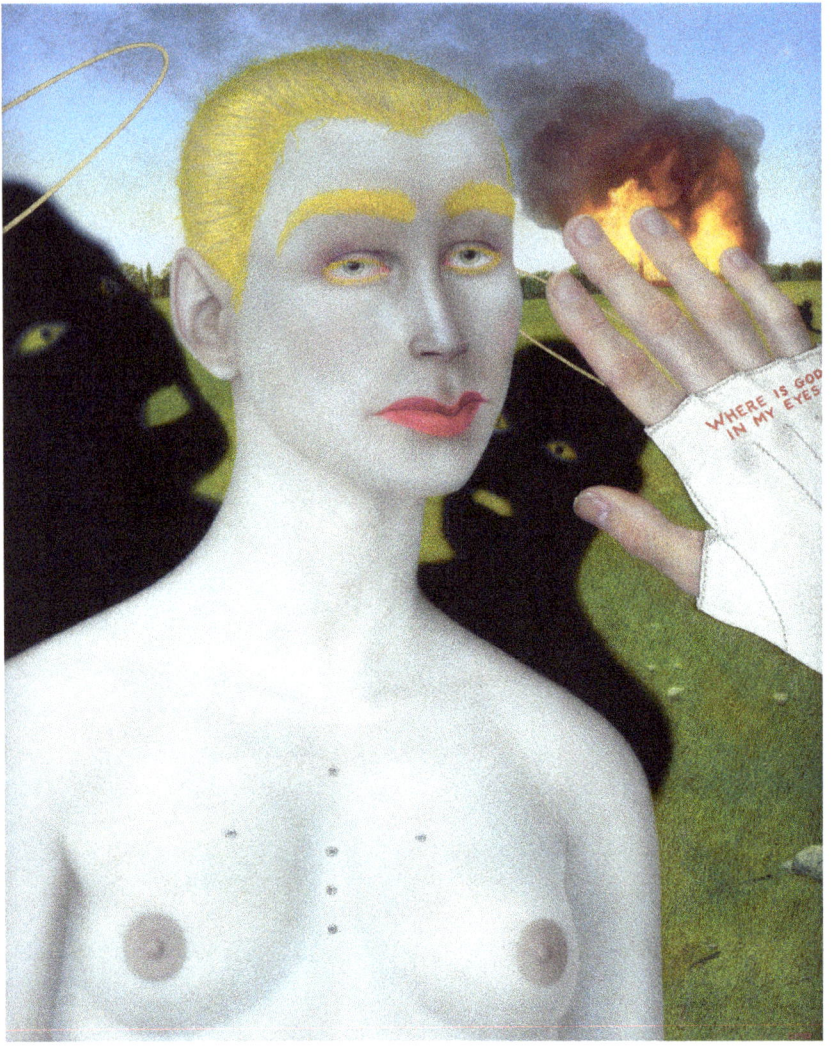

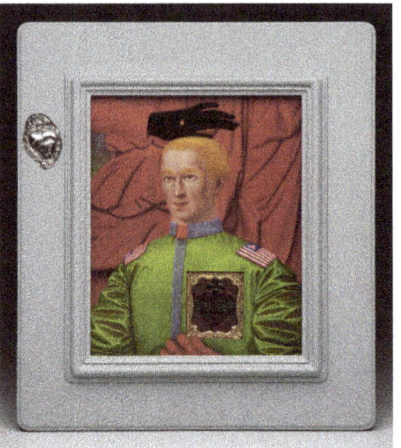

(Left) *A Presence in Dreams*. 1987. Colored pencil, acrylic, leather, rhine-stones, gold leaf, 10 x 8 in.
(Right) *Beyond Other Worlds*. 1992. Colored pencil, acrylic, brass, stained glass, Mylar, 14 x 11 x 1/4 in.

of funerals for gay men who had died of AIDS. In 2009, Demeulenaere retroactively created a triptych of works illustrating his journey through this stage of his life. His 1980 work ***The Past in Myth*** shows some early hints of ambiguous sexuality, and the influence of the pre-Raphaelite and High Renaissance painters he had studied during an influential trip to Europe. His 1987 image ***A Presence in Dreams*** shows an androgynous Demeulenaere staring into his own hand while in the background stand three dark, sinister figures and a burning church. Demeulenaere sees this piece as showing his acceptance of his homosexuality and reconciliation with the Catholic Church on his own terms. ***Beyond Other Worlds*** (1992) uses the figure of an unequivocally gay saint/astronaut to imply a future world of limitless possibility.

Demeulenaere's installations typically employ an archetypal structure (e.g., the church in the DIA installation ***Sanctuary*** or the house in ***Little White House*** [both 1993]) to contain a collection of miniatures that talk from his perspective as a gay man to the institutions that the structures represent. For example, see ***Noli Me Tangere*** (1992), which draws an analogy between Christ and a gay man dying from AIDS; ***Unto Us a Child Is Born*** (1993), which shows a gay male couple as parents; and ***Kouros*** (1993), which references the Greek term for ideal man. The works are often homoerotic and undoubtedly transgressive, but never gratuitously shocking. Demeulenaere walks a fine line. Not coincidentally, the structures also allow Demeulenaere, ever the perfectionist, to control both the lighting and the viewer's relationship to the work. Little is left to chance.

Latterly, Demeulenaere has broadened his subject matter to include other minority groups that have endured prejudice through history. For example, the *Arcada Triptych* (2010–13) draws parallels between the treatment of Moors in Inquisition-era Spain and contemporary conflicts. Demeulenaere sees these works as both expressions of solidarity with other persecuted groups and experiments in imagining what their experience would be like. In these and earlier works, Demeulenaere has often used his art to explore a fluid identity, shifting between different genders and races long before it was fashionable to do so. One senses, in fact, that he is contemptuous of fashion, just as he is of what he considers "political correctness," and of artists whose craft doesn't meet his exacting standards. Ultimately his work is about

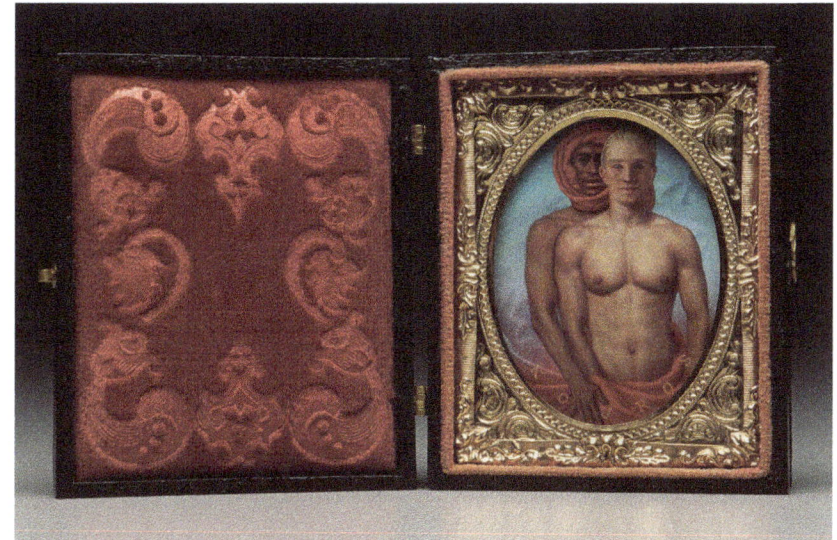

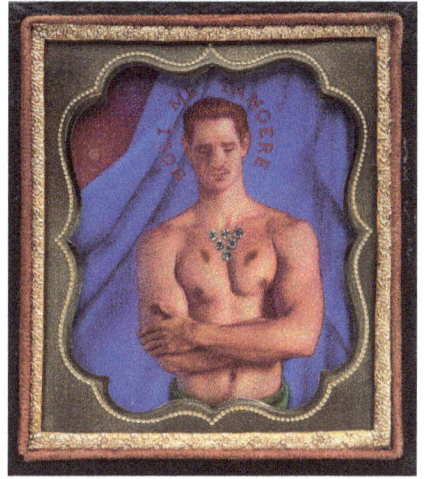
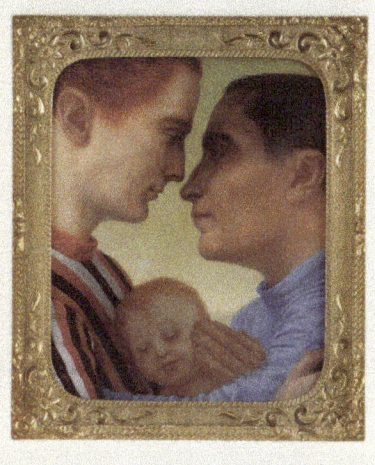

(Top) Kouros. 1993. Opened case, acrylic on panel, brass, velvet, wood, 4 x 6 in. Courtesy of the Detroit Institute of Arts.
(Bottom, Left) Noli Me Tangere. 1992. Colored pencil, rhinestones, brass, velvet, wood case, 4 x 3 1/2 in. Courtesy of the Detroit Institute of Arts.
(Bottom, right) Unto Us a Child Is Born. 1993. Oil on panel, brass, Corian, 4 x 3 1/2 in.

tolerance, but for someone so uncompromising, this doesn't always come naturally; or as he puts it, "I have to keep reminding myself."

STEVE PANTON, JULY 2016

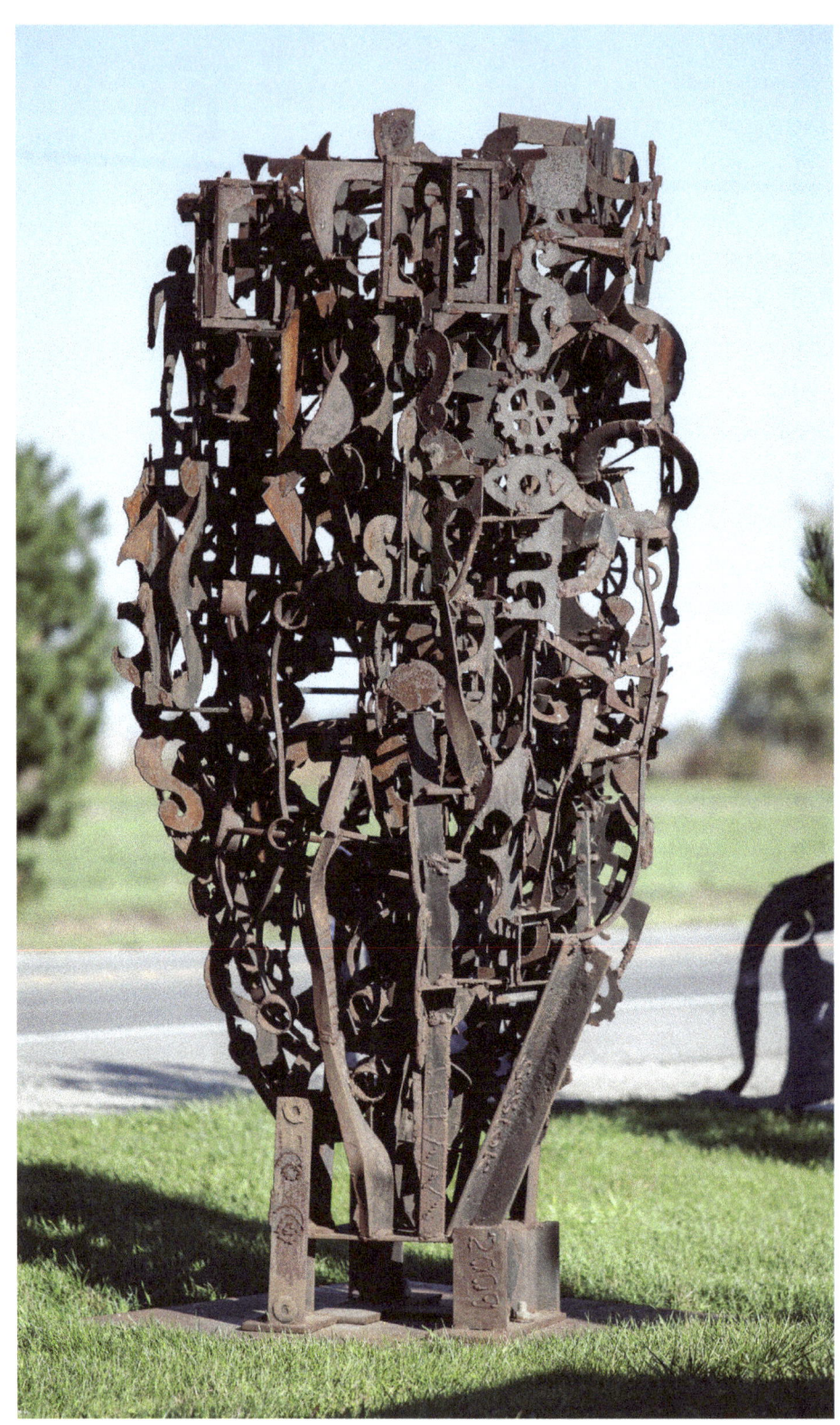

Dream Machine. 2009. Welded steel, 140 x 72 x 72 in.

57 // ROBERT SESTOK

Born Detroit, 1946
Studied College for Creative Studies;
Haystack Mountain School of Crafts,
Maine; Cranbrook Academy of Art
Lives in Detroit

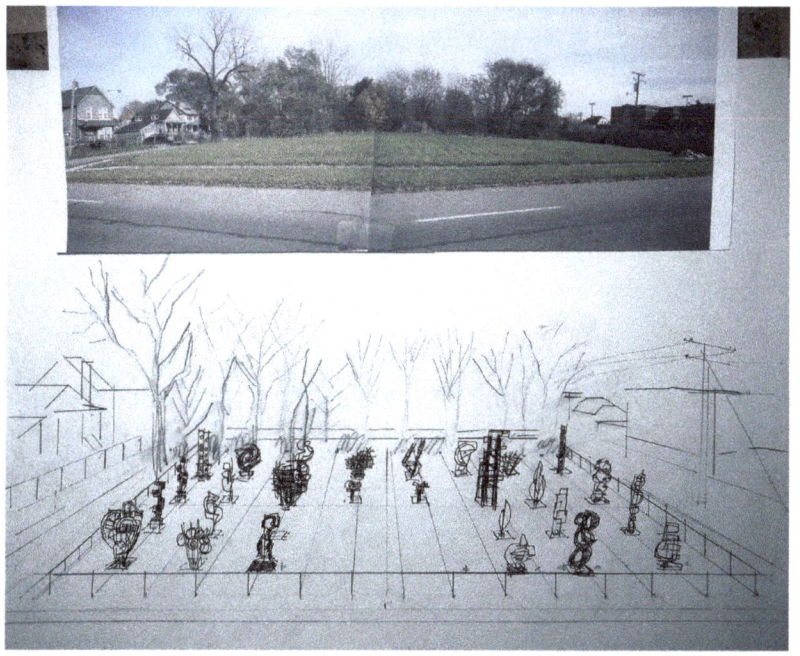

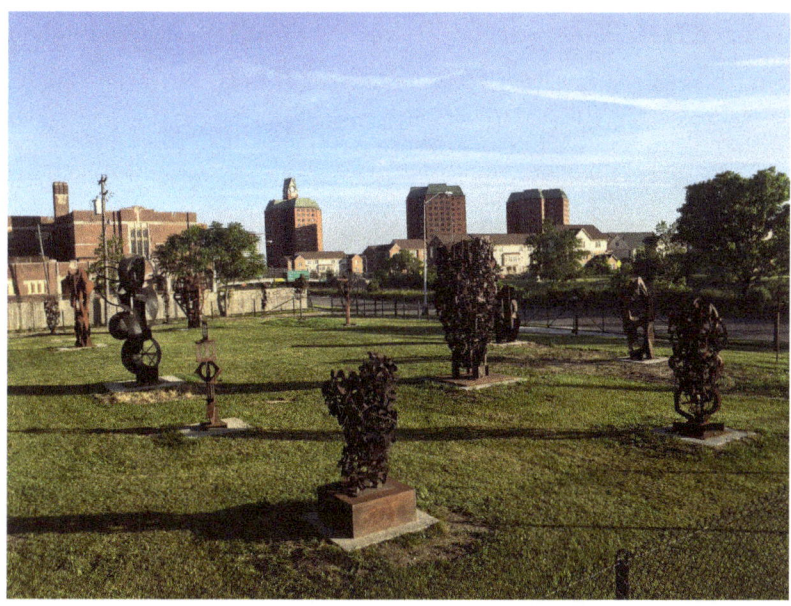

Rarely does one get to see a full bore display of an artist's oeuvre, all at once and all in one place. Robert Sestok counts as the standout exception in the Motor City, where he has engineered, from purchase and design to sodding and installing, an open-air anthology of his sculptural practice. His **City Sculpture** park, located at Alexandrine and the Lodge Freeway northbound service drive, features an array of some three dozen sculptures, each centered on concrete pads laid out in a grid. Encompassing four contiguous city lots, and furnished with Sestok-built benches to offer a respite and meditative break from strolling about, this expansive public-private sward—it is open seven days a week—is a

(Top) City Sculpture (design and plan). 2014. Ink on paper, photograph, 20 x 24 in.
(Bottom) City Sculpture (overview). 2015. 100 x 150 ft.

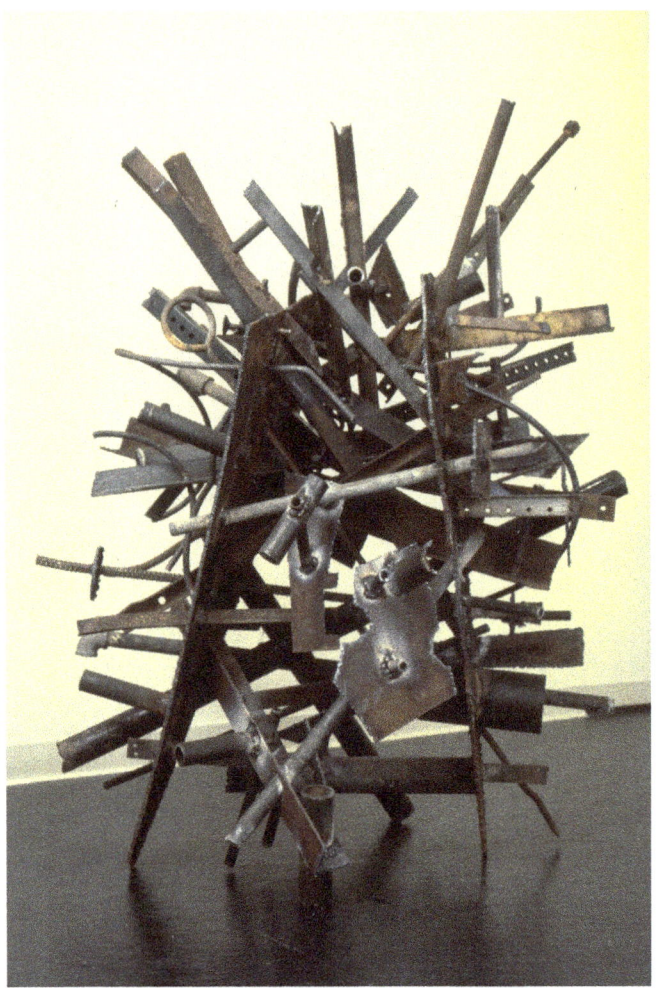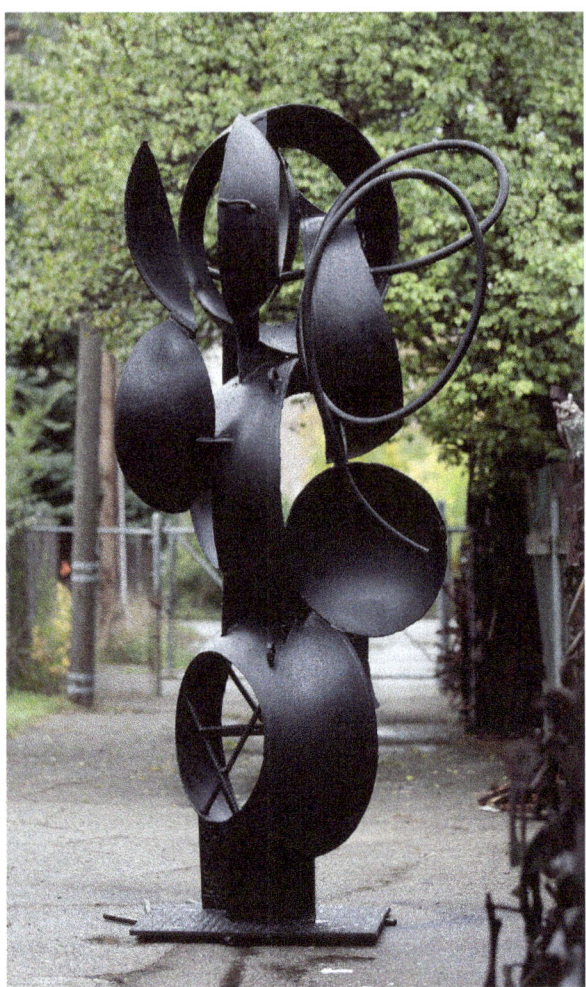

(Left) Conductivity. 1980. Welded steel, 56 x 30 x 38 in.
(Right) Triosphere. 2010. Welded steel, 144 x 72 x 65 in. Photography by R. H. Hensleigh.

welcome oasis within Detroit's Cass Corridor neighborhood.

Although *City Sculpture* is just a little over a year old, sculptor and painter Sestok has been embedded in the Detroit art scene from the early, simmering days of the "Corridor," which saw the influx of a group of artists who established studios along Cass Ave. Sestok continues to be an active participant in the downtown Detroit universe, having participated in the last several years in no fewer than eight group shows and three solos. As a prime protagonist of the indefatigable do-it-yourself Detroit work ethic then and now, Sestok's art and activism within the community has climaxed in the thirty-six-year survey on view in his self-made park. Ranging in date from 1980 to 2016, the totems on view include his breakthrough, found-object sculpture **Conductivity** (1980), tucked protectively under the trees at the back of the property. Its bristling porcupine silhouette, dark in hue, rife with jutting, salvaged pipes and poles, establishes the idiom for all that follows: abstract, welded steel sculpture. It summarizes as well the "deconstructivist" aesthetic that he avows is fundamental to his art and that of other like-minded bricoleurs: "The downtown environment seemed to

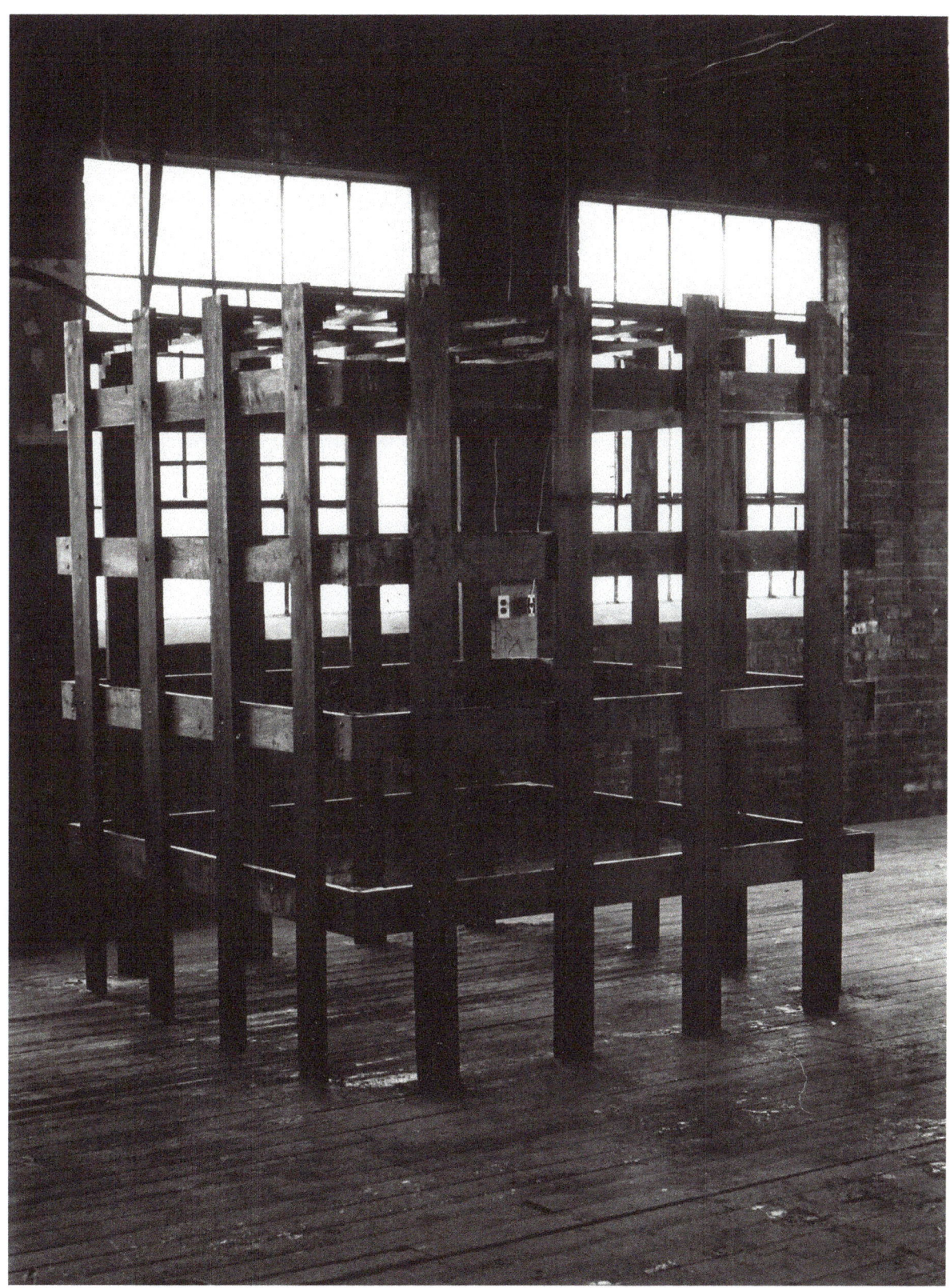

Cage. 1972. Wood and tar, 96 x 96 x 96 in.

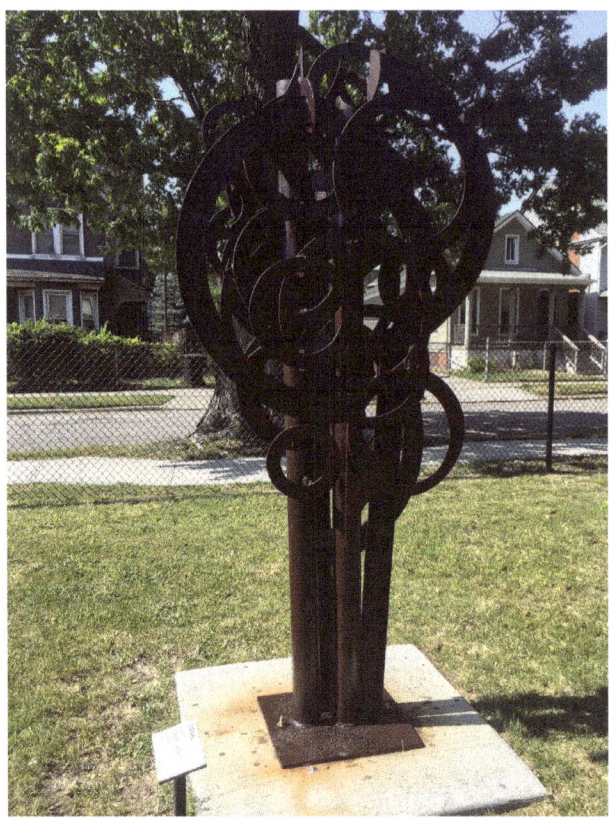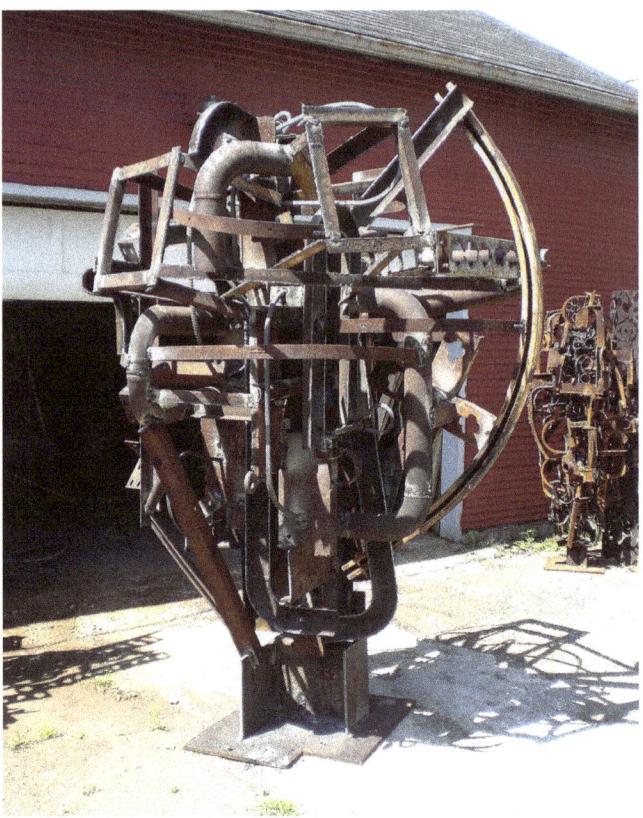

(Left) Signal. 2004. Welded steel, 108 x 36 x 24 in.
(Right) Save the Planet. 2010. Welded steel, 120 x 96 x 96 in.

inspire a deconstructivist view of art. In the past, art was more contained and easily defined; now rules were being broken…. Many artists in the group were tearing things apart and reconstructing them. It was these methods that made artists from the Cass Corridor seem different."

Pride of place in Sestok's exposition goes to some of the tallest deconstructivist denizens nearest the entrance, from the emphatically black **Triosphere** (2010) towering twelve feet high, its curvaceous arcs having been cut from propane storage tanks,

to the densely packed **Dream Machine** of the previous year, replete with innumerable small elements—sprockets, pipes, and French curves among them. Near the top a mask/face implies the progenitor of the swarming imagery below. Then there's the bulbous **Save the Planet** (2010) and lithe, wiry **Tomahawk Heart** (2007), with its kinetic inner life—delineated by a twisting steel rod—safeguarded by thick, enveloping contours. **Signal**, off to the side, and slightly earlier—2004— suggests railroad crossings, but also a lighthearted, effervescent

fizzing and bubbling. Equally tall (nine feet), but glistening and reflective is **New Gold Standard #1**, recently fashioned (2015) from discarded sheets of golden-hued, anodized aluminum. After wham-banging and crumpling them with a bat, Sestok threaded each distressed section onto a supporting rod, like a necklace or kebab, to create a shiny, hollow column of battered bling.

As much of a piece as Sestok's parade of sculpture seems, as a rule, the origins of an artistic practice evolve from contrary sources. At one point, when

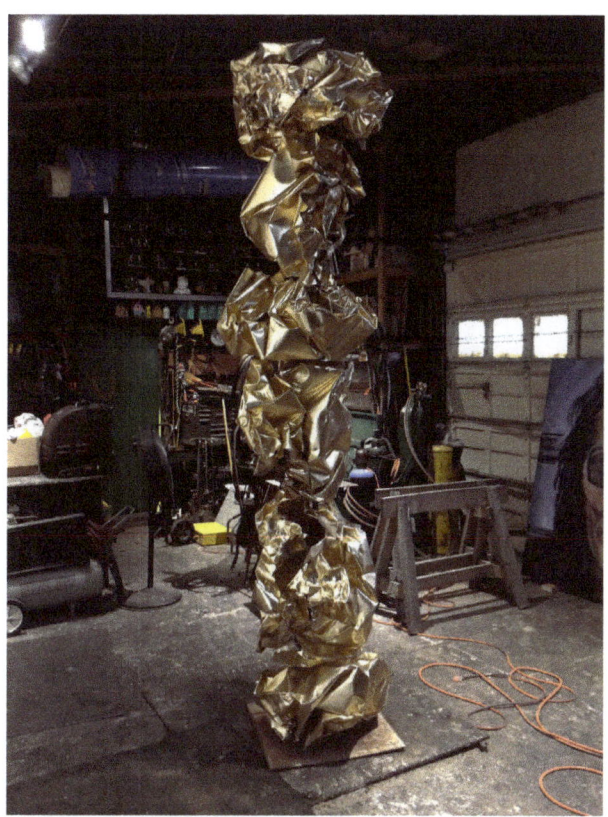
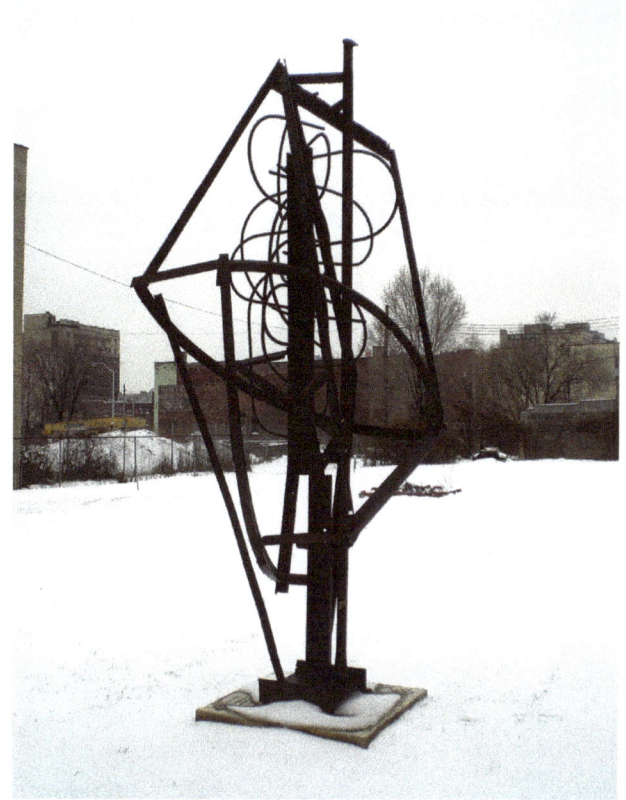

(Top, left) New Gold Standard #1. 2015. Anodized aluminum, 110 x 28 x 24 in. Photography by R. H. Hensleigh.
(Top, right) Tomahawk Heart. 2007. Welded steel, 132 x 72 x 72 in.
(Bottom, right) Rock and Roll. 1978–79. Painted canvas mounted on wood, aluminum, LED Lights,
52 1/2 x 165 x 16 in. Collection of Wayne State University Art Collection/Gift of James Pearson Duffy.

the grid was god in the seventies, Sestok constructed several crisp, modular structures of wood slathered with tar, such as *Cage* in 1972. Later, he fabricated a number of mixed-media reliefs, loose and kicky like *Rock and Roll* (1978–79), now installed in Cobo Center, before *Conductivity* came along in 1980. Other reliefs, post-1980, followed at intervals, but fully three-dimensional structures soon held sway.

Clearly, Sestok has always "forged ahead, never backward,"

steadily assembling sculptures with salvaged materials that came to hand, building two studios and launching a sculpture park over the years. Unsurprisingly, he is not yet done, continuing to harbor a fantasy that one day, perhaps in the broad, open space at the entrance to *City Sculpture*, he will weld together a monumental mashup of the homeless sculptures still stored in his studio and adjacent alley into a single entity. Is that, perhaps, why he left the center

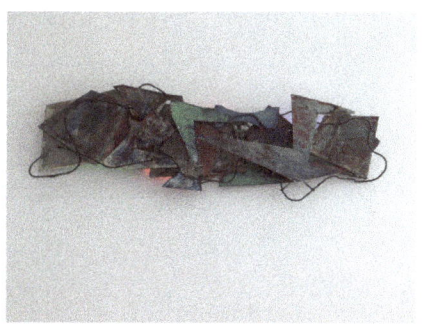

of the grid incomplete? Daring himself, and us, he proposes "sticking all this stuff together, all the work into one big ball."

DENNIS ALAN NAWROCKI,
AUGUST 2016

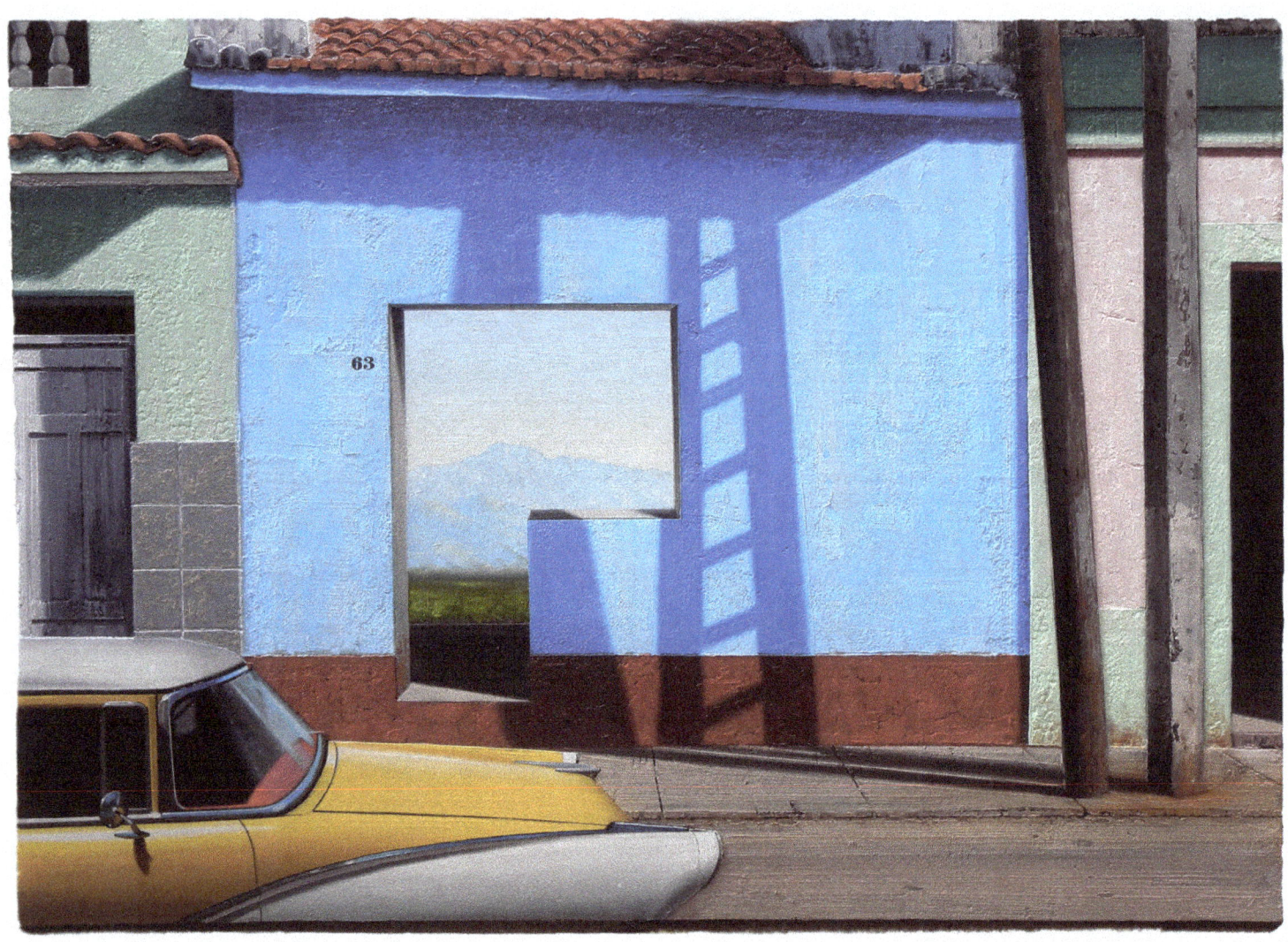

La patria. 2013. Oil on panel, 32 x 48 in.

Born Des Moines, Iowa, 1950
BFA, Drake University, Iowa; MFA,
Tyler School of Art, Pennsylvania
Lives in Royal Oak, Michigan

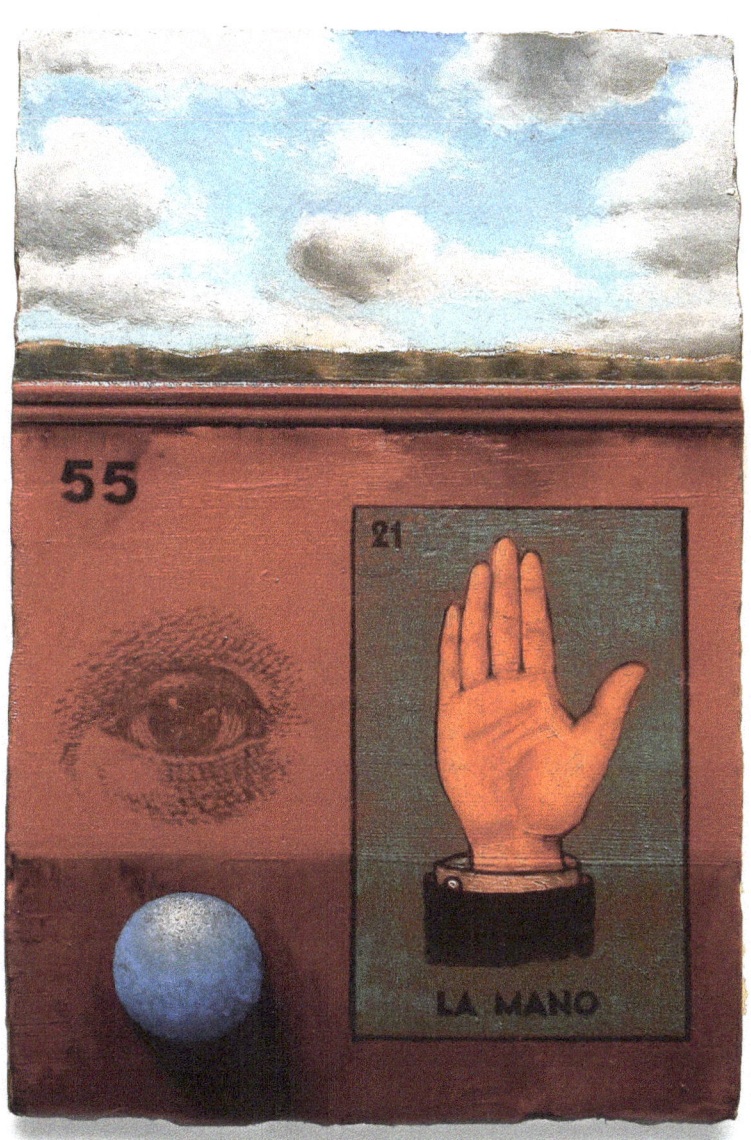

With their luscious surfaces, painstakingly lifelike textures, and subtly surreal depictions of almost-possible places, the oil paintings of Mel Rosas invite and reward both close attention and long-view contemplation. Rosas, an influential professor of painting at Wayne State University, is one of those painters who draws knowingly from the deep well of art history (Vermeer, Hopper, and Magritte are three signal antecedents), as well as an idiosyncratic assortment of wider cultural influences. The expansive body of work that has obsessed him for more than thirty years is also an object lesson in the use of art as a tool to explore, expand, and communicate the self. Rosas's paintings are portals that offer the artist passage into his Latin American ancestry and the viewer into a lush and evocative dream world.

Clairvoyance. 2005. Oil on panel, 4 x 6 in.

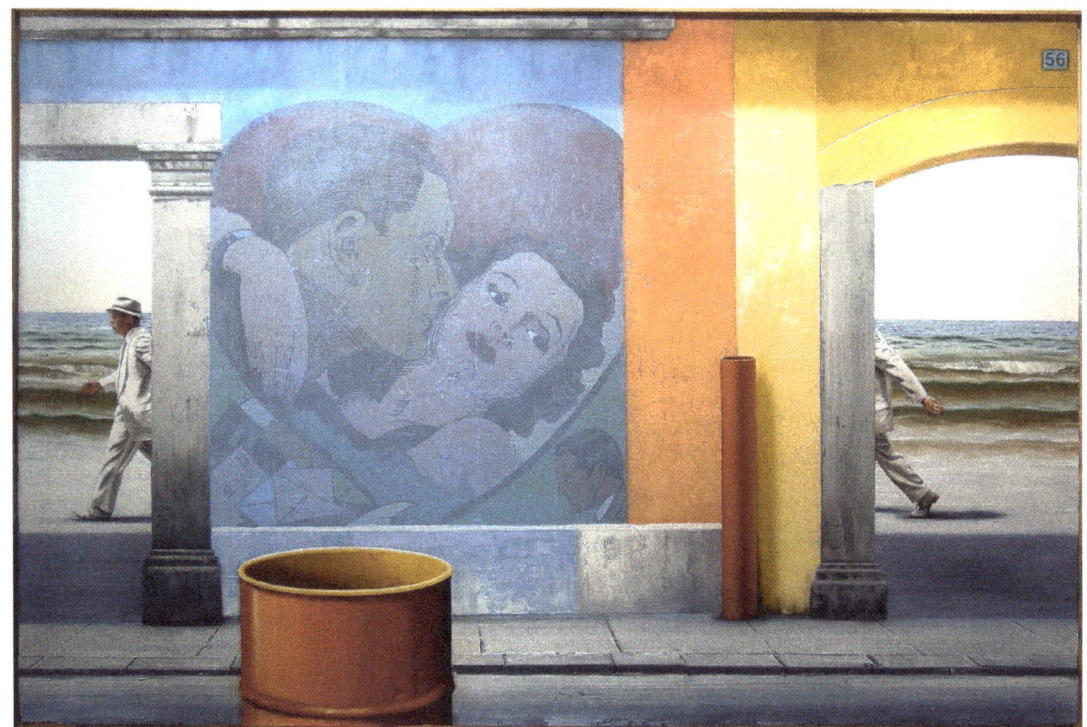

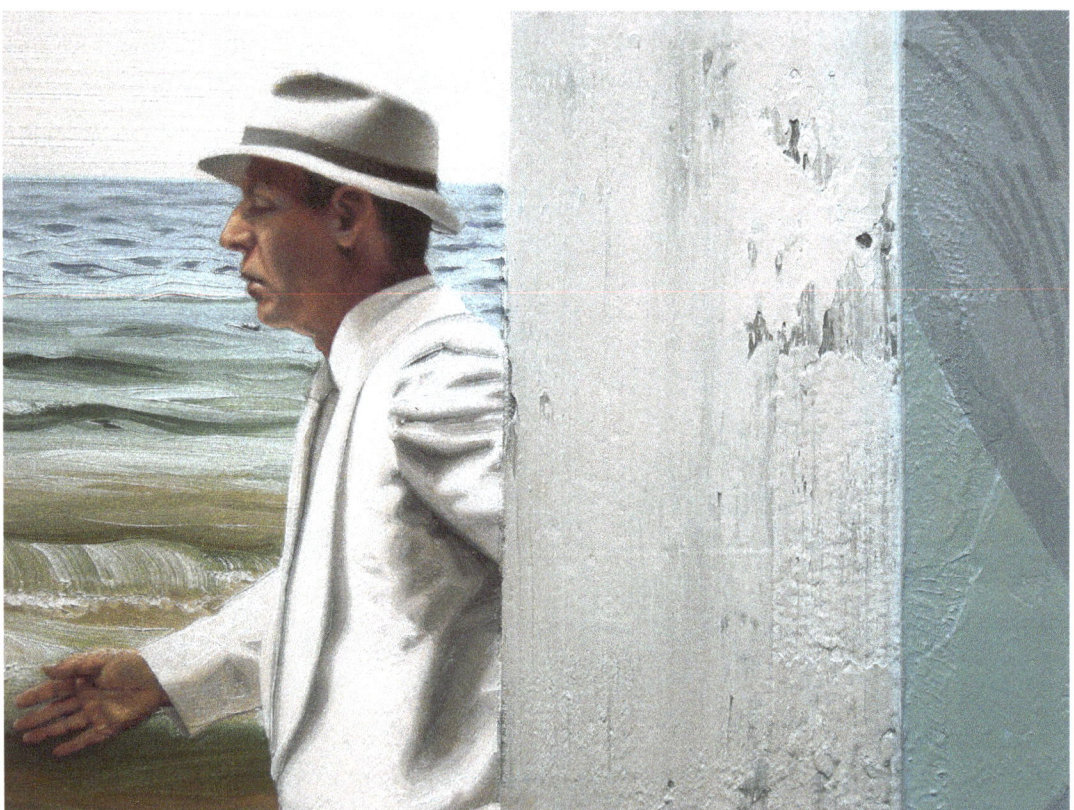

(Top) Searching for the Romantic. 2006. Oil on canvas, 48 x 72 in.
(Bottom) Searching for the Romantic (detail). 2006. Oil on canvas, 48 x 72 in.

The portal, in fact, is one of Rosas's dominant motifs, puncturing again and again the richly textured walls that tend to fill his compositions. In a typical painting, such a facade— invariably worn with age, often stained, scored, graffitied, but nonetheless alive with color—is depicted as if viewed from the street in front of it. Beyond it, glimpsed through various openings, are either voids (as in **El regreso**, 2001) or, more commonly, fragmented scenes of sublime natural beauty: oceans, mountains, forests, and vast skies—see **Despues de la lluvia** (2004) and **Jabon del amor** (2005). The portals are often the first clues that the meticulous *realism* of Rosas's scenarios belies their truly surreal nature. Consider **La patria** (2013), in which the improbable opening (at once a doorway *and* a window) seems to have been carefully excised from the vibrant cerulean wall. From there, notice the shadow of a ladder, cast, impossibly, by a post. It is only gradually that a fundamental truth about the work becomes clear: this is not a depiction of reality. These walls are not the walls of *buildings*. They're just . . . walls.

In speaking about his practice, Rosas mentions his concern

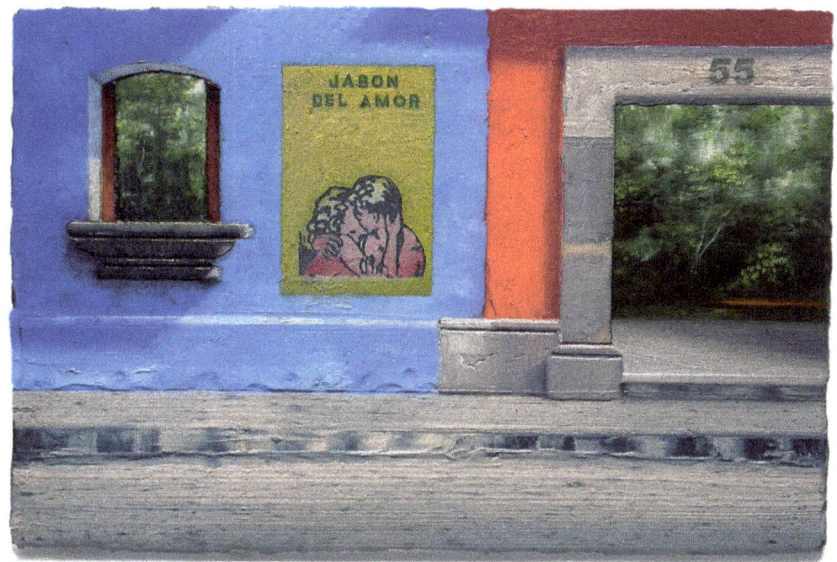

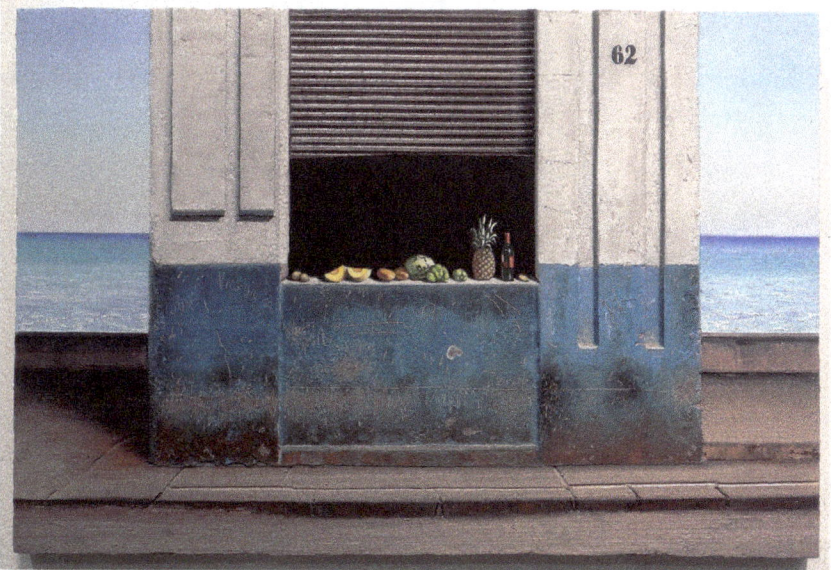

(Top) Jabon del amor. 2005. Oil on panel, 4 x 6 in.
(Bottom) La naturaleza muerta. 2012. Oil on panel, 12 x 18 in.

with "beingness," "being present," and "altered states," and with their typical (though not complete) absence of figures, his enigmatic scenes do invite a psychospiritual reading. In most of the works mentioned above, the viewer is on one side, the void or the immense impersonality of nature is on the other, and between them is a wall: a man-made surface, time worn and marked by cultural signifiers, that *seems* more than it is. The viewer (the subject, in this reading) can seemingly access transcendence, but only incompletely (through the portals), as long as the wall (personality, the ego) stands.

Rosas's paintings, which he thinks of as "fictions," are each the culmination of a

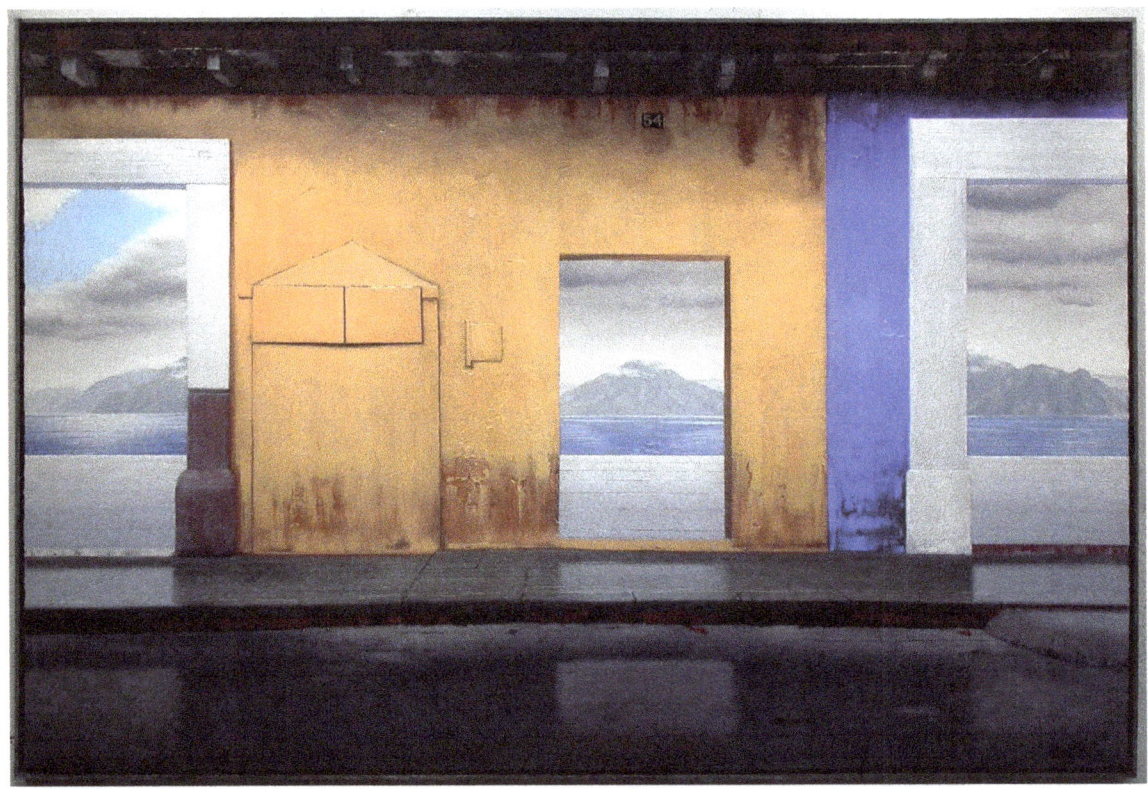

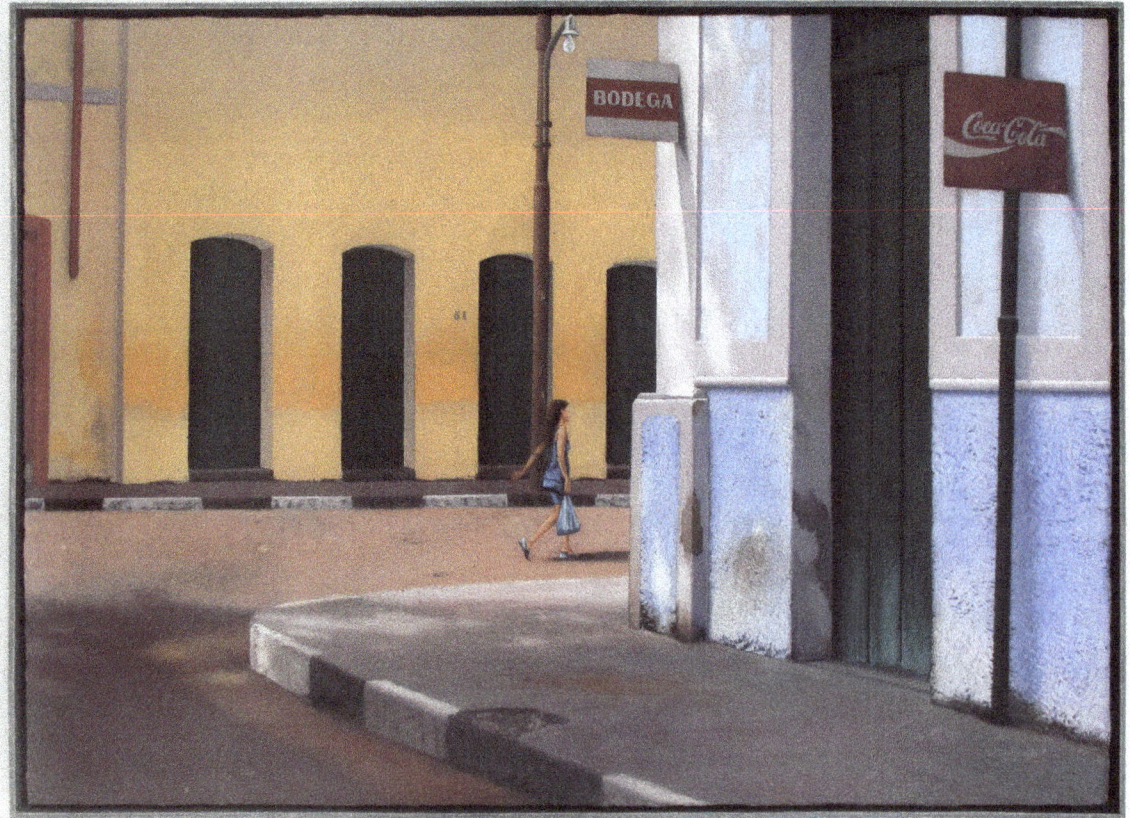

(Top) Despues de la lluvia. 2004. Oil on canvas, 48 x 72 in.
(Bottom) El regreso. 2001. Oil on panel, 24 x 36 in.

lengthy process of travel, observation, documentation, and imaginative recontextualization. Their imagery is collaged from photographs the artist makes on regular research trips to Latin America, solo excursions during which he roams, eavesdrops, takes copious notes and pictures, and ultimately enters an "almost transcendental state." While the keen observational quality of his work speaks to his position as an outsider in these cultures, Rosas, whose mother was American and whose father was from Panama, says that his practice is also a way of coming to terms with his Latino heritage, which, as a child and young man, he attempted to downplay, even hide, in order to blend in in mostly white Des Moines.

Today, his work is inextricably linked with Latin America, where Rosas encounters communities that embrace the supernatural (consider the hypnotic mysticism of *Clairvoyance*, 2005) and "almost surreal" experiences that find a natural home in his paintings. (The panther trotting past the canopied portal in 2015's ***Day of the Panther***, for instance, originated in a real-life moment in Panama, when a groggy Rosas stopped his car

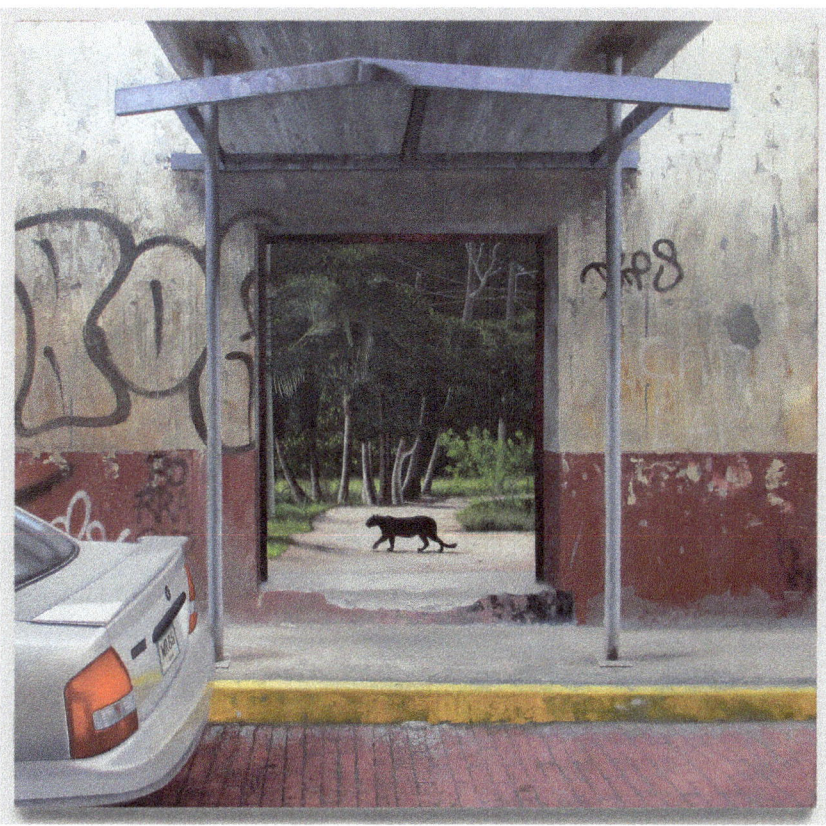

Day of the Panther. 2015. Oil on panel, 48 x 48 in.

after a long drive and watched, amazed, as a panther crossed in front of him.) Rosas sometimes inserts himself into these scenes, either overtly, as in ***Searching for the Romantic*** (2006)—in which the bifurcated figure, striding past a suspended sea, is a self-portrait—or more subtly, as in any number of works featuring a two-digit street number, which mirrors the artist's age during the period he made the painting.

Perhaps the most fundamental link between Rosas and his father's small-town Latino culture is a certain sympathy of

texture. Look, for instance, at ***La naturaleza muerta*** (2012), with its astonishing reproduction in oil of the intricate surface of an aging fruit stand. This is the kind of detail that Rosas is drawn to in Latin America, and that he masterfully recreates in service of his fantastic vision.

MATTHEW PIPER, AUGUST 2016

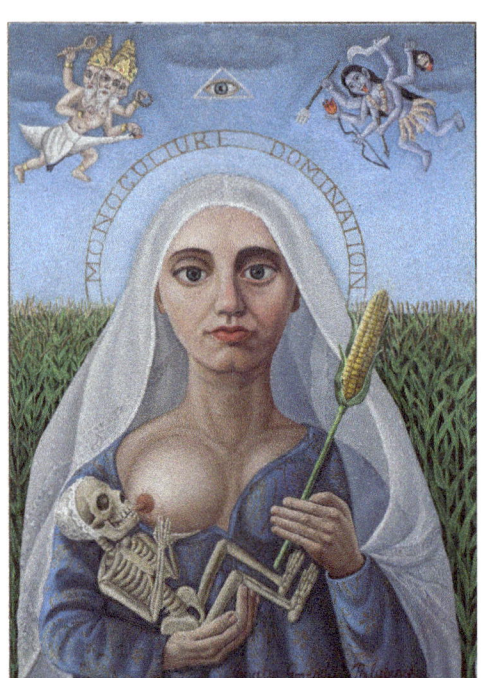 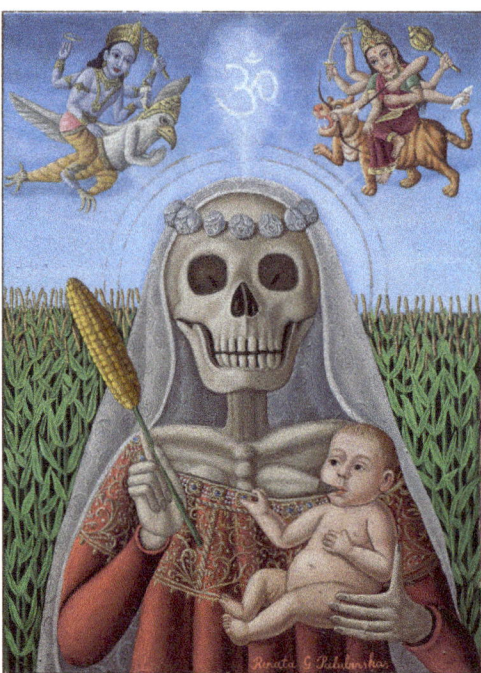 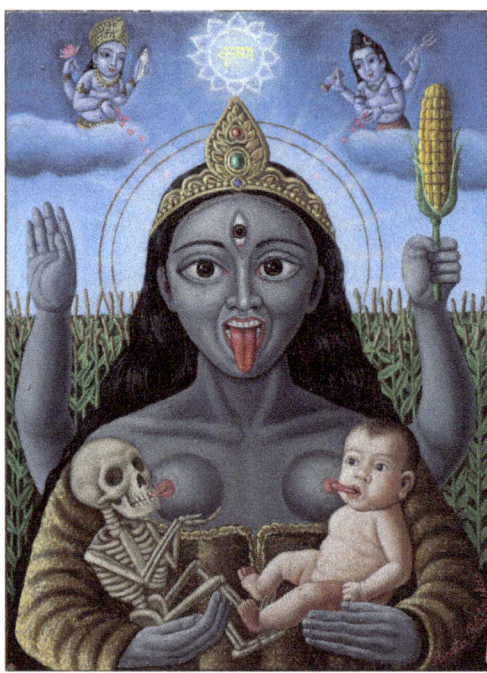

(Left) Monoculture Domination (left side). 2014. Oil on board, triptych, each piece 17 1/2 x 22 in.
(Middle) Monoculture Domination (center). 2014. Oil on board, triptych, each piece 17 1/2 x 22 in.
(Right) Monoculture Domination (right side). 2014. Oil on board, triptych, each piece 17 1/2 x 22 in.

59 // RENATA PALUBINSKAS

Born Kaunas, Lithuania, 1968
Diploma in Fine Art and Restoration,
St. Zukas Technium of Applied Arts,
Kaunus, Lithuania
Lives in Beverley Hills, Michigan

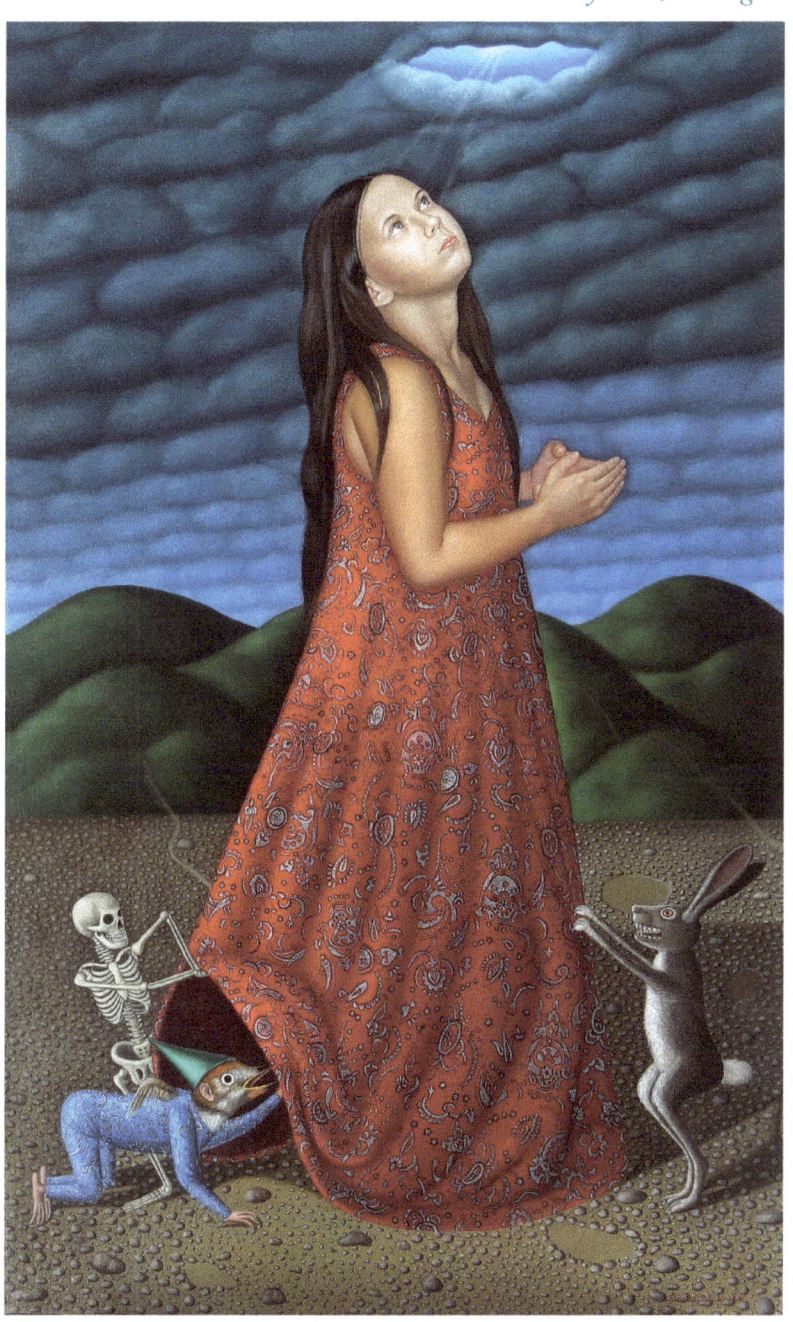

Lithuania, Renata Palubinskas confides, was the last place in Europe to embrace Christianity, maintaining its pantheistic pagan beliefs as late as the fourteenth century. A similar sense, of being out of sync with prevailing currents, and instead embracing the richness of the distant past, pervades Palubinskas's own extensive body of paintings. She is an especially wholehearted artist, making full use of a rigorous Eastern European education in traditional painting and drawing techniques to take on big topics, such as mortality and the search for enlightenment, with great joy. Her quest is a spiritual one, drawing insights from all religions but finding the most compelling answers in writings from the Hindu tradition. She talks of the beauty she finds in martial arts,

Unexpected. 2004. Oil on canvas, 68 x 36 in.

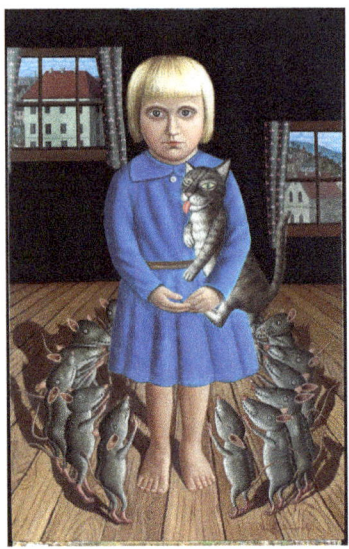 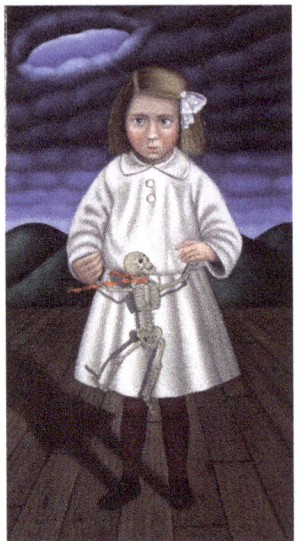 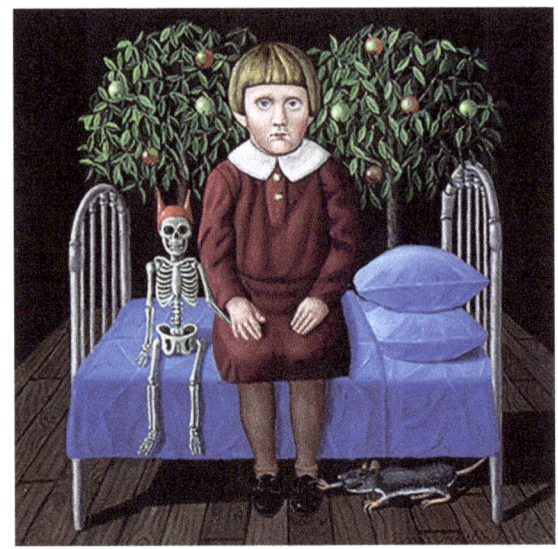

(Left) Outsider. 2006. Oil on canvas. *(Middle) Captured.* 2005. Oil on canvas, 25 x 15 in. *(Right) From the Little Girl's Diary.* 2006. Oil on board, 12 x 12 in.

and if pressed, will admit to having a black belt in karate.

Palubinskas's works are allegorical but have a lightness of touch that often belies their intense subject matter. In her worlds, human, mythical, and animal characters appear and reappear in different combinations. She makes particular use of pubescent children, whom she sees as symbolizing the transitional stage at which the Self starts to emerge and begins to question the purpose of life. For Palubinskas, the path beyond this point is paved with threats of many kinds and uncertain emotions, but must be pursued in order to potentially transcend the limited existence of the material world. In her paintings, the threat of the unknown is often represented by "monsters

lurking in the dark," and the possibility for transcendence is often expressed by a ray of light breaking through a hole in the clouds.

It is the tension between the "light" and "dark" that is at the base of many of Palubinskas's compositions. See, for example, 2005's **Captured**, 2000's *Death Chases Time*, or especially 2004's **Unexpected**. In the latter, the young girl is shown both in the glow of, and staring through, a hole in the clouds; her hands are shown cupped in a seemingly devotional gesture, while at her feet a skeleton and a clothed, mammal-like figure wearing a party hat peer under her dress threateningly. The rabbit, another common presence in Palubinskas's work, tugs at the fabric, and displays sharp teeth—even the most benign creature may pose

an unexpected hazard on life's journey. The light, as with many of Palubinskas's paintings, has a bright but unsettling, dream-like quality; the girl's shoulder glows with a pre-Raphaelite intensity. The overall effect is a haunting combination of masterful painting and both psychological and narrative prompts.

Others of Palubinskas's paintings are still more mysterious. In **From the Little Girl's Diary** (2006), a young, archaically dressed woman stares impassively, perhaps even knowingly, at the viewer, while gently holding the hand of a skeleton sitting beside her in a windowless bedroom. In the background stands the Tree of Knowledge, while at the girl's feet, a rat reaches out to touch her. Or see **Outsider** (2006), in which a barefoot

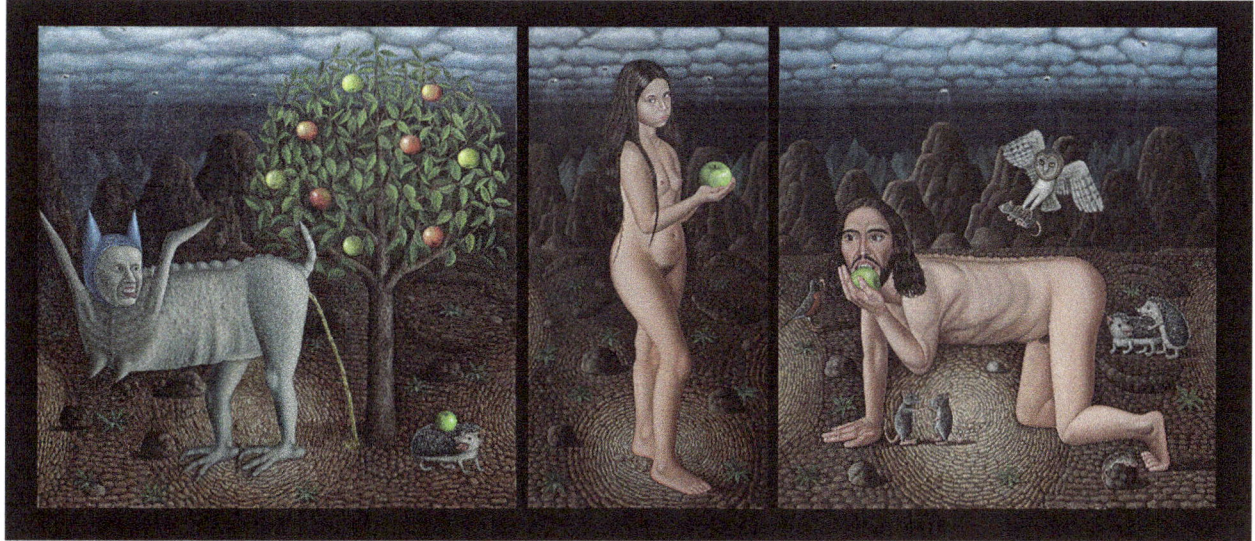

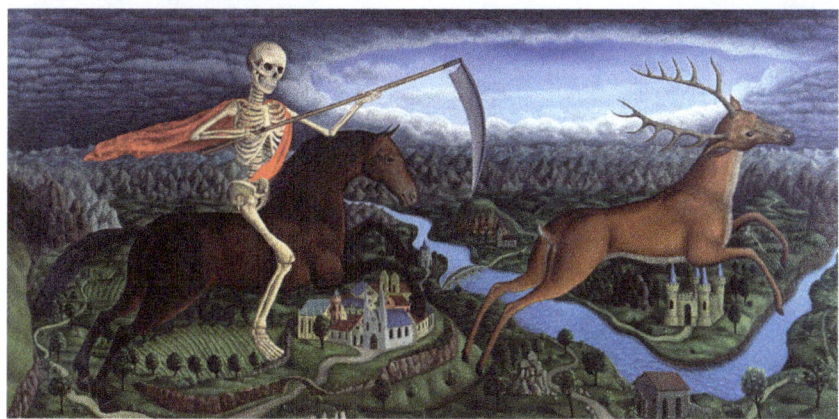

(Top) Desecration of the Self. 1999/2015. Oil on canvas, triptych, 52 x 134 in.
(Bottom) Death Chases Time. 2000. Oil on canvas, 36 x 72 in.

young girl protectively cradles a cat, while surrounded by a circle of finger-pointing rats. In the background, two windows look out across a medieval cityscape. There is a Gothic quality to the works, but not gratuitously so.

Although Palubinskas draws extensively from Eastern philosophy, the themes she considers are universal, and hence she is able to frame them using Western symbology familiar to a local audience. More recently, she has started to directly incorporate Hindu deities and symbols into her work, and also to explicitly address specific contemporary issues. The triptych *Monoculture Domination* (2014) illustrates this latter point by including contemporary material issues, such as genetic modification and the risks of prioritizing the demands of capitalism above the need for crop diversity, alongside universal themes such as life, death, and the need for harmony.

Most recently, Palubinskas has indicated a desire to create large-scale works, and has started the process with the triptych *Desecration of the Self* (1999/2015), which tips the scales at a little over eleven feet wide. Created for a general audience at the Grand Rapids annual ArtPrize competition, it conflates the classic Adam and Eve tale with the contemporary cautionary tale of British comedian Russell Brand. Palubinskas is fascinated with Brand because of his openness about his hedonistic past and his attempts to replace it with a more spiritual quest. Most likely she hopes that we see the work and question our own materially centered lives.

STEVE PANTON, SEPTEMBER 2016

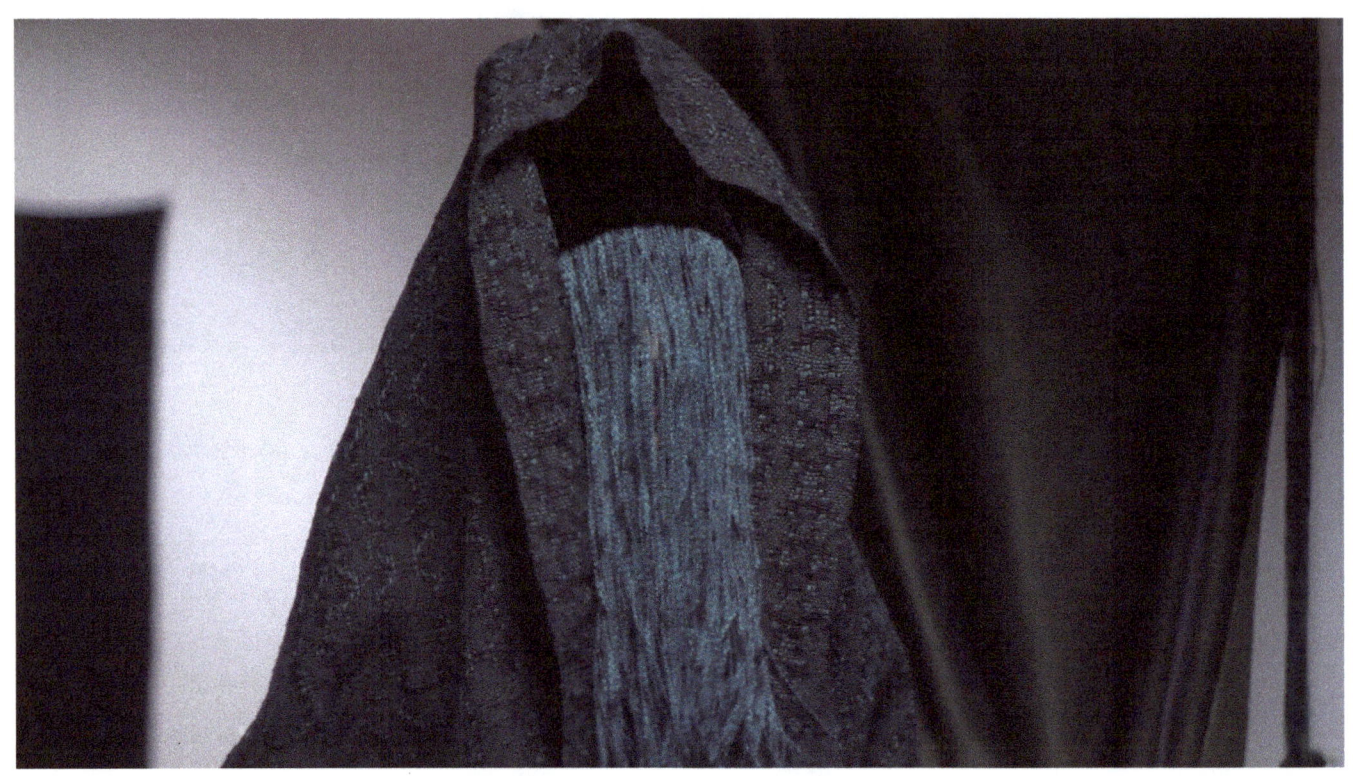

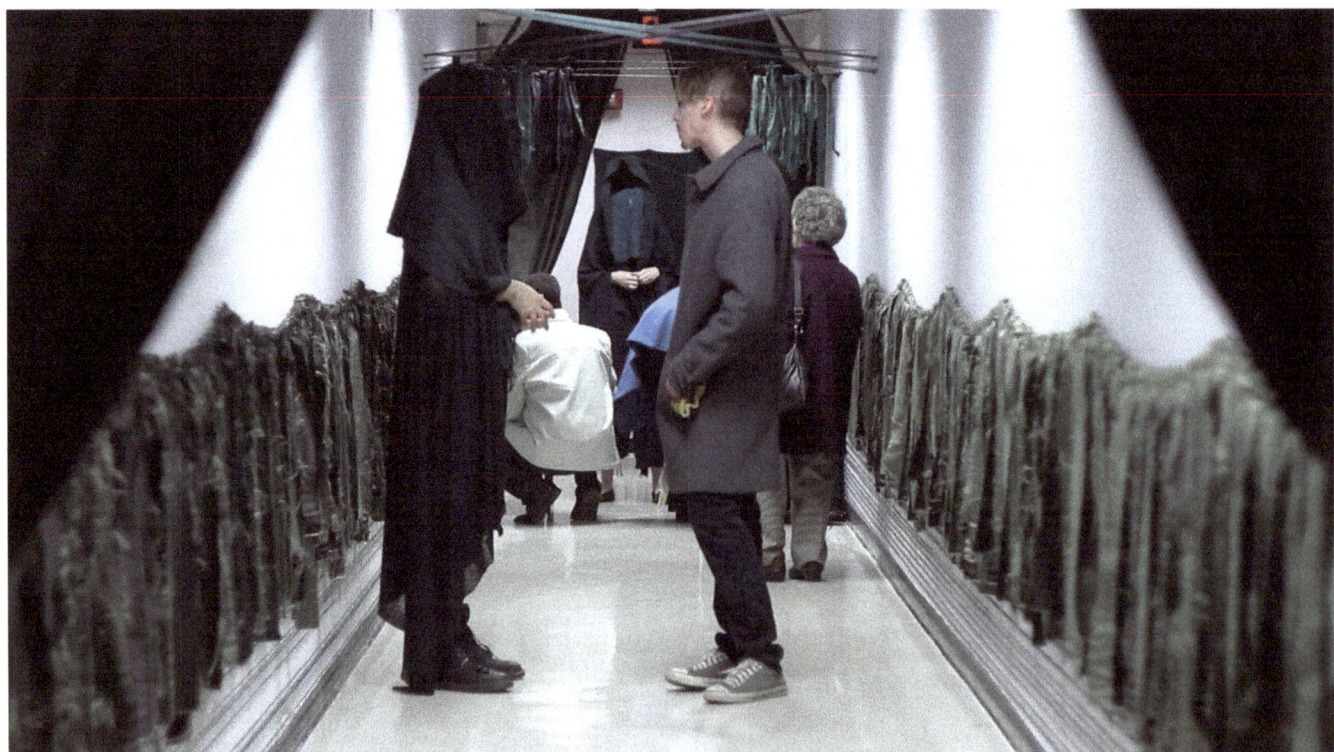

Daraz\Amanor. 2016. Installation/performance. Photography by Oksana Mirzoyan.

Born New York, New York, 1988
BA (Anthropology), Wayne State Uni-
versity; BFA, College for
Creative Studies
Lives in Detroit

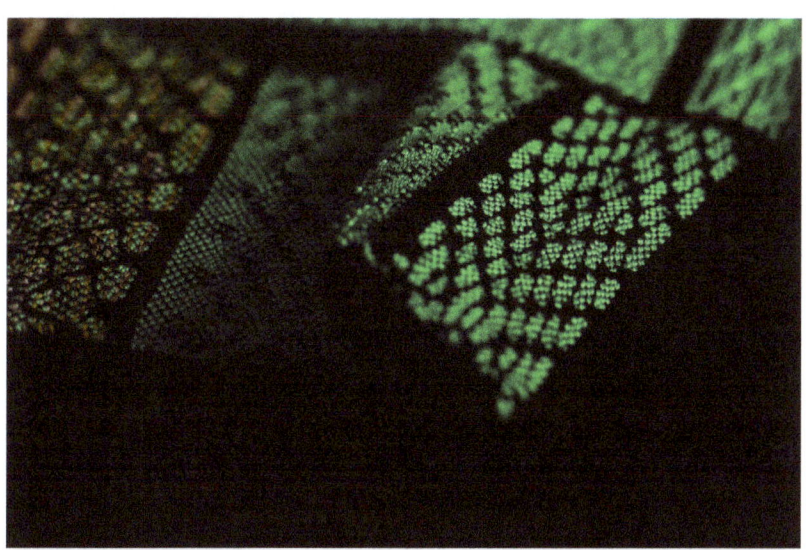

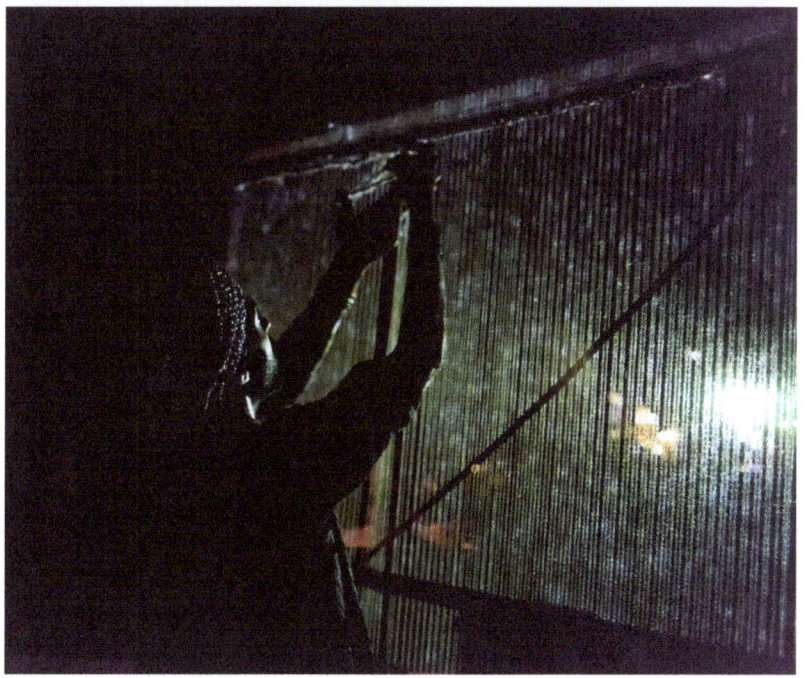

The art of weaving has long inspired metaphors for nothing less than the nature of human existence—from the mythic Fates, literally weaving each individual's destiny, to Ishmael's musing in *Moby Dick* that the "mingled, mingling threads of life are woven by warp and woof: calms crossed by storms, a storm for every calm." The age-old link between weaving and living is of paramount significance to Levon Kafafian, a young artist and teacher for whom this ancient way of making is at the center of a vital, unfolding, multimodal

(Top) Black Forest (detail). 2014. Cotton, linen, and rayon, 14 in. x 8 ft. x 3 in. (with 26 in. corded fringe). Photography by Samantha Otto.
(Bottom) Nightweaving. 2016. Performance. Photography by Bruno Vanzieleghem.

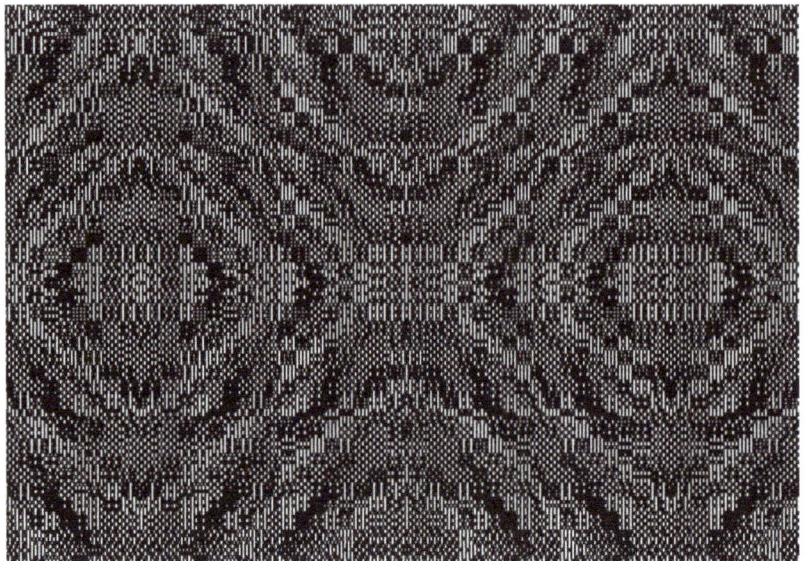
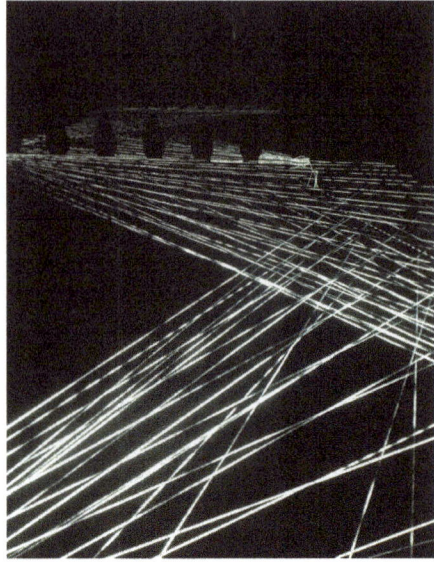

(Left) Endless Becoming. 2015. Video still.
(Right) In the Garden by Loomlight. 2016. Installation, reflective thread. Photography by Levon Kafafian.

practice—a practice that seeks to connect people more deeply to the natural world, one another, and their own lived experience.

Kafafian is a skilled craftsman, a deft weaver of sensitive, distinctive fabrics that revel in their handmade quality—see, for instance, the imperfect, entangling intricacies of 2014's **Spirit of Spring** and **Black Forest**. But for Kafafian, objects—no matter how soulful—are inert, ineffective; they only become activated when used. "One of the reasons I started weaving was to move away from mass production and be more in tune with sustainability," he says, "but as time went on, I realized that I was still just making *stuff*."

Kafafian continues to make stuff and, at the Fringe Society, his loom-filled home and studio, to teach others how to do the same. But more often than not, what he makes now has a function, whether protective (as in his numerous scarves and shawls), or ceremonial (as in the fabrics, garments, and **pottery** produced for his ongoing series of interactive performances), or else as constituent elements of short video pieces. The work in the latter two categories at once depends on Kafafian's foundational weaving *and* notably departs from it,

engaging participants in ways that objects alone never could.

In his 2015 video trilogy *Interlacing*, for instance, Kafafian animates the act of weaving in support of another, personally developed metaphor: textile processes as life cycle. **Endless Becoming**, the first of the trilogy, is an entirely digital rumination on gestation created using textile drafting software, in which the artist devised a design, then repeatedly stepped it forward and shifted it, overlapping and animating the resulting patterns in layers that pulse, expand, contract, and drift. **Unbound and Undone**, meanwhile, inspired by

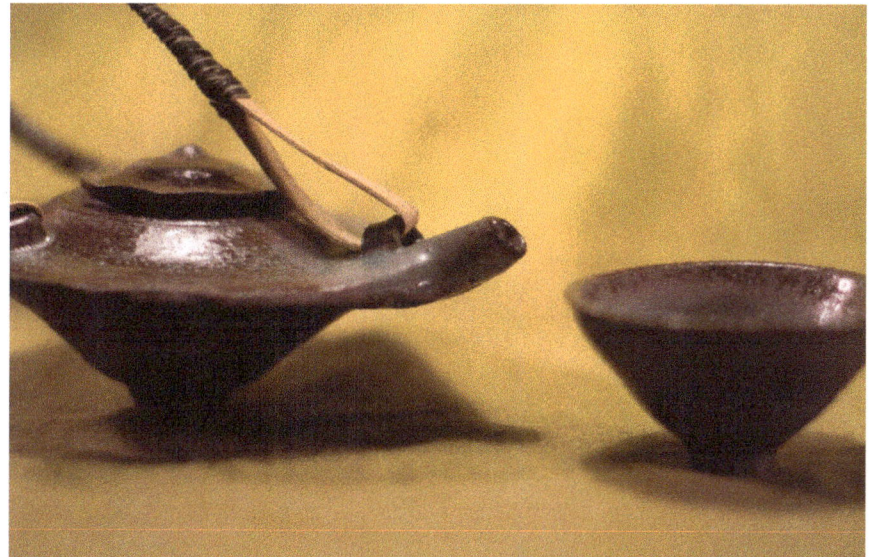
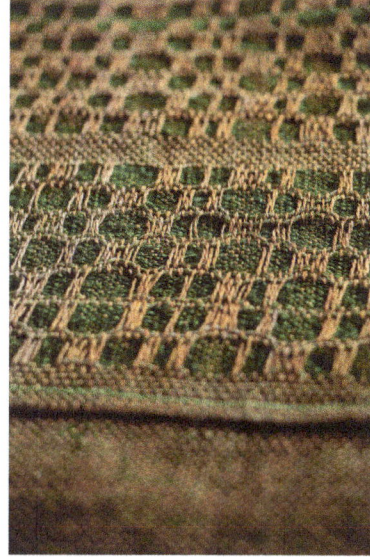

(Left) Dragon Well Spring tea service *(detail)*. 2015. Salt-fired temmoku body, waxed linen, reed.
(Right) Spirit of Spring (detail). 2014. Linen, 10 x 38 in. Photography by Samantha Otto.

the death of Kafafian's mother, is a sensuous, close-up look at the unraveling of a piece of fabric—a duplicate, in fact, of the burial shroud he wove for her. As installed, each of the works that make up *Interlacing* contained additional textile elements: *Unbound and Undone*, for instance, was accompanied in the gallery by the pile of unwound fabric depicted, as well as a bowl of incense that gallery-goers were invited to light.

That invitation marks the first time that Kafafian encouraged participation in his work, an engagement he has continued to develop into what he terms "participatory rituals." One such event was ***Daraz|Amanor*** (2016), held near the spring equinox, in which the artist, draped in a handmade costume inspired by Ottoman-era womenswear, invited people to consider what had recently died in their lives, "and from that death, what seed emerged to create new growth?" Participants wrote their responses on strips of fabric and tied them to cords strung above their heads.

Kafafian says that through such rituals, he hopes to provide "alternative perspectives" and to help people see that "things are possible between the notions that they carry." He also wants to introduce some magic into their lives. Inspired by a desire to take weaving "into the dark," he has recently been staging nighttime performances that incorporate installations made with reflective thread. Related work includes ***Nightweaving*** (2016), a performance at the nightclub Tires, during which he wove on a large frame loom, dazzling partygoers who realized that they could make the thread glow by shining their phones onto it, as well as ***In the Garden by Loomlight*** (2016), an immersive installation created during this year's Sidewalk Festival. He has also been known to don traditional

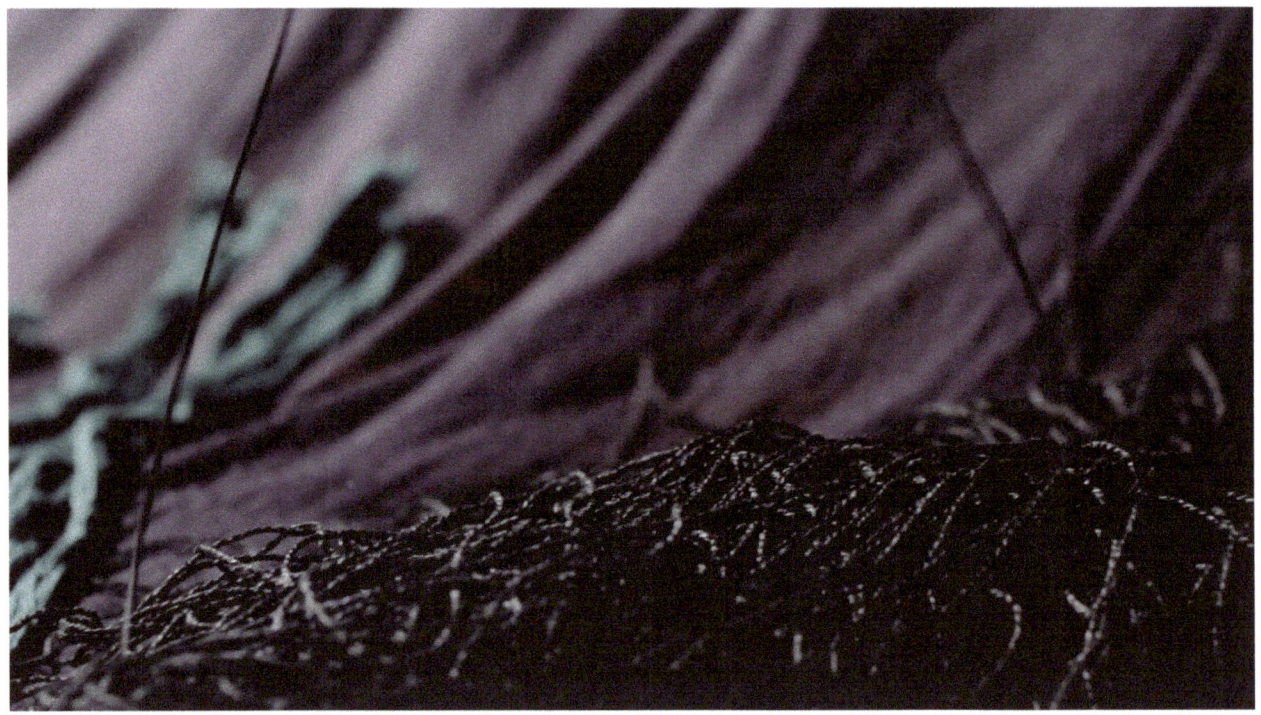

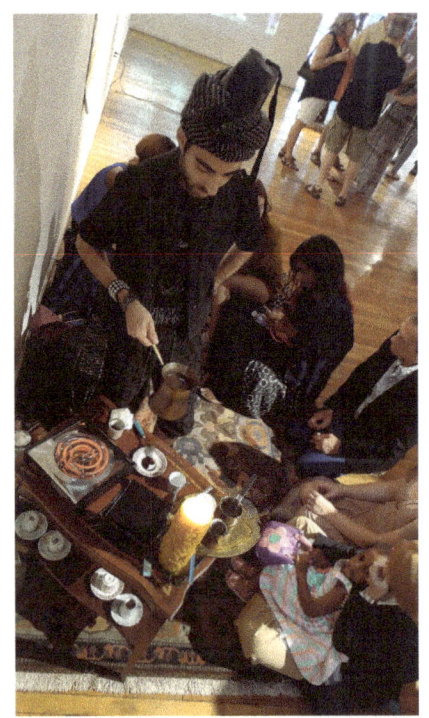

(Top) Unbound and Undone. 2015. Video still. Videography by Matthew Shuert.
(Bottom) Coffee ground reading ceremony at N'Namdi Gallery. 2016. Photography by Michel Soucisse.

Armenian costume, serve Arabic coffee, and ***read participants' fortunes*** in the grounds.

Kafafian's Armenian heritage is a strong influence in his work, but so is a self-described liminality. After all, despite being steeped in his parents' cultural traditions, he was born and raised in the United States. As a queer artist, he also comfortably embodies both the masculine and the feminine. ("Women's work," he says with pride. "It's what I do.") Ancient/contemporary, craft/fine art, studio/social practice: Kafafian is most at home in the spaces between.

MATTHEW PIPER,
SEPTEMBER 2016